T0184075

Lecture Notes in Computer Science 11181

More information about this series at http://www.springer.com/series/7407

Mohamed Faouzi Atig · Saddek Bensalem
Simon Bliudze · Bruno Monsuez (Eds.)

Verification and Evaluation of Computer and Communication Systems

12th International Conference, VECoS 2018
Grenoble, France, September 26–28, 2018
Proceedings

Editors
Mohamed Faouzi Atig
Uppsala University
Uppsala
Sweden

Simon Bliudze
Inria Lille - Nord Europe
Villeneuve d'Ascq
France

Saddek Bensalem
Grenoble Alpes University
St Martin d'Hères
France

Bruno Monsuez
École Nationale Superieure
de Techniques Avancées
Palaiseau
France

ISSN 0302-9743 ISSN 1611-3349 (electronic)
Lecture Notes in Computer Science
ISBN 978-3-030-00358-6 ISBN 978-3-030-00359-3 (eBook)
https://doi.org/10.1007/978-3-030-00359-3

Library of Congress Control Number: 2017950042

LNCS Sublibrary: SL1 – Theoretical Computer Science and General Issues

This Springer imprint is published by the registered company Springer Nature Switzerland AG
The registered company address is: Gewerbestrasse 11, 6330 Cham, Switzerland

Preface

This volume contains the papers presented at the 12th International Conference on Verification and Evaluation of Computer and Communication Systems (VECoS 2018) held during September 26–28, 2018, at the Université Grenoble Alpes in Grenoble, France.

The aim of the VECoS conference is to bring together researchers and practitioners in the areas of verification, control, performance, and dependability evaluation in order to discuss the state of the art and challenges in modern computer and communication systems in which functional and extra-functional properties are strongly interrelated. Thus, the main motivation for VECoS is to encourage cross-fertilization between various formal verification and evaluation approaches, methods, and techniques, and especially those developed for concurrent and distributed hardware/software systems.

The Program Committee (PC) of VECoS 2018 included researchers from 18 countries. We received 23 full submissions from 15 countries and each paper was evaluated by at least three reviewers (except one paper which received two reviews). After a thorough and lively discussion phase, the PC decided to accept 11 papers (which represented an acceptance rate of 48%).

The conference program also included three invited talks. The invited speakers for VECoS 2018 were: Parosh Aziz Abdulla from the Uppsala University, Sweden; Axel Legay of Inria Rennes, France; and Alexandra Silva from the University College London, UK.

We are grateful to all members of the PC and organizing committee, to all referees for their cooperation, and to Springer for their professional support during the publication phase of the proceedings.

Finally, we would like to thank the sponsoring institutions without whom VECoS 2018 could not have been realized. We are also thankful to all authors of submitted papers and to all participants of the conference. Their interest in this conference and contributions to the discipline are greatly appreciated.

September 2018

Mohamed Faouzi Atig
Saddek Bensalem
Simon Bliudze
Bruno Monsuez

Organization

Steering Committee

Djamil Aissani	University of Bejaia, Algeria
Hassane Alla	GIPSA-lab and Grenoble INP, France
Kamel Barkaoui (Chair)	CNAM, France
Hanifa Boucheneb	École Polytechnique de Montréal, Canada
Francesco Flammini	Ansaldo STS, Italy
Belgacem Ben Hedia	CEA-LIST, France
Mohamed Kaaniche	LAAS-CNRS, France
Bruno Monsuez	ENSTA ParisTech, France
Nihal Pekergin	Université Paris-Est-Créteil, France
Tayssir Touili	CNRS, and Université Paris 13, France

Organizing Committee

Belgacem Ben Hedia (Publicity Co-chair)	CEA-LIST, France
Saddek Bensalem (Co-chair)	University of Grenoble Alpes and VERIMAG, France
Marius Bozga	CNRS and VERIMAG, France
Jacques Combaz	CNRS and VERIMAG, France
Bruno Monsuez (Co-chair)	ENSTA ParisTech, France
Ayoub Nouri	University of Grenoble Alpes, France
Vladimir-Alexandru Paun (Publicity Co-chair)	ENSTA ParisTech, France

Program Committee

Djamil Aissani	University of Bejaia, Algeria
Yamine Ait Ameur	IRIT, INPT-ENSEEIHT, France
Mohamed Faouzi Atig (Co-chair)	Uppsala universitet, Sweden
Eric Badouel	Inria Rennes - Bretagne Atlantique, France
Kamel Barkaoui	CNAM, France
Imen Ben Hafaiedh	Institut supérieur d'Informatique (ISI) and LIP2, Tunisia
Belgacem Ben Hedia	CEA-LIST, France
Saddek Bensalem	University of Grenoble Alpes and VERIMAG, France
Adel Benzina	Tunisia Polytechnic School, Tunisia
Simon Bliudze (Co-chair)	Inria Lille - Nord Europe, France
Patrice Bonhomme	Université François Rabelais de Tours, France

Hanifa Boucheneb	École Polytechnique de Montréal, Canada
Florian Brandner	Télécom ParisTech, France
Yu-Fang Chen	Institute of Information Science, Academia Sinica, Taiwan
Feng Chu	Université d'Evry-Val-d'Essonne, France
Gabriel Ciobanu	Romanian Academy, Institute of Computer Science, Iasi, Romania
Mohamed Escheikh	Enit, Tunisia
Alessandro Fantechi	Università di Firenze, Italy
Marc Frappier	Université de Sherbrooke, Canada
Fabio Gadducci	Università di Pisa, Italy
Annie Geniet	Lias/Ensma, France
Mohamed Ghazel	IFSTTAR - COSYS/ESTAS, France
Serge Haddad	ENS Paris-Saclay, CNRS, and Inria, France
Mohamad Jaber	American University of Beirut, Lebanon
Abderrazak Jemai	Insat, Tunisia
Mohamed Jmaiel	Digital Research Center of Sfax, Tunisia
Jorge Julvez	University of Cambridge, UK, and University of Zaragoza, Spain
Mohamed Kaaniche	LAAS-CNRS, France
Panagiotis Katsaros	Aristotle University of Thessaloniki, Greece
Igor Konnov	Inria Nancy - Grand Est and LORIA, France
Lars Kristensen	Western Norway University of Applied Sciences, Norway
Alberto Lluch Lafuente	Technical University of Denmark, Denmark
Eric Madelaine	Université Côte d'Azur and Inria Sophia Antipolis Méditerranée, France
Roland Meyer	TU Braunschweig, Germany
Ali Mili	NJIT, USA
Bruno Monsuez	ENSTA ParisTech, France
Ayoub Nouri	University of Grenoble Alpes, France
Claire Pagetti	ONERA and IRIT-ENSEEIHT, France
Vladimir-Alexandru Paun	ENSTA ParisTech, France
Ahmed Rezine	Linköping University, Sweden
Krishna S.	IIT Bombay, India
Paola Spoletini	Kennesaw State University, USA
Sofiene Tahar	Concordia University, Canada
Tayssir Touili	CNRS and Université Paris 13, France
Bernard van Gastel	Open University of the Netherlands, The Netherlands
Roger Villemaire	Université du Québec à Montréal, Canada
Qiang Wang	National University of Defense Technology, China
Karsten Wolf	Universität Rostock, Germany
Faiez Zalila	Inria Lille - Nord Europe, France

Additional Reviewers

Kevin Delmas
Iulia Dragomir
Yassmeen Elderhalli
He Junkai
Slim Kallel
Victor Khomenko
Li Yantong
Afef Maâlej
Huu Vu Nguyen
Adrien Pommellet
Adrian Puerto Aubel
Prakash Saivasan

Sponsors

Université Grenoble Alpes

VERIMAG

Inria Lille – Nord Europe

Grenoble INP

CNRS

Formal Methods Europe

Commissariat à l'Énergie Atomique et aux Énergies Alternatives

Automated Black-Box Verification of Networking Systems (Invited Talk)

Alexandra Silva

University College London, UK

Abstract. Our society is increasingly reliant on complex networking systems, consisting of several components that operate in a distributed and concurrent fashion, exchange data that may be highly sensitive, and are implemented with a mix of open and closed-source code. In this talk, we will present a broad overview of techniques and tools to automate the modelling and verification of networking software systems. We will focus mainly on the model learning paradigm, originally proposed in artificial intelligence, to automatically build an automaton model of a running system in a black-box fashion — purely via interactions with the running system.

Contents

Invited Papers

The State of Fault Injection Vulnerability Detection

Thomas Given-Wilson, Nisrine Jafri, and Axel Legay(✉)

Inria Rennes - Bretagne Atlantique, Rennes, France
{thomas.given-wilson,nisrine.jafri,axel.legay}@inria.fr

Abstract. Fault injection is a well known method to test the robustness and security vulnerabilities of software. Fault injections can be explored by simulations (cheap, but not validated) and hardware experiments (true, but very expensive). Recent simulation works have started to apply formal methods to the detection, analysis, and prevention of fault injection attacks to address verifiability. However, these approaches are adhoc and extremely limited in architecture, fault model, and breadth of application. Further, there is very limited connection between simulation results and hardware experiments. Recent work has started to consider broad spectrum simulation approaches that can cover many fault models and relatively large programs. Similarly the connection between these broad spectrum simulations and hardware experiments is being validated to bridge the gap between the two approaches. This presentation highlights the latest developments in applying formal methods to fault injection vulnerability detection, and validating software and hardware results with one another.

Keywords: Fault injection · Vulnerability · Model checking
Formal methods · Simulation

1 Introduction

Fault injection is a commonly used technique to test the robustness or vulnerability of systems against potential physical fault injection attacks. Testing for system robustness is generally applied for systems that are deployed in hostile environments where faults are likely to occur. Such environments include aviation, military, space, etc. where atmospheric radiation, EMP, cosmic rays etc. may induce faults. Vulnerability against attacks is usually used to detect places where a malicious attacker may attempt to exploit a system with a targeted fault injection. Since the underlying mechanism of a fault causing undesirable behaviour is common to both of these scenarios, the detection of potential *fault injection vulnerabilities* is an important area of research.

To support this research requires being able to reproduce the effect of some kind of fault in an experimental environment. There are two broad classes of approaches used to reproduce such faults, either simulating the fault injection

M. F. Atig et al. (Eds.): VECoS 2018, LNCS 11181, pp. 3–21, 2018.
https://doi.org/10.1007/978-3-030-00359-3_1

using a *software based approach*, or (re)producing the fault injection with some specialised equipment as a *hardware based approach.*

The software based approach was first proposed as an alternative to the requiring specialised hardware to (re)produce a fault [4,16,39]. The typical software approach is to perform a simulation based upon a chosen *fault model*; a model of how the fault effects the system. The main advantage of software based approaches are that they are cheap and fast to implement since they require only development skills and normal computing systems without any specialised hardware. The main challenge for software based approaches are that they have not been validated against hardware based approaches to verify that their results coincide, i.e. that the vulnerabilities found by the software based approaches are genuine.

The hardware based approach was proposed as a technique to study potential vulnerabilities which may be created by environmental factors or potential malicious attacks [21]. The hardware based approach consists of using specialised hardware to induce an actual fault on a specific device. Some examples include: setting up a laser that can target specific transistors in a chip [33], setting up an X-ray beam to target a transistor [2], mounting an EMP probe over a chip to disrupt normal behaviour [23], and many others [3,5,37]. The main advantage of such hardware based approaches are that any detected vulnerability is guaranteed to be genuine and potentially reproducible. The main challenge for such hardware based approaches are the cost of specialised hardware and expertise to configure such an environment and conduct the experiments.

Since both software and hardware based approaches have advantages (and disadvantages), research has proceeded using both approaches. Thus, there are many works that explore the software based approach [8,20,25], and also many works that explore hardware based approaches [5,26,34], but none that explore both. However, due to the relative cost and also the potential for broader and faster results, the more recent focus has been on improving software based approaches [14,25,27].

One recent development in the software based approaches is the use of formal methods that can provide stronger claims about the existence (or more often absence) of a fault injection vulnerability [13,14]. The benefit of formal methods is that the results allow for strong positive statements about the properties that have been proved (or disproved) formally. Thus, results can show that a particular attack cannot succeed [14], or that a particular counter-measure is effective against an attack [24].

However, a significant challenge for the software based approaches is in their breadth of applicability. Many software based approaches are only able to perform simulations of produce results for a single hardware architecture [11,25]. Similarly, many are only able to produce results for a single fault model, that is they can only detect vulnerabilities against one kind of fault injection attack [27]. Further, some software based approaches only aim to formalise that very small fragments of a program are not vulnerable to fault injection attack (or that a counter-measure is effective), but cannot produce results on even whole functions (let alone whole programs) [24]. Lastly, many approaches do not operate on the binary and hardware model itself, but instead on a (higher-level) language that is significantly abstracted away from the hardware and actual fault injections [9].

Another significant challenge for the software based approaches are in the accuracy and breadth of the tools they use. Various works have applied techniques that build upon exploiting tools to transform between languages or models [14,15] or that rely on tools for checking or verifying [27]. However, many of these tools have their own limitations.

Recent works have started to address the above challenges by using an automated process to find fault injection vulnerabilities over whole functions and with many fault models [13,14]. However, despite these showing good results they are still challenges due to the tools used, and are still targeting a single architecture (albeit upon the binary itself).

Similar issues appear in the hardware based approaches. For example, demonstrating a vulnerability by flipping a bit with a laser on one chip, says nothing about robustness or vulnerability: against flipping a different bit with the same laser; being able to flip the same bit with an X-ray beam; flipping the same bit on a different chip; or against EMP attacks, etc. Here the search for breadth in results is significantly harder to achieve, since testing every possible transistor of a single chip is already infeasible, let alone reasoning over all chips on the market.

Further to the above challenges, to date there has been no significant effort to correlate the software and hardware approaches on a common case study. Thus, there is very little information on whether the two approaches coincide, and whether many of the assumptions made about the approaches hold in practice.

This work provides an overview of some of these recent and significant developments and the general state of the art of fault injection vulnerability detection. This covers a background on the key components of fault injection vulnerability detection, and an overall explanation of how the software based and hardware based approaches operate. The main focus here is on the capabilities and challenges for the state of the art, with a view towards how to develop improved approaches to this area in future.

The latest in automated approaches that can be applied more generally to binary programs are also recalled. This highlights the strengths and capabilities of automating fault injection vulnerability detection, and recent developments in the software based approach. These results are able to show several vulnerabilities in cryptographic implementations. Significantly formal methods were able to be applied to relatively complex program behaviour to produce useful results with reasonable cost.

This paper also discusses the approach of ongoing work on connecting the software and hardware based approaches together by experimenting on the same case study. This overviews the requirements to yield useful results from these experiments, and also identifies some open questions that can be addressed by the results of this ongoing work.

More broadly this paper looks to the future of fault injection vulnerability detection and how to improve the approaches. Longer term the goal should be to raise fault injection vulnerability detection from a niche and specialised area of software quality, to something that can be applied in the manner that we currently apply bug detection and standards compliance. That is, a future where fault injection vulnerability detection can be automated into development environments and processes to seamlessly integrate with the development environment and identify vulnerabilities efficiently and with negligible cost.

The structure of the paper is as follows. Section 2 recalls background information helpful for understanding this work. Section 3 recalls recent related works on various approaches to fault injection vulnerability detection. Section 4 discusses challenges for current approaches and tools. Section 5 overviews some recent results on broad spectrum software approaches to detecting fault injection vulnerabilities. Section 6 considers how to combine software and hardware based approaches and the questions being addressed in ongoing work. Section 7 considers the future directions in fault injection vulnerability detection. Section 8 concludes.

2 Background

This sections recalls useful background information for understanding the rest of the paper. This includes an overview of the definition of fault injection and how to reason about fault injection by fault models and their typical classification. The two approaches (software and hardware) are both overviewed, along with their main advantages and disadvantages.

2.1 Fault Injection

Fault injection is any modification at the hardware level which may change normal program execution. Fault injection can be unintentional (e.g. background radiation, power interruption [4,21]) or intentional (e.g. induced EMP [10,23], rowhammer [29,35,41]).

Unintentional fault injection is generally attributed to the environment [12,21] An example of this is one of the first observed fault injections where radioactive elements present in packing materials caused bits to flip in chips [4].

Intentional fault injection occurs when the injection is done by an *attacker* with the intention of changing program execution [23,29,35,41]. For example, fault injection attacks performed on cryptographic algorithms (e.g. RSA [9], AES [33], PRESENT [40]) where the fault is introduced to reveal information that helps in computing the secret key.

A fault injection *vulnerability* is a fault injection that yields a change to the program execution that is useful from the perspective of an attacker. This is in contrast to other effects of fault injection that are not useful, such as simply crashing a program, causing an infinite loop, or changing a value that is subsequently over-written. Observe that the definition of a vulnerability is not necessarily trivial or stable, the above example of a program crash may be a vulnerability if the attacker desires to achieve a denial of service attack.

One challenge in understanding and reasoning about fault injection is to be able to understand the effect that different kinds of faults can have upon the system that is effected. This requires some definition of how to characterise a fault and its behaviour in a manner that can be used experimentally.

2.2 Fault Model

Fault models are used to specify the nature and scope of the induced modification. A fault model has two important parameters, location and impact. The location includes the spatial and temporal location of fault injection relating to the execution of the target program. The impact depends on the type and granularity of the technique used to inject the fault, the granularity can be at the level of bit, byte, or multiple bytes.

According to their granularity fault models can be classified into the following kinds [31]. Bit-wise models: in these fault models the fault injection will manipulate a single bit. One can distinguish five types of bit-wise fault model [31]: bit-set, bit-flip, bit-reset, stuck-at and random-value. Byte-wise models: in these fault models the fault injection will modify eight contiguous bits at a time (usually in the same byte from the program or hardware perspective, *not* spread across multiple bytes). One can distinguish three types of byte-wise fault model: byte-set, byte-reset or random-byte. Wider models: in these fault models the fault injection will manipulate an entire word (defined for the given architecture). For this fault model a sequence of 8 to 64 bits will be modified depending on the architecture, e.g. changing the value of an entire word at once. This will typically target the modification of an entire instruction or single word value.

Based on the fault model classification presented in the paragraph above, a list of fault models used in the experiment results presented in Sect. 5.2 are as follows. The *bit flip* (FLP) fault model that flips the value of a single bit, either from 0 to 1 or from 1 to 0, this fault model is an example of a Bit-wise model. The *zero one byte* (Z1B) fault model that sets a single byte to zero (regardless of initial value), this fault model is an example of a Byte-wise model. The *unconditional jump* (JMP) and *conditional jump* (JBE) fault models that change the value of a single byte in the target of an unconditional or conditional jump instruction (respectively), these are examples of Byte-wise fault models. The *non-operation* (NOP) fault model that sets a byte to a non-operation code for the chosen architecture, this is an example of a Byte-wise fault model (but can also be implemented as a Wider model by changing the value of the whole instruction word). The *zero one word* (Z1W) fault model that sets a whole word to have the value zero (regardless of prior value), this is an example of the Wider model.

2.3 Software-Based Fault Injection Approaches

Software-based approaches consists of reproducing at software level the effect that would have been produced by injecting a fault at the hardware level. Software based approaches can be achieved in a number of ways, two common ones are described below. The first common approach is to simulate the program execution (sometimes including simulating the entire hardware stack as well) and then simulate the fault injection as part of the simulation [17]. The results of the simulation are then used to indicate the behaviour of the program under the fault injection performed. The second common approach is to take the program and use software to build a model of its behaviour [18]. The faults may be injected into the program before or after the model is constructed, but the model is then tested for specific behaviours or properties and the results used to reason about the behaviour of the program. The second is becoming more popular in recent works [13,14] as formal methods can be used on the model that allow for reasoning about all possible outcomes, and verifying when properties of the model may hold. Note that a vulnerability can be defined rather abstractly in many software based approaches since no clearly observable behaviour is required, merely some definition of how to define vulnerability for the simulation or model.

The advantages of software-based approaches are in cost, automation, and breadth. Software-based simulations do not require expensive or dedicated hardware and can be run on most computing devices easily [26]. Also with various software tools being developed and matured, limited expertise is needed to plug together a toolchain to do fault injection vulnerability detection [13,14]. Such a toolchain can then be automated to detect fault injection vulnerabilities without direct oversight or intervention. Further, simulations can cover a wide variety of fault models that represent different kinds of attacks and can therefore test a broad range of attacks with a single system. Combining all of the above allows for an easy automated process that can test a program for fault injection vulnerabilities against a wide variety of attack models, and with excellent coverage of potential attacks.

The disadvantages of software-based approaches are largely in their implementations or in the veracity of their results. Many software-based approaches have shown positive results, but are often limited by the tools and implementation details, with limitations in architecture, scope, etc. However, the biggest weakness is the lack of veracity of the results: software-based approaches have not been proven to map to actual vulnerabilities in practice.

2.4 Hardware-Based Fault Injection Approaches

Hardware-based approaches consists of disturbing the hardware at physical level, using hardware materiel (e.g. EMP, Laser, Temperature, etc.). Hardware based approaches are usually achieved by configuring the specific hardware to be experimented on and loading the program to be tested for vulnerabilities. A special device is then used to perform fault injection on the hardware during execution, e.g. EMP a chip, laser a transistor, overheat a chip. The result of the execution of the program is observed under this fault injection, with some particular outcomes considered to be "vulnerable" and thus a vulnerability is considered to have been achieved. One typical requirement for this approach is to have idea of how a vulnerability is observable from program execution, since otherwise it is unclear whether the outcome of execution is a vulnerability or merely some normal or faulty behaviour.

The advantages of hardware-based approaches are in the quality of the results. A fault injection that has been demonstrated in practice with hardware cannot be denied to be genuine.

The disadvantages of hardware-based approaches are the cost, automation, and breadth. To do hardware-based fault injection vulnerability detection requires specialised hardware and expertise to conduct the experiments. This is compounded when multiple kinds of attacks are to be considered; since different equipment is needed to perform different kinds of fault injection (e.g. EMP, laser, power interrupt). Further, hardware-based approaches tend to be difficult to automate, since the experiments must be done with care and oversight, and also the result can damage or interrupt the hardware in a manner that breaks the automation. Lastly, hardware-based approaches tend to have limited breadth of application; this is due to requiring many different pieces of hardware to test different architectures, attacks, etc. and also due to the time and cost to test large numbers of locations for fault injection vulnerability.

3 Existing Work

This section recalls recent works related to the detection of fault injection vulnerabilities. These are divided according to their general approach as being either software or hardware based.

3.1 Software Based Approach

This section recalls recent related works that use software based approaches for detection of fault injection vulnerabilities.

One recent work which uses formal methods to detect vulnerabilities is [19]. Here the authors presents a symbolic LLVM-based Software-implemented Fault Injection (SWiFI) evaluation framework for resilience evaluation. InSWiFI the fault injection simulation and the vulnerability detection are done on the intermediate language LLVM-IR, which limits accurate simulation of fault models closely related to low level hardware effects.

The Symbolic Program Level Fault Injection and Error Detection Framework (SymPLFIED) [25] is a program-level framework to identify potential vulnerabilities in software. The vulnerabilities are detected by combining symbolic execution and model checking techniques. The SymPLFIED framework is limited as SymPLFIED only supports the MIPS architecture [28].

Lazart [27] is a tool that can simulate a variety of fault injection attacks and detect vulnerabilities using formal methods. The Lazart process begins with the source code which is compiled to LLVM-IR. The simulated fault is created by modifying the control flow of the LLVM-IR. Symbolic execution is then used to detect differences in the control flow, and thus detect vulnerabilities. One of the main limitations of Lazart is that it is unable to reason about or detect fault injection attacks that operate on binaries rather than the LLVM-IR.

In [32] the authors propose combining the Lazart process with the Embedded Fault Simulator (EFS) [6]. This extends from the capabilities of Lazart alone by adding lower level fault injection analysis that is also embedded in the chip with the program. The simulation of the fault is performed in the hardware, so the semantics of the executed program correspond to the real execution of the program. However, EFS is limited to only considering instruction skip faults (equivalent to NOPs of Sect. 2.2).

An entirely low level approach is taken by Moro et al. [24] who use model checking to formally prove the correctness of their proposed software countermeasures schemes against fault injection attacks. The focus is on a very specific and limited fault injection model that causes instruction skips and ignores other kinds of attacks. Further, the model checking is over only limited fragments of the assembly code, and not the program as a whole.

A less formal approach is taken in [1] where experiments are used for testing the TTP/C protocol in the presence of faults. Rather than attempting to find fault injection attacks, they injected faults to test robustness of the protocol. They combined both hardware testing and software simulation testing, comparing the results as validation of their approach.

A fault model inference focused approach is taken by Dureuil et al. [11]. They fix a hardware model and then test various fault injection attacks based upon this hardware model. Fault detection is limited to EEPROM faults on the ARMv7-M architecture. The fault model is then inferred from the parameters of the attack and the embedded program. The faults are simulated upon the assembly code and the results checked with predefined oracles on the embedded program.

3.2 Hardware Based Approach

This section recalls recent related works that use software based approaches for detection of fault injection vulnerabilities.

In [34] the authors applies the electromagnetic and the optical attacks to the RSA algorithm, a well known algorithm used in various cryptographic systems. The authors presented a successful attack on the RSA algorithm implementation over an 8-bit architecture micro-controller. Experiments showed that the faults can affect program flow as well as the SRAM content and the flash memory.

Skorobogatov [36] showed using a laser, one can effect certain memory cells SRAM and cause them to switch. The experiments were conducted on an PIC16F84 micro-controller. The advantage of using a laser is that they can accurately target a single bit to modify.

In [7] the authors presents a practical laser fault attack which target creating fault in the Deep Neural Networks (DNN) on a low-cost micro-controller.

An other type of hardware attack was presented in [5] where the authors showed that they can perform successful attacks by alternating the power supply. The experiments were performed on a software implementation of the AES and RSA crypto algorithm running on a ARM9 CPU. The result showed that it was possible to retrieve the full 256-bit key of the AES crypto algorithm, and reproduce with cheaper equipment a known attack against RSA.

In [26,42] the authors present a survey of the different hardware based approach techniques used to inject a fault. The authors also refer to relevant works where the various fault injection techniques are used. For many other recent and older works on hardware fault injection and their approaches we refer the reader to these works.

4 Challenges

This section discusses common challenges for fault injection vulnerability detection and how they impact the current state of the art in this and closely related areas.

Historically informal approaches (i.e. those that do not employ formal methods) while using a software based approach are unable to provide strong guarantees about the absence of fault injection vulnerabilities [30]. A similar challenge faces hardware based approaches that cannot guarantee that their inability to find a vulnerability ensures that no such vulnerability exists.

One solution to the above challenge is the employment of formal methods in the vulnerability detection approach [14,25]. This allows results to guarantee that if no vulnerability is found, then no vulnerability exists in the program that was analysed. However, in practice most of these approaches are only able to formally show the lack of vulnerability for a very specific case, or the effectiveness of a counter-measure with limited scope. Thus they are still challenged to produce broad or general results that have the guarantee of formal correctness.

More generally another key challenge for both software and hardware based approaches is the limited scope considered. For either approach the results tend to be highly specific with respect to the architecture being considered [11,25]. That is, although the results may be complete and correct for one program, they only hold for a single implementation executed on a single specific chip and against a single fault injection technique or fault model [27]. Although this does not limit the significance of finding a fault injection vulnerability, the absence of any vulnerability is not a particularly strong claim under these conditions. Thus the challenge here for both software and hardware based approaches is to find some way to generalise beyond very small and highly specific case studies.

To some extent the software based approaches can be generalised to incorporate multiple fault models and so offer broader coverage and vulnerability detection. However, this requires a software based approach that can be scaled effectively to multiple fault models [13,14].

For the hardware based approaches the fault model is inherent to the attack and so does not need to be considered. On the other hand, there is limited opportunity to transfer or generalise results. Demonstrating a vulnerability with a laser offers very limited information about whether a vulnerability can be produced with an EMP. Thus a challenge here is to find ways to be able to transfer or compare both positive and negative results between different kinds of hardware attacks.

Considering this, recent broad spectrum approaches to fault injection vulnerability detection by using automated software approaches show significant promise [13,14]. However, even these are still limited to some specific architectures and known or implemented fault models.

This identifies yet another challenge area for the software based approaches: the limitations of the tools used in their software process. For many software based approaches there are specific tools developed for them, that tend to lack breadth and maturity [15,27]. For others that employ tools (often from other domains), these tools tend to have limitations of their own such as being unable to handle everything required (e.g. not supporting all instructions of a given architecture), or being unreliable or inconsistent in their results [13,14].

5 Broad Spectrum Simulation

This section recalls some recent approaches to addressing the various challenges discussed above. In particular, the focus here is on recent broad spectrum simulations that adopt an automated scalable formal process for detecting fault injection vulnerabilities in binary files [13,14]. These works address some of the challenges described above and progress towards approaches that vastly reduce their limitations, and thus are more widely applicable.

5.1 Process

This section recalls the core concepts of the process used in [13,14] for the broad spectrum detection of fault injection vulnerabilities. One of the main contributions of these works is in the development of this automated process that can apply formal verification techniques to the detection of fault injection vulnerabilities in binary files. An overview of the key concepts of the process is depicted in Fig. 1, the rest of this section discusses the key points of implementation and application of this process.

The process begins with a binary file that is to be checked for fault injection vulnerabilities. In [13,14] the properties that define the correct and vulnerable behaviours are also in this file as annotations maintained by the compiler. (These properties may also define other behaviours such as incorrect or crashed, but these are used for exploration and precision rather than detection of fault injection vulnerabilities.)

The binary file is then translated into a model that represents the behaviour of the binary program in an intermediate language suitable for a formal verification tool. In [13,14] this translation is done to LLVM-IR as an intermediate language that is then used by a model checker (see below). This translation to

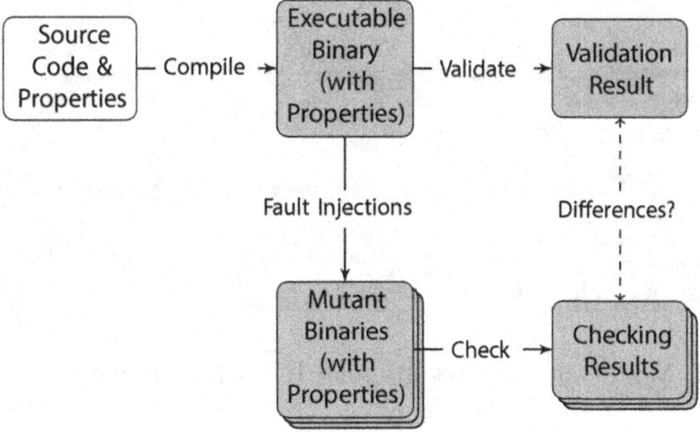

Fig. 1. Software process diagram

LLVM-IR also maintains the properties and converts them to known properties for the model checker.

The properties are then checked by a model checker to validate that they do indeed hold on the original binary program. In [13,14] this is done using LLBMC a bounded model checker for LLVM-IR. The purpose of this step is to verify that the properties hold and are correctly defined for the binary program, and so that later results can be compared with the validation.

The binary is then injected with a simulated fault injection according to a choice of fault model. This can include many different fault models, and they can be injected in many different locations within the binary. Each possible fault injection combination (of fault model and location) yields a new mutant binary. Note that some care is taken here to ensure fault injection does not effect the property annotations.

The mutant binary is then translated to a model in LLVM-IR, and this model is then checked with LLBMC, both of these are done in the same manner as for the original binary program. The results of this checking on the mutant binary are compared with the validation results for the original program, with any changes being attributed to the fault injection. Thus, the introduction of a "vulnerable" result by the simulated fault injection indicates a fault injection vulnerability.

Note that in [13] this process is refined to be vastly more efficient, but the core concepts are the same in both works.

5.2 Results

This section recalls the main results of these broad spectrum experiments and their implications for detecting fault injection vulnerabilities. The above process was applied to the PRESENT and SPECK cryptographic algorithm implementations. In both cases these algorithms are significantly complex and would be infeasible for a human to check for fault injection vulnerabilities manually. This infeasibility is particularly true for some of the more unusual fault injection

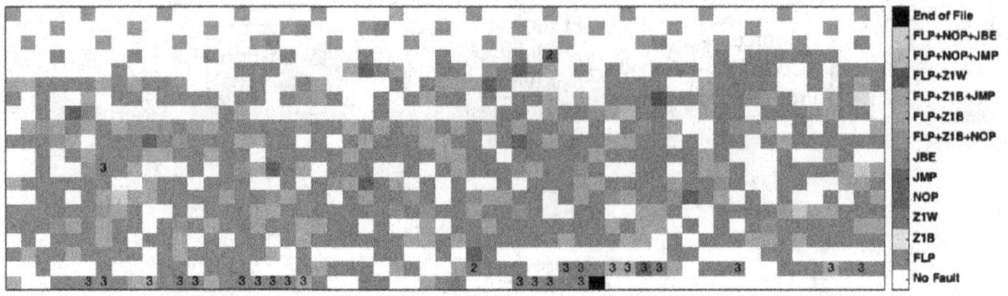

Fig. 2. Model checking results for PRESENT (taken from [13])

mutations that cause instructions to be accessed at a different offset and so interpreted as different instructions.

An overview of the results of applying the process to PRESENT with six fault models described in Sect. 2.2 (flipping one bit FLP, zeroing one byte Z1B, zeroing one word Z1W, nopping one instruction NOP, modifying a on-conditional jump address JMP, and modifying a conditional jump address JBE) can be seen in Fig. 2. Each square in the diagram indicates a byte of the program that was analysed, with white indicating no impact on execution. Overall 73 vulnerabilities to various properties were found in PRESENT using this automated fault injection vulnerability detection process. Only a small number of these (9 occurrences, indicated with a "2" on the square in the diagram) were found to violate a property that allowed an attacker to send the plaintext in place of the ciphertext. The majority (64 occurrences, indicated with a "3" on the square in the diagram) were crypto-analytical vulnerabilities that allow the encryption key to be calculated from a number of ciphertexts by an attacker. The remaining non-white squares indicated a different "incorrect" behaviour due to fault injection. (Note that a square with a "2" may contain multiple fault injection vulnerabilities depending on the fault model used.)

Overall these broad spectrum experiments indicated that several significant fault injection vulnerabilities existed in the PRESENT algorithm. Further, the results indicated which fault model and location would be able to implement a successful fault injection attack in practice.

The same process with the same six fault models (from Sect. 2.2) was applied to SPECK yielding the results overviewed in Fig. 3. Overall there were only 9 vulnerabilities found in SPECK, and all of them were fault injection vulnerabilities that allowed the attacker to directly access the plaintext (indicated by a "2" on the square corresponding to the byte in the program in the diagram). Other colours are as described above for PRESENT.

Again these results indicated there exist vulnerabilities in the SPECK implementation, as well as the exact fault model and location to implement the attack.

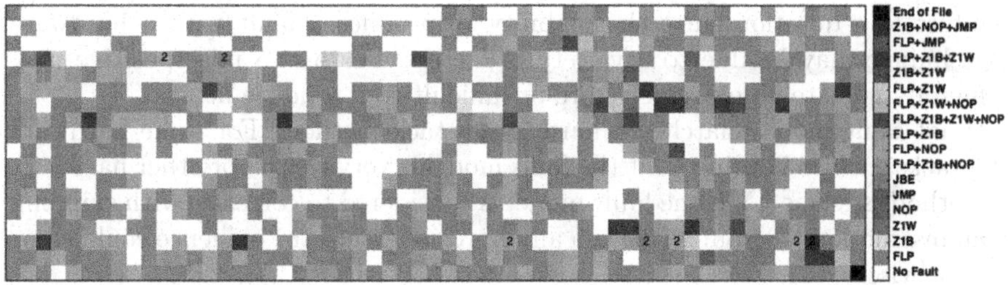

Fig. 3. Model checking results for SPECK (taken from [13]) (Color figure online)

6 Connection to Hardware

Another major challenge is the lack of connection between the software and hardware experiments in fault injection vulnerability detection. The natural progression in this area would be to combine the software based simulations with hardware based experiments. This section presents some of the key concepts of ongoing work, and the questions being addressed by this work.

The experimental approach used is to take a case study that has a variety of behaviours, and includes weaknesses that are believed to be vulnerable to some kinds of fault injection (i.e. some fault models). This case study is then experimented on using both software and hardware based approaches. The braod spectrum software based approach of Sect. 5.1 is applied to *the whole program* with a variety of fault models. A hardware based fault injection technique is also used to test *the whole program* for fault injection vulnerabilities.

This combined approach requires significantly more experimental work than is typically conducted. The software based experiments must cover the whole program and a wide variety of (or ideally all known) fault models to be able to reason about and compare the results well. This is in contrast to many prior works where merely checking a specific location, fault model, or counter-measure was the goal. Similarly, the hardware experiments must cover the whole program (and with enough repetitions to be reliable) to ensure that all possible configurations have been tested, and that they can be compared with all the software results. Again this differs from prior work where the hardware approach typically focuses only on very specific (known to be potentially vulnerable) code points and exploits the expert knowledge of the experimenter.

The results of such experiments on a common case study and with coverage of the whole program allows for many interesting questions to be addressed including those below.

- Do the software and hardware based approaches coincide? That is, do the results actually match each other, or are the two unrelated in where they find vulnerabilities and how they explain such vulnerabilities.
- Do the software results have false negatives or positives? In theory using a (correct) formal approach should never yield false negative results since this would imply the formalism is incorrect. However, false positives are a more

interesting question since the inability to produce a fault with a hardware technique may be due to a variety of factors. Further, a false positive may merely indicate an extremely rare or difficult to reproduce attack.
- What fault model matches a hardware attack method? For some hardware attacks such as lasering a bit the fault model is very clear. For other hardware methods such as EMP the fault model is considered to correlate with skipping an instruction [22], but with such an imprecise attack the evidence could show otherwise.
- Can combining both software and hardware improve vulnerability detection? Although having access to both approaches (particularly for a variety of hardware attacks) is not feasible, knowing how to make the most efficient use of the available resources could be an advantage gained by knowing the coincidence between software and hardware. That is, software could indicate where to attempt to fault the hardware in a program without a known (or suspected) weakness.

These and other open questions can be addressed by conducting such combined experiments, yielding deeper insight into both the software and hardware aspects of fault injection vulnerability detection.

7 Looking Forward

Recent works have shown significant advances in detecting fault injection vulnerabilities using software, hardware, and combined approaches. However, there are still many opportunities for progress and areas that need significant effort to be able to make fault injection vulnerability detection a reliable and easily applicable part of software development.

One significant challenges for many of the recent and current approaches is the underlying tools that they depend upon. For example, the translation tools used for the results highlighted here rely upon MC-Sema [38] that has various limitations with instruction sets, or failures to correctly translation behaviour. Similarly, in many other works [15,25] the tools limit the applicability of the technique to some limited scope, limited architecture, limited size, etc. Thus, in many areas the tools used require refinement and maturity, and in other areas the tools simply do not exist and would need to be created. Another example is of the limitations of applying some of the tools in the manner used here, such as LLBMC as used in [14] is not able to produce a counter-example to the property and thus indicate which combination of inputs were vulnerable for a given fault injection vulnerability, further in [13] LLBMC was shown to be inconsistent when producing results. Here an alternative model checker (and likely alternative intermediate language and so translation tools) could yield much more precise results.

Another main area of improvement would be in the automation of fault injection vulnerability detection. Although some recent works highlighted here [13,14] have begun to address automation, most approaches have not. Being able to automate the the search for vulnerabilities allows fault injection vulnerability detection to be changed from a highly manual process, to another quality or verification process used during software development. Indeed, this would allow fault injection vulnerability to be considered along with other quality checks such as: bug detection, standards compliance, verification, correctness-by-construction, etc.

Another area to advance in would be in the application of formal methods. Many of the current approaches use highly specific and limited applications of formal methods [14,25,27], or a heavy technique that does not exploit domain specific information. For example, the model checking highlighted here does not take into account prior results, or modularity of sub-components. Thus, an incremental approach may yield significant efficiency returns. Similarly, developing and exploiting formal methods that focus on the exact problems considered in vulnerability detection could yield much more precise results than those that are currently state of the art.

Work on strongly connecting the software and hardware based approaches is clearly a goal for future research and development. A strong foundation of understanding of the relations between different kinds of software and hardware based approaches will enrich and improve the results of both. Further, by connecting these results, software based results can be validated to be genuine by reproducing them with hardware experiments. In the other direction, hardware based experiments will demonstrate the efficacy and accuracy of the software based approaches.

Finally, many existing works in the domain of fault injection vulnerabilities and their detection work on examples or programs where a vulnerability is already known to exist. The goal of the work is to (re)produce a known attack (or exploit one that has been intentionally designed in) to demonstrate the efficacy of the approaches used. However, finding vulnerabilities that were not even suspected in advance, or devising approaches that allow the finding of such vulnerabilities in an efficient manner is a clear requirement for practical application in the future.

8 Conclusion

Fault injection represent a serious threat to the robustness and security of many software systems used in daily life. There are two main approaches to detecting fault injection vulnerabilities and testing system robustness; software and hardware based. Both approaches have yielded useful results and can make useful contributions. Software based approaches are good for simulation and being able to cheaply implement, albeit at the cost of the ability to demonstrate a fault injection vulnerability is genuine and can be exploited. Hardware based approaches are good for proving genuine exploitability, but are expensive in time, equipment, and expertise to conduct.

Many recent software based approaches propose the use of formal methods in the process of detecting fault injection vulnerabilities. However, these solutions still have challenges regarding the proposed process as an whole or the tools used in their implementation. Although some of the most recent works attempt to broaden the abilities of software based approaches, in combination with formal methods, there are still challenges ahead for the underlying tools.

Recently proposed and evaluated software approaches have shown their efficiency in detecting potential fault injection vulnerabilities. These software approaches were applied to a variety of systems, working on different architectures, embedding different types of programs. Further, these software approaches have demonstrated scalability in being able to be applied to many fault models in many locations on non-trivial real-world programs with previously unknown vulnerabilities.

Despite these software approach's good results, they can not guarantee that the detected vulnerabilities correspond to real vulnerabilities in practice. The fact that the fault injection are simulated gives no guarantee that in a real physical fault injection attack on the system will have the same effect. Thus the challenge of combining both software and hardware based approaches on a single case study to explore how the two approaches connect. Such experiments should improve our understanding of how to interpret software based approaches: do they produce false positives, false negatives, how reproducible the claimed fault injection vulnerabilities are, and other questions. Similarly, such experiments will allow the fault models of hardware based approaches to be more accurately determined. Further, combining both approaches may yield vastly more effective techniques to find vulnerabilities by exploiting the strengths of each approach.

There are many challenges open in the domain of fault injection vulnerability detection. In addition to those explicitly mentioned above, the broader goal can be to have fault injection vulnerability detection reach the maturity and confidence of other software quality approaches. Developing tools that can integrate into development environments or build processes to automatically detect (potential) fault injection vulnerabilities in the near future is a desirable goal.

References

1. Ademaj, A., Grillinger, P., Herout, P., Hlavicka, J.: Fault tolerance evaluation using two software based fault injection methods. In: Proceedings of the Eighth IEEE International On-Line Testing Workshop, pp. 21–25. IEEE (2002)
2. Anceau, S., Bleuet, P., Clédière, J., Maingault, L., Rainard, J., Tucoulou, R.: Nanofocused X-ray beam to reprogram secure circuits. In: Fischer, W., Homma, N. (eds.) CHES 2017. LNCS, vol. 10529, pp. 175–188. Springer, Cham (2017). https://doi.org/10.1007/978-3-319-66787-4_9
3. Balasch, J., Gierlichs, B., Verbauwhede, I.: An in-depth and black-box characterization of the effects of clock glitches on 8-bit MCUs. In: 2011 Workshop on Fault Diagnosis and Tolerance in Cryptography (FDTC), pp. 105–114. IEEE (2011)
4. Bar-El, H., Choukri, H., Naccache, D., Tunstall, M., Whelan, C.: The sorcerer's apprentice guide to fault attacks. IACR Cryptology ePrint Archive, 2004:100 (2004)
5. Barenghi, A., Bertoni, G.M., Breveglieri, L., Pelosi, G.: A fault induction technique based on voltage underfeeding with application to attacks against AES and RSA. J. Syst. Softw. **86**(7), 1864–1878 (2013)

6. Berthier, M., Bringer, J., Chabanne, H., Le, T.-H., Rivière, L., Servant, V.: Idea: embedded fault injection simulator on smartcard. In: Jürjens, J., Piessens, F., Bielova, N. (eds.) ESSoS 2014. LNCS, vol. 8364, pp. 222–229. Springer, Cham (2014). https://doi.org/10.1007/978-3-319-04897-0_15
7. Breier, J., Hou, X., Jap, D., Ma, L., Bhasin, S., Liu, Y.: Practical fault attack on deep neural networks. arXiv preprint arXiv:1806.05859 (2018)
8. Carreira, J., Madeira, H., Silva, J.G., et al.: Xception: software fault injection and monitoring in processor functional units. Dependable Comput. Fault Toler. Syst. **10**, 245–266 (1998)
9. Christofi, M., Chetali, B., Goubin, L.: Formal verification of an implementation of CRT-RSA vigilant's algorithm. In: PROOFS Workshop: Pre-proceedings, p. 28 (2013)
10. Dehbaoui, A., Dutertre, J.-M., Robisson, B., Orsatelli, P., Maurine, P., Tria, A.: Injection of transient faults using electromagnetic pulses-practical results on a cryptographic system-. IACR Cryptology EPrint Archive, 2012:123 (2012)
11. Dureuil, L., Potet, M.-L., de Choudens, P., Dumas, C., Clédière, J.: From code review to fault injection attacks: filling the gap using fault model inference. In: Homma, N., Medwed, M. (eds.) CARDIS 2015. LNCS, vol. 9514, pp. 107–124. Springer, Cham (2016). https://doi.org/10.1007/978-3-319-31271-2_7
12. Ecoffet, R.: In-flight anomalies on electronic devices. In: Velazco, R., Fouillat, P., Reis, R. (eds.) Radiation Effects on Embedded Systems, pp. 31–68. Springer, Dordrecht (2007). https://doi.org/10.1007/978-1-4020-5646-8_3
13. Given-Wilson, T., Heuser, A., Jafri, N., Lanet, J.-L., Legay, A.: An automated and scalable formal process for detecting fault injection vulnerabilities in binaries (2017)
14. Given-Wilson, T., Jafri, N., Lanet, J., Legay, A.: An automated formal process for detecting fault injection vulnerabilities in binaries and case study on PRESENT. In: 2017 IEEE Trustcom/BigDataSE/ICESS, Sydney, Australia, 1–4 August 2017, pp. 293–300. IEEE (2017)
15. Höller, A., Krieg, A., Rauter, T., Iber, J., Kreiner, C.: QEMU-based fault injection for a system-level analysis of software countermeasures against fault attacks. In: 2015 Euromicro Conference on Digital System Design (DSD), pp. 530–533. IEEE (2015)
16. Hsueh, M.-C., Tsai, T.K., Iyer, R.K.: Fault injection techniques and tools. Computer **30**(4), 75–82 (1997)
17. Johansson, A.: Software implemented fault injection used for software evaluation. In: Building Reliable Component-Based Systems (2002)
18. Kooli, M., Di Natale, G.: A survey on simulation-based fault injection tools for complex systems. In: 2014 9th IEEE International Conference on Design and Technology of Integrated Systems In Nanoscale Era (DTIS), pp. 1–6. IEEE (2014)
19. Le, H.M., Herdt, V., Große, D., Drechsler, R.: Resilience evaluation via symbolic fault injection on intermediate code. In: Design, Automation and Test in Europe Conference and Exhibition (DATE), pp. 845–850. IEEE (2018)
20. Marinescu, P.D., Candea, G.: LFI: a practical and general library-level fault injector. In: IEEE/IFIP International Conference on Dependable Systems and Networks, DSN 2009, pp. 379–388. IEEE (2009)
21. May, T.C., Woods, M.H.: A new physical mechanism for soft errors in dynamic memories. In: 16th Annual Reliability Physics Symposium, pp. 33–40. IEEE (1978)
22. Moro, N.: Sécurisation de programmes assembleur face aux attaques visant les processeurs embarqués. Ph.D. thesis, Université Pierre et Marie Curie-Paris VI (2014)

23. Moro, N., Dehbaoui, A., Heydemann, K., Robisson, B., Encrenaz, E.: Electromagnetic fault injection: towards a fault model on a 32-bit microcontroller. In: 2013 Workshop on Fault Diagnosis and Tolerance in Cryptography (FDTC), pp. 77–88. IEEE (2013)
24. Moro, N., Heydemann, K., Encrenaz, E., Robisson, B.: Formal verification of a software countermeasure against instruction skip attacks. J. Cryptogr. Eng. **4**(3), 145–156 (2014)
25. Pattabiraman, K., Nakka, N., Kalbarczyk, Z., Iyer, R.: SymPLFIED: symbolic program-level fault injection and error detection framework. In: 2008 IEEE International Conference on Dependable Systems and Networks with FTCS and DCC (DSN), pp. 472–481. IEEE (2008)
26. Piscitelli, R., Bhasin, S., Regazzoni, F.: Fault attacks, injection techniques and tools for simulation. In: Sklavos, N., Chaves, R., Di Natale, G., Regazzoni, F. (eds.) Hardware Security and Trust, pp. 27–47. Springer, Cham (2017). https://doi.org/10.1007/978-3-319-44318-8_2
27. Potet, M.-L., Mounier, L., Puys, M., Dureuil, L.: Lazart: a symbolic approach for evaluation the robustness of secured codes against control flow injections. In: 2014 IEEE Seventh International Conference on Software Testing, Verification and Validation, pp. 213–222. IEEE (2014)
28. Price, C.: MIPS IV instruction set (1995)
29. Qiao, R., Seaborn, M.: A new approach for rowhammer attacks. In: 2016 IEEE International Symposium on Hardware Oriented Security and Trust (HOST), pp. 161–166. IEEE (2016)
30. Quisquater, J.-J.: Eddy current for magnetic analysis with active sensor. In: Proceedings of ESmart, pp. 185–194 (2002)
31. Rivière, L., Bringer, J., Le, T.-H., Chabanne, H.: A novel simulation approach for fault injection resistance evaluation on smart cards. In: 2015 IEEE Eighth International Conference on Software Testing, Verification and Validation Workshops (ICSTW), pp. 1–8. IEEE (2015)
32. Rivière, L., Potet, M.-L., Le, T.-H., Bringer, J., Chabanne, H., Puys, M.: Combining high-level and low-level approaches to evaluate software implementations robustness against multiple fault injection attacks. In: Cuppens, F., Garcia-Alfaro, J., Zincir Heywood, N., Fong, P.W.L. (eds.) FPS 2014. LNCS, vol. 8930, pp. 92–111. Springer, Cham (2015). https://doi.org/10.1007/978-3-319-17040-4_7
33. Roscian, C., Dutertre, J.-M., Tria, A.: Frontside laser fault injection on cryptosystems-application to the AES, last round. In: 2013 IEEE International Symposium on Hardware-Oriented Security and Trust (HOST), pp. 119–124. IEEE (2013)
34. Schmidt, J.-M., Hutter, M.: Optical and EM fault-attacks on CRT-based RSA: Concrete results, na (2007)
35. Seaborn, M., Dullien, T.: Exploiting the DRAM rowhammer bug to gain kernel privileges. In: Black Hat (2015)
36. Skorobogatov, S.: Optically enhanced position-locked power analysis. In: Goubin, L., Matsui, M. (eds.) CHES 2006. LNCS, vol. 4249, pp. 61–75. Springer, Heidelberg (2006). https://doi.org/10.1007/11894063_6
37. Skorobogatov, S.: Optical fault masking attacks. In: 2010 Workshop on Fault Diagnosis and Tolerance in Cryptography (FDTC), pp. 23–29. IEEE (2010)
38. Trail of bits. Mc-semantics (2016). https://github.com/trailofbits/mcsema
39. Verbauwhede, I., Karaklajic, D., Schmidt, J.-M.: The fault attack jungle-a classification model to guide you. In: 2011 Workshop on Fault Diagnosis and Tolerance in Cryptography (FDTC), pp. 3–8. IEEE (2011)

40. Wang, G., Wang, S.: Differential fault analysis on present key schedule. In: 2010 International Conference on Computational Intelligence and Security (CIS), pp. 362–366. IEEE (2010)
41. Yim, K.S.: The rowhammer attack injection methodology. In: 2016 IEEE 35th Symposium on Reliable Distributed Systems (SRDS), pp. 1–10. IEEE (2016)
42. Yuce, B., Schaumont, P., Witteman, M.: Fault attacks on secure embedded software: threats, design, and evaluation. J. Hardw. Syst. Secur. **2**(2), 111–130 (2018). https://doi.org/10.1007/s41635-018-0038-1. ISSN 2509-3436

Replacing Store Buffers by Load Buffers in TSO

Parosh Aziz Abdulla[1(✉)], Mohamed Faouzi Atig[1], Ahmed Bouajjani[2], and Tuan Phong Ngo[1]

[1] Uppsala University, Uppsala, Sweden
{parosh,mohamed_faouzi.atig,tuan-phong.ngo}@it.uu.se
[2] IRIF Université Paris Diderot - Paris 7, Paris, France
abou@irif.fr

Abstract. We consider the weak memory model of Total Store Ordering (TSO). In the classical definition of TSO, an unbounded buffer is inserted between each process and the shared memory. The buffers contains pending store operations of the processes. We introduce a new model where we replace the store buffers by load buffers. In contrast to the classical model, the buffers now contain load operations. We show that the models have equivalent behaviors in the sense that the processes reach identical sets of states when the input program is run under the two models.

Keywords: Program verification · Weak memory models · TSO

1 Introduction

Designers of concurrent programs traditionally assume Sequential Consistency (SC) [36]. Under SC, the results of any execution is the same as if the operations of all the processors were executed in some sequential order, and the operations of each individual processor appear in this sequence in the order specified by its program. However, to optimize performance, modern architectures and compilers implement memory models that weaken the guarantees given by SC, by allowing various processes to execute instructions out-of-order, and also by allowing access to memory stores by different processes in different orders. In the context of *sequential* programming, this out-of-order execution is transparent to the programmer since one can still work under the SC model. However, this is not true any more when we consider concurrent processes that share the memory. In fact, it turns out that concurrent algorithms such as mutual exclusion and producer-consumer protocols may not behave correctly any more. Therefore, program verification is a relevant (and difficult) task in order to prove correctness under the new semantics. The out-of-order execution of instructions has led to the invention of new program semantics, so called *Weak (or Relaxed) Memory Models* (WMMs), by allowing permutations between certain types of memory operations. Examples include the Intel x86 [31] and SPARC [49] processors that use the TSO [43] (total store order) memory model. SPARC also defines

M. F. Atig et al. (Eds.): VECoS 2018, LNCS 11181, pp. 22–28, 2018.
https://doi.org/10.1007/978-3-030-00359-3_2

two other weak memory models: PSO (Partial Store Order) and RMO (Relaxed Memory Order). The Power [30] and ARM [14] architectures employ memory models that are even more relaxed [13,38,40,41]. Moreover, compilers, such as Java [39] and C++ [15], reorder commands to prefetch values from memory and fill the processor's execution line. In all these weak or relaxed memory models, different processes can observe different memory states at the same time. This implies that programs when run under weak or relaxed memory models display some behaviours which are not possible in SC.

2 Total Store Ordering

Total Store Ordering (TSO) is a classical model corresponding to the relaxation adopted by Sun's SPARC multiprocessors [49] and to formalizations of the x86-TSO memory model [42,44]. In TSO, a *store buffer* is inserted between each process and the main memory. The buffer behaves like an unbounded perfect (non-lossy) FIFO channel that carries the pending store operations of the process. When a process performs a write (store) operation, it appends it to the end of its buffer. These operations are propagated to the shared memory non-deterministically in a FIFO manner. When a process reads a variable, it searches its buffer for a pending store operation on that variable. If no such a store operation exists, it fetches the value of the variable from the main memory. The unboundedness of the buffers implies that the state space of the system is

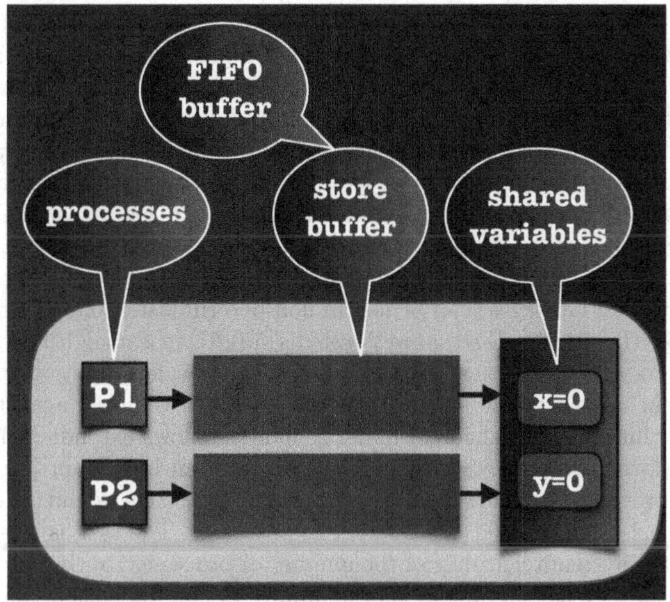

Fig. 1. The classical operational semantics for TSO.

infinite even in the case where the input program is finite-state. Therefore, verifying programs running on the TSO memory model poses a difficult challenge. Decidability of safety properties has been obtained by constructing equivalent models that replace the perfect store buffer by *lossy* channels [2,16,17]. However, these constructions are complicated and involve several ingredients that lead to inefficient verification procedures. For instance, they require each message inside a lossy channel to carry (instead of a single store operation) a full snapshot of the memory representing a local view of the memory contents by the process. Furthermore, the reductions involve non-deterministically guessing the lossy channel contents. The guessing is then resolved either by consistency checking [16] or by using explicit pointer variables (each corresponding to one process) inside the buffers [2], causing a serious state space explosion problem (Fig. 1).

3 Load-Buffer Semantics

We introduce an alternative semantics which we call the *load buffer* semantics, where we replace the store buffers by *load buffers* that contain pending load operations. The pending load operations represent values that will potentially be taken by forthcoming load operations. The flow of information will now be in the reverse direction, i.e., store operations are performed by the processes atomically on the main memory, while values of variables are propagated non-deterministically from the memory to the load buffers of the processes. When a process performs a load operation, it can fetch the value of the variable from the head of its load buffer. The load-buffer semantics is equivalent to the original store-buffer semantics in the sense that any given set of processes will reach the same set of local states under both semantics. This alternative TSO semantics allows us to understand the original model in a different way compared to the classical semantics. Furthermore, the load-buffer semantics offers several important advantages from the point of view of formal reasoning and program verification. First, it allows transforming the load buffers to *lossy* channels without adding the costly overhead that was necessary in the case of store buffers. This means that we can assume w.l.o.g. that any message in the load buffers (except a finite number of messages) can be lost in non-deterministic manner. Hence, we can apply the theory of *well-structured systems* [5,6,27] in a straightforward manner leading to a much simpler proof of decidability of safety properties. Second, the absence of extra overhead means that we obtain more efficient algorithms and better scalability. Finally, the load-buffer semantics allows extending the framework to perform *parameterized verification* which is an important paradigm in concurrent program verification. A *parameterized system*, e.g. a mutual exclusion protocol, consists of an arbitrary number of processes. The task is to show correctness of the system regardless of the number of processes. In the case of TSO, this means that we have a system that is infinite in two dimensions: we have an unbounded number of processes each of which is equipped with an unbounded buffer (Fig. 2).

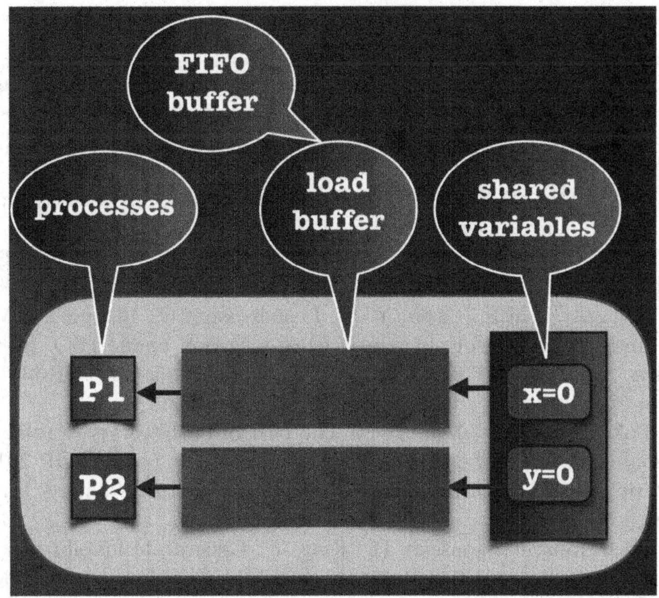

Fig. 2. The load-buffer semantics for TSO.

4 Related Work

There have been a lot of works related to the analysis of programs running under WMMs (e.g., [2,8–10,19–24,28,32–35,37,47,48,50]). Some of these works propose precise analysis techniques for checking safety properties or stability of finite-state programs under WMMs (e.g., [2,4,10,19,26]). Others propose context-bounded analyzing techniques (e.g., [7,18,45,46]) or stateless model-checking techniques (e.g., [1,25,29,51]) for programs under TSO and PSO. Different other techniques based on monitoring and testing have also been developed during these last years (e.g., [21,22,37]). There are also a number of efforts to design bounded model checking techniques for programs under WMMs (e.g., [11,12,20,50]) which encode the verification problem in SAT/SMT.

The closest works to ours are those presented in [2,3,16,17] which provide precise and sound techniques for checking safety properties for finite-state programs running under TSO. However, these techniques are complicated and cannot be extended, in a straightforward manner, to the verification of parameterized systems (as it is the case of the developed techniques for the Dual TSO semantics).

References

1. Abdulla, P.A., Aronis, S., Atig, M.F., Jonsson, B., Leonardsson, C., Sagonas, K.: Stateless model checking for TSO and PSO. In: Baier, C., Tinelli, C. (eds.) TACAS 2015. LNCS, vol. 9035, pp. 353–367. Springer, Heidelberg (2015). https://doi.org/10.1007/978-3-662-46681-0_28
2. Abdulla, P.A., Atig, M.F., Chen, Y.-F., Leonardsson, C., Rezine, A.: Counter-example guided fence insertion under TSO. In: Flanagan, C., König, B. (eds.) TACAS 2012. LNCS, vol. 7214, pp. 204–219. Springer, Heidelberg (2012). https://doi.org/10.1007/978-3-642-28756-5_15
3. Abdulla, P.A., Atig, M.F., Chen, Y.-F., Leonardsson, C., Rezine, A.: MEMORAX, a precise and sound tool for automatic fence insertion under TSO. In: Piterman, N., Smolka, S.A. (eds.) TACAS 2013. LNCS, vol. 7795, pp. 530–536. Springer, Heidelberg (2013). https://doi.org/10.1007/978-3-642-36742-7_37
4. Abdulla, P.A., Atig, M.F., Ngo, T.-P.: The best of both worlds: trading efficiency and optimality in fence insertion for TSO. In: Vitek, J. (ed.) ESOP 2015. LNCS, vol. 9032, pp. 308–332. Springer, Heidelberg (2015). https://doi.org/10.1007/978-3-662-46669-8_13
5. Abdulla, P., Cerans, K., Jonsson, B., Tsay, Y.: General decidability theorems for infinite-state systems. In: LICS 1996, pp. 313–321. IEEE Computer Society (1996)
6. Abdulla, P.A.: Well (and better) quasi-ordered transition systems. Bull. Symb. Log. **16**(4), 457–515 (2010)
7. Abdulla, P.A., Atig, M.F., Bouajjani, A., Ngo, T.P.: Context-bounded analysis for POWER. In: Legay, A., Margaria, T. (eds.) TACAS 2017. LNCS, vol. 10206, pp. 56–74. Springer, Heidelberg (2017). https://doi.org/10.1007/978-3-662-54580-5_4
8. Abdulla, P.A., Atig, M.F., Chen, Y.-F., Leonardsson, C., Rezine, A.: Automatic fence insertion in integer programs via predicate abstraction. In: Miné, A., Schmidt, D. (eds.) SAS 2012. LNCS, vol. 7460, pp. 164–180. Springer, Heidelberg (2012). https://doi.org/10.1007/978-3-642-33125-1_13
9. Abdulla, P.A., Atig, M.F., Jonsson, B., Leonardsson, C.: Stateless model checking for POWER. In: Chaudhuri, S., Farzan, A. (eds.) CAV 2016. LNCS, vol. 9780, pp. 134–156. Springer, Cham (2016). https://doi.org/10.1007/978-3-319-41540-6_8
10. Abdulla, P.A., Atig, M.F., Lång, M., Ngo, T.P.: Precise and sound automatic fence insertion procedure under PSO. In: Bouajjani, A., Fauconnier, H. (eds.) NETYS 2015. LNCS, vol. 9466, pp. 32–47. Springer, Cham (2015). https://doi.org/10.1007/978-3-319-26850-7_3
11. Alglave, J., Kroening, D., Nimal, V., Tautschnig, M.: Software verification for weak memory via program transformation. In: Felleisen, M., Gardner, P. (eds.) ESOP 2013. LNCS, vol. 7792, pp. 512–532. Springer, Heidelberg (2013). https://doi.org/10.1007/978-3-642-37036-6_28
12. Alglave, J., Kroening, D., Tautschnig, M.: Partial orders for efficient bounded model checking of concurrent software. In: Sharygina, N., Veith, H. (eds.) CAV 2013. LNCS, vol. 8044, pp. 141–157. Springer, Heidelberg (2013). https://doi.org/10.1007/978-3-642-39799-8_9
13. Alglave, J., Maranget, L., Tautschnig, M.: Herding cats: modelling, simulation, testing, and data mining for weak memory. ACM TOPLAS **36**(2), 7:1–7:4 (2014)
14. ARM: ARM architecture reference manual ARMv7-A and ARMv7-R edition (2012)
15. ISO/IEC 14882:2014. Programming language C++ (2014)

16. Atig, M.F., Bouajjani, A., Burckhardt, S., Musuvathi, M.: On the verification problem for weak memory models. In: POPL (2010)
17. Atig, M.F., Bouajjani, A., Burckhardt, S., Musuvathi, M.: What's decidable about weak memory models? In: Seidl, H. (ed.) ESOP 2012. LNCS, vol. 7211, pp. 26–46. Springer, Heidelberg (2012). https://doi.org/10.1007/978-3-642-28869-2_2
18. Atig, M.F., Bouajjani, A., Parlato, G.: Getting rid of store-buffers in TSO analysis. In: Gopalakrishnan, G., Qadeer, S. (eds.) CAV 2011. LNCS, vol. 6806, pp. 99–115. Springer, Heidelberg (2011). https://doi.org/10.1007/978-3-642-22110-1_9
19. Bouajjani, A., Derevenetc, E., Meyer, R.: Checking and enforcing robustness against TSO. In: Felleisen, M., Gardner, P. (eds.) ESOP 2013. LNCS, vol. 7792, pp. 533–553. Springer, Heidelberg (2013). https://doi.org/10.1007/978-3-642-37036-6_29
20. Burckhardt, S., Alur, R., Martin, M.M.K.: CheckFence: checking consistency of concurrent data types on relaxed memory models. In: PLDI, pp. 12–21. ACM (2007)
21. Burckhardt, S., Musuvathi, M.: Effective program verification for relaxed memory models. In: Gupta, A., Malik, S. (eds.) CAV 2008. LNCS, vol. 5123, pp. 107–120. Springer, Heidelberg (2008). https://doi.org/10.1007/978-3-540-70545-1_12
22. Burnim, J., Sen, K., Stergiou, C.: Testing concurrent programs on relaxed memory models. In: ISSTA, pp. 122–132. ACM (2011)
23. Dan, A.M., Meshman, Y., Vechev, M., Yahav, E.: Predicate abstraction for relaxed memory models. In: Logozzo, F., Fähndrich, M. (eds.) SAS 2013. LNCS, vol. 7935, pp. 84–104. Springer, Heidelberg (2013). https://doi.org/10.1007/978-3-642-38856-9_7
24. Dan, A., Meshman, Y., Vechev, M., Yahav, E.: Effective abstractions for verification under relaxed memory models. Comput. Lang. Syst. Struct. **47**(Part 1), 62–76 (2017)
25. Demsky, B., Lam, P.: Satcheck: sat-directed stateless model checking for SC and TSO. In: OOPSLA 2015, pp. 20–36. ACM (2015)
26. Derevenetc, E., Meyer, R.: Robustness against power is PSpace-complete. In: Esparza, J., Fraigniaud, P., Husfeldt, T., Koutsoupias, E. (eds.) ICALP 2014. LNCS, vol. 8573, pp. 158–170. Springer, Heidelberg (2014). https://doi.org/10.1007/978-3-662-43951-7_14
27. Finkel, A., Schnoebelen, P.: Well-structured transition systems everywhere!. Theor. Comput. Sci. **256**(1–2), 63–92 (2001)
28. He, M., Vafeiadis, V., Qin, S., Ferreira, J.F.: Reasoning about fences and relaxed atomics. In: 24th Euromicro International Conference on Parallel, Distributed, and Network-Based Processing, PDP 2016, Heraklion, Crete, Greece, 17–19 February 2016, pp. 520–527 (2016)
29. Huang, S., Huang, J.: Maximal causality reduction for TSO and PSO. OOPSLA, pp. 447–461 (2016)
30. IBM (ed.): Power ISA v. 2.05 (2007)
31. Inc, I.: Intel^{TM}64 and IA-32 Architectures Software Developer's Manuals
32. Kuperstein, M., Vechev, M.T., Yahav, E.: Automatic inference of memory fences. In: FMCAD, pp. 111–119. IEEE (2010)
33. Kuperstein, M., Vechev, M.T., Yahav, E.: Partial-coherence abstractions for relaxed memory models. In: PLDI, pp. 187–198. ACM (2011)
34. Lahav, O., Vafeiadis, V.: Owicki-Gries reasoning for weak memory models. In: Halldórsson, M.M., Iwama, K., Kobayashi, N., Speckmann, B. (eds.) ICALP 2015. LNCS, vol. 9135, pp. 311–323. Springer, Heidelberg (2015). https://doi.org/10.1007/978-3-662-47666-6_25

35. Lahav, O., Vafeiadis, V.: Explaining relaxed memory models with program transformations. In: Fitzgerald, J., Heitmeyer, C., Gnesi, S., Philippou, A. (eds.) FM 2016. LNCS, vol. 9995, pp. 479–495. Springer, Cham (2016). https://doi.org/10.1007/978-3-319-48989-6_29
36. Lamport, L.: How to make a multiprocessor computer that correctly executes multiprocess programs. IEEE Trans. Comput. **C–28**(9), 690–691 (1979)
37. Liu, F., Nedev, N., Prisadnikov, N., Vechev, M.T., Yahav, E.: Dynamic synthesis for relaxed memory models. In: PLDI 2012, pp. 429–440 (2012)
38. Mador-Haim, S., et al.: An axiomatic memory model for POWER multiprocessors. In: Madhusudan, P., Seshia, S.A. (eds.) CAV 2012. LNCS, vol. 7358, pp. 495–512. Springer, Heidelberg (2012). https://doi.org/10.1007/978-3-642-31424-7_36
39. Manson, J., Pugh, W., Adve, S.V.: The Java memory model. In: POPL2005, pp. 378–391. ACM (2005)
40. McKenney, P.E.: Memory ordering in modern microprocessors, part II. Linux J. **137**, 5 (2005)
41. Nieplocha, J., Carpenter, B.: ARMCI: a portable remote memory copy library for distributed array libraries and compiler run-time systems. In: Rolim, J., et al. (eds.) IPPS 1999. LNCS, vol. 1586, pp. 533–546. Springer, Heidelberg (1999). https://doi.org/10.1007/BFb0097937
42. Owens, S., Sarkar, S., Sewell, P.: A better x86 memory model: x86-TSO. In: Berghofer, S., Nipkow, T., Urban, C., Wenzel, M. (eds.) TPHOLs 2009. LNCS, vol. 5674, pp. 391–407. Springer, Heidelberg (2009). https://doi.org/10.1007/978-3-642-03359-9_27
43. Owens, S., Sarkar, S., Sewell, P.: A better x86 memory model: x86-TSO (extended version). Technical report. UCAM-CL-TR-745, University of Cambridge (2009)
44. Sewell, P., Sarkar, S., Owens, S., Nardelli, F.Z., Myreen, M.O.: x86-tso: a rigorous and usable programmer's model for x86 multiprocessors. CACM **53**, 89–97 (2010)
45. Tomasco, E., Lam, T.N., Fischer, B., Torre, S.L., Parlato, G.: Embedding weak memory models within eager sequentialization, October 2016. http://eprints.soton.ac.uk/402285/
46. Tomasco, E., Lam, T.N., Inverso, O., Fischer, B., Torre, S.L., Parlato, G.: Lazy sequentialization for TSO and PSO via shared memory abstractions. In: FMCAD16, pp. 193–200 (2016)
47. Travkin, O., Wehrheim, H.: Verification of concurrent programs on weak memory models. In: Sampaio, A., Wang, F. (eds.) ICTAC 2016. LNCS, vol. 9965, pp. 3–24. Springer, Cham (2016). https://doi.org/10.1007/978-3-319-46750-4_1
48. Vafeiadis, V.: Separation logic for weak memory models. In: Proceedings of the Programming Languages Mentoring Workshop, PLMW@POPL 2015, Mumbai, India, 14 January 2015, p. 11:1 (2015)
49. Weaver, D., Germond, T. (eds.): The SPARC Architecture Manual Version 9. PTR Prentice Hall, Englewood Cliffs (1994)
50. Yang, Y., Gopalakrishnan, G., Lindstrom, G., Slind, K.: Nemos: a framework for axiomatic and executable specifications of memory consistency models. In: IPDPS. IEEE (2004)
51. Zhang, N., Kusano, M., Wang, C.: Dynamic partial order reduction for relaxed memory models. In: PLDI, pp. 250–259. ACM (2015)

Distributed Systems and Protocols

Orchestration Synthesis for Real-Time Service Contracts

Davide Basile[1,2(✉)], Maurice H. ter Beek[2], Axel Legay[3], and Louis-Marie Traonouez[3]

[1] University of Florence, Florence, Italy
[2] ISTI–CNR, Pisa, Italy
{davide.basile,maurice.terbeek}@isti.cnr.it
[3] Inria Rennes, Rennes, France
{axel.legay,louis-marie.traonouez}@inria.fr

Abstract. Service contracts offer a way to define the desired behavioural compliance of a composition of services, characterised by the fulfilment of all requirements (e.g. service requests) by obligations (e.g. service offers). Depending on their granularity, requirements may vary according to their criticality and contain real-time aspects (e.g. service expiration time). Synthesis of safe orchestrations, the standard method to refine spurious compositions into compliant ones, is of paramount importance. Ideally, safe orchestrations solve competition among matching requests/offers, respecting criticalities and time constraints, in the best possible way. The contribution of this paper is (i) the introduction of timed service contract automata, a novel formalisation of service contracts with (ii) real-time constraints and (iii) service requests with varying levels of criticality, and a means to compute their (iv) composition and (v) safe orchestration. Orchestration is based on the synthesis of the most permissive controller from supervisory control theory, computed using the concept of zones from timed games. An intuitive example illustrates the contribution.

1 Introduction

Service computing is concerned with the creation, publication, discovery and orchestration of services [1]. A typical application is an orchestration of services created and published by different organisations that are dynamically discovered. In the recent Service Computing Manifesto [2], *service design* is listed as one of the four emerging research challenges in service computing for the next 10 years.

Formal models of service contracts are surveyed in [3]. These offer specification frameworks to formalise the externally observable behaviour of services in terms of obligations (i.e. *offers*) and requirements (i.e. *requests*) to be matched. Contracts that are fulfilled characterise *agreement* among services as an *orchestration* (i.e. composition) based on the satisfaction of all requirements through obligations. Orchestrations must be able to dynamically adapt to the discovery of new services, to service updates and to services that are no longer available [4].

M. F. Atig et al. (Eds.): VECoS 2018, LNCS 11181, pp. 31–47, 2018.
https://doi.org/10.1007/978-3-030-00359-3_3

In this paper, we include notions of time in one such model, viz. (service) contract automata [5]. Such an automaton represents either a single service (called a principal) or a multi-party composition of services. The goal of each principal is to reach an accepting (final) state by matching its requests with corresponding offers of other principals. The underlying composition mechanism is orchestration. Service interactions are implicitly controlled by an orchestrator synthesised from the principals, which directs them in such a way that only finite executions in agreement actually happen. The (verifiable) notion of *agreement* characterises safe executions of services (i.e. all requests are matched by corresponding offers).

In [6], service contract automata were equipped with modalities distinguishing *necessary* and *permitted* requests to mimick the uncontrollable and controllable actions, respectively, as known from Supervisory Control Theory (SCT) [7].

Contribution. We introduce *timed service contract automata* (TSCA) by endowing service contract automata with *real-time constraints*. TSCA also allow to specify different types of necessary requests, called *urgent*, *greedy* and *lazy*, with decreasing levels of criticality as in [8], which are key aspects to ensure that certain necessary requests must *always* be satisfied (e.g. in each possible context) while others must *eventually* be satisfied (e.g. in specific contexts). To handle this in a synthesis algorithm for TSCA, a notion of *semi-controllability* is used, which encompasses both the notion of controllability and that of uncontrollability as used in classical synthesis algorithms from SCT. Our synthesis algorithm mixes and extends techniques from SCT with notions from timed games [9,10].

A TSCA orchestration thus solves multi-party competitions on service actions and on the associated timing constraints, a natural scenario in service computing. Moreover, TSCA offer a lot of flexibility in the design of service systems through different levels of critical requests and, in particular, by allowing to indicate those service offers and requests that can possibly be (temporarily) ignored in an orchestration to avoid it becoming unsafe. This neatly delimits the fragments (i.e. executions) of service compositions allowed in safe orchestrations (cf. Fig. 4 discussed in Sect. 4). By changing the timing constraints or criticality levels, designers can fine-tune such fragments according to their specific needs.

We summarise our contribution: (i) we introduce TSCA, a new formalisation of service contracts with (ii) real-time constraints and (iii) service requests with varying criticality levels, and a means to compute TSCA (iv) composition and (v) safe orchestration. We are not aware of other formalisms for service contracts or component-based software engineering with native support for these features. We illustrate its functioning with a TSCA model of a Hotel reservation system.

Related Work. Formalisms for service contracts and session types are surveyed in [11]: all of them lack an explicit notion of time and different levels of criticality.

Component-based formalisms like *Interface automata* [12] and *(timed) (I/O) automata* [13–15] cannot model contracts that compete for the same service offer or request, a key feature of TSCA, and also do not allow different criticality levels. Modal I/O automata [16] distinguish may and must modalities, thus admitting some actions to be more critical than others, but the other differences remain. The accidentally homonym *contract automata* of [17] were introduced to model generic natural language legal contracts between two parties: they are not compositional and do not focus on synthesising orchestrations of services in agreement.

Finally, the synthesis algorithm for TSCA (introduced in Sect. 3) resembles a *timed game*, but differs from classical timed game algorithms [9,10]: it solves both reachability and safety problems, and a TSCA might be such that all 'bad' configurations are unreachable (i.e. it is safe), while at the same time no final configuration is reachable (i.e. the resulting orchestration is empty). TSCA strategies are defined as relations: the orchestration is the maximal winning strategy, which is computable since only finite traces are allowed [18] and all services terminate by definition. The orchestrator enforces only fair executions.

2 Modelling Real-Time Service Contracts

Contract automata were introduced to describe and compose service contracts [5]. A contract automaton represents the behaviour of a set of principals (possibly a singleton) which can either request, offer or match services (a match is a pair of complementary request-offer services) or remain idle. The number of principals in a contract automaton is called its rank. The states and actions labelling the transitions of a contract automaton (of rank n) are vectors (of rank n) over the states of its principals and over the actions that each performs, respectively.

Notation. The complement of a finite set S is denoted by $\overline{S}$; the empty set by $\emptyset$. For a vector $\boldsymbol{v} = (e_1, \ldots, e_n)$ of *rank* $n \geq 1$, denoted by $r_{\boldsymbol{v}}$, its ith element is denoted $\boldsymbol{v}_{(i)}$, $1 \leq i \leq r_{\boldsymbol{v}}$. Concatenation of m vectors $\boldsymbol{v}_i$ is denoted by $\boldsymbol{v}_1 \cdots \boldsymbol{v}_m$.

The set of basic actions of a contract automaton is defined as $\Sigma = \mathsf{R} \cup \mathsf{O} \cup \{\bullet\}$, where $\mathsf{R} = \{a, b, \ldots\}$ is the set of *requests*, $\mathsf{O} = \{\overline{a}, \overline{b}, \ldots\}$ is the set of *offers*, $\mathsf{R} \cap \mathsf{O} = \emptyset$, and $\bullet \notin \mathsf{R} \cup \mathsf{O}$ is a distinguished element representing an *idle* move. We define the involution $co(\cdot) : \Sigma \mapsto \Sigma$ s.t. $co(\mathsf{R}) = \mathsf{O}$, $co(\mathsf{O}) = \mathsf{R}$ and $co(\bullet) = \bullet$.

We stipulate that in an action vector $\boldsymbol{a}$ over Σ there is either a single offer or a single request, or a single pair of request-offer that matches, i.e. there exist i, j such that $\boldsymbol{a}_{(i)}$ is an offer and $\boldsymbol{a}_{(j)}$ is the complementary request or vice versa; all the other entries of $\boldsymbol{a}$ contain the symbol $\bullet$ (meaning that the corresponding principals remain idle). Let $\bullet^m$ denote a vector $(\bullet, \ldots, \bullet)$ of rank m.

Definition 1 (Actions). *Let $\boldsymbol{a}$ be an action vector over Σ. Let $n_1, n_2, n_3 \geq 0$.*

If $\boldsymbol{a} = \bullet^{n_1} \alpha \bullet^{n_2}$, then $\boldsymbol{a}$ is a request (action) *on α if $\alpha \in \mathsf{R}$, whereas $\boldsymbol{a}$ is an* offer (action) *on α if $\alpha \in \mathsf{O}$.*

If $\boldsymbol{a} = \bullet^{n_1} \alpha \bullet^{n_2} co(\alpha) \bullet^{n_3}$, then $\boldsymbol{a}$ is a match (action) *on α, with $\alpha \in \mathsf{R} \cup \mathsf{O}$.*

Actions $\boldsymbol{a}$ and $\boldsymbol{b}$ are complementary, *denoted by $\boldsymbol{a} \bowtie \boldsymbol{b}$, iff the following holds: (i) $\exists\, \alpha \in \mathsf{R} \cup \mathsf{O}$ s.t. $\boldsymbol{a}$ is either a request or offer on α; (ii) $\boldsymbol{a}$ is an offer on α implies $\boldsymbol{b}$ is a request on $co(\alpha)$; (iii) $\boldsymbol{a}$ is a request on α implies $\boldsymbol{b}$ is an offer on $co(\alpha)$.*

In [6], the contract automata of [5] were equipped with action variability via *necessary* ($\Box$) and *permitted* ($\Diamond$) modalities that can be used to classify requests (and matches), while all offers are by definition permitted. Permitted requests and offers reflect optional behaviour and can thus be discarded in compositions.

2.1 Timed Service Contract Automata

In this paper, the set of necessary requests of the service contract automata of [6] is partitioned in *urgent*, *greedy* and *lazy* requests as in [8]. These must be matched to reach agreement, thus adding a layer of 'timed' variability: a means to specify 'when' certain (service) requests must be matched in a composition (contract). Table 1 depicts the different types of actions considered in this paper.

Table 1. Classification of (basic) actions of timed service contract automata

Permitted offers	Permitted requests	Necessary requests		
		lazy	*greedy*	*urgent*
$\overline{a}$	$a\Diamond$	$a\Box_\ell$	$a\Box_g$	$a\Box_u$

We borrow notation concerning clocks from [10]. Let X be a finite set of real-valued variables called clocks. Let $C(X)$ denote the set of constraints φ generated by the grammar $\varphi ::= x \sim k \mid x - y \sim k \mid \varphi \wedge \varphi$, where $k \in \mathbb{Z}$, $x, y \in X$ and $\sim \in \{<, \leq, =, >, \geq\}$. Let $B(X)$ denote the subset of $C(X)$ that uses only rectangular constraints of the form $x \sim k$. For simplicity, we consider only such constraints. A *valuation* of the variables in X is a mapping $X \mapsto \mathbb{R}_{\geq 0}$. Let $\mathbf{0}$ denote the valuation that assigns 0 to each clock. For $Y \subseteq X$, let $v[Y]$ denote the valuation assigning 0 for any $x \in Y$ and $v(x)$ for any $x \in X \setminus Y$. Let $v + \delta$ for $\delta \in \mathbb{R}_{\geq 0}$ denote the valuation s.t. for all $x \in X$, $(v + \delta)(x) = v(x) + \delta$. For $g \in C(X)$ and $v \in \mathbb{R}^X_{\geq 0}$, we write $v \models g$ if v satisfies g and $[g]$ denotes the set of valuations $\{v \in \mathbb{R}^X_{\geq 0} \mid v \models g\}$. A *zone* Z is a subset of $\mathbb{R}^X_{\geq 0}$ s.t. $[g] = Z$ for some $g \in C(X)$.

Definition 2 (TSCA). *A timed service contract automaton $\mathcal{A}$ (TSCA for short) of rank $n \geq 1$ is a tuple $\langle Q, \mathbf{q_0}, A^\Diamond, A^{\Box_u}, A^{\Box_g}, A^{\Box_\ell}, A^o, X, T, F\rangle$, in which*

- *$Q = Q_1 \times \cdots \times Q_n$ is the product of finite sets of states*
- *$\mathbf{q_0} \in Q$ is the initial state*
- *$A^\Diamond, A^{\Box_u}, A^{\Box_g}, A^{\Box_\ell} \subseteq \mathsf{R}$ are (pairwise disjoint) sets of permitted, urgent, greedy and lazy requests, respectively, and we denote the set of requests by $A^r = A^\Diamond \cup A^\Box$, where $A^\Box = A^{\Box_u} \cup A^{\Box_g} \cup A^{\Box_\ell}$*
- *$A^o \subseteq \mathsf{O}$ is the finite set of offers*
- *X is a finite set of real-valued clocks*
- *$T \subseteq Q \times B(X) \times A \times 2^X \times Q$, where $A = (A^r \cup A^o \cup \{\bullet\})^n$, is the set of transitions partitioned into* permitted *transitions $T^\Diamond$ and* necessary *transitions $T^\Box$ with $T = T^\Diamond \cup T^\Box$ s.t., given $t = (\mathbf{q}, g, \mathbf{a}, Y, \mathbf{q}') \in T$, the following holds:*
  - *$\mathbf{a}$ is either a request or an offer or a match*
  - *$\forall i \in 1 \dots n : \mathbf{a}_{(i)} = \bullet$ implies $\mathbf{q}_{(i)} = \mathbf{q}'_{(i)}$*
  - *$t \in T^\Diamond$ iff $\mathbf{a}$ is either a request or a match on $a \in A^\Diamond$ or an offer on $\overline{a} \in A^o$; otherwise $t \in T^\Box$*
- *$F \subseteq Q$ is the set of final states*

A principal *TSCA (or just* principal*) has rank 1 and $A^r \cap co(A^o) = \varnothing$.*

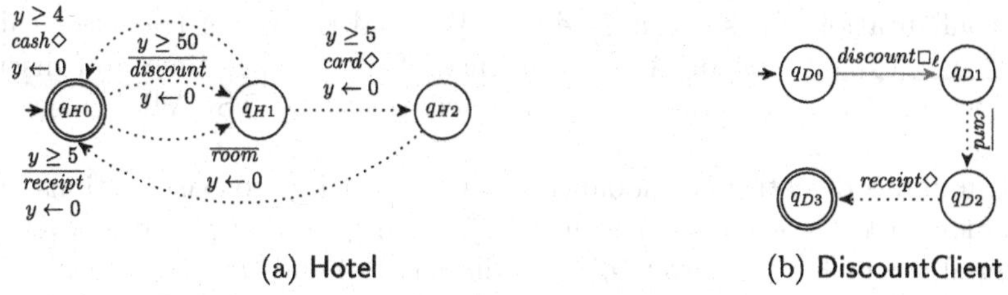

Fig. 1. TSCA: (a) hotel booking system; (b) discount client

For brevity, unless stated differently, in the sequel we assume a fixed TSCA $\mathcal{A} = \langle Q_{\mathcal{A}}, \boldsymbol{q_0}_{\mathcal{A}}, A^{\diamond}_{\mathcal{A}}, A^{\square_u}_{\mathcal{A}}, A^{\square_g}_{\mathcal{A}}, A^{\square_\ell}_{\mathcal{A}}, A^{o}_{\mathcal{A}}, X_{\mathcal{A}}, T_{\mathcal{A}}, F_{\mathcal{A}}\rangle$ of rank n. Subscript $\mathcal{A}$ may be omitted when no confusion can arise. Moreover, if not stated otherwise, each operation $op(A^r)$ (e.g. union) is intended to be performed homomorphically on $op(A^{\diamond})$, $op(A^{\square})$, $op(A^{\square_u})$, $op(A^{\square_g})$ and $op(A^{\square_\ell})$. Finally, abusing notation, we may write $T^{\diamond\cup\square}$ as shorthand for $T^{\diamond} \cup T^{\square}$ and likewise for other transition sets, and we may write a transition t as a request, offer or match, if its label is such.

Pictorially, offer actions are overlined while request actions are not. Moreover, permitted actions label dotted transitions and are suffixed by $\diamond$, whereas urgent, greedy and lazy necessary actions label red, orange and green transitions and are suffixed by $\square_u$, $\square_g$ and $\square_\ell$, respectively (cf. Table 1).[1]

Example 1. Figure 1 shows two TSCA. The one in Fig. 1a depicts a hotel booking system offering two room types (normal and discount) and requests payment from clients. The discount room is only available upon waiting at least 50 time units (t.u. for short). Then the hotel requests payment, either in cash (which takes at least 4 t.u.) or by card (at least 5 t.u.). In the latter case only, the hotel offers a receipt after at least 5 t.u. The TSCA in Fig. 1b depicts a hotel client, who requests a discount room, offers to pay by card and requests a receipt.

2.2 Semantics

A TSCA recognises a trace language over actions and their modalities. Let $\mathcal{A}$ be a TSCA and let $\bigcirc \in \{\diamond, \square_u, \square_g, \square_\ell\}$. From now on we use $\bigcirc$ as placeholder for necessary ($\square$) and permitted ($\diamond$) transitions. A *configuration* of a TSCA is a tuple $(w, \boldsymbol{q}, v) \in (A \cup \{\bigcirc\})^* \times Q \times \mathbb{R}^X_{\geq 0}$ consisting of a recognised trace, a state and a valuation of clocks. Recognised traces are such that from a configuration $(w, \boldsymbol{q}, v)$, a TSCA either lets time progress or performs a discrete step to reach a new configuration. This is formally defined by the transition relation $\rightarrow$ by which a step $(w, \boldsymbol{q}, v) \xrightarrow{a\bigcirc} (w', \boldsymbol{q}', v')$ is fired iff $w = \boldsymbol{a}\bigcirc\, w'$ and $(\boldsymbol{q}, g, \boldsymbol{a}, Y, \boldsymbol{q}') \in T^{\bigcirc}$, where $v \models g$ and $v' = v[Y]$ or else, for some $\delta \geq 0$, we have $(w, \boldsymbol{q}, v) \xrightarrow{\delta} (w, \boldsymbol{q}, v')$ if $v' = v + \delta$. Time progress δ is a silent action in languages recognised by TSCA.

The semantics of a TSCA $\mathcal{A}$ is a labelled transition system $TS_{\mathcal{A}} = (\mathbb{C}, c_0, \rightarrow)$, where $\mathbb{C} = (A \cup \{\bigcirc\})^* \times Q \times \mathbb{R}^X_{\geq 0}$ is the set of configurations, $c_0 = (w, \boldsymbol{q}_0, \boldsymbol{0})$ is the

[1] In this paper, there are no examples of greedy necessary actions.

initial configuration, for some $w \in (A \cup \{\bigcirc\})^*$, and the set of transition labels is $(A\{\bigcirc\}) \cup \mathbb{R}_{\geq 0}$. A *run* of $\mathcal{A}$ is a sequence of alternating time and discrete transitions in TS_A. Note that the traces recognised by TSCA languages are finite.

By an abuse of notation, modalities can be attached to basic actions or to their action vector (e.g. $(a\Box_\ell, \overline{a}) \equiv (a, \overline{a})\Box_\ell$). We may write $(\boldsymbol{q}, v)$ whenever w is immaterial, $(\boldsymbol{q}, v)\xrightarrow{\boldsymbol{a}\bigcirc}$ whenever $(\boldsymbol{q}', v')$ is immaterial and $(w, \boldsymbol{q}, v) \rightarrow (w', \boldsymbol{q}', v')$ whenever $\boldsymbol{a}\bigcirc$ or δ are immaterial. Let $\rightarrow^*$ denote the reflexive and transitive closure of $\rightarrow$. The language of $\mathcal{A}$ is $\mathscr{L}(\mathcal{A}) = \{\, w \mid (w, \boldsymbol{q_0}, \boldsymbol{0}) \rightarrow^* (\epsilon, \boldsymbol{q}, v),\ \boldsymbol{q} \in F \,\}$.

Behavioural analysis is based on exploring a (finite) *simulation graph*, whose nodes are *symbolic configurations*, defined as pairs $(\boldsymbol{q}, Z)$, where $\boldsymbol{q} \in Q$ and Z is a zone of $\mathbb{R}^X_{\geq 0}$. Let $C \subseteq \mathbb{C}$ be a set of configurations and let $\boldsymbol{a} \in A$. Then we define the $\boldsymbol{a}$-successor of X by $Post_{\mathcal{A},\boldsymbol{a}}(C) = \{\, c' \mid \exists c \in C : c\xrightarrow{\boldsymbol{a}\circ}c' \,\}$ and the $\boldsymbol{a}$-predecessor $Pred_{\mathcal{A},\boldsymbol{a}}(C) = \{\, c \mid \exists c' \in C : c\xrightarrow{\boldsymbol{a}\circ}c' \,\}$. We moreover define the *match/offer predecessor* as $moPred_{\mathcal{A}}(C) = \bigcup_{\boldsymbol{a}\ match\ or\ offer} Pred_{\mathcal{A},\boldsymbol{a}}(C)$.

The timed successors and timed predecessors of C are defined by $C^{\nearrow} = \{\, (\boldsymbol{q}, v + \delta) \mid (\boldsymbol{q}, v) \in C,\ \delta \in \mathbb{R}_{\geq 0} \,\}$ and $C^{\swarrow} = \{\, (\boldsymbol{q}, v - \delta) \mid (\boldsymbol{q}, v) \in C,\ \delta \in \mathbb{R}_{\geq 0} \,\}$, respectively. Let $\rightarrow$ be the transition relation defined on symbolic configurations by $(\boldsymbol{q}, Z)\xrightarrow{\boldsymbol{a}\bigcirc}(\boldsymbol{q}', Z')$ if $(\boldsymbol{q}, g, \boldsymbol{a}, Y, \boldsymbol{q}') \in T^{\bigcirc}$ and $Z' = ((Z \cap [g])[Y])^{\nearrow}$.

2.3 Composition

A set of TSCA is *composable* iff their sets of clocks are pairwise disjoint.

Definition 3 (Composable TSCA). *A set* $\{\, \mathcal{A}_i \mid i \in 1 \ldots n \,\}$ *of TSCA is said to be* composable *iff* $\forall X_i, X_j, i \neq j : X_i \cap X_j = \varnothing$.

The operands of the composition operator are either principals or composite services. Intuitively, a composition interleaves the actions of all operands, with only one restriction: if two operands are ready to execute two complementary actions, then only their match is allowed wheras their interleaving is prevented. The formal definition precedes an intuitive explanation. Recall from Definition 2 that the set of actions is $A \subseteq (A^r \cup A^o \cup \{\bullet\})^m$. Also recall that we set $\bigcirc \in \{\Diamond, \Box\}$.

Definition 4 (Composition). *Let* $\mathcal{A}_i$ *be composable TSCA of rank* r_i, $i \in 1 \ldots n$. *The* composition $\bigotimes_{i \in 1 \ldots n} \mathcal{A}_i$ *is the TSCA* $\mathcal{A}$ *of rank* $m = \sum_{i \in 1 \ldots n} r_i$, *where*

- $Q = Q_1 \times \cdots \times Q_n$, *with* $\boldsymbol{q_0} = \boldsymbol{q_{0_1}} \cdots \boldsymbol{q_{0_n}}$
- $A^r = \bigcup_{i \in 1 \ldots n} A^r_i$, $\quad A^o = \bigcup_{i \in 1 \ldots n} A^o_i$, $\quad X = \bigcup_{i \in 1 \ldots n} X_i$
- $T^{\bigcirc} \subseteq Q \times B(X) \times A \times 2^X \times Q$ *s.t.* $(\boldsymbol{q}, g, \boldsymbol{a}, Y, \boldsymbol{q}') \in T^{\bigcirc}$ *iff, when* $\boldsymbol{q} = \boldsymbol{q}_1 \cdots \boldsymbol{q}_n \in Q$, *either case (1) or case (2) holds:*
  1. $\exists i, j, 1 \leq i < j \leq n$, *s.t.* $(\boldsymbol{q}_i, g_i, \boldsymbol{a}_i, Y_i, \boldsymbol{q}'_i) \in T^{\bigcirc}_i$, $(\boldsymbol{q}_j, g_j, \boldsymbol{a}_j, Y_j, \boldsymbol{q}'_j) \in T^{\bigcirc \cup \Diamond}_j$, $\boldsymbol{a}_i \bowtie \boldsymbol{a}_j$ *holds, and*

$$\begin{cases} \boldsymbol{a} = \bullet^u \boldsymbol{a}_i \bullet^v \boldsymbol{a}_j \bullet^z, \textit{ with } u = r_1 + \cdots + r_{i-1},\ v = r_{i+1} + \cdots + r_{j-1}, \\ z = r_{j+1} + \cdots + r_n,\ |\boldsymbol{a}| = m,\ g = g_i \wedge g_j,\ Y = Y_i \cup Y_j, \\ \textit{and } \boldsymbol{q}' = \boldsymbol{q}_1 \cdots \boldsymbol{q}_{i-1}\ \boldsymbol{q}'_i\ \boldsymbol{q}_{i+1} \cdots \boldsymbol{q}_{j-1}\ \boldsymbol{q}'_j\ \boldsymbol{q}_{j+1} \cdots \boldsymbol{q}_n \end{cases}$$

or

$$\begin{cases} k, k' \in \{i, j\},\ k \neq k',\ g = g_k \wedge \neg g_{k'},\ Y = Y_k, \\ \boldsymbol{a} = \bullet^u \boldsymbol{a}_k \bullet^v, \textit{with } u = r_1 + \cdots + r_{k-1},\ v = r_{k+1} + \cdots + r_n,\ |\boldsymbol{a}| = m, \\ \textit{and } \boldsymbol{q}' = \boldsymbol{q}_1 \cdots \boldsymbol{q}_{i-1}\ \boldsymbol{q}'_i\ \boldsymbol{q}_{i+1} \cdots \boldsymbol{q}_n \end{cases}$$

2. $\exists i, 1 \leq i \leq n$, *s.t.* $(\boldsymbol{q}_i, g_i, \boldsymbol{a}_i, Y_i, \boldsymbol{q}'_i) \in T_i^{\bigcirc}$ *and* $\forall j \neq i, 1 \leq j \leq n$, *s.t.* $(\boldsymbol{q}_j, g_j, \boldsymbol{a}_j, Y_j, \boldsymbol{q}'_j) \in T_j^{\bigcirc \cup \Diamond}$, $\boldsymbol{a}_i \bowtie \boldsymbol{a}_j$ *does not hold, and*

$$\begin{cases} \boldsymbol{a} = \bullet^u \boldsymbol{a}_i \bullet^v, \textit{with } u = r_1 + \cdots + r_{i-1},\ v = r_{i+1} + \cdots + r_n,\ |\boldsymbol{a}| = m, \\ g = g_i,\ Y = Y_i,\ \textit{and } \boldsymbol{q}' = \boldsymbol{q}_1 \cdots \boldsymbol{q}_{i-1}\ \boldsymbol{q}'_i\ \boldsymbol{q}_{i+1} \cdots \boldsymbol{q}_n \end{cases}$$

– $F = \{\boldsymbol{q}_1 \cdots \boldsymbol{q}_n \in Q \mid \boldsymbol{q}_i \in F_i,\ i \in 1 \ldots n\}$

The composition of (untimed) contract automata has been carefully revisited in Definition 4. Case (1) generates match transitions starting from complementary actions of two operands' transitions, say $\boldsymbol{a}_i \bowtie \boldsymbol{a}_j$. If $(\boldsymbol{q}_j, g_j, \boldsymbol{a}_j, Y_j, \boldsymbol{q}'_j) \in T^{\Box}$, then the resulting match transition is marked necessary (i.e. $(\boldsymbol{q}, g, \boldsymbol{a}, Y, \boldsymbol{q}') \in T^{\Box}$), with $g = g_i \wedge g_j$ the conjunction of the guards. If both $\boldsymbol{a}_i$ and $\boldsymbol{a}_j$ are permitted, then so is their resulting match transition t. All principals not involved in t remain idle. In case $\boldsymbol{a}_i \bowtie \boldsymbol{a}_j$ as before, but only one guard (i.e. either g_i or g_j) is satisfied, then only the interleaving is possible and guard $g = g_k \wedge \neg g_{k'}$ requires the guard of principal k (either g_i or g_j) to be satisfied and that of principal $k' \neq k$ not.

Case (2) generates all interleaved transitions if no complementary actions can be executed from the composed source state (i.e. $\boldsymbol{q}$). Now one operand executes its transition $t = (\boldsymbol{q}_i, g_i, \boldsymbol{a}_i, Y_i, \boldsymbol{q}'_i)$ and all others remain idle: only the guard of principal i must be satisfied. The resulting transition is marked necessary (permitted) only if t is necessary (permitted, respectively). Note that condition $\boldsymbol{a}_i \bowtie \boldsymbol{a}_j$ excludes pre-existing match transitions of the operands to generate new matches.

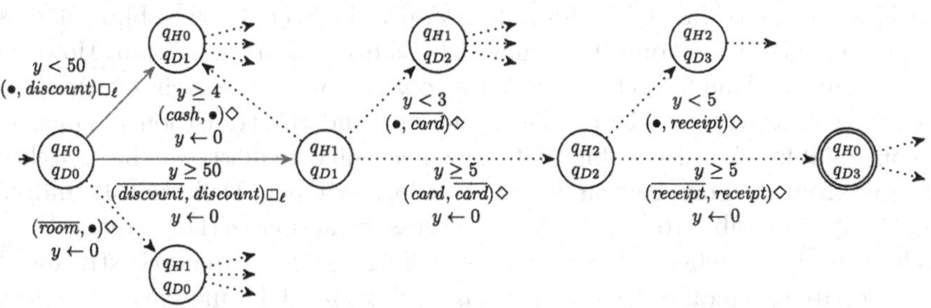

Fig. 2. Excerpt of composition Hotel ⊗ DiscountClient of the two TSCA in Fig. 1

Example 2. Figure 2 shows excerpts of the TSCA composition of the hotel and client TSCA of Fig. 1. The more relevant part is depicted, viz. whose semantics is an orchestration (from initial to final state). Note that request $\textit{discount}\,\Box_\ell$ can either be matched with the offer $\overline{\textit{discount}}$ if $y \geq 50$ or not matched if $y < 50$.

2.4 Controllability

We now discuss the different types of actions of TSCA (cf. Table 1) in light of the orchestration synthesis algorithm we will present in Sect. 3. To begin with, we define dangling configurations, i.e. those that are either not reachable or from which no final state can be reached (i.e. not successful). The orchestration synthesis will be specified as a safety game, in which reachability of final states is satisfied through the dangling predicate. The definition makes use of a set C of 'bad' configurations that are not to be traversed. Recall that $\mathcal{A}$ is a fixed TSCA.

Definition 5 (Dangling configuration). *Let $\mathcal{A}$, $C \subseteq \mathbb{C}$ and $c = (\boldsymbol{q}, v) \in C$.*

We say that c is reachable *in $\mathcal{A}$ given C, denoted as $c \in \mathit{Reachable}_{\mathcal{A}}(C)$, iff $(\boldsymbol{q}_0, \mathbf{0}) \xrightarrow{w}{}^{*} c$ without traversing configurations $(\boldsymbol{q}_r, v_r) \in C$.*

We say that c is successful *in $\mathcal{A}$ given C, denoted as $c \in \mathit{Successful}_{\mathcal{A}}(C)$, iff $c \xrightarrow{w}{}^{*} (\boldsymbol{q}_f, v') \in F$ without traversing configurations $(\boldsymbol{q}_r, v_r) \in C$.*

The set of dangling configurations *in $\mathcal{A}$ given C is defined as $\mathit{Dangling}_{\mathcal{A}}(C) = \overline{\mathit{Reachable}_{\mathcal{A}}(C) \cap \mathit{Successful}_{\mathcal{A}}(C)}$.*

In the sequel, abusing notation, we simply say that a state $\boldsymbol{q} \in Q$ is *dangling* (in $\mathcal{A}$ given C), denoted by $\boldsymbol{q} \in \mathit{Dangling}_{\mathcal{A}}(C)$, iff $(\boldsymbol{q}, v) \in \mathit{Dangling}_{\mathcal{A}}(C)$ for all possible evaluations v. Moreover, we set $\mathit{Dangling}(\mathcal{A}) = \mathit{Dangling}_{\mathcal{A}}(\varnothing)$.

Orchestration synthesis for (service) contract automata resembles that of the most permissive controller from SCT; in fact, [6] provided a correspondence between *controllable*/*uncontrollable* actions from SCT and permitted/necessary requests of contract automata. Intuitively, the aim of SCT is to synthesise a most permissive controller enforcing 'good' computations, i.e. runs reaching a final state without traversing any given *forbidden* state. To do so, SCT distinguishes *controllable* events (those the controller can disable) from *uncontrollable* events (those always enabled). Ideally, actions ruining a so-called safe orchestration of service contracts (a notion formally defined in Sect. 3, resembling a most permissive controller) should be removed by the synthesis algorithm. However, this can only be done for actions that are controllable in the orchestration.

We now characterise when a TSCA action (and the transition it labels) is (un)controllable. We also define 'when' a necessary request can be matched, stemming from the composition of TSCA (interleavings in Definition 4). Indeed, in TSCA it is possible to require that a necessary action (either a request or a match) must be matched in every possible configuration of the orchestration. It is also possible to require that a necessary action must be matched in at least one configuration from which it is fired. In the latter situation, it is possible to safely remove those requests (or matches) from the orchestration, as long as they appear as part of a match in some other transition of the orchestration. Such necessary actions are called *semi-controllable*, basically a controllable action becomes uncontrollable in case all possible matches are removed, but not vice versa. Table 2 summarises the controllability of requests and matches of TSCA.

Recall that all offers are permitted. All permitted actions (offers, requests and matches) are fully controllable. Necessary actions (*urgent*, *greedy* and *lazy*

Table 2. Controllability of request actions and match actions

Action	Requests	Matches
Urgent $\Box_u$	Uncontrollable	Uncontrollable
Greedy $\Box_g$	Semi-controllable	Uncontrollable
Lazy $\Box_\ell$	Semi-controllable	Semi-controllable
Permitted $\Diamond$	Controllable	Controllable

requests) have an increasing degree of (semi-)controllability. An urgent request must be matched in every possible state in which it can be executed. Accordingly, urgent requests and urgent matches are uncontrollable. A greedy request can be disabled by the controller as long as it is matched elsewhere; once it is matched, it can no longer be disabled. In this case, greedy requests are semi-controllable while greedy matches are uncontrollable. Finally, a lazy action only requires to be matched: its matches are controllable in the orchestration, provided at least one match is available (i.e. lazy requests and lazy matches are semi-controllable).

In the rest of this section, we characterise semi-controllability of transitions (cf. Definition 6). Since we deal with real-time systems, this notion is defined on configurations. Note from Table 2 that permitted actions are always controllable, while urgent actions are always uncontrollable.

A semi-controllable transition t is either a (greedy or lazy) request or a lazy match, and it is controllable in TSCA $\mathcal{A}$ given C if there exists a (greedy or lazy) match transition t' in $\mathcal{A}$, which is reachable given C, and in both t and t' the same principal, in the same local state, does the same request, and additionally the target configuration is successful given C. Otherwise, t is uncontrollable.

Definition 6 (Semi-controllable transition). *Let $\mathcal{A}$ be a TSCA, let $C \subseteq \mathbb{C}$ and let $t = (\boldsymbol{q}_1, g_1, \boldsymbol{a}_1, Y_1, \boldsymbol{q}'_1)$ be a transition of $\mathcal{A}$. Then t is* semi-controllable *if it is a request on $a \in A^{\Box_g} \cup A^{\Box_\ell}$ or a match on $a \in A^{\Box_\ell}$.*

At the same time, t is either controllable or uncontrollable in $\mathcal{A}$ given C.

We say that t is controllable *in $\mathcal{A}$ given C if $\exists t' = (\boldsymbol{q}_2, g_2, \boldsymbol{a}_2, Y_2, \boldsymbol{q}'_2) \in T^{\Box}$, s.t. $\boldsymbol{a}_2$ is a match, $\exists v$ s.t. $(\boldsymbol{q}_2, v) \in Reachable_{\mathcal{A}}(C)$, $(\boldsymbol{q}'_2, v') \in Post_{\mathcal{A},\boldsymbol{a}_2}((\boldsymbol{q}_2, v)^{\nearrow})$, $(\boldsymbol{q}'_2, v') \in Successful_{\mathcal{A}}(C)$, $\boldsymbol{q}_{1(i)} = \boldsymbol{q}_{2(i)}$ and $\boldsymbol{a}_{1(i)} = \boldsymbol{a}_{2(i)} \in \mathsf{R} \cap (A^{\Box_g} \cup A^{\Box_\ell})$; otherwise t is* uncontrollable *in $\mathcal{A}$ given C.*

In Definition 6, it does not suffice to require $\boldsymbol{q}_2$ or $\boldsymbol{q}'_2$ to be in $Dangling_{\mathcal{A}}(C)$: it could be the case that $\boldsymbol{q}'_2$ is only reachable from a trace not passing through transition t', while $\boldsymbol{q}_2$ only reaches a final configuration through a trace not traversing t'. Hence, we need to require that for some v, $(\boldsymbol{q}_2, v)$ is reachable, and $(\boldsymbol{q}'_2, v')$ is a (timed) successor of $(\boldsymbol{q}_2, v)$ that reaches a final configuration.

Example 3. In Fig. 2, all transitions are permitted, except for the lazy discount actions. The transition $(\bullet, \mathit{discount})\Box_\ell$ is thus a controllable lazy request, as the same request of $\mathsf{DiscountClient}$ is matched in the transition $(\overline{\mathit{discount}}, \mathit{discount})\Box_\ell$. In the resulting orchestration (cf. Sect. 4) this will be the only match available for such a necessary action.

We call a transition *uncontrollable* if one of the above cases holds (i.e. urgent or greedy match, uncontrollable greedy or lazy request or uncontrollable lazy match).

3 Orchestration Synthesis

In this section, we define synthesis of safe orchestrations of TSCA, considering both timing constraints and service requests with different levels of criticality. We carefully adapt the synthesis algorithm for (modal) service contract automata defined in [6], which was based on the synthesis of the most permissive controller from SCT. To respect the timing constraints, the synthesis algorithm of TSCA presented below is computed using the notion of zones from timed games [9,10].

The algorithm we will propose differs from the ones presented in [9,10] by combining two separate games, viz. *reachability* games and *safety* games. Indeed, as said before, the orchestration synthesis of TSCA is based on the synthesis of the *most permissive controller* from SCT, which ensures that (i) forbidden states are never traversed (a.k.a. a safety game) and (ii) marked states must be reachable (a.k.a. a reachability game). In the TSCA framework, marked states are the final states of the composition of contracts, whereas bad states are those states that spoil an agreement among contracts (cf. Definitions 7 and 9 below).

We recall *(modal) agreement* and *safety* on languages of service contract automata [6]. Intuitively, a trace is in agreement if it is a concatenation of matches, offers and their modalities, while a TSCA is safe if all traces of its language are in agreement, and it admits agreement if at least one of its traces is.

Definition 7 (Agreement, safety). *Let $\mathcal{A}$ be a TSCA. A trace accepted by $\mathcal{A}$ is in* agreement *if it belongs to the set*

$$\mathfrak{A} = \{\, w \in (\Sigma^n \bigcirc)^* \mid \forall i \text{ s.t. } w_{(i)} = \boldsymbol{a}\bigcirc,\ \boldsymbol{a} \text{ is a match or an offer},\ n > 1 \,\}$$

$\mathcal{A}$ *is* safe *if* $\mathscr{L}(\mathcal{A}) \subseteq \mathfrak{A}$*; else* unsafe. *If* $\mathscr{L}(\mathcal{A}) \cap \mathfrak{A} \neq \varnothing$, *then* $\mathcal{A}$ admits agreement.

Basically, an orchestration of TSCA enables the largest sub-portion of a composition of TSCA that is safe. Given the timed setting, the orchestration must consider clock evaluations for each contract. Hence, the underlying transition system of a TSCA is inspected by the synthesis algorithm. The orchestration will be rendered as a strategy on this transition system such that only traces in agreement are enforced. We start by introducing the notion of strategy on TSCA and that of a well-formed strategy: a strategy avoiding dangling configurations.

Definition 8 (Strategy). *Let $\mathcal{A}$ be a TSCA. A* strategy *f is a relation defined as $f : (\Sigma^n\{\bigcirc\} \cup \mathbb{R}^X_{\geq 0})^* \times (\Sigma^n\{\bigcirc\} \cup \mathbb{R}^X_{\geq 0})$ mapping traces to actions or delays s.t. given $(\boldsymbol{q}_0, \boldsymbol{0}) \xrightarrow{w}{}^{*} (\boldsymbol{q}, v)$, then $(\boldsymbol{q}, v) \xrightarrow{\lambda} (\boldsymbol{q}', v')$, for some $\lambda \in f(w)$, $(\boldsymbol{q}', v') \in \mathbb{C}$.*

Furthermore, f is well-formed *given $C \subseteq \mathbb{C}$ if never $(\boldsymbol{q}', v') \in Dangling_{\mathcal{A}}(C)$. The language recognised by $\mathcal{A}$ following the strategy f is denoted by $\mathscr{L}_f(\mathcal{A})$ and $f^{\mathbb{C}}$ denotes the strategy allowing to traverse all and only configurations in $\mathbb{C}$.*

We discuss further differences compared to timed games. A TSCA game can be seen as a 2-player game. A controller (i.e. orchestrator) fires controllable transitions to enforce agreement among contracts. An opponent fires uncontrollable transitions to drive the orchestrator to some 'bad' configuration, from which an agreement can no longer be enforced (cf. Definition 9). The opponent has precedence over the orchestrator, as long as its uncontrollable transitions are enabled (i.e. satisfied clock guards). Finally, fairness of TSCA guarantees that a final state is eventually reached, as traces recognised by TSCA languages are finite.

In timed games, strategies cannot prevent uncontrollable transitions from being fired. This follows from the notion of *outcome* of a strategy, which is used to characterise winning strategies. In TSCA, winning strategies are defined as those avoiding 'bad' configurations while at the same time enforcing agreement among contracts. Next we will formally define bad configurations, i.e. configurations in *uncontrollable disagreement*. Basically, a configuration is in uncontrollable disagreement if the orchestrator cannot prevent a request of a principal from being fired without a corresponding offer (i.e. no match). In such configurations, the controller loses: the orchestration is unsafe. Note that the opponent can only win by reaching one such configuration. Indeed, unfair traces are ruled out in TSCA.

Definition 9 (Configuration in uncontrollable disagreement). *Let $\mathcal{A}$ be a TSCA and let $C \subseteq \mathbb{C}$. A transition $t = \boldsymbol{q} \xrightarrow{a} \in T_{\mathcal{A}}$ is* forced *in a configuration $(\boldsymbol{q}, v)$ given C iff $(\boldsymbol{q}, v) \xrightarrow{a}$ and (i) t is uncontrollable in $\mathcal{A}$ given C or (ii) $\boldsymbol{q} \notin F$ and no other $t' = \boldsymbol{q} \xrightarrow{a'} \in T_{\mathcal{A}}$ is s.t. $(\boldsymbol{q}, v) \xrightarrow{\delta} (\boldsymbol{q}, v') \xrightarrow{a'}$ for some delay δ.*

A configuration $(\boldsymbol{q}, v_1) \notin Dangling_{\mathcal{A}}(C)$ is in uncontrollable disagreement *in $\mathcal{A}$ given C iff $(\boldsymbol{q}, v_1) \xrightarrow{w}{}^{*} (\boldsymbol{q}_1, v_2)$ s.t. only timed or forced transitions are enabled and either (i) $w \notin \mathfrak{A}$ or (ii) some configuration in C was traversed or (iii) $\nexists w' \in \mathfrak{A}$ s.t. $(\boldsymbol{q}_1, v_2) \xrightarrow{w'}{}^{*} (\boldsymbol{q}_f, v_3)$ with $\boldsymbol{q}_f \in F_{\mathcal{A}}$ without traversing configurations in C.*

A safe orchestration of TSCA can be interpreted as a *winning strategy* in terms of timed games, and it is defined below. Basically, a winning strategy enforces agreement among contracts: no bad configurations will ever be traversed.

Definition 10 (Winning strategy). *Let $\mathcal{A}$ be a TSCA, f be a strategy given $C \subseteq \mathbb{C}$ and U its set of configurations in uncontrollable disagreement in $\mathcal{A}$ given C. Then f is a* winning strategy *given C if it is well-formed given C, it never traverses configurations in U and $\mathscr{L}_f(\mathcal{A}) \subseteq \mathfrak{A}$. A winning strategy f given C is* maximal *if there is no winning strategy f' given C s.t. $\mathscr{L}_f(\mathcal{A}) \subseteq \mathscr{L}_{f'}(\mathcal{A})$.*

Before defining the synthesis of a safe orchestration, we introduce some useful notions. Given a set of configurations $C \subseteq \mathbb{C}$ of a TSCA $\mathcal{A}$, the *uncontrollable predecessor* predicate $uPred_{\mathcal{A}}(C)$ is defined as all configurations from which some configuration in C is reachable by firing an uncontrollable transition. Formally:

$$uPred_{\mathcal{A}}(C) = \{\, c \mid \exists c' \in C,\ c \xrightarrow{a\square} c' \text{ uncontrollable in } \mathcal{A} \text{ given } C \,\}$$

We borrow the notion of *safe timed predecessor* of a set $C_1 \subseteq \mathbb{C}$ with respect to a set $C_2 \subseteq \mathbb{C}$ from [10]. Intuitively, a configuration c is in $Pred_{\mathcal{A},t}(C_1, C_2)$ if from c it is possible to reach a configuration $c' \in C_1$ by time elapsing and the trace from c to c' avoids configurations in C_2. Formally:

$$Pred_{\mathcal{A},t}(C_1, C_2) = \{ c \in \mathbb{C} \mid \exists\, \delta \in \mathbb{R}_{\geq 0} \text{ s.t. } c \xrightarrow{\delta} c',\ c' \in C_1 \text{ and } Post_{\mathcal{A},[0,\delta]}(c) \subseteq \overline{C_2} \},$$
$$\text{where } Post_{\mathcal{A},[0,\delta]}(c) = \{ c' \in \mathbb{C} \mid \exists\, t \in [0,\delta] \text{ s.t. } c \xrightarrow{t} c' \} \text{ and } \overline{C_2} = \mathbb{C} \setminus C_2$$

We can now specify the synthesis of a safe orchestration of TSCA. Let $\hat{\mathcal{A}}$ denote the TSCA obtained from $\mathcal{A}$ by replacing $T_{\mathcal{A}}$ with $T_{\hat{\mathcal{A}}} = \{ t = \boldsymbol{q} \xrightarrow{\boldsymbol{a}\,\circ} \mid t \in T_{\mathcal{A}} \text{ and } (\circ \neq \diamond \vee \boldsymbol{a} \text{ not request}) \}$, i.e. all permitted requests are pruned from $\mathcal{A}$.

Definition 11 (Safe orchestration synthesis). *Let $\mathcal{A}$ be a TSCA and let $\phi : 2^{\mathbb{C}} \to 2^{\mathbb{C}}$ be a monotone function on the cpo $(2^{\mathbb{C}}, \subseteq)$ s.t. $\phi(\mathbb{C}_{i-1}) = \mathbb{C}_i$, where $\mathbb{C}_0 = \{ c \mid c \in \mathbb{C},\ c \xrightarrow{\boldsymbol{a}\,\square},\ \boldsymbol{a}$ uncontrollable request in $\hat{\mathcal{A}}$ given $\varnothing \}$ and*

$$\mathbb{C}_i = Pred_{\hat{\mathcal{A}},t}(\mathbb{C}_{i-1} \cup uPred_{\hat{\mathcal{A}}}(\mathbb{C}_{i-1}), moPred_{\hat{\mathcal{A}}}(\overline{\mathbb{C}_{i-1}})) \cup Dangling_{\hat{\mathcal{A}}}(\mathbb{C}_{i-1}) \cup \mathbb{C}_{i-1}$$

Finally, let $\mathbb{C}^* = sup(\{ \phi^n(\mathbb{C}_0) \mid n \in \mathbb{N} \})$ be the least fixed point of ϕ. Then the safe orchestration *of $\mathcal{A}$ is the strategy:*

$$f^* = \begin{cases} \bot & \textit{if } (\boldsymbol{q}_0, \boldsymbol{0}) \in \mathbb{C}^* \\ f^{\overline{\mathbb{C}^*}} & \textit{otherwise} \end{cases}$$

This definition is such that whenever the initial configuration belongs to $\mathbb{C}^*$, then the orchestration is *empty*: no strategy exists to enforce agreement among contracts while avoiding configurations in uncontrollable disagreement. Otherwise, $\overline{\mathbb{C}}^*$ identifies a winning strategy characterising a safe orchestration of contracts. This strategy allows as many transitions as possible without traversing configurations in $\mathbb{C}^*$. The controller can avoid principals reaching bad configurations in $\mathbb{C}^*$, while guaranteeing all requirements to be satisfied. $\overline{\mathbb{C}}^*$ moreover identifies the maximal winning strategy, i.e. f^* allows all controllable match/offer transitions to configurations not in $\mathbb{C}^*$ (recall f^* is not a function). Note that f^* is computable due to finiteness of the symbolic configurations and monotonicity of the fixed-point computation [10]: it is the maximal well-formed winning strategy.

Theorem 1 (Maximal winning strategy). *Let $\mathcal{A}$ be a TSCA and f^* be the strategy computed through Definition 11. If $f^* = \bot$, then there exists no well-formed winning strategy f given $\mathbb{C}^*$. Otherwise, f^* is the maximal well-formed winning strategy in $\mathcal{A}$ given $\mathbb{C}^*$.*

Example 4. Recall the composition Hotel⊗DiscountClient in Fig. 2. We can apply the synthesis algorithm to compute its safe orchestration f^*. In f^*, the request transition $(\bullet, discount\square_\ell)$ is removed because it is controllable (cf. Example 3). The language recognised by f^* is the singleton $\mathscr{L}_{f^*}(\mathsf{Hotel} \otimes \mathsf{DiscountClient}) = \{(\overline{discount}, discount)\square_\ell(card, \overline{card})\diamond(\overline{receipt}, receipt)\diamond\}$.

In [10] (Theorem 4) the computation of $Pred_{\mathcal{A},t}$ is reduced to the following basic operations on zones: $Pred_{\mathcal{A},t}(C_1, C_2) = (C_1^{\swarrow} \setminus C_2^{\swarrow}) \cup ((C_1 \cap C_2^{\swarrow}) \setminus C_2)^{\swarrow}$. Similarly, we now provide procedures for computing the newly introduced sets $moPred_{\mathcal{A}}$, $uPred_{\mathcal{A}}$ and $Dangling_{\mathcal{A}}$ using basic operations on zones. Together these provide an effective procedure for computing $\mathbb{C}^*$ (hence a safe orchestration). The set $moPred_{\mathcal{A}}$ can be computed from $Pred_{\mathcal{A}}$ by only considering discrete steps that are not requests. Conversely, both $uPred_{\mathcal{A}}$ and $Dangling_{\mathcal{A}}$ require visiting the symbolic configurations of $\mathcal{A}$, and can be computed as follows.

Theorem 2 (Compute dangling configuration). *Let $\mathcal{A}$ be a TSCA, $C \subseteq \mathbb{C}$ and ϕ be as in Definition 11 s.t. $\phi(\mathbb{C}_{i-1}) = \mathbb{C}_i$ and $\mathbb{C}^* = sup(\{\, \phi^n(\mathbb{C}_0) \mid n \in \mathbb{N} \,\})$.*

1. *The* reachable configurations *in $\mathcal{A}$ given C are computed as $Reachable_{\mathcal{A}}(C) = \mathbb{C}^*$, where $\mathbb{C}_0 = (\boldsymbol{q}_0, \boldsymbol{0})^{\nearrow} \setminus C^{\nearrow}$ and $\mathbb{C}_i = \bigcup_{\boldsymbol{a}} (Post_{\mathcal{A},\boldsymbol{a}}(\mathbb{C}_{i-1})^{\nearrow} \setminus C^{\nearrow}) \cup \mathbb{C}_{i-1}$*
2. *The* successful configurations *in $\mathcal{A}$ given C are computed as $Successful_{\mathcal{A}}(C) = \mathbb{C}^*$, where $\mathbb{C}_0 = \{\, (\boldsymbol{q}_f, v) \mid \boldsymbol{q}_f \in F_{\mathcal{A}}$ and $v \in \mathbb{R}_{\geq 0}^{X_{\mathcal{A}}} \,\} \setminus C$ and $\mathbb{C}_i = Pred_{\mathcal{A},t}(\mathbb{C}_{i-1} \cup (Pred_{\mathcal{A}}(\mathbb{C}_{i-1}) \setminus C), C) \cup \mathbb{C}_{i-1}$*
3. *The* dangling configurations *in $\mathcal{A}$ given C are computed as $Dangling_{\mathcal{A}}(C) = \overline{Successful_{\mathcal{A}}(C \cup \overline{Reachable_{\mathcal{A}}(C)})}$*

Note that the dangling configurations are efficiently computed by combining a forward exploration (i.e. reachable configurations) with a backward exploration (i.e. successful configurations): it is then possible to ignore unreachable successful configurations. We thus determined an effective procedure to compute $Dangling_{\mathcal{A}}(C)$ that uses basic operations on zones. Finally, we define a procedure for computing the set of uncontrollable predecessors using Theorem 2.

Lemma 1 (Compute uncontrollable predecessors). *Let $\mathcal{A}$ be a TSCA and $C \subseteq \mathbb{C}$. Then the set of* uncontrollable predecessors *of C in $\mathcal{A}$ is computed as*

$$uPred_{\mathcal{A}}(C) = \{\, c \in \mathbb{C} \mid \exists c' \in C : c \xrightarrow{\boldsymbol{a}\Box} c' \in unc_{\mathcal{A}}(C) \,\},$$

where $unc_{\mathcal{A}}(C) = \{\, (\boldsymbol{q}, v) \xrightarrow{\boldsymbol{a}\Box} \mid (\boldsymbol{q}, v) \in \mathbb{C} \wedge (\boldsymbol{a}$ urgent $\vee \boldsymbol{a}$ greedy match $\vee\ (\nexists (\boldsymbol{q}_2, v) \in Reachable_{\mathcal{A}}(C), (\boldsymbol{q}_2', v') \in Successful_{\mathcal{A}}(C).(\boldsymbol{q}_2', v') \in Post_{\mathcal{A},\boldsymbol{a}'}(\boldsymbol{q}_2, v)^{\nearrow} \wedge \boldsymbol{a}_{(i)} = \boldsymbol{a}'_{(i)} = a \in \mathsf{R} \wedge \boldsymbol{a}'$ match $\wedge\ \boldsymbol{q}_{(i)} = \boldsymbol{q}_{2(i)})) \,\}$

With our results, safe TSCA orchestrations can be implemented using libraries for timed games [19,20] with primitive zone operations (i.e. $\cup$, $\cap$, $\setminus$, $^{\nearrow}$ and $^{\swarrow}$).

4 Running Example Revisted

We continue our running example with a PriviledgedClient, depicted in Fig. 3a, optionally asking for a discount room via a permitted request, but after 8 t.u. (in its initial state) urgently requests a normal room. In orchestration f^* of composition (Hotel $\otimes$ DiscountClient) $\otimes$ PriviledgedClient, the discount request of DiscountClient could be matched before one of the requests of PriviledgedClient. But, this interaction is prevented in f^*. Let $\boldsymbol{a} = (\overline{discount}, discount, \bullet)\Box_{\ell}$,

$\boldsymbol{b} = (\bullet, \bullet, room)\Box_u$, $t1 = ((q_{H0}, q_{D0}, q_{P0}), y \geq 50, \boldsymbol{a},\ y \leftarrow 0, (q_{H1}, q_{D1}, q_{P0}))$ and $t2 = ((q_{H1}, q_{D1}, q_{P0}), x \geq 8, \boldsymbol{b}, \varnothing, (q_{H1}, q_{D1}, q_{P1}))$. Now $t1$ is not enabled by f^* or else we can reach a configuration c_2 in uncontrollable disagreement via $c_0 \xrightarrow{\delta = 50} c_1 \xrightarrow{a} c_2 \xrightarrow{\delta = 0} c_2 \xrightarrow{b}$. In c_2, the uncontrollable transition t_2 is enabled, but urgent request $\boldsymbol{b}$ is not matched, thus violating agreement. The first transition enabled in f^* is $((q_{H0}, q_{D0}, q_{P0}), x \geq 8, (\overline{room}, \bullet, room)\Box_u$, $y \leftarrow 0, (q_{H1}, q_{D0}, q_{P1}))$.

Thus, PriviledgedClient interacts with Hotel prior to DiscountClient, who is served successively. This is only possible as both lazy request $(\bullet, \mathit{discount})\Box_\ell$ and lazy match $(\overline{\mathit{discount}}, \mathit{discount})\Box_\ell$ of Hotel $\otimes$ DiscountClient are semi-controllable and are delayed in the orchestration of (Hotel$\otimes$DiscountClient)$\otimes$PriviledgedClient.

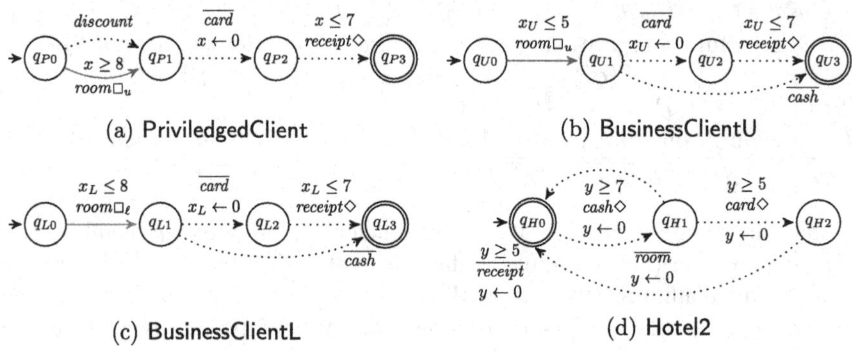

Fig. 3. TSCA: (a) priviledged, (b) urgent (c) lazy business clients, (d) hotel2

Next consider the TSCA of Fig. 3b–d, variants of the previous contracts: BusinessClientU requests urgently a room within 5 t.u., BusinessClientL requests lazily a room within 8 t.u, while Hotel2 offers only a normal room (no discount).

First look at the (Hotel2 $\otimes$ BusinessClientL) $\otimes$ BusinessClientU orchestration. It is empty (i.e. no agreement). In the initial state of Hotel2 $\otimes$ BusinessClientL, the room offer is available only after 8 t.u., otherwise it is matched by BusinessClientL's lazy room request. As BusinessClientU's urgent room request must be matched within 5 t.u., it cannot be matched prior to BusinessClientL's lazy room request: a violation, so the initial configuration is in uncontrollable disagreement.

Next look at (Hotel2 $\otimes$ BusinessClientU) $\otimes$ BusinessClientL's orchestration f^*. Part of the behaviour allowed by f^* is depicted in Fig. 4 in the fragment marked with ✓ (in this figure, a transition is fired as soon as it is enabled). Now BusinessClientU performs the transaction with the hotel first. In case of card payments, the minimum time required to reach state $\boldsymbol{q} = (q_{H0}, q_{U3}, q_{L0})$ is $5 + 5 = 10$ t.u., with clocks evaluation $v = (y = 0, x_U = 5, x_L = 10)$. In $(\boldsymbol{q}, v)$ (the top leftmost configuration in Fig. 4), the (lazy) necessary room request of BusinessClientL can no longer be satisfied as it should have been matched within 8 t.u., so violating agreement. Thus f^* forbids card payments of BusinessClientU. Note that also the two previous configurations (contained in the fragment marked with ϟ in Fig. 4) are forbidden in f^*, as they are in uncontrollable disagreement.

If, however, BusinessClientU pays cash, then the minimum time required to reach state $\boldsymbol{q}$ is 7 t.u., with clocks evaluation $v' = (y = 0, x_U = 7, x_L = 7)$. Indeed, in configuration $(\boldsymbol{q}, v')$ (the central rightmost configuration in the fragment marked with ✓ in Fig. 4) the lazy room request of BusinessClientL can be matched by the room offer of Hotel2, and successively the orchestration enables this client to pay either by cash or by card. Therefore, to satisfy BusinessClientL's lazy room request, in the resulting safe orchestration BusinessClientU is only allowed to pay with cash.

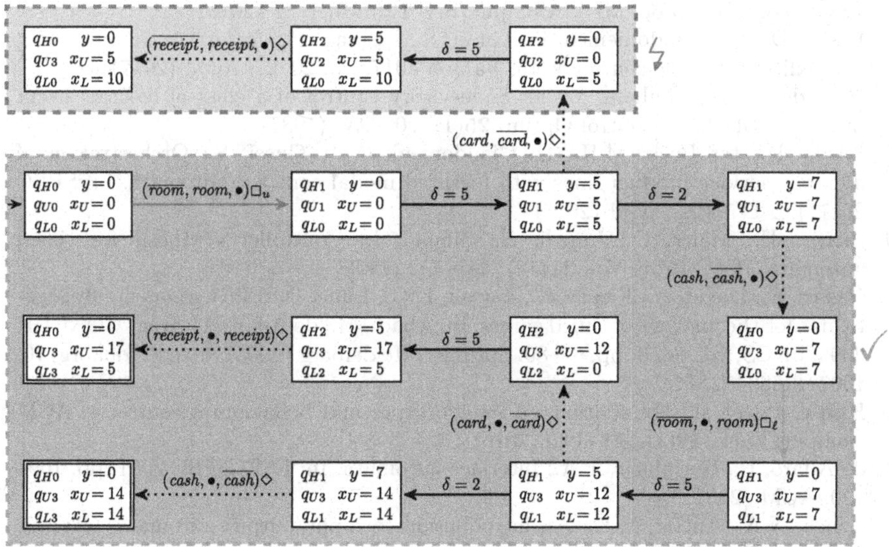

Fig. 4. Excerpt of $TS_{(\mathsf{Hotel2} \otimes \mathsf{BusinessClientU}) \otimes \mathsf{BusinessClientL}}$, whose fragment marked with ✓ is allowed in the safe orchestration whereas the one marked with ϟ is not

5 Conclusions and Future Work

We have presented TSCA, a new formalism for specifying *service contracts* with *real-time constraints*, and for *synthesising* their *safe orchestration* in the presence of service requests with different levels of criticality (viz. *urgent*, *greedy* and *lazy*).

We plan to implement the theory in a prototype, extending tools for contract automata [21–23] and reusing libraries from timed games for operations on zones [19,20], to which orchestration synthesis has been reduced (cf. Theorem 2). We would also like to equip the formalism with weighted actions, e.g. to specify the prices of hotel rooms or how much clients are willing to pay for their room.

References

1. Georgakopoulos, D., Papazoglou, M.P.: Service-Oriented Computing. MIT, Cambridge (2008)
2. Bouguettaya, A., et al.: A service computing manifesto: the next 10 years. Commun. ACM **60**(4), 64–72 (2017)
3. Bartoletti, M., Cimoli, T., Zunino, R.: Compliance in behavioural contracts: a brief survey. In: Bodei, C., Ferrari, G.-L., Priami, C. (eds.) Programming Languages with Applications to Biology and Security. LNCS, vol. 9465, pp. 103–121. Springer, Cham (2015). https://doi.org/10.1007/978-3-319-25527-9_9
4. Basile, D., Degano, P., Ferrari, G.L.: A formal framework for secure and complying services. J. Supercomput. **69**(1), 43–52 (2014)
5. Basile, D., Degano, P., Ferrari, G.L.: Automata for specifying and orchestrating service contracts. Log. Meth. Comput. Sci. **12**(4:6), 1–51 (2016)
6. Basile, D., Di Giandomenico, F., Gnesi, S., Degano, P., Ferrari, G.L.: Specifying variability in service contracts. In: VaMoS 2017, pp. 20–27. ACM (2017)
7. Ramadge, P.J., Wonham, W.M.: Supervisory control of a class of discrete event processes. SIAM J. Control Optim. **25**(1), 206–230 (1987)
8. Basile, D., ter Beek, M.H., Di Giandomenico, F., Gnesi, S.: Orchestration of dynamic service product lines with featured modal contract automata. In: SPLC 2017, pp. 117–122. ACM (2017)
9. Asarin, E., Maler, O., Pnueli, A., Sifakis, J.: Controller synthesis for timed automata. IFAC Proc. Vol. **31**(18), 447–452 (1998)
10. Cassez, F., David, A., Fleury, E., Larsen, K.G., Lime, D.: Efficient on-the-fly algorithms for the analysis of timed games. In: Abadi, M., de Alfaro, L. (eds.) CONCUR 2005. LNCS, vol. 3653, pp. 66–80. Springer, Heidelberg (2005). https://doi.org/10.1007/11539452_9
11. Hüttel, H., et al.: Foundations of session types and behavioural contracts. ACM Comput. Surv. **49**(1), 3:1–3:36 (2016)
12. de Alfaro, L., Henzinger, T.A.: Interface automata. In: ESEC/FSE 2001, pp. 109–120. ACM (2001)
13. Lynch, N.A., Tuttle, M.R.: An introduction to input/output automata. CWI Q. **2**(3), 219–246 (1989)
14. Alur, R., Dill, D.L.: A theory of timed automata. Theoret. Comput. Sci. **126**(2), 183–235 (1994)
15. David, A., Larsen, K.G., Legay, A., Nyman, U., Wąsowski, A.: Timed I/O automata. In: HSCC 2010, pp. 91–100. ACM (2010)
16. Larsen, K.G., Nyman, U., Wąsowski, A.: Modal I/O automata for interface and product line theories. In: De Nicola, R. (ed.) ESOP 2007. LNCS, vol. 4421, pp. 64–79. Springer, Heidelberg (2007). https://doi.org/10.1007/978-3-540-71316-6_6
17. Azzopardi, S., Pace, G.J., Schapachnik, F., Schneider, G.: Contract automata. Artif. Intell. Law **24**(3), 203–243 (2016)
18. Bouyer, P., Markey, N., Sankur, O.: Robust reachability in timed automata: a game-based approach. In: Czumaj, A., Mehlhorn, K., Pitts, A., Wattenhofer, R. (eds.) ICALP 2012. LNCS, vol. 7392, pp. 128–140. Springer, Heidelberg (2012). https://doi.org/10.1007/978-3-642-31585-5_15
19. David, A., et al.: UPPAAL DBM Library (2017)
20. Legay, A., Traonouez, L.-M.: PyEcdar: towards open source implementation for timed systems. In: Van Hung, D., Ogawa, M. (eds.) ATVA 2013. LNCS, vol. 8172, pp. 460–463. Springer, Cham (2013). https://doi.org/10.1007/978-3-319-02444-8_35

21. Basile, D., Degano, P., Ferrari, G.-L., Tuosto, E.: Playing with our CAT and communication-centric applications. In: Albert, E., Lanese, I. (eds.) FORTE 2016. LNCS, vol. 9688, pp. 62–73. Springer, Cham (2016). https://doi.org/10.1007/978-3-319-39570-8_5
22. Basile, D., Di Giandomenico, F., Gnesi, S.: FMCAT: supporting dynamic service-based product lines. In: SPLC 2017, pp. 3–8. ACM (2017)
23. Basile, D., ter Beek, M.H., Gnesi, S.: Modelling and analysis with featured modal contract automata. In: SPLC 2018. ACM (2018)

Modelling and Verification of Dynamic Role-Based Access Control

Inna Vistbakka[1(✉)] and Elena Troubitsyna[1,2]

[1] Åbo Akademi University, Turku, Finland
inna.vistbakka@abo.fi
[2] KTH, Stockholm, Sweden
elenatro@kth.se

Abstract. Controlling access to resources is essential for ensuring correctness of system functioning. Role-Based Access Control (RBAC) is a popular authorisation model that regulates the user's rights to manage system resources based on the user's role. In this paper, we extend the traditional static approach to defining RBAC and propose as well as formalise a dynamic RBAC model. It allows a designer to explicitly define the dependencies between the system states and permissions to access and modify system resources. To facilitate a systematic description and verification of the dynamic access rights, we propose a contract-based approach and then we demonstrate how to model and verify dynamic RBAC in Event-B. The approach is illustrated by a case study – a reporting management system.

1 Introduction

Modern software systems become increasingly resource-intensive. It is essential to guarantee that the authorised users have an access to the eligible resources and the resources are protected from an access by the unauthorised users. This aspect of the system behaviour is addressed by the access control policy.

Role-Based Access Control (RBAC) [4] is a widely used access control model. It regulates users' access to computer resources based on their role in an organisation. The standard RBAC framework adopts a static, state-independent approach to define the access rights to the system resources. However, it is often insufficient for correct implementation of the desired system functionality and should be augmented with the dynamic, i.e., a state-dependant view on the access control.

In this paper, we propose a dynamic RBAC model, which allows a designer to explicitly define the rights to access a certain resource based on the resource state and the system workflow. We formalise the dynamic RBAC and propose a systematic contract-based approach to defining the rights to access the system resources. We rely on the design-by-contract approach [8] to explicitly define the dynamic access rights for each role over resource. Moreover, we propose an approach that allow us to verify the consistency of the desired system workflow,

M. F. Atig et al. (Eds.): VECoS 2018, LNCS 11181, pp. 48–63, 2018.
https://doi.org/10.1007/978-3-030-00359-3_4

described by the scenarios, with the static and dynamic RBAC constraints. The workflow is described using UML use case and activity diagrams, which serve as a middle-hand between the textual requirements description and their formal Event-B model.

Event-B [2] is a state-based formalism for the correct-by-construction system development. It allows us to specify both dynamic and static aspects of system behaviour. The dynamic behaviour, defined by the events, models the workflow scenarios, which we want to analyse. The static component of the specification models the interdependencies between the roles, resources and the users. The Rodin platform and Pro-B plug-in [10,14] allow us to automate the verification of consistency between the dynamic RBAC and the desired system workflow. The approach is illustrated by a case study – a reporting management system.

2 From Static to Dynamic RBAC

RBAC: Basic Concepts. Role-Based Access Control (RBAC) [4] is one of the main mechanisms for ensuring data integrity in a wide range of computer-based systems. The authorisation model defined by RBAC regulates users' access to computer resources based on their role in an organisation.

RBAC is built around the notions of users, roles, rights and protected system resources. A *resource* is an entity, e.g., data, access to which should be controlled. A user can access a resource based on an assigned role, where a role is usually seen as a job function performed by a user within an organisation. In their turn, rights define the specific actions that can be applied to the resources. RBAC can be defined as a table that relates roles with the allowed rights over the resources. RBAC (depicted in Fig. 1) has the following elements:

- `USERS` is a set of users;
- `ROLES` is a set of available user roles;
- `RESOURSES` is a set of protected system resources;
- `RIGHTS` is a set of all possible rights over the resources;
- `PERMISSIONS` is a set of permissions over the resources.

Moreover, `US_ASSIGN` defines a *user assignment* to roles, while `RO_PERM` is *permission assignment* to roles. Next we discuss all these notions in details.

Let $\mathtt{USERS} = \{\mathtt{u}_1, \mathtt{u}_2, ..., \mathtt{u}_n\}$ be a set of users. In general, a concept of a user may stand for a person in the organisation, an administrative entity or a non-person entity, such as a computing (sub)system. A user can access a resource based on the assigned role.

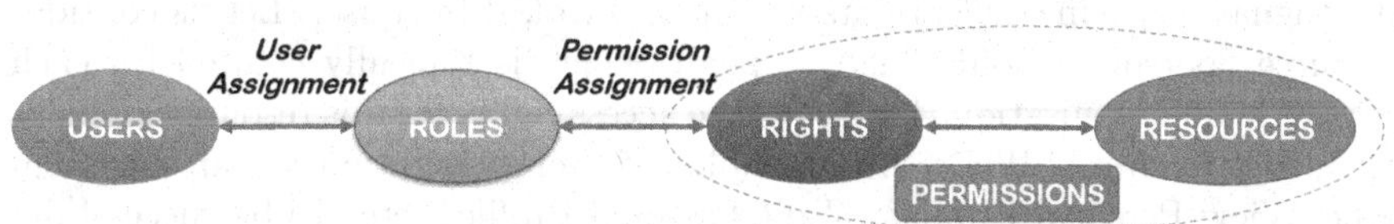

Fig. 1. RBAC structure

Let $\mathtt{ROLES} = \{\mathtt{r}_1, \mathtt{r}_2, ..., \mathtt{r}_\mathtt{m}\}$ be a set of possible user roles within the system. A role is usually seen as a job function performed by a user within an organisation. For example, often, a role is used to indicate the job-related access rights to a resource.

The protected system resources are denoted by the set $\mathtt{RESOURCES} = \{\mathtt{re}_1, \mathtt{re}_2, ..., \mathtt{re}_\mathtt{k}\}$. The notion of the resource depends on the system, i.e., it can denote OS files or directories; data base columns, rows or tables; disk space or just simple lock mechanisms.

Let $\mathtt{RIGHTS} = \{\mathtt{ri}_1, \mathtt{ri}_2, ..., \mathtt{ri}_\mathtt{l}\}$ be a set of possible rights over the system resource. Rights are defined as specific manipulations that can be performed with the resources. For example, for a resource database, the access rights can be *Update, Insert, Append, Delete*; for a resource file – *Create, View, Print.*

A user can access resources based on the assigned roles. A user authorisation list – *user assignment* – can be defined as the mapping between users and roles:

$$\mathtt{US\_ASSIGN} : \mathtt{USERS} \rightarrow \mathbb{P}(\mathtt{ROLES}),$$

which assigns to a given user a set of possible roles. A user can play (i.e., be mapped to) a number of roles, and a role can have many users. The notation $\mathbb{P}(\mathtt{ROLES})$ stands for the powerset (set of all subsets) type over elements of the type ROLES.

Static RBAC. Access control in RBAC is realised in terms of (static) *permissions.* A permission is an ability of a holder of a permission to perform some action(s) in the system. To formally define all possible permissions, we introduce the relation PERMISSIONS as follows:

$$\mathtt{PERMISSIONS} : \mathtt{RESOURCES} \leftrightarrow \mathtt{RIGHTS}$$

It describes relationships between a certain system resource and the rights that can be applied to it.

Permission assignments to a role are defined based on the job authority and responsibilities within the job function. To formally define permissions that are provided by the system to the different user roles, we define the function RO_PERM that maps each user role to a set of allowed rights over the resources:

$$\mathtt{RO\_PERM} : \mathtt{ROLES} \rightarrow \mathbb{P}(\mathtt{PERMISSIONS}).$$

In the paper, we make a distinction between rights and operations. The operations (or *use cases*) define the specific tasks, which a user may perform in the system. Therefore, an "operation" is a more general concept than a "right" and designates specific basic rights which are invoked by a user. Let us consider a resource "personal profile page" – page, which is typically created for each employee in an organisation. The set of the access rights for this resource includes *Create, Delete, Read, Write.* An examples of user's operation within a system can be "View Personal Profile", "Edit Personal Profile", etc. To be successfully executed, the operation "View Personal Profile" requires the *Read* right, while the "Edit Personal Profile" operation requires both *Read* and *Write* rights.

Usually RBAC gives a static view on the access rights associated with each role, i.e., it defines the permissions to manipulate certain resources "in general", i.e., without referring to the system state. Therefore, rights define the necessary conditions for an operation to be executed. However, we argue, that these conditions are insufficient for a correct implementation of the intended system functionality. For instance, assume that a user with a specific role `User` has *Read* and *Write* rights to the personal profile page `page`, where a user with the role `Admin` has *Read*, *Write* as well as *Create* and *Delete* rights to the resource `page`. Even though `User` has rights to *Read* and *Write* the profile page, s/he cannot use them if `Admin` has not created the web-page before using his/her right *Create* or has already deleted it using *Delete* right.

It is easy to see that the access rights depend not only on the role but also on the state of the resource. Therefore, the static view on RBAC should be complemented with an explicit definition of the *dynamic state-dependant* conditions.

Dynamic RBAC. Let us now discuss a formalisation of the dynamic view on RBAC. Each resource can be characterised by its state, i.e., we can introduce the set $\mathtt{STATES} = \{\mathtt{st}_1, ..., \mathtt{st}_j\}$ defining all possible states of the resources. Then we can define *dynamic (state-dependant) permissions* as the following function:

$$\mathtt{DYN\_PERM} : \mathtt{RESOURCES} \times \mathtt{STATES} \rightarrow \mathbb{P}(\mathtt{RIGHTS}).$$

For each resource and its specific state, DYN_PERM returns access rights applicable to the resource in each of its states. Let us note, that DYN_PERM is defined for all allowed access rights that can be applied to the resources. Then *dynamic role permissions* can be defined as the function DYN_RO_PERM:

$$\mathtt{DYN\_RO\_PERM} : \mathtt{ROLES} \rightarrow \mathbb{P}(\mathtt{DYN\_PERM}).$$

Essentially, it maps the assigned dynamic permissions to the roles.

Let us now return to our personal profile page example. Assume that the resource `page` can be in three states: *null* (before it is created), *locked* (after it is deleted) or *unlocked*. Then, when `page` is in the state *null*, `User` has no rights over this resource. However, when `page` is in the state *unlocked*, `User` has *Read* and *Write* rights, and when `page` is in the state *locked*, `User` role has *Read* right.

The dynamic and static views on RBAC are intrinsically interdependent. The permissions defined by the static and dynamic constraints constitute the necessary and sufficient constraints the user has over the operations execution. In the next section, we discuss how to verifying these conditions using the design-by-contract approach.

3 Reasoning About Dynamic RBAC Using Contracts

The dynamic view on RBAC, advocated in this paper, aims at defining conditions enabling a successful execution of an operation with respect to both –

static access rights defined by RBAC and system dynamics defined by its workflow. Typically, the workflow is described by the *scenarios*. A scenario defines a sequence of operations – *use cases* – that should be performed over the resources to implement the desired functionality. A scenario consists of individual steps that combine the operations executed over the resources in a certain order.

Usually a scenario involves a single or multiple actors (users) that perform the operations over the resources. The users performing the operations in a scenario must have all the permissions required to complete every single step of a given scenario. Thus we should verify consistency between the defined RBAC and the control flow implemented by the desired scenarios. For each operation in the scenario, we define the correctness conditions as the *contract for operation*. We follow the design-by-contract approach [8], i.e., define each contract as a combination of a *precondition* (the conditions on the operational input) and a *postcondition* (conditions to be satisfied as a result of the operation execution).

A Concept of an Operation Contract. Let $OPERATIONS$ be a set representing all possible operations within a system execution. Each operation represents an interaction of a user with the system. We assume that the state of a system is represented by a collection of variables denoted as v. Then the user operations result in changing the system state.

For each operation we define a **pre**- and **post**-condition pair. Figure 2 presents a generic from of an operation structure definition. An operation $oper_i$ might have parameters p_i that are defined in the **params** clause. The **pre**-clause defines the assumptions about the state of the system before the execution of the operation. The **post**-clause defines the state of the system after the completion of the operation. Here postconditions describe the actual changes in the state of the resource. The operation as such is a state transition resulting in the change of the variables values from v to v'.

A precondition represents the static and dynamic constraints that should be satisfied by each operation. If precondition of an operation is not satisfied then the scenario containing it is deadlocked indicating an inconsistency between the formulated constrains and the desired workflow.

Defining Consistency Conditions. Let us now investigate how to use contracts to derive consistency conditions. We start by introducing the function $ScenarioSeq$ such that

$$ScenarioSeq \in SCENARIOS \rightarrow \mathtt{seq}(OPERATIONS),$$

```
Operation oper_i                  // <name of an operation>
  params p_i                      // <list of parameters>
  pre Pre_i(p_i, v)               // <list of predicates>
  post Post_i(p_i, v, v')         // <list of predicates>
end
```

Fig. 2. General structure of an operation contract

where **seq** is a sequence constructor to represent composite steps within a scenario. Here *SCENARIOS* is a set of scenario ids.

Lets consider a scenario S, where $S \in SCENARIOS$. We say that a scenario S is *executable* if the final state of a scenario S is reachable from its initial state. Since a scenario is defined as a sequence of the corresponding operations, and the operations, in their turn, are defined as state transitions, we can define a scenario execution as follows:

$$\sigma^S_{init} \leadsto^S \sigma^S_{fin}, \tag{1}$$

where σ^S_{init} and σ^S_{fin} denote the initial and final states of a scenario S respectively.

Let a scenario S be a sequence consisting of m operations:

$$ScenarioSeq(S) = [oper_1, oper_2, ..., oper_m], \tag{2}$$

We use the definition of an operation contract to explicitly formulate the consistency property of a scenario control flow. A scenario S is executable (i.e., a scenario control flow is consistent) if the following properties are hold:

$$Pre(oper_{i+1}) \subseteq Post(oper_i), i = 1...m-1, \tag{3}$$

$$Pre(oper_1) \subseteq \sigma^S_{init}, \tag{4}$$

$$\sigma^S_{fin} \subseteq Post(oper_m) \tag{5}$$

Essentially, these properties require that all sequences of the scenario steps are enabled. Property (3) requires that any next operation should be *enabled* by the previously executed operation. Property (4) describes the consistency conditions imposed on the initial state of a scenario, i.e., verifies that the first operation is enabled. Property (5) requires for the final state of the scenario to be a subset of the states in which the last operation in the scenario terminates.

The above definitions formalise the constraints that should be verified to ensure that the operations of a given scenario can be executed in the desired order. If any of the conditions is violated then an inconsistency is detected, which should be eradicated either by inspecting the requirements or their formalisation. Next we will discuss how to use the proposed formalisation in the context of dynamic RBAC.

Operation Implementation Under RBAC. The generic structure of an operation description is given in Fig. 2. In the RBAC context, an operation defines user action over a system resource. Upon an operation execution, the state of the resource might be changed. Consequently, it might result in changing the (dynamic) access rights for a particular role over resources. Thus, in the context of RBAC, we can define an operation as shown in Fig. 3.

Below we give an explanation of each clause:

- **params** *clause.* The user operation over the system resource has following parameters: a user *us*, a user role *ro* and a resource *res*.
- **pre** *clause.* Predicates over

```
Operation oper_i
  params us, res, ro
  pre  Resource_State(res) = state
       US_ASSIGN(us) = ro
       rights(ro) ∈ DY_RO_PERM(ro)(res, state)
  post Resource_State(res) = state'
       rights' [roles] = DY_RO_PERM [roles](res, state')
end
```

Fig. 3. A generic operation implementation for RBAC

  - a current *state* of the resource *res*;
  - required access *rights* of the role ro over the resource *res* to perform the operation.
- **post** *clause.* Predicates over
  - modified *state* of a resource *res*;
  - revised access *rights* for all *roles* over the resource *res*.

The precondition aims at verifying that the resource is in the correct state before the operation execution, the user has a role that makes him/her eligible for executing this operation, and the operation can be executed with respect to the current resource state and the role. The postcondition postulates that the state of the resource might change as well as the dynamic rights for the system roles. Let us observe, that the input parameter role *ro* does not change as a result of the operation execution. However, it should be defined since the same operation would typically have different contracts for different roles.

In this section, we have defined the conditions which should be verified to ensure consistency of desired scenarios and static and dynamic RBAC constraints. To automate the proposed approach, we propose to use Event-B framework. In the next section, we give its brief overview.

4 Background: Event-B and ProB

The Event-B formalism [2] is a state-based formal approach that promotes the correct-by-construction system development and formal verification by theorem proving. In Event-B, a system model is specified as an *abstract state machine* [2]. An abstract state machine encapsulates the model state, represented as a collection of variables, and defines state operations, i.e., it describes the dynamic system behaviour. Types of variables and other properties are defined in the *Invariants* clause. A machine also has an accompanying component, called *context*, which includes user-defined sets, constants and their properties given as model axioms.

The dynamic behaviour of the system is defined by a collection of atomic *events*. Generally, an event has the following form:

$$e \;\widehat{=}\; \textbf{any}\ a\ \textbf{where}\ G_e\ \textbf{then}\ R_e\ \textbf{end},$$

where e is the event's name, a is the list of local variables, G_e is the event *guard*, and R_e is the event action. The *guard* G_e is a predicate over the local variables of the event and the state variables of the system. The body of an event is defined by a *multiple* (possibly nondeterministic) assignment over the system variables. The guard defines the conditions under which the event is *enabled*, i.e., its body can be executed. If several events are enabled at the same time, any of them can be chosen for execution nondeterministically.

The system behaviour in Event-B is modelled by a set of events. We can transform this representation into the pre- postcondition format, as we did in [16] and then establish the correspondence between the definitions of an operation contract and an Event-B event. To perform it we can rely on our previous work presented, e.g., in [6].

Refinement in Event-B. Event-B employs a top-down refinement-based approach to system development. Development typically starts from an abstract specification that nondeterministically models most essential functional requirements. In a sequence of refinement steps, we gradually reduce nondeterminism and introduce detailed design decisions. The consistency of Event-B models, i.e., verification of well-formedness, invariant preservation as well as correctness of refinement steps, is demonstrated by proving the relevant verification theorems – proof obligations [2].

Tool Support for Development and Model Checking. Modelling, refinement and verification in Event-B is supported by an automated tool – Rodin platform [14]. The platform provides the designers with an integrated modelling environment, supporting automatic generation and proving of the proof obligations. Moreover, various Rodin extensions allow the modeller to transform models from one representation to another. They also give access to various verification engines (theorem provers, model checkers, SMT solvers).

For instance, the ProB extension [10] of Rodin supports automated consistency checking of Event-B machines via model checking, constraint based checking, and animation. ProB supports analysis of liveness properties (expressed in linear or computational tree logic (LTL/CTL)), invariant violations as well as the absence of deadlocks. A model checker systematically explores the state space, looking for various errors in the model under consideration [7].

In this paper, we argue that modelling with Event-B provides us with a suitable verification dynamic policies of RBAC.

5 Verification of System Scenarios Under Dynamic RBAC

In Sects. 2 and 3 we discussed the dynamic extension of RBAC and defined the conditions for verifying scenario consistency. In this section, we propose a formal Event-B based approach that implements these ideas to identify possible scenarios violating consistency. Our approach uses the graphical modelling in UML as the front-end. Graphical models are used to describe the general structure of the system and its scenarios. They serve as a middle-hand between the textual requirements description and formal specification. The proposed approach is shown in Fig. 4. It consists of the following six steps:

STEP 1: *Define RBAC model.* Define the system roles and operations over the system resources for each role. Represent the actors as roles, the operations as use cases and create the UML use case diagram of a system. Create an activity diagram representing the intended system workflow.

STEP 2: *Define/modify operation implementations.* Define all possible states of the system resources and create a state diagram representing how execution of each actor's operation changes the state of the resources. Then using the created state diagram, create an abstract specification in Event-B that defines the resource states and the corresponding state transitions. Each defined state transition should correspond to a realisation of the user operation.

Next, for each operation, define (or modify) its contract. Represent all the required elements: resource state, a role, required basic access rights for a role to perform an operation and the id of the accessed resource. Incorporate into the Event-B model the defined contracts by specifying the Event-B events.

STEP 3: *Compose a scenario and check it for consistency.* Compose/modify a scenario over the operations defined in the STEP 2. All the dynamic characteristics of a system are formulated in terms of the model variables and the required properties as the model invariants. All the static system properties are defined in the model context (e.g., a sequence of evolved scenario steps). Then simulate execution of a chosen scenario in Event-B and model check this model in ProB looking for inconsistencies in its execution. Any violations of the control flow consistency conditions (3)–(5) lead to deadlocking the model, which in turn indicate such inconsistencies in the operation definitions.

STEP 4: *Scenario analysis.* If a deadlock in the previous STEP 3 is found for a certain scenario, then analyse the operations involved in the scenario execution. The purpose of a such analysis is to come up with one or several recommendations for modification of the operation implementation. Then return to the STEP 2 for necessary modifications of one or several operations.

STEP 5: *Storing a valid scenario.* A checked valid scenario is stored as the corresponding command sequence in the Event-B context. Return back to STEP 3 until a scenario model is complete.

The resulting Event-B model (specification) can be used as an input for the next system development steps. Event-B specification can be refined further to introduce detailed requirements representation. Since the consequent refinement steps depend on the nature of the system to be developed, we omit their consideration in this paper.

In the next section, we illustrate the proposed approach by an example.

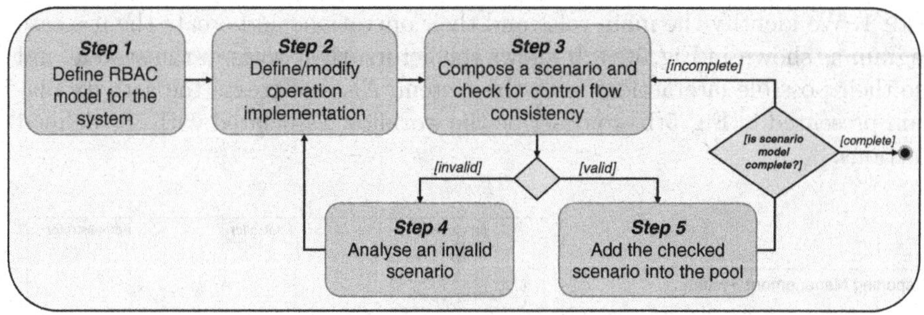

Fig. 4. Steps of the approach

6 Formal Modelling of a Reporting Management System

The Reporting Management System (RMS) is used by different employees in an organisation to send periodic (e.g., monthly) work reports. Below we summarise the access control-related requirements:

- *There are three roles in the system* – employee, controller and administrator;
- *Functionality associated with the roles*:
  - An employee can create a new report, modify an existing one or delete a non-approved report, as well as submit a report to its controller;
  - A controller can read the submitted report received from one of the associated employees, and can either approve or disapprove it;
  - An administrator has an access to all the reports of all her/his associated controllers, and it is her/his responsibility to register the reports approved by the controllers.
- *Report access policies*:
  - Until a report is submitted, the employee can modify or delete it.
  - As soon as a report is submitted, it cannot be altered or deleted by the employee any longer.
  - Upon the controller's approval, the report is registered by the administrator.
  - In case of disapproval, the report is returned back to the employee and can be further modified or deleted.

Let us note that each actor operation requires certain basic access rights. For instance, an employee, to execute `Modify Report` operation, should have *Read* and *Write* access rights to the report file. In its turn, the employee's supervisor – controller – should have *Read* and *Write* access rights to the same file to execute `Approve Report` operation. However, as soon as an employee submits a report to a controller, she/he can have only *Read* access right to the report file.

System Modelling and Verification. To specify and verify RMS, we follow the steps described in Sect. 5:

STEP 1. We identify the main roles and their operations and create the use case diagram as shown in Fig. 5(a). It shows the actors, their roles in the system and also their possible interactions with the system. Also we create the activity diagram presented in Fig. 5(b) to describe the workflow associated with the defined functions.

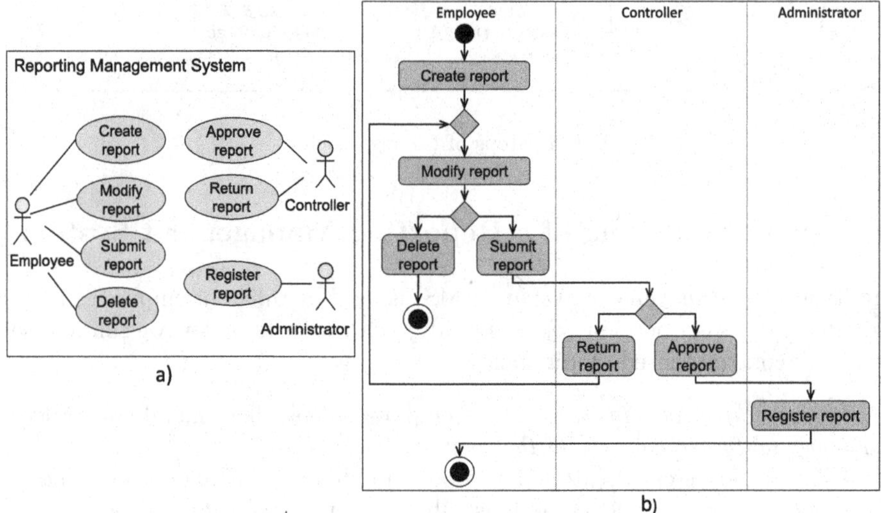

Fig. 5. Reporting management system: (a) Use case diagram, (b) Activity diagram

STEP 2. Each actor's function changes the state of a certain report. Hence, the overall behaviour of the system, for each particular report, can be considered as a set of transitions between all the possible states of the report. The corresponding state diagram is represented in Fig. 6.

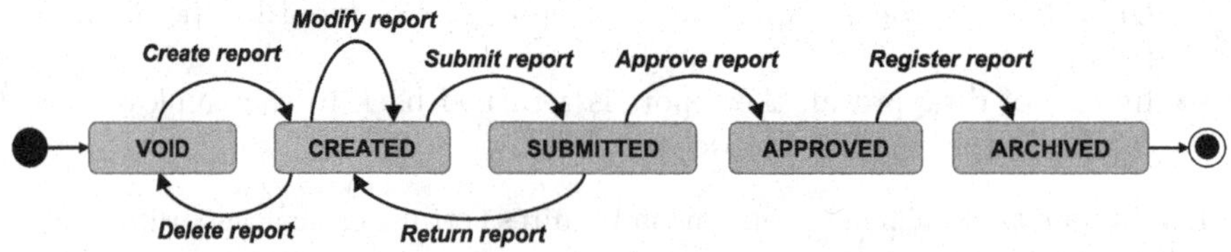

Fig. 6. State diagram – reporting management system

Then, we use the state diagram and create an abstract specification in Event-B that defines the state of reports and the corresponding state transitions. To represent a current state for each report we define a function *report_state*:

$$report\_state \in REPORTS \rightarrow STATES.$$

Initially each report has the state *VOID*. The actual report creation is modelled by the event CreateReport that changes the state of a single report *rp* to *CREATED*. Then the events ModifyReport, DeleteReport and SubmitReport become enabled. When the report is submitted, its state changes to *SUBMITTED*. Upon report approval, its state is changed to *APPROVED*, otherwise, if the report is rejected, it returns back to the state *CREATED*. Finally, once the administrator registers already approved report, the report goes to its final state *ARCHIVED*.

Next we link each role with the set of operations that correspond to it. Moreover, for each role, we will define the required basic access rights – *Create, Read, Write, Delete* – modelled as *C, R, W, D* values, respectively.

To specify dynamic permissions for the introduced roles, we define a variable *dPerm* with the following properties:

$$dPerm \in ROLES \times REPORTS \rightarrow \mathbb{P}(RIGHTS),$$
$$\forall\, r \in REPORTS \cdot dPerm(\texttt{Employee}, r) \subseteq \{C, R, W, D\} \land$$
$$dPerm(\texttt{Controller}, r) \subseteq \{R, W\} \;\land\; dPerm(\texttt{Administrator}, r) \subseteq \{R, W\}.$$

The variable *dPerm* is a function that assigns to each role and a report a set of possible access rights that can be associated with the role.

Obviously, for each role, the set of available access rights to a report depends on the current state of this report. For instance, a controller can have *Read* (*R*) and *Write* (*W*) rights only over the submitted reports. Moreover, when the report that has been submitted for approval, it cannot be further modified by the employee until the end of the approval period. Therefore, during the approval period, the employee has only *Read* right to this particular report. Hence, we should restrict the set of enabled rights depending on the report's state. In the corresponding Event-B events which model the change of a report state, the values of role permissions will be updated. For brevity, we omit showing the whole Event-B specification – its excerpt is presented in Fig. 7. For more details, please see our previous work [20].

Let us note that the variables *dPerm* and *report_state* together represent the *dynamic role permissions* `RO_DYN_PERM` discussed in Sect. 2. We use these two variables instead of one just to avoid nested data structures (function of function) in Event-B specification.

STEP 3: SCENARIO VERIFICATION. In this step, we analyse the desired system scenarios associated with RMS. For example, we consider a simple scenario as the following chain of operations performed by an employee and a controller:

CreateReport → ModifyReport → SubmitReport → ReturnReport → ModifyReport

We represent this chain as the corresponding command sequence and define it in the context. Then, in the machine part of the Event-B specification of RMS, we simulate the scenario execution by accumulating the information about the sequence of the corresponding scenario steps in *Scenario*. To implement it, we define a number of events – Start, Next, Finish – that simulate the scenario execution (see Fig. 8). The sequence of operations is built by starting from the first operation and simulating the execution sequenceleading to the last operation.

The scenario execution process is completed when the last command of the scenario is executed.

We formulate the invariant property *finish=TRUE⇒ CurScenario=Scenario* stating that if the scenario execution has been completed then the scenario contains all the steps (i.e., is equal to the executed steps). In the case, when the resulting command sequence does not match to the required sequence (*CurScenario*), a violation is found by model checking. Consequently, a found scenario sequence becomes an input for STEP 4.

STEP 4: ANALYSIS AND OPERATION MODIFICATIONS. In our example, we have found a deadlock – the scenario execution deadlocks on the execution of the event ReturnReport. We analysed the operation and discovered that in the implementation of ReturnReport the access rights for `Employee` upon the operation execution are set to R (*Read* right). However, the operation ModifyReport requires for a role `Employee` to have R, W, D access rights (*Read*, *Write* and *Delete*, respectively) to the report file. As a result, we modify the operation ReturnReport and check again this scenario for consistency.

STEP 5: STORING A SCENARIO. The checked scenario from *CurScenario* is then added to the set of checked scenarios *CheckedScenarios*. Then we repeat phases STEP 3–5 until we verify all the scenarios in the desired system workflow represented in the activity diagram.

As a result of the described process, we arrive at an Event-B model of RMS. We specify and verify dynamic access control via allowed rights over the resources according to the system policies.

7 Related Work and Conclusions

Recently the problem of modelling and analysing the access control policies has attracted a significant research attention. Milhau et al. [9] have proposed

```
Machine RMS_abs
Events...
CreateReport ≙
 any rep, u
 where report_state(rep) = VOID
   US_ASSIGN(u) = Employee
   C ∈ dPerm(Employee, rep)
 then
   report_state(rep) := CREATED
   dPerm(Employee, rep) := {R, W, D}
 end
ModifyReport ≙
 any rep, u
 where report_state(rep) = CREATED
   US_ASSIGN(u) = Employee
   {R, W, D} ⊆ dPerm(Employee, rep)
 then
   skip
 end

SubmitReport ≙
  any rep, u
  where report_state(rep) = CREATED
     US_ASSIGN(u) = Employee
     R ∈ dPerm(Employee, rep)
  then
     report_state(rep) := SUBMITTED
     dPerm := dPerm ⊲- ({Employee ↦ rep ↦ {R}} ∪
                        {Controller ↦ rep ↦ {R, W}})
  end
ReturnReport ≙
 any rep, u
 where report_state(rep) = SUBMITTED
    US_ASSIGN(u) = Controller
    R ∈ dPerm(Controller, rep)
 then
    report_state(rep) := CREATED
    dPerm := dPerm ⊲- ({Employee ↦ rep ↦ {R}} ∪
                       {Controller ↦ rep ↦ ∅})
 end
 ...
```

Fig. 7. Event-B specification of RMS (with possible inconsistencies)

```
Start ≙
any u_c, r
where num=0 ∧ u_c = CurScenario(1) ∧
      r = ReqRole(u_c) ∧
      CurRights(r) = ReqRights(u_c) ∧ ...
then
  Scenario := {1 ↦ u_c}
  CurRights := RightsUpdate(u_c)
  num := 1
  finish := bool(num = card(CurScenario))
end
```

```
Next ≙
any u_c, r
where finish = FALSE ∧ num > 1 ∧
      u_c = CurScenario(num+1) ∧
      r = ReqRole(u_c) ∧
      CurRights(r) = ReqRights(u_c) ∧ ...
then
  Scenario := Scenario ∪ {num + 1 ↦ u_c}
  CurRights := RightsUpdate(u_c)
  num := num + 1
  finish := bool(num = card(CurScenario))
end
```

Fig. 8. STEP 3: some events of the formalisation

a methodology for specifying access control policies using a family of graphical frameworks and translating them into the B. The main aim of the work has been to formally specify an access control filter that actually regulates access control to the data. In this work, the dynamics is mainly considered with respect to the operation execution order, while, in our work, the dynamic view on the access policies depends on the system state, in particular, on the state of a resource.

The basic RBAC model has been extended in a variety of ways [1,5,13]. The problem of spatio-temporal RBAC model is discussed in [1]. The authors considered role-based access control policies under time and location constraints. Moreover, they demonstrated how the proposed model can be represented and analysed using UML and OCL. Ray et al. [13] proposed location-aware RBAC model that incorporates location constraints in user-role activation. In our work we consider dynamic, state-dependent constraints within the access control model.

A number of works uses UML and OCL based domain specific language to design and validate the access control model. For instance, in the work [15] UML is used to describe security properties. In contrast to our work, here the authors transform UML models to Alloy for analysis purpose. A domain-specific language for modelling RBAC and translating graphical models in Event-B was proposed in [19].

Verification of behaviour aspects of software models defined using the design-by-contract approach has been discussed, e.g., in [3]. The goal of this work has been to detect the defects in the definition of the operations. Formal verification has been performed over the declarations of the operations in the UML/OCL models. In contrast, in our work, the defined operational contracts are used to model the scenario execution sequences and formulate the consistency properties. A contract-based approach to modelling and verification of RBAC for cloud was proposed in [11]. An approach to integrating UML modelling and Event-B to reason about behaviour and properties of web-services was proposed in [12].

A data-flow oriented approach to graphical and formal modelling has been proposed in [17,18,21]. These works use the graphical modelling to represent system architecture and the data flow. The diagrams are translated into Event-B, to verify the impact of security attacks on the invariant system properties.

In this paper, we have done two main research contributions. Firstly, we have defined a formal model of dynamic RBAC and proposed a contract-based approach to verification of consistency of scenarios with respect to the static and dynamic RBAC constraints. Secondly, we have proposed an integrated approach incorporating verification of dynamic RBAC into Event-B. In our approach, graphical models are used as a middle hand between the textual requirements description and a formal model. They help a designer to identify the scenarios and define the system workflow.

In this paper, we have used a combination of proving and model checking to verify consistency between the scenarios and the constraints of dynamic RBAC. Event-B and the Rodin platform have offered us a suitable basis for the formalisation and automation of our approach. The provers have been used to verify correctness of the data structure definitions and the Pro-B model checker to find violations in the scenario models. Moreover, model animation has facilitated analysis of the scenarios as well as identifying the recommendations for operation implementation specifications. We have validated our approach by a case study – Reporting Management System. We believe that the proposed approach facilitates an analysis of complex access control policies.

As a future work, we are planing to consider more complex variants of dynamic RBAC. For instance, we will model the situations when several users can get simultaneous or partial access to some parts of a data resource depending on their roles and resource states. Moreover, we are planing to work on an extension of the proposed approach for modelling and verification of dynamic RBAC and formalise it as Event-B specification patterns.

References

1. Abdunabi, R., Al-Lail, M., Ray, I., France, R.B.: Specification, validation, and enforcement of a generalized spatio-temporal role-based access control model. IEEE Syst. J. **7**(3), 501–515 (2013)
2. Abrial, J.R.: Modeling in Event-B. Cambridge University Press, Cambridge (2010)
3. Cabot, J., Clarisó, R., Riera, D.: Verifying UML/OCL operation contracts. In: Leuschel, M., Wehrheim, H. (eds.) IFM 2009. LNCS, vol. 5423, pp. 40–55. Springer, Heidelberg (2009). https://doi.org/10.1007/978-3-642-00255-7_4
4. Ferraiolo, D.F., Sandhu, R.S., Gavrila, S.I., Kuhn, D.R., Chandramouli, R.: Proposed NIST standard for role-based access control. ACM Trans. Inf. Syst. Secur. **4**(3), 224–274 (2001)
5. Fuchs, L., Pernul, G., Sandhu, R.S.: Roles in information security - a aurvey and classification of the research area. Comput. Secur. **30**(8), 748–769 (2011)
6. Laibinis, L., Troubitsyna, E.: A contract-based approach to ensuring component interoperability in Event-B. In: Petre, L., Sekerinski, E. (eds.) From Action Systems to Distributed Systems - The Refinement Approach, pp. 81–96. Chapman and Hall/CRC (2016)
7. Leuschel, M., Butler, M.J.: ProB: an automated analysis toolset for the B method. STTT **10**(2), 185–203 (2008)
8. Meyer, B.: Design by contract: the Eiffel method. Proc. Tools **26**, 446 (1998)

9. Milhau, J., Idani, A., Laleau, R., Labiadh, M., Ledru, Y., Frappier, M.: Combining UML, ASTD and B for the formal specification of an access control filter. ISSE **7**(4), 303–313 (2011)
10. ProB: Animator and Model Checker. https://www3.hhu.de/stups/prob/index.php/. Accessed 06 June 2018
11. Rauf, I., Troubitsyna, E.: Generating cloud monitors from models to secure clouds. In: DSN 2018. IEEE Computer Society (2018, in print)
12. Rauf, I., Vistbakka, I., Troubitsyna, E.: Formal verification of stateful services with REST APIs using Event-B. In: IEEE ICWS 2018. IEEE (2018, in print)
13. Ray, I., Kumar, M., Yu, L.: LRBAC: a location-aware role-based access control model. In: Bagchi, A., Atluri, V. (eds.) ICISS 2006. LNCS, vol. 4332, pp. 147–161. Springer, Heidelberg (2006). https://doi.org/10.1007/11961635_10
14. Rodin: Event-B platform. http://www.event-b.org/. Accessed 06 June 2018
15. Sun, W., France, R.B., Ray, I.: Rigorous analysis of UML access control policy models. In: POLICY 2011, pp. 9–16. IEEE Computer Society (2011)
16. Tarasyuk, A., Troubitsyna, E., Laibinis, L.: Integrating stochastic reasoning into Event-B development. Formal Asp. Comput. **27**(1), 53–77 (2015)
17. Troubitsyna, E., Laibinis, L., Pereverzeva, I., Kuismin, T., Ilic, D., Latvala, T.: Towards security-explicit formal modelling of safety-critical systems. In: Skavhaug, A., Guiochet, J., Bitsch, F. (eds.) SAFECOMP 2016. LNCS, vol. 9922, pp. 213–225. Springer, Cham (2016). https://doi.org/10.1007/978-3-319-45477-1_17
18. Troubitsyna, E., Vistbakka, I.: Deriving and formalising safety and security requirements for control systems. In: SAFECOMP 2018. LNCS. Springer, Cham (2018, in print)
19. Vistbakka, I., Barash, M., Troubitsyna, E.: Towards creating a DSL facilitating modelling of dynamic access control in Event-B. In: Butler, M., Raschke, A., Hoang, T.S., Reichl, K. (eds.) ABZ 2018. LNCS, vol. 10817, pp. 386–391. Springer, Cham (2018). https://doi.org/10.1007/978-3-319-91271-4_28
20. Vistbakka, I., Troubitsyna, E.: Towards integrated modelling of dynamic access control with UML and Event-B. In: IMPEX/FM&MDD 2017. EPTCS, vol. 271, pp. 105–116 (2018)
21. Vistbakka, I., Troubitsyna, E., Kuismin, T., Latvala, T.: Co-engineering safety and security in industrial control systems: a formal outlook. In: Romanovsky, A., Troubitsyna, E.A. (eds.) SERENE 2017. LNCS, vol. 10479, pp. 96–114. Springer, Cham (2017). https://doi.org/10.1007/978-3-319-65948-0_7

Performance Evaluation of Dynamic Load Balancing Protocols Based on Formal Models in Cloud Environments

Roua Ben Hamouda[1], Sabrine Boussema[2(✉)], Imene Ben Hafaiedh[2], and Riadh Robbana[3]

[1] Faculty of Sciences of Tunis (FST), University of Tunis El Manar (UTM), 2092 Tunis, Tunisia

[2] Higher Institute of Computer Science (ISI), UTM, 2080 Tunis, Tunisia
boussemasabbrine@gmail.com

[3] National Institute of Applied Science and Technology (INSAT), University of Carthage (UC), 1080 Tunis, Tunisia

Abstract. Cloud computing has recently emerged as a new paradigm for hosting and delivering services over the Internet. It is an attracting technology in the field of computer science since it allows starting from the small and increases resources only when there is a rise in service demand. Load balancing can improve the Quality of Service (QoS) metrics, including response time, cost, throughput, performance and resource utilization in Cloud environments. It can be described as an optimization problem and should be adapting nature due to the changing needs. In this paper, we propose a first step towards formal verification of dynamic load balancing protocols in the Cloud. The proposed approach offers a way to easily implement, analyze and compare different load balancing protocols, based on a generic model. We focus on the study of centralized and dynamic load-balancing protocols. We propose a high-level model allowing to specify a set of well known load balancing protocols. A formal and QoS evaluations has been performed automatically, using Uppaal framework.

Keywords: Formal model · Cloud computing · Load balancing
Task migration · Dynamic load balancing · Performance analysis

1 Introduction

Cloud Computing has become one of the most popular technology adopted by both industry and academia and in which shared resources, information services, software and other services are provided in a flexible and efficient way to users according to their need at exact time [1]. Load balancing [2] is a key aspect of cloud computing as it allows to avoid the situation in which some nodes become overloaded while the others are underloaded or even idle. Load balancing can improve the QoS metrics, including response time, cost, throughput, performance and resource utilization [3]. Thus, it becomes imperative to develop

M. F. Atig et al. (Eds.): VECoS 2018, LNCS 11181, pp. 64–79, 2018.
https://doi.org/10.1007/978-3-030-00359-3_5

an algorithm which can improve the system performance by balancing the work load among different nodes. Indeed, Service Level Agreement (SLA) and user satisfaction could be provided by choosing excellent load balancing techniques. Therefore, providing the efficient load-balancing algorithms and mechanisms is a key to the success of cloud computing environments. Several researches have been done in the field of load balancing and task scheduling in cloud environments and different load-balancing strategies have been proposed [4]. In general, load balancing algorithms are classified following two main categories namely Static and Dynamic. Static algorithms segregate the traffic equally among the different nodes in the cloud environment. In this approach, the division of the traffic is easier and consequently it will lead to imperfect circumstances. Indeed, such algorithms are used in the environment where there are few load variations as it does not take into consideration the real-time information about the system while distributing the load thereby making things simpler. But, they are not capable to handle the load changes during run-time [5,6]. Dynamic algorithms [7] continuously check the different properties of the nodes such as their capabilities, network bandwidth, processing power, memory and storage capacity and other parameters thereby assigning suitable weights to the nodes.

Dynamic algorithms could be implemented either in a distributed or a centralized (non-distributed) way. It depends on whether their models are based on a main controller (non-distributed) or a set of local controllers (distributed) to gather and analyze information about the system status continuously which provides a basis for choosing the right load balancing strategy dynamically.

In centralized load balancing technique, all the allocation and scheduling decisions are made by a single node. This node is responsible for storing knowledge base of entire cloud network. Therefore, in cloud systems, such decisive nodes should provide the application users with robustness, fault tolerance, execution automation, and powerful computing facilities which implies various cloud service requirements to be maintained. Therefore, several verification challenges arise throughout the design development and deployment of these systems. In addition, unlike conventional software and hardware systems, a wide range of different properties and design requirements arise in the cloud based systems. Thus, providing efficient load-balancing algorithms and mechanisms is a key to the success of cloud computing environments. The analysis of the efficiency of different load-balancing techniques and their comparison results could be achieved through different techniques and approaches.

Formal methods and techniques [8] are based on mathematical models for the analysis of computing, communication, and industrial systems in order to establish system correctness with mathematical rigor. Such methods are highly recommended verification techniques for safety critical systems. In particular, after the promising recently developed verification tools and techniques which facilitate the early detection of defects and hence enhance the design quality. In this work, we provide a generic formal model allowing the description of load balancing mechanisms in cloud architecture. Our proposition allows to easily specify different dynamic and centralized load balancing protocols. We have conducted formal verification through model-checking such as for deadlock freedom, invariance and a set of CTL properties using UPPAAL Framework [9]. We have also performed a series of experiments to evaluate, analyze and compare the QoS of the modeled protocols under a set of real-time executions for different configurations and metrics.

The rest of this paper is organized as follows. Section 2 discusses related works and presents the proposed approach. In Sect. 3, we depict the different concepts of the UPPAAL tool adopted to design the proposed formal model. In Sect. 4, we describe our formal model for the specification of dynamic load-balancing algorithms, in particular the modeling of three well-known algorithms namely; Weighted Round-Robin (WRR), Weighted least connection (WLC) and the Exponential Smooth Forecast based on Weighted Least Connection (ESWLC). In Sect. 5, we provide and discuss the different verification and analysis results. Section 6 concludes the paper and discusses possible perspectives.

2 Related Work and Approach

2.1 Related Work

In [10,11], authors have studied state of the art load balancing techniques and the necessary requirements and considerations for designing and implementing suitable load-balancing algorithms for cloud environments. They have also evaluated them based on different metrics. However, their work suffers from the lack of simulating the load balancing techniques by simulator tools. Authors in [12] discussed some basic concepts of cloud computing and load balancing by studying some of the existing load balancing algorithms applied to clouds. However, their approach does not pertain time optimization. In many other researches as in [5,6], evaluation and comparison of load balancing algorithms are performed based on simulation tools like CloudSim [13]. In [14], various algorithms are analyzed using an analysis tool, namely, cloud analyst, which is also a simulation tool allowing the user to run multiple simulations. These conventional simulation methods that are used in the context of Cloud cannot provide full coverage for complex systems, therefore, formal methods are used in addition to simulation to improve the quality and the reliability of cloud systems. Most of the existing researches addressing formal modeling and verification of cloud environments, are focusing on security issues like in [15] where authors introduced cloud calculus, a process algebra based on structural congruence and a reduction relation, for the specification of security aspects in the cloud. Different other issues in Cloud computing have been formally studied like Elasticity [16], Data Inconsistency, Misconfiguration [17]. To the best of our knowledge, there is no researches addressing the formal modeling and verification of load balancing algorithms in Cloud environments.

2.2 Approach

In this work, we propose a generic formal model allowing to easily describe at a high-level different load-balancing policies (see Fig. 1). We first give a formal model for the description of cloud architecture based on a set of timed automata and communication channels provided by UPPAAL framework [9]. Second, we define a particular function called *LB_Policy*() implementing the load balancing policy of the algorithm under study. Modeling formally a given algorithm is reduced to coding the corresponding strategy in the *LB_Policy*() function. Once the load balancing policy is implemented, the model could be formally checked for a set of properties described as CTL formulas. Moreover, a set of performance measures could be easily performed using the simulator integrated in UPPAAL. In this work, we provide a model considering centralized and dynamic load balancing algorithms. Then, to apply our approach, we consider in particular three well-known centralized and dynamic protocols:

- Weighted Round Robin (WRR): adapts the most important advantage of the traditional Round-Robin (RR) algorithm [18]. Therefore, it was developed to improve the critical issues of round robin. In weighted round robin algorithm each server is assigned a weight and according to the highest weight they receive more connections. In a situation, when all the weights become equal, servers will receive balanced traffic.
- Weighted Least Connection (WLC): assigns the performance weight to each real node and selects least weighted real node. The real node with a higher weight receives more requests and more connections than others [19].
- Exponential Smooth Forecast based on Weighted Least Connection (ESWLC): improves WLC by taking into account the time series and trials. That is ESWLC builds the conclusion of assigning a certain task to a node after having a number of tasks assigned to that node and getting to know the node capabilities. ESWLC builds the decision based on the experience of the node's CPU power, memory, number of connections and the amount of disk space currently being used. Thus, it allocates the resource with least weight to a task and takes into account node capabilities [20].

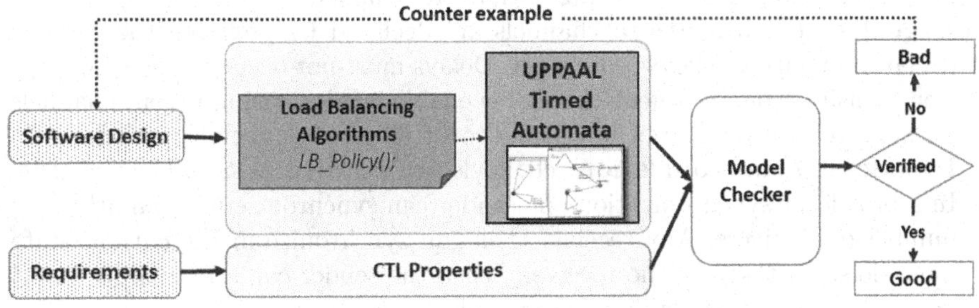

Fig. 1. Modeling and verification approach of load-balancing protocols

3 Preliminaries

In this section, we give an overview about the modeling formalism and the framework, we use for the description of real-time load balancing protocols in cloud environment. We choose to specify our model using the Uppaal framework [9], which is a toolbox for verification of real-time systems. It consists of three main parts:

- A description language: serves as a modeling or design language to describe system behavior as networks of timed automata extended with data variables.
- A simulator: enables examination in an interactive and graphical fashion of possible dynamic executions of a system during early modeling (or design) stages and thus provides an inexpensive mean of fault detection.
- A model-checker: checks whether the property (a system requirement) holds for the model of a system. It takes as input a network of automata in the textual-format and a CTL formula.

A system description consists of a collection of timed automata, extended with integer variables in addition to clock variables. Each automaton consists of a set of control nodes (states) which are defined by automata's locations, value of clocks, and the value of all local and global variables. It can use a dense-time model where a clock variable evaluates to a real number. Each edge may have a guard, a synchronization and updates of some variables. A guard is a side-effect free expression that evaluates to a boolean and it must be satisfied when the transition is fired. It can contain predicates on clocks, integer and boolean variables. When a transition is fired, a set of variables are updated by means of a set of user defined functions. In Uppaal, a transition may be labeled by a synchronization of the form *Sync*! or *Sync*? where *Sync* evaluates to a channel. Uppaal description language provides three types of synchronization:

- **Binary synchronization:** channels are declared as *chan c*. An edge labelled with *c*! synchronizes with another *c*?. A synchronization pair is chosen non-deterministically if several combinations are enabled.
- **Urgent synchronization:** channels are declared by prefixing the channel declaration with the keyword urgent. Delays must not occur if a synchronization transition on an urgent channel is enabled. Edges using urgent channels for synchronization cannot have time constraints, i.e., no clock guards.
- **Broadcast synchronization:** channels are declared as *broadcast chan c*. In a broadcast synchronization one sender can synchronize with an arbitrary number of receivers. Any receiver then can synchronize in the current state must do so. If there are no receivers, then the sender can still execute the *c*! action, i.e. broadcast sending is never blocking.

4 A Generic Formal Model of Load-Balancing Protocols

Our purpose is to provide generic formal model of load-balancing protocols in cloud architecture. In this section, using the already presented notions of Uppaal, we first provide the detailed description of a generic model of the cloud architecture. Then, we describe how this model could be adapted to model different load-balancing protocols.

4.1 The Overall Architecture of the Proposed Model

In centralized load balancing techniques, all the allocation and scheduling decisions are made by a single controller named Load Balancer (LB). This latter is responsible for storing knowledge based of entire cloud network and can apply static or dynamic approach for load balancing. Thus, it must be linked to all existing virtual machines which process its given tasks by interacting with its associated cores. The recent is the processing unit that receives instructions and performs calculations, or actions, based on those instructions. Figure 2, describes the overall structure of our model which is the same for modeling any centralized load-balancing protocol. In other words, components, their behaviors and channels are the same for all protocols. Each protocol is coded and encapsulated in a particular function called *LB_Policy*(). For this reason, we first give the description of the generic model, depicted in Fig. 2. Then, we give how it can be easily extended to a particular load balancing protocol such as WRR, WLC and ESWLC protocols. Hence, the architecture of our generic model is given by the superposition of three layers, where each layer defines a different type of component namely: *LB*, Virtual Machine (*VM*) and Core (*C*) (see Fig. 2).

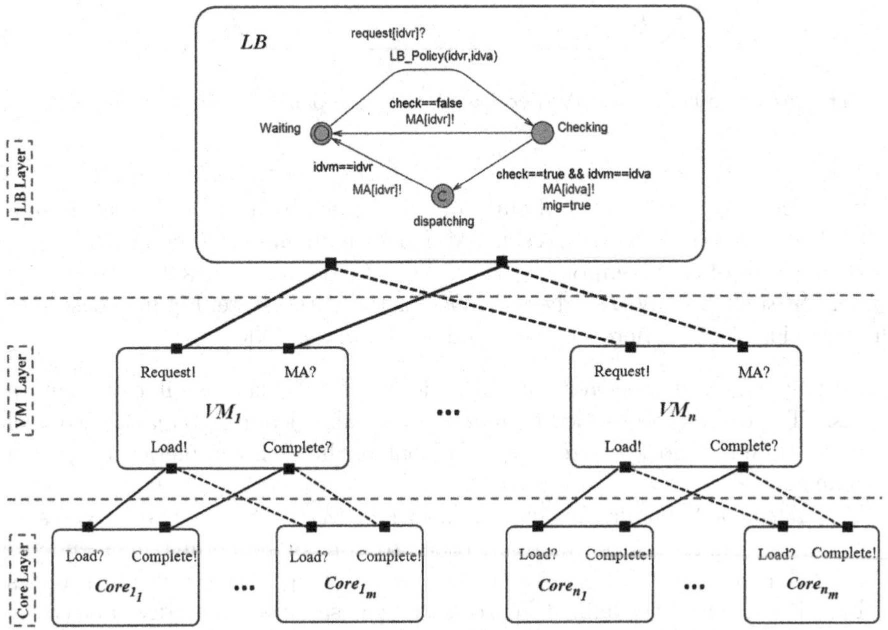

Fig. 2. The overall architecture of the proposed model

To detail our proposed model, we proceed in a bottom-up manner through the different layers. Note that, in our model, all components communicate with each other over a set of binary synchronizations (see Sect. 3).

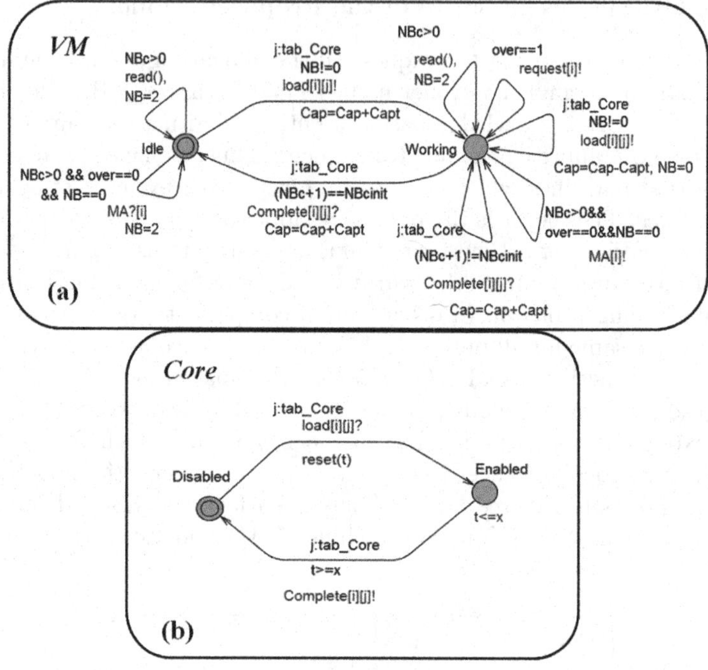

Fig. 3. (a) The behavior of VM component (b) the behavior of core component

Core Layer: The lower layer of our model is defined by a set of Uppaal components defining the set of cores of each VM. For each virtual machine $\{VM_i\}_{i \in [1..n]}$ we define a set of core components $\{C_{i_1}, .., C_{i_m}\}$. This latter has 2 control nodes namely $\{disabled, enabled\}$, where *disabled* is the initial state. Figure 3 describes the behavior of C_{i_j}, where $i \in [1..n]$ and $j \in [1..m]$, as follows:

- Initially, C_{i_j} is in *disabled* control node, until VM_i chooses it to execute a task. Then, the edge labeled by $load[i][j]?$ is taken leading to *enabled* control node. Here the clock t is reset to 0 to control the task completion execution time x.
- In *enabled* control node, we define an invariant $Inv = (t \leqslant x)$, which expresses constraint on the clock values in order to control remaining in a *enabled* control node. Thus, C_{i_j} can stay in this node as long as the value of t satisfies Inv. Then, once the defined guard $[t \geqslant x]$ is satisfied, the edge labeled by $complete[i][j]!$ can be taken leading back to the initial state.

Virtual Machine Layer: The medium layer of our generic model consists of a set of virtual machines defined as a set of n components $\{VM_1, .., VM_n\}$. A VM component has 2 control nodes namely *idle* and *working*, where *idle* is the initial state. All the VMs have the same behavior thus technically we can easily instantiate as many VMs as needed. For each VM, we define a set of channels allowing interacting between a VM and the rest of components. Figure 3 describes the behavior of a VM_i, where $i \in [1..n]$, as follows:

- Initially, VM_i is in *idle* control node where a first local edge must be taken up allowing to initialize the different VM variables. In particular, these latter are: VM initial capacity cap_i^{init}, the number of its associated cores nb_c and its assigned queue of tasks.
- After initialization, VM_i can fire up an local loop edge labeled $read(i)$, allowing to scroll task from its assigned queue. In this case, VM_i checks if it has available cores to compute a task by the defined guard $[nb_c > 0]$, else it waits the current task instance to complete. This edge can be taken in *idle* and in *working* control nodes.
- In its both control nodes a VM_i can fire up an external loop edge labeled $MA[i]?$, allowing to accept a task from other VM assigned by LB. To do that, a VM_i checks that it has not yet a task scrolled to compute $[nb = 0]$, that it is not overloaded $[over = 0]$ and that it has available core $[nb_c > 0]$. This edge can be taken in *idle* and in *working* control nodes.
- Once VM_i has a task to compute, it checks that it has sufficient resource capacity cap_i to begin task execution and so it can fire up $load[i][j]!$ edge, where $j \in [1..m]$. If it is in *idle* control node, it takes up the *load* edge and goes to *working* control node. Else it can take up the *load* loop edge in *working* control node. In both cases, VM_i decreases its current capacity value cap_i to reserve the scrolled task needed capacity cap_t.
- If C_{ij} complete a task execution, it interrogates the $complete[i][j]!$ external edge, thus, VM_i take up its $complete[i][j]!$ edge. If C_{ij} is the only core under execution, then by taken up *complete* edge, VM_i goes from *working* control node to the *idle* one. Else, it fires up the loop *complete* edge in *working* control node. In both cases, VM_i increases its current capacity value cap_i.

Load Balancer Layer: The top layer of our proposed model consists of LB component, which is the central component in the architecture. It has 2 control nodes namely *waiting* and *checking*, where *waiting* is the initial state. LB has different local and external edges. These latter are defined to allow interacting with VM components. Note that, all VMs characteristics are globally declared, thus LB has full visibility of their current values. In other word, VM data is passed via globally declared shared variables and synchronization is achieved via channels. Figure 2 describes the behavior of LB as follows:

- At LB definition we have initialized, by collecting initial capacities cap_i^{init} of underloaded VMs, in a queue, where $i \in [1..n]$. At the beginning of each cycle, LB is in *waiting* control node. Once a request is received from an overloaded

VM, with unique identifier id_vr, LB takes up an edge labeled $request[id_{vr}]?$ to go then to *checking* control node. To model mapping (load balancing) between an overloaded VM and an underloaded one, we define the function $LB\_Policy(id_{vr}, id_{va})$. This function is performed one a request for migration is received. It models the fact of checking the existence of an underloaded VM in the current queue, then comparing the selected VM capacity cap_a, depending on the coded load-balancing policy, with the needed task capacity cap_t.

- In *checking* control node, $LB\_Policy()$ function is already performed, and thus depending on its result, LB can go back to *waiting* control node or go to *dispatching* control node. More precisely, if there is no VM with enough capacity ($check = false$), LB comes back to *waiting* control node. However, if there is at least one suitable VM, with unique identifier id_{va}, to run the task ($check = true$), then LB goes to *dispatching* control node by taken up $MA[id_{va}]!$. This edge allows synchronization with the selected VM. Thereafter, LB returns to *waiting* control node by taken up $MA[id_{vr}]!$ allowing to synchronize with VM which requested for migration. This synchronization is needed to respond VM for its request.

4.2 Modeling Dynamic Load-Balancing Protocols

Now that, the overall architecture is given, implementing a given load-balancing strategy is reduced to code the corresponding policy in the $LB\_Policy()$ function.

Modeling WRR Protocol: In this protocol, the Load balancer considers only the resource capabilities in mapping between the overloaded VM and the underloaded one. Which means that, once the existence of an underloaded VM in the current queue is checked, LB executes its $LB\_Policy()$ function performed while taken up *request* edge, to search for suitable VM capacity $[cap_a \geq cap_t]$, where cap_a is the current capacity of VM, which will accept migration and cap_t is task needed capacity. Then, it assigns task to the selected VM.

Modeling WLC Protocol: In this protocol, the Load balancer does not consider current VMs capacities, however it considers the current number of free cores in VMs. In other words, once the existence of an underloaded VM in the current queue is checked, LB executes its $LB\_Policy()$ function, to search for suitable VM having the least free resources nb_c considering migrated task needs. Then, it assigns task to the selected VM.

Modeling ESWLC Protocol: In this protocol, the Load balancer allocates the resource with least weight to a task and takes into account current VMs capacities. Thus, ESWLC protocol is the merge of previous load balancing protocols. Particularly, once the existence of an underloaded VM in the current queue is checked, LB executes its $LB\_Policy()$ function, to search for suitable VM having the least free resources nb_c and a suitable current capacity $[cap_a \geq cap_t]$. Then, it assigns task to the selected VM.

5 Performance Analysis

As already detailed in Sect. 4, the proposed model, have been parametrized and adapted to specify three well-known load-balancing protocols. Note that, specifying other algorithms could be easily performed based on the same approach. Now a comparative analysis of the specified protocols is performed and different experiments could be easily extracted using the automatically generated code of our models. In this section, we perform the formal analysis of these models to compare them and to prove a set of formally defined properties like deadlock-freedom and invariance. All experiments were performed on a 2.6 Ghz Intel Core i5 with 8 GB of RAM.

5.1 Formal Evaluation

Based on Uppaal Model-checker, we have proven a set of formally defined properties (Deadlock, Invariance, Safety and Liveness properties) of the specified load-balancing algorithms at a high level of abstraction with no need to code generation. Extending our proposed model to any number of components is easily performed. Thus, we have generated several versions of our models for different numbers of components and we have studied the performance of the modeled algorithms for different configurations.

Deadlock-Freedom: is an important property to be checked when it comes to resource allocation protocols in general and dynamic load-balancing ones in particular. Indeed, in dynamic systems where behaviors and configurations may change at run time deadlock situations have to be avoided. Such situations cannot be proven using simulations. Table 1 summarizes the verification time taken for checking deadlock freedom of the 3 specified algorithms (WRR, WLC and ESWLC). Unfortunately and due to the state space explosion problem, deadlock-freedom becomes undecidable when increasing considerably the number of components of the model. However, in the context of load-balancing in the cloud, several other properties are also very interesting to evaluate, in particular when increasing the system load.

Invariance: is also an important issue when studying dynamic load balancing protocols. Indeed, task scheduling and load balancing in the cloud are defining on which resources a given task is executed and when. Thus, ensuring the satisfaction of time constraints related to these scheduled or migrated tasks is mandatory. In our model, we have defined cores as a set of timed automata in order to specify tasks execution to a predefined execution time. More precisely, we define an invariant for each Core component in its state named *Executing*, which guarantees that a core cannot execute a given task for more than the predefined worst-case execution time x of that task. This invariant is formally described using Temporal-Logic as follow:

$$\forall i : VM_{id}, j : Core_{id},$$
$$A[]\ (Core(i,j).enabled \implies (Core(i,j).t \leq V[i].task[j].x)$$

Table 1. Verification time of deadlock-freedom

Nbr of components	WRR	WLC	ESWLC
6	0,015 s	0,016 s	0,032 s
9	30,124 s	34,387 s	42,384 s
10	220,289 s	253,36 s	251,577 s
12	558,374 s	693,309 s	695,961 s

Figure 4(a), shows the verification-time of invariance when increasing the number of VMs in WRR, WLC and ESWLC protocols. Figure 4(b), shows the verification-time for the invariance verification when increasing the number of cores with a configuration of 10 VMs. Extending our model to a large number of components (VMs or Cores) provides a way to study at a high-level how load balancing protocols may react in the context of more complex architectures.

CTL Properties: Any desired property expressed as a CTL formula could be automatically checked over the proposed model and thus on the different specified load-balancing protocols.We have specified a set of properties and checked them using UPPAAL model-checker. Verification results are computed for a configuration of 100 VMs and are given in Table 2:

- Property 1: Load-balancing algorithm terminates and returns a result.

$$A[]\ (\text{LB.Checking} \implies A <> \text{LB.Waiting})$$

- Property 2: Whenever a task is read, it will be eventually loaded or scheduled for migration

$$\forall i : VM_{id}, \forall j : Task_{id}\ A[]\ (VM(i).R(j) = 1 \implies A <> (VM(i).req(j) = true \text{ or } VM(i).load(j) = true))$$

- Property 3: Whenever a VM requested is Task for migration, it will be eventually loaded or migrated

$$\forall i : VM_{id}, \forall j : Task_{id}\ A[]\ VM(i).req(j) = true \implies A <> VM(i).load(j) = true \text{ or } IdVR(i)(j) = true$$

- Property 4: Whenever a VM is overloaded, it will be eventually become underloaded.

$$\forall i : VM_{id}\ A[]\ (VM(i).over = true \implies A <> VM(i).over = false)$$

All specified properties have been proven to be satisfied by the studied protocols, except the Property 1 for the WLC protocol.

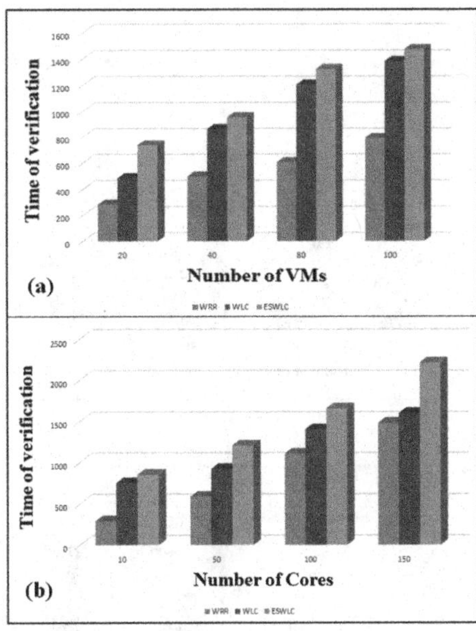

Fig. 4. Invariance verification-time (second) for dynamic load balancing protocols: (a) when increasing the number of VMs (b) when increasing the number of cores

Table 2. Verification-time (second) of variety of CTL properties

Protocols	WRR	WLC	ESWLC
Property 1	42.72	5.116 (not satisfied)	47.51
Property 2	3.869	4.399	4.337
Property 3	3.85	5.679	4.306
Property 4	3.916	4.368	4.321

5.2 Performance Evaluation

In order to evaluate and compare the described load-balancing algorithms, a series of experiments have been conducted using simulations set up in Uppaal. For each load balancing algorithm different metrics could be measured in different possible configurations. In Fig. 5, we have measured different metrics, such as the number of migration, number of requests for migration. Such aspects are very interesting in the context of load-balancing as they allow to have an idea about the throughput of the studied protocols and their performance. In Fig. 6(a), we measure the completion execution time of the total number of tasks for the different load-balancing protocols by increasing the number of VMs. Similarly, in Fig. 6(b) we measure the same metric but by increasing the number of tasks. We can see through these measures that ESWLC protocol performs better in terms of completion time. The model we have proposed, allows to define easily different

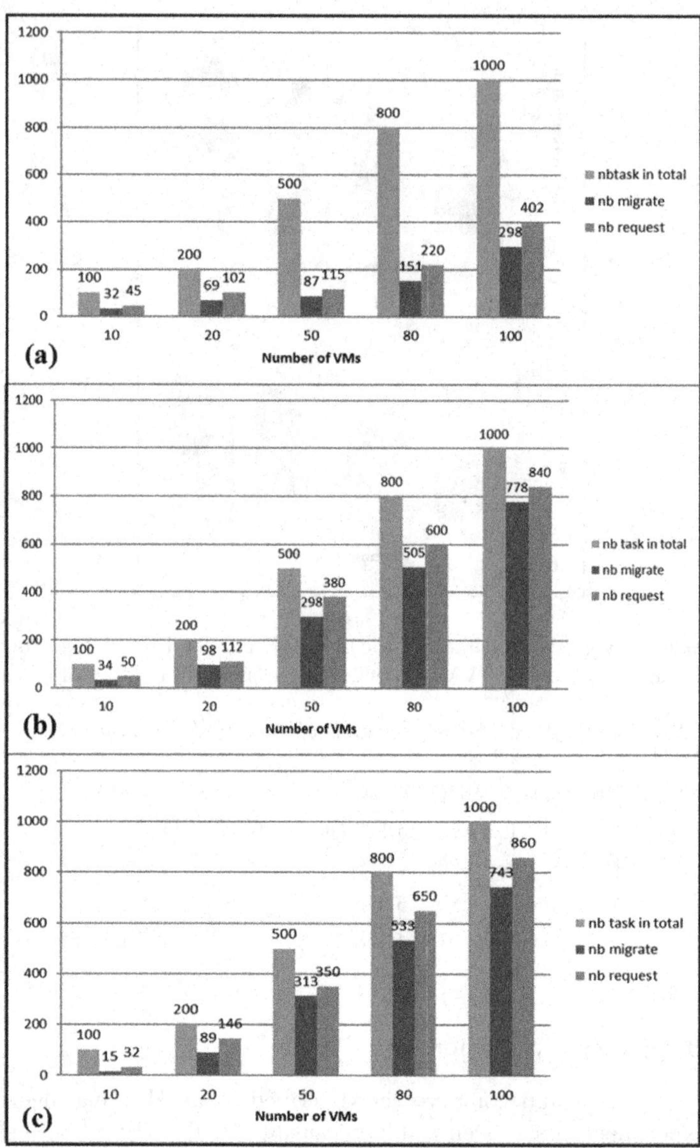

Fig. 5. Number of migrations and requests for migration for (a) WRR, (b) WLC, (c) ESWLC

set of configurations providing a way to compare different load-balancing strategies. Even though, VMs are modeled by the same Uppaal component, one can define different VM *types* which allows to specify heterogeneous configurations. Figure 7 provides the completion time measured for different heterogeneous configurations.

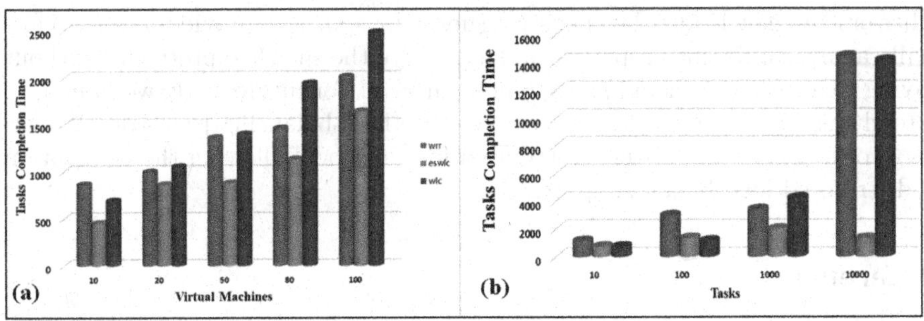

Fig. 6. Completion execution-time: (a) when increasing the number of VMs (b) when increasing the number of tasks

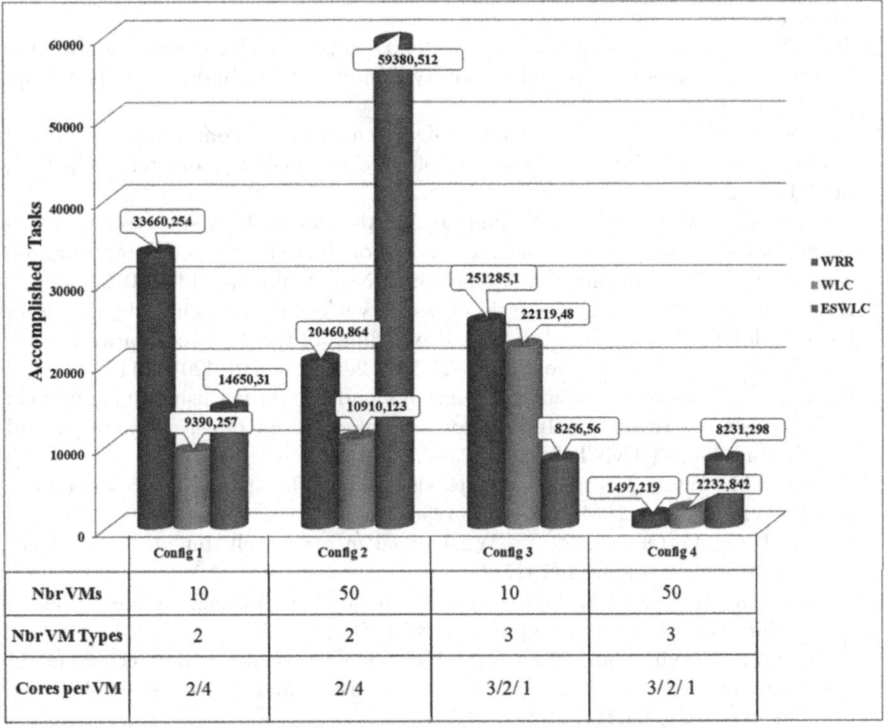

Fig. 7. Completion-time for different configurations.

6 Conclusion

In this work we have proposed a formal generic model for the specification of dynamic Load Balancing protocol in a centralized environment. The model has been parametrized so that it can specify different load balancing protocols namely WRR, WLC and ESWLC. This model could be easily adapted to specify other or even new load-balancing strategies. Our approach provides a way to formally analyze different properties and aspects of the specified protocols, without having to implement them in a concrete platform. For future work, we intend, to extend this model, to take into account other load-balancing protocols. We are also working on a completely distributed formal model allowing the description of distributed load-balancing protocols.

References

1. Armbrust, M., et al.: A view of cloud computing. Commun. ACM **53**(4), 50–58 (2010)
2. Rimal, B.P., Choi, E., Lumb, I.: A taxonomy and survey of cloud computing systems. In: 2009 Fifth International Joint Conference on INC, IMS and IDC, pp. 44–51 (2009)
3. Joshi, S., Kumari, U.: Load balancing in cloud computing: challenges issues. In: 2nd International Conference on Contemporary Computing and Informatics (IC3I), pp. 120–125 (2016)
4. Aslam, S., Shah, M.A.: Load balancing algorithms in cloud computing: a survey of modern techniques. In: 2015 National Software Engineering Conference (NSEC), pp. 30–35 (2015)
5. Nuaimi, K.A., Mohamed, N., Nuaimi, M.A., Al-Jaroodi, J.: A survey of load balancing in cloud computing: challenges and algorithms. In: Second Symposium on Network Cloud Computing and Applications, NCCA, pp. 137–142 (2012)
6. Radojevic, B., Zagar, M.: Analysis of issues with load balancing algorithms in hosted (cloud) environments. In: 2011 Proceedings of the 34th International Convention MIPRO, Opatija, Croatia, 23–27 May 2011, pp. 416–420 (2011)
7. Panwar, R., Mallick, B.: Load balancing in cloud computing using dynamic load management algorithm. In: International Conference on Green Computing and Internet of Things (ICGCIoT), pp. 773–778 (2015)
8. Clarke, E.M., Wing, J.M.: Formal methods: state of the art and future directions. ACM Comput. Surv. **28**(4), 626–643 (1996)
9. Larsen, K.G., Pettersson, P., Yi, W.: Uppaal in a nutshell. Int. J. Softw. Tools Technol. Transf. **1**, 134–152 (1997)
10. Mesbahi, M., Rahmani, A.: Load balancing in cloud computing: a state of the art survey. Int. J. Mod. Educ. Comput. Sci. **8**(3) (2016)
11. Milani, A.S., Navimipour, N.J.: Load balancing mechanisms and techniques in the cloud environments: systematic literature review and future trends. J. Netw. Comput. Appl. **71**, 86–98 (2016)
12. Padhy, R.P., Rao, P.: Load balancing in cloud computing systems. PhD thesis (2011)
13. Ray, S., De Sarkar, A.: Execution analysis of load balancing algorithms in cloud computing environment. Int. J. Cloud Comput.: Serv. Arch. (IJCCSA) **2**(5), 1–13 (2012)
14. Volkova, V.N., Chemenkaya, L.V., Desyatirikova, E.N., Hajali, M., Khodar, A., Osama, A.: Load balancing in cloud computing. In: IEEE Conference of Russian Young Researchers in Electrical and Electronic Engineering (EIConRus), pp. 387–390 (2018)

15. Jarraya, Y., Eghtesadi, A., Debbabi, M., Zhang, Y., Pourzandi, M.: Cloud calculus: security verification in elastic cloud computing platform. In: 2012 International Conference on Collaboration Technologies and Systems, CTS 2012, Denver, CO, USA, 21–25 May 2012, pp. 447–454 (2012)
16. Naskos, A., et al.: Cloud elasticity using probabilistic model checking. CoRR (2014)
17. Kikuchi, S., Aoki, T.: Evaluation of operational vulnerability in cloud service management using model checking. 2013 IEEE Seventh International Symposium on Service-Oriented System Engineering, pp. 37–48 (2013)
18. Samal, P., Mishra, P.: Analysis of variants in round robin algorithms for load balancing in cloud computing. Int. J. Comput. Sci. Inf. Technol. **4**, 416–419 (2013)
19. Choi, D.J., Chung, K.S., Shon, J.G.: An improvement on the weighted least-connection scheduling algorithm for load balancing in web cluster systems. In: Kim, T., Yau, S.S., Gervasi, O., Kang, B.-H., Stoica, A., Ślęzak, D. (eds.) FGIT 2010. CCIS, vol. 121, pp. 127–134. Springer, Heidelberg (2010). https://doi.org/10.1007/978-3-642-17625-8_13
20. Bakde, K.G., Patil, B.: Survey of techniques and challenges for load balancing in public cloud. Int. J. Tech. Res. Appl. **4**, 279–290 (2016)

A Protocol for Constraint Automata Execution in a Synchronous Network of Processors

Alireza Farhadi[1(✉)], Mohammad Izadi[2], and Jafar Habibi[2]

[1] Kish International Campus, Sharif University of Technology, Tehran, Iran
alirezafarhadi@ce.sharif.edu

[2] Computer Engineering Department, Sharif University of Technology, Tehran, Iran
{izadi,jhabibi}@sharif.edu

Abstract. In service oriented computing we encounter the problem of coordinating autonomous services (e.g., micro-services) communicate within the deployment environments (e.g., multi-cloud infrastructures) but participate for the functional requirements. While the environments have the deployment concerns like real-time, security, privacy or even energy consumption constraints, for the sake of brevity, the formal models of coordination in service oriented systems generally abstract away these concerns and focus on the functional ones such as synchronization, data and context dependency constraints. In this paper, we consider Constraint Automata (CA) as a formal model of the functional behaviours for the Reo coordination networks without any buffered channel. We devise a distributed protocol to model execution the CA subject to the deployment constraints on the messaging within a network of processors derived from the Reo network structure. We assume the constraints are satisfied while the protocol messages go through the shortest paths in the network. The protocol itself is modelled by another formal model Network of Timed Automata (NTA) with the untimed transitions implemented by the UPPAAL tool. Our protocol models the message passing along the shortest paths for performing a CA's transition by all the participant processors. The protocol guarantees all the processors do the same CA's transition as a consensus in the same round of execution.

Keywords: Reo coordination language · Constraint Automata
Deployment constraints · UPPAAL tool

1 Introduction

One of the challenges in service-oriented computing is that autonomous services are deployed on remote machines and must cope with the existence of the time delays in the network. However, the overall behaviour of the system must conform to the designer's intent. Reo coordination language [1] is a notation for modelling service composition which can also be used for executing service oriented systems. Services are assumed to have no knowledge about each other and

M. F. Atig et al. (Eds.): VECoS 2018, LNCS 11181, pp. 80–94, 2018.
https://doi.org/10.1007/978-3-030-00359-3_6

Reo networks constructed from Reo *channels* and *nodes*, model coordination of all interactions among the services without a-priori knowledge of their internal details.

Problem. In the presence of the time delays and asynchronous communications imposed by the deployment concerns, enforcing a network to behave in a time delay agnostic and synchronous manner is not a trivial task [15]. The existing coordination models have difficulties in dealing with some real world challenges, such as carrying out transactions subject to the deployment constraints. These challenges become more formidable when the models of coordination are used for concrete implementations.

Motivation. In [8,11,13] the authors show Constraint Automta (CA) as an operational semantic model of Reo for which a proposed distributed protocol forces a particular communication order among specific regions within a Reo network. The regions contain stateless channels connected by nodes that decide collectively on their behaviour in synchronous manner. The regions are separated by channels with a buffer of size of one [20] and called *synchronous regions.* Each synchronous region acts as an autonomous component. The behaviour of such a region is modelled as a constraint automaton with a single state that can interact with the other regions. Reo network structure is a suitable model that makes synchronous regions explicit to the designers of the distributed applications. The authors in [8,10,11,13] propose an algorithm for detecting synchronous regions within a Reo network and a distributed semantics for composing them.

As a motivation, fully distributing Reo nodes within synchronous regions because of hardware requirements (see Sect. 6.5.4 in [19]), is in analogy to migrating service oriented architectures to micro-service architectures [7] where autonomous big services can be decomposed into more finer and stateless ones because of non-functional requirements. In fact, micro-services actually must communicate asynchronously with real-time, security, privacy or even energy consumption constraints.

The deployment constraints of the behaviour of the synchronous region are ensured by the messaging along the shortest paths, therefore, our protocol can be used as the more concrete implementation of the synchronous regions that targets the deployment concerns.

For example, in micro-service architecture, cost efficiency in deploying such services is a vital need in multi-cloud native applications, so we need to combine both service coordination and deployment complexities while keeping the micro-services small and simple. Reo networks can model coordination logics, then based on the result of our work, each corresponding synchronous region can be implemented as a new set of coordinating micro-services (here processors) that are deployed on the multi-cloud computing environment. In our protocol, specific constraints of the deployment environment can be considered together with coordination logics in the implementation of the coordinating micro-services.

Contribution. In this paper, we propose a generic fully distributed protocol for ensuring that a static network of processors executes high-level user-defined specifications in the form of a CA with a single state. The observed computations in the underlying generic protocol represent a refinement of the user-defined specification [18] that takes into account not only the constraints imposed by the higher behavioural model, i.e. CA, but also the deployment constraints rooted in asynchronous nature of the communication over the actual paths for the messaging. In fact, low-level messages should go through shortest paths to satisfy the latter constraints. In our setting the deployment constraints are realized over link costs between the actual processors.

We assume that all the processors hold the same CA model and collectively run that model. It is guaranteed that the same results (cf. next paragraph) are achieved by each processor independently. Each processor knows (*i*) the behaviour of the synchronous region specified by the CA, (*ii*) the shortest paths to the other processors for the messaging (*iii*) and, executes the proposed generic protocol. In this way, we show, in formal setting, how the behaviour of the CA and the deployment constraints in messaging along the shortest paths within a network of the Reo synchronous region are preserved together.

For modelling the distributed execution of the Reo synchronous regions, we assign each node of the corresponding Reo network to a processor that is running on a separate machine [15]. These processors concurrently exchange a number of messages through the shortest paths during a limited period called *round* to inform each other about their statuses, decide which transition of the CA as a consensus must be executed in the current round and execute it.

The UPPAAL Network of Timed Automata (NTA) with the untimed transitions can be a suitable tool to model this distributed execution since it has the UPPAAL synchronization channels capable of modelling the message passing across the network of the automata [16] with plenty of variables and methods which can be used in the guard and update sections of their transitions, as well as the facilities for the design and validation of the protocol. The facilities are model checking, simulation and trace tracking features [6]. Furthermore, we derive a detailed semantic model consisting of four relations induced from the CA and the deployment constraints. The relations collectively are used in the protocol coded in the UPPAAL tool and some properties of the protocol execution are verified in an example by using the UPPAAL model checker.

For the rest of the paper, the structure is as follows. In Sect. 2, we provide the background about the Reo coordination language, networks, synchronous regions and the Reo operational formal semantics in terms of CA. The summary of the related works are reviewed in Sect. 3. In Sects. 4 and 5, we introduce our protocol for the distributed execution of a Reo synchronous region and explain its implementation in the UPPAAL tool. In Sect. 6, we elaborate on the semantic models of the proposed protocol. Finally in Sect. 7, we give a conclusion of our work.

2 Reo Coordination Language

The Reo coordination language has a user-friendly notation [1,2] that consists of two types of building block elements. With these building blocks, one can construct a Reo network. The first type of the basic elements in Reo is *channel*; this type is used for showing the data items flow over the network. Some of the channels are illustrated in the top of Fig. 1. In general, the data item can represent the actual or control data. By convention, the channels in Reo are the entities that have exactly two ends, which can be either the *source* (input) or *sink* (output) end.

The channel ends are used for accepting or dispensing the data items. In the *Sync* channel, when two ends are ready to interact, then the data item flows from the input to the output end. The *Filter* channel applies a data constraint in addition to the synchronization one forced by the Sync channel. Whenever the synchronization constraint is satisfied, the data item can flow if it belongs to the relation set induced by the data constraint (e.g., $\mathbb{R}_{>0}$ for the data items with positive real number values). Otherwise, the data item is accepted at the input end but it is lost when flowing towards the output end. The *LossySync* channel behaves like the Sync channel, when their two ends are ready to interact. But if the input end is ready to interact and the output one is not, then the data item is lost and not delivered to the output end.

The other type of the building blocks in Reo is called *node* (see bottom Fig. 1). The elements of this type are located on the channel ends and used for connecting the channels along the network. The behaviours of the nodes in absorbing the ingoing data items and synchronously dispensing the outgoing ones can be different but they generally fall into three categories: *Replicator*, *Merger* and *Join* nodes. In the Replicator node, the selected input is dispensed into all the outputs. In the Merger node, one of the incoming data items is non-deterministically allowed to be dispensed over all the outgoing channels. The Join node has a different way in absorbing the data item; it combines all the incoming data items into a tuple which consists of all the data items received, and then sends the tuple into all of the outgoing channels.

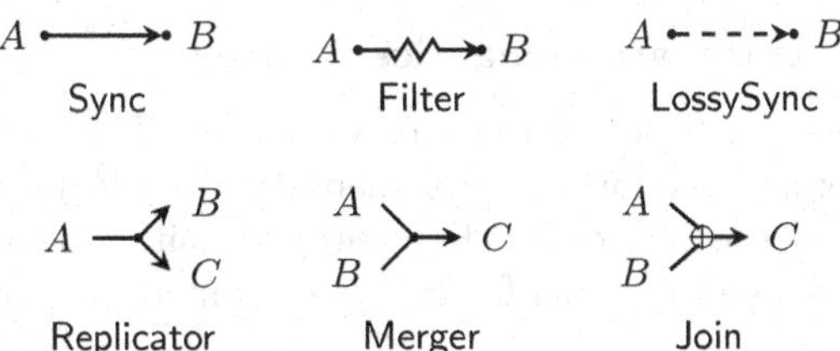

Fig. 1. Graphical representation of some basic Reo channels and nodes

A Reo network composed of the connecting building blocks elements has an internal structure. The structure can have complex behaviours, and communicate with its external environment only through its boundary nodes. In the Reo networks, the boundary nodes are connected directly to the external components' ports. The ports are used for reading or writing the data items from/to the networks; therefore, from the surrounding components' point of view, the internal behaviours and structures of the networks are not important. This feature scales up the design capability of protocol designers and simplifies the overall system design by doing it in several layers of abstraction.

2.1 Synchronous Regions of Reo Networks

The data flow over the Reo network takes place in a stepwise fashion. This means that in each step, based on the structure of interconnection among the elements and the existence of the data items on the boundary nodes; the data items can flow synchronously within the synchronous regions. The observed behaviour of the whole network can be expressed by the sequences of the data flows which exist in the synchronous regions along the consecutive steps. Such sequences obey a set of the constraints grouped as *synchronization*, *data*, *context-sensitive* constraints.

The synchronization constraints determine which boundary nodes participate in the current step by reading or writing the data items initiated by the connected components' ports, and the data constraints specify the relation between the input and output data items during the data flow. Meanwhile context-sensitive constraints deal with not only what happens on boundary nodes but also what cannot happen on them. The other type of constraints like time, cost and priority are good candidates to be used in specifying behaviours of the Reo networks [3].

The constraints over the sequences can be studied by automata theory. For example, The automata model for the synchronization constraints over the data flow in a Reo network have a set of states that formally corresponds to the set of the synchronous regions of the network. Moreover, for each state, we can define a union set of the labels on its outgoing transitions that resembles the Reo nodes and their stateless connected channels within the corresponding region (see Sect. 5.1 in [10]). Here, a transition models an instantaneous step of the data flow over a set of the Reo nodes labelled on it.

2.2 Constraint Automata Semantics for Reo

Several semantic models have been proposed for Reo. They serve different purposes (model checking, simulation, implementation) or focus on the behaviour of various subsets of the Reo channels (context-sensitive, timed, probabilistic, etc.). The popular semantic model for Reo is presented in a form of Constraint Automata (CA) [5].

By definition, since a Reo network keeps running as long as the input data arrived, so there are no final states in its respective CA. In CA, each state shows an evaluation for the internal buffer. The transitions of the CA are labelled by the port names which model the Reo nodes and the constraints over the data item values on those ports.

Definition 1 *[Constraint Automata (CA)]. A constraint automaton* $A = (S, \mathcal{N}, \rightarrow, s_0)$ *consists of a set of states S, a set of port names* $\mathcal{N}$*, a transition relation* $\rightarrow \subseteq S \times 2^{\mathcal{N}} \times DC \times S$*, where DC is the set of data constraints over an infinite data domain Data, and an initial state* $s_0 \in S$*.*

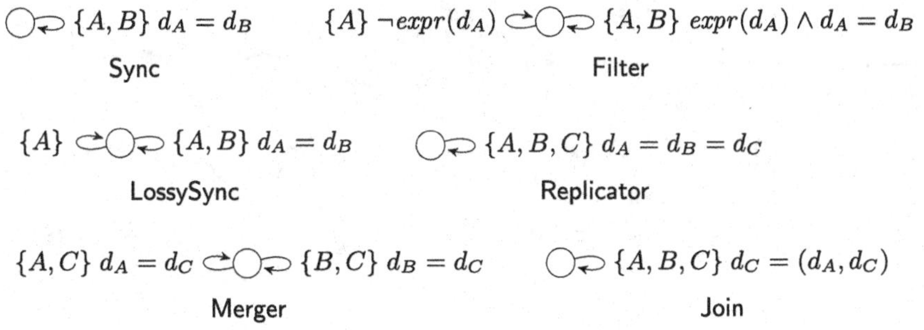

$\{A,B\}\ d_A = d_B$

Sync

$\{A\}\ \neg expr(d_A)$ $\{A,B\}\ expr(d_A) \wedge d_A = d_B$

Filter

$\{A\}$ $\{A,B\}\ d_A = d_B$

LossySync

$\{A,B,C\}\ d_A = d_B = d_C$

Replicator

$\{A,C\}\ d_A = d_C$ $\{B,C\}\ d_B = d_C$

Merger

$\{A,B,C\}\ d_C = (d_A, d_C)$

Join

Fig. 2. CA for some basic Reo channels and nodes

The data constraints set DC is formally defined by a set of dcs with the following grammar:

$$dc ::= dc_1 \wedge dc_2 \mid \neg dc \mid \top \mid data(n) = (d_1, d_2, \cdots, d_i) \\ \text{where } n \in \mathcal{N} \text{ and } d \in Data \text{ and } i \geq 1 \tag{1}$$

Informally, $data(n) = (d_1, d_2, \cdots, d_i)$ can be used as a syntax for denoting the flow of the data tuple $(d_1, d_2, \cdots, d_i)$ through the port name n [9]. We often use $d_A = d_B$ and $expr(d_A)$ to show the derived data constraints which means that the data items on the sample ports A and B are the same and the boolean expression $expr$ over the data item on the sample port A is evaluated to true, respectively.

A transition relation can be written as $q \xrightarrow{(N,g)} p$ instead of $(q, N, g, p) \in \rightarrow$. Figure 2 shows the CA for the basic Reo channels and nodes given in Fig. 1. The behaviour of any Reo network composed of these elements can be obtained by computing the product of their corresponding CAs. It is customary to make the composed automaton amenable by hiding the unimportant port names during compositional design [5].

For example, a Reo network that consists of a Merger node connected to a Filter channel on `C` port, and its composed behaviour in the CA with one state and four transitions are shown on the left and right sides of Fig. 3, respectively. Note that `C` port in the CA is hidden. Intuitively, the network routes non-deterministically the data item, from the boundary nodes `A` or `B` to the node `D` via the internal node `C`, where the data value is greater than value `d1`, otherwise the data item will be lost and not received by the node `D`.

The CA can be used in the implementations in which the Reo networks are deployed on a centralized machine and there is no deployment constraints for the message passing between the ports [17]. Therefore, it cannot be used for modelling real coordination problems. This means centralized implementations of the CA can probably be used if the deployment constraints are negligible, but they are not suitable for the distributed service coordination in the presence of the deployment constraints (e.g., communication delays [14]).

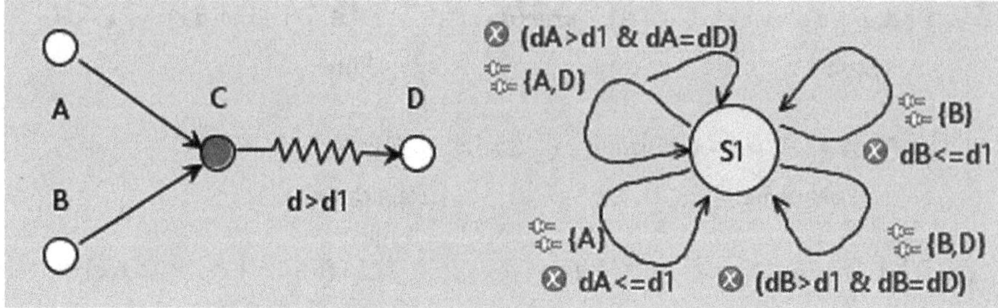

Fig. 3. Merger-Filter Reo network and its CA

3 Related Works

Since most implementations of the current semantics of Reo are centralized [9], they assume that all nodes that participate in a synchronous act of the coordination are located on one machine and there is no communication hop between any two nodes. In contrast with works in [8,10,11,13] that each synchronous region itself is assumed to be sequential event-handling code, Reo nodes within a synchronous region can be considered as distinct coordinating processors that are distributed across the Reo network of the region and communicate asynchronously in presence of deployment constraints.

All the previous distributed execution models proposed for the Reo implementations show the complexity in extracting from the global models the separate local behavioural models which are suitable for deployment on the separate distributed processors [10,15,20]. In our approach, it's assumed that a Reo network can be splitted to separate synchronous region(s). We only deal with a single synchronous region with its behaviour modelled by a single state CA.

4 Execution Protocol

Our aim in this section is to show a distributed execution protocol among a set of components. The protocol models the execution of the Reo network of the synchronous region with the single state CA as its operational semantics, over the network of the processors categorized into two groups. The internal processors are connected in a free-form topology that can be like the Reo network structure. The second group consists of the boundary processors that each of them interact with an adjacent component and an internal processor.

All the boundary processors contain the same *CA representation* of the behaviour of the network. This representation includes the synchronization and data constraints sections for each CA's transition. The processors and communication links among them in the network resemble the corresponding nodes and channels in the Reo network of the synchronous region. In this protocol, the CA's port names are also the same as the processor names. We formally define the CA representation in Sect. 6.

After a message passing period during a round of the execution protocol, consumption or production of the data items over the boundary processors obey the synchronous region behaviour model specified by the corresponding CA's transition, which is selected by all the boundary processors after reaching a *consensus*.

In fact, the processors of the network are committed to do that transition. Some of the processors take an action (that is either consumption or production of the data items) in the execution of the CA's transition if they correspond to the CA's port names in the synchronization constraints and the values of the data items satisfy the data constraints of that transition. Such processors are called the *active* participant processors during the round. The rest of the processors do not take any action and are called the *inactive* processors.

During each round of the protocol, all the boundary processors communicate and route their messages using the shortest paths through the network of the internal processors. But the message passing between the component ports and the corresponding boundary processors are considered simultaneous in the protocol.

All the messages exchanged between each two processors have the same format, consisting of

(i) an item showing whether there is a pending request from the adjacent component port on the corresponding boundary processor,
(ii) the data item provided by the component which may be *null*, and
(iii) a random transition number that is selected randomly by the boundary processor from all the possible CA's transitions.

This last item can be used as a suggestion to decide the final selected transition at the end of the round as the consensus.

In the protocol, all the processors begin from the same round number zero and increase it by one after selecting and executing the consensus transition at the end of the current round and repeat the process described above in the next round. The maximum number of the rounds is equal to one less than the number of the boundary processors and when the round number reaches the maximum value, it gets back to zero.

4.1 Protocol Properties

In each round, there is a specific processor whose initial random transition number must be used to decide the consensus transition. In other words all the boundary processors take a chance in a round robin order, to force the other boundary processors to use its initial random transition number as a starting point for searching within the possible transitions list, therefore, the protocol is *fair*.

After all the boundary processors' messages reach their destination during a round, each processor starts to check which transition can be selected as a consensus transition. This search is done based on the received statuses and the available data items from all the other boundary processors. Since the search starts from a common agreed starting point in the possible CA's transition list, it is guaranteed that all processors will agree on the same transition or no transition because of the identical conditions happened during the current round. When the consensus transition is selected, the boundary processors execute it.

It is also obvious by design of the protocol that there is no active boundary processor by the end of each round that has not already received any request from its corresponding component's port during that round.

In Sect. 5, an illustrative example comes with the implementation details in the UPPAAL tool. There, we also show the correctness of the proposed protocol by using the model checker of the UPPAAL to verify two CTL properties.

5 Implementation in UPPAAL

The UPPAAL tool is used to model and verify a wide range of applications from communication protocols to multimedia applications [6]. Networks of Timed Automata (NTA) extended with the bounded integer and Boolean variables, the user defined functions and the channel synchronizations make the UPPAAL suitable for the design and the implementation of the distributed protocols.

In the protocol implementation there are two important UPPAAL templates named `BoundaryNode` and `InternalNode`, for modelling the behaviour of the processors, one for the boundary and another for the internal processors. Here, the term node is used instead of the term processor in the UPPAAL implementation.

Based on our assumption a boundary processor can interact with an adjacent components port and an internal processor. But the internal processors can be connected to any number of the other internal processors according to the Reo network structure.

The UPPAAL template `BoundaryNode` has three parameters that specify the index of the instantiated processor, the type of the boundary processor, and the internal processor that is connected to the boundary processor. In contrast, the `InternalNode` template has just two parameters, one shows the index of the instantiated internal processor and the other corresponds to the index of the boundary processor that its message can be sent to that internal processor to be routed forward.

Since it is possible for the messages of all the boundary processors to pass through an internal processor, the number of times the `InternalNode` template is instantiated equals the number of the boundary processors. The pseudo-codes of the instantiated boundary and internal processors are listed in Algorithms 1 and 2, respectively. Informally, the NTA of the proposed protocol behave in three phases within a round of execution:

(i) determining the status of the boundary nodes,
(ii) routing the messages by internal nodes, and
(iii) calculating and executing the consensus CA's transition.

Algorithm 1. Algorithm of Boundary Processor *i*

```
procedure BoundaryProcessor
  adjacentComponentPort ← the adjacent component port
  connectedInternalProcessor ← the connected internal processor
  numOfBoundaryProcess ← the number of the boundary processors
  maxTransition ← the maximum number of the transition of the CA rep.
  while true do
    foreach currentRound ∈ [1..maxTransition] do
idle:
      if Is there any request from adjacentComponentPort then
        informs the connectedInternalProcessor by the message encoded as:
        boundaryNodeStatus[i] ← true
        boundaryNodeDataItem[i] ← the data on the writeradjacentComponentPort
        selectedRandomTransitionIndex[i] ← rand([1..maxTransition])
      else
        informs the connectedInternalProcessor by the message encoded as:
        boundaryNodeStatus[i] ← false
        boundaryNodeDataItem[i] ← null
        selectedRandomTransitionIndex[i] ← rand([1..maxTransition])
committing, suspend:
      foreach receivedMessageNo ∈ [1..numOfBoundaryProcess] do
        get informed by the connectedInternalProcessor
consensus:
      consensusTransition ← compute the consensus transition based on the CA
    rep. and received messages during the currentRound
      if consensusTransition is not found then
        progress to the next round.
      else
        execute the consensusTransition based on the CA rep.
        It may update the reader adjacentComponentPort
```

Illustrative Example. Here we define a system with four processors `A_Node`, `B_Node`, `D_Node` and (three instances of) `C_Node`, where `A_Node` and `B_Node` receive data from the adjacent component's ports. For the sake of modelling

Algorithm 2. Algorithm of Internal Processor *i*

```
procedure InternalProcessor
  correspondingBoundaryProcessor ← boundary processor whose message can be
  received
  numOfBoundaryProcess ← number of the boundary processors
free:
  exitNodeNumber ← calculating the exit nodes based on the shortest paths for
  routing the messages of correspondingBoundaryProcessor
  while exitNodeNumber ≠ 0 do
lock:
    Pick an exit node and inform it
```

the component's port, we introduce two other templates named WriterPort and ReaderPort for the writer and reader component's ports, respectively. The boundary processors A_Node, B_Node are connected to the internal processor C_Node which in turn connects to the boundary processor D_Node that sends the received data item to its adjacent component's port Reader_D.

This network of processors operates as a Reo network shown in Fig. 3. The Uppaal system declaration is encoded as follows and the complete code of this example is available at http://ce.sharif.edu/~alirezafarhadi/MergerFilter.xml.

```
Writer_A = WriterPort(A);
Writer_B = WriterPort(B);
Reader_D = ReaderPort(D);
A_Node = BoundaryNode(A, writer, C);
B_Node = BoundaryNode(B, writer, C);
D_Node = BoundaryNode(D, reader, C);
C_Node_For_A = InternalNode(C,A);
C_Node_For_B = InternalNode(C,B);
C_Node_For_D = InternalNode(C,D);
system
Writer_A, Writer_B, Reader_D,
A_Node, B_Node, D_Node,
C_Node_For_A, C_Node_For_B, C_Node_For_D;
```

Example Evaluation. By using the model checker of the Uppaal tool, we can verify correctness of our protocol implementation for the current example. Since the protocol model must be tractable for the model checker, we determined a maximum number of the round in our example implementation. This makes the result NTA finally encounter a deadlock situation when the round number reaches the maximum.

The following CTL property specifies if there is a situation where the protocol finishes the maximum round while one of the boundary processors (in this case, D_Node) is not in its consensus state. This property is not satisfied by the model checker.

```
E<> A_Node.consensus and B_Node.consensus
and not D_Node.consensus and deadlock
```

As a second property we check if there is a situation where all the boundary processors with pending requests and data items on them are committed to participate in a specific transition but it is not executed. The Uppaal model checker shows the property is not valid. Both the above properties are provided in companion with the code of the example.

In a random simulation run generated by the Uppaal simulator, Writer_B and Reader_D component's ports participate during a single round but Writer_A has not any request. A sequence chart available at http://ce.sharif.edu/~alirezafarhadi/MSC.png shows all the boundary nodes receive the messages of the others through the corresponding connected internal nodes and reach to their consensus states. Note that A_Node sends its message only after receiving the message of D_Node.

6 Semantic Models

To model the proposed protocol formally, let us consider the protocol representation of the synchronization and data constraints in CA in more details. For the synchronization constraints, we construct a set of the node statuses. In this section, we use term node instead of terms port and processor.

Definition 2 *[Transition Nodes Participations (TNP)]. A transition nodes participation relation over a constraint automaton $C = (S, \mathcal{N}, \rightarrow, s_0)$ is a set of tuples of the form $(Tr, \phi_{Tr}(\mathcal{N}))$ where $Tr \in \rightarrow$ is a transition in the $\rightarrow$, the transition relation in the C, and $\phi_{Tr} : \mathcal{N} \rightarrow P_{Tr}$ is a function from $\mathcal{N}$, a set of all node names, to a set P_{Tr} which determines status of participation (active or inactive) for each node $A \in \mathcal{N}$ in the Tr and is defined as below:*

$P_{Tr} = \{A | A \in \mathcal{N}$, where A has the active role in the $Tr\} \cup \{\overline{A} | A \in \mathcal{N}$, where A has the inactive role in the $Tr\}$

For modelling the data constraints over a transition in the CA in our protocol, we must distinguish between the disjoint sets of the input nodes $\mathcal{I}$ and the output nodes $\mathcal{O}$. The internal nodes can be removed from the CA's transitions by the hiding operator [5], therefore, we formally have $\mathcal{N} = \mathcal{I} \cup \mathcal{O}$. For the data constraints, we define two separate relations:

1. The *input data constraints* relation that shows what evaluation over the data items in the input nodes is valid in a transition.
3. The *output data assignments* relation that determine for each output node which data items can be consumed based on each valid input data evaluation.

Definition 3 *[Input Data Constraints (IDC)]. An input data constraint relation over a constraint automaton $C = (S, \mathcal{N}, \rightarrow, s_0)$ is a set of tuples of the form $(Tr, \eta_{Tr}(\mathcal{I}))$ where $Tr \in \rightarrow$ is a transition in the $\rightarrow$, the transition relation in the C, and $\eta_{Tr}(\mathcal{I})$ is a set of all allowable data evaluations over the set of input nodes $\mathcal{I} \subseteq \mathcal{N}$ for the transition Tr. For each member of $\eta_{Tr}(\mathcal{I})$, we have a set of tuples of the form (A, d_A) where $A \in \mathcal{I}$ is an input node and $d_A \in$ Data is the corresponding data item. For this member, the Tr's data constraints for the input nodes are satisfied.*

This relation is interpreted as the data items provided by the adjacent writer components' ports and consumed by the network in the active input nodes during the related transition Tr. An evaluation in $\eta_{Tr}(\mathcal{I})$ assigns the data items to all active nodes in the set $\mathcal{I}$. The data items are from the data value domain *Data* of the CA. The value *nil*, is used for the inactive nodes in $\mathcal{I}$.

Intuitively we can see the IDC relation which models a part of the data constraints set *DC* of the CA as the simpler version of the constraints where the *dc*s over the output nodes are replaced by *true*. The other part of the data constraints in CA must be modelled as the output data assignments relations.

Definition 4 *[Output Data Assignments (ODA)]. An output data assignment relation over a constraint automaton $C = (S, \mathcal{N}, \rightarrow, s_0)$ is a set of tuples of the form $(Tr, \eta_{Tr}(\mathcal{I} \cup \mathcal{O}))$ where $Tr \in \rightarrow$ is a transition in the $\rightarrow$, the transition relation in the C, and $\eta_{Tr}(\mathcal{I} \cup \mathcal{O})$ is a set of all allowable data evaluations over the set of input and output nodes $\mathcal{I} \cup \mathcal{O} = \mathcal{N}$ for the transition Tr. For each member of $\eta_{Tr}(\mathcal{I} \cup \mathcal{O})$, we have a set of tuples of the form (A, d_A) where $A \in \mathcal{I} \cup \mathcal{O}$ and $d_A \in Data$ is the corresponding data item. For this member, the Tr's data constraints for all the input and output nodes are satisfied.*

This relation is the extended version of the IDC. It also has information about the data item provided by the network in active output ports and consumed by adjacent reader components during the related transition Tr. An evaluation in $\eta_{Tr}(\mathcal{I} \cup \mathcal{O})$, in contrast to $\eta_{Tr}(\mathcal{I})$, assigns data items to all active nodes in the set $\mathcal{I} \cup \mathcal{O}$.

In addition to the CA-based models above, another useful concept in running the proposed distributed protocol is the *shortest path nodes* relation. Given two nodes, this relation maps them to a set of intermediate nodes, which must be traversed in order to stay on the shortest path between the two nodes. The message passing based on the relation preserves the deployment constraints.

Definition 5 *[Shortest Path Nodes (SPN)]. A SPN relation is a set of tuples of the form $(A, B, \sigma(A, B))$ in which $A, B \in \mathcal{N}$ and $\sigma(A, B)$ is a sequence of node names of the CA that shows a path with the minimum cost among all the other possible paths in the corresponding graph of the Reo network.*

Based on the semantic models described in this section, we can deal with the protocol correctness. First, we can formally introduce a language to specify the behaviour of the CA and NTA associated with nodes running the protocol. Then we can make sufficient statements about the progress of the protocol over time and definitiveness of reaching a consensus. Finally, in a theorem we can show that there is an equivalence relation [4] between the CA and the corresponding NTA, thus showing the correctness of the whole protocol.

7 Conclusion

In this paper we devise a protocol for the distributed execution of the CA of the synchronous regions, among the processors within which passing the messages conforms the deployment constraints by going through the shortest paths. The protocol is deployed on the machines located in a network resembling the Reo network of the synchronous region, with deployment constraints on the message passing over the links in the network.

We use the network of the UPPAAL timed automata with untimed transitions to model each processor which communicates with the other processors by the UPPAAL channels during a round period. They finally select a consensus CA's transition based on the collected messages and the functional constraints imposed by the CA. The protocol simply guarantees that all the processors execute the transition at the end of the round.

By using our proposed protocol, previous works on automatically generating the centralized and distributed coordination codes for the SOAP-based web services [12] in service oriented architecture, are suitable to be extended to communication protocols in micro-service architecture (e.g., REST and web socket technologies). In the future works we intend to extend our distributed protocol with the context dependent Reo semantics. In this setting the distributed Reo synchronous regions that are related by the context dependency constraints must communicate with each other to reach a consensus transition.

References

1. Arbab, F.: Reo: a channel-based coordination model for component composition. Math. Struct. Comput. Sci. **14**(3), 329–366 (2004)
2. Arbab, F.: Puff, the magic protocol. In: Agha, G., Danvy, O., Meseguer, J. (eds.) Formal Modeling: Actors, Open Systems, Biological Systems: Essays Dedicated to Carolyn Talcott on the Occasion of Her 70th Birthday. LNCS, vol. 7000, pp. 169–206. Springer, Heidelberg (2011). https://doi.org/10.1007/978-3-642-24933-4_9
3. Arbab, F., Chothia, T., Meng, S., Moon, Y.-J.: Component connectors with QoS guarantees. In: Murphy, A.L., Vitek, J. (eds.) COORDINATION 2007. LNCS, vol. 4467, pp. 286–304. Springer, Heidelberg (2007). https://doi.org/10.1007/978-3-540-72794-1_16
4. Baier, C., Katoen, J.P.: Principles of Model Checking, vol. 950. The MIT press, Cambridge (2008)
5. Baier, C., Sirjani, M., Arbab, F., Rutten, J.: Modeling component connectors in Reo by constraint automata. Sci. Comput. Program. **61**(2), 75–113 (2006)
6. Behrmann, G., David, A., Larsen, K.G.: A tutorial on UPPAAL. In: Bernardo, M., Corradini, F. (eds.) SFM-RT 2004. LNCS, vol. 3185, pp. 200–236. Springer, Heidelberg (2004). https://doi.org/10.1007/978-3-540-30080-9_7
7. Fowler, M., Lewis, J.: Microservices. ThoughtWorks (2014). http://martinfowler.com/articles/microservices.html. Accessed 7 Dec 2017
8. Jongmans, S.-S.T.Q., Arbab, F.: Global consensus through local synchronization: a formal basis for partially-distributed coordination. Sci. Comput. Program. **115**, 199–224 (2016)
9. Jongmans, S.-S.T.Q., Arbab, F.: Overview of thirty semantic formalisms for Reo. Sci. Ann. Comput. Sci. **22**(1), 201–251 (2012)
10. Jongmans, S.-S.T.Q., Clarke, D., Proença, J.: A procedure for splitting processes and its application to coordination. arXiv preprint arXiv:1209.1422 (2012)
11. Jongmans, S.-S.T.Q., Santini, F., Arbab, F.: Partially distributed coordination with Reo and constraint automata. Serv. Oriented Comput. Appl. **9**(3–4), 311–339 (2015)
12. Jongmans, S.-S.T.Q., Santini, F., Sargolzaei, M., Arbab, F., Afsarmanesh, H.: Orchestrating web services using Reo: from circuits and behaviors to automatically generated code. Serv. Oriented Comput. Appl. **8**(4), 277–297 (2014)
13. Jongmans, S.-S.T.Q., Arbab, F.: Global consensus through local synchronization. In: Canal, C., Villari, M. (eds.) ESOCC 2013. CCIS, vol. 393, pp. 174–188. Springer, Heidelberg (2013). https://doi.org/10.1007/978-3-642-45364-9_15

14. Kokash, N., Changizi, B., Arbab, F.: A semantic model for service composition with coordination time delays. In: Dong, J.S., Zhu, H. (eds.) ICFEM 2010. LNCS, vol. 6447, pp. 106–121. Springer, Heidelberg (2010). https://doi.org/10.1007/978-3-642-16901-4_9
15. Kokash, N.: Handshaking protocol for distributed implementation of Reo. arXiv preprint arXiv:1504.03553 (2015)
16. Kokash, N., Jaghoori, M.M., Arbab, F.: From timed Reo networks to networks of timed automata. Electron. Notes Theor. Comput. Sci. **295**, 11–29 (2013)
17. Maraikar, Z., Lazovik, A., Arbab, F.: Building mashups for the enterprise with SABRE. In: Bouguettaya, A., Krueger, I., Margaria, T. (eds.) ICSOC 2008. LNCS, vol. 5364, pp. 70–83. Springer, Heidelberg (2008). https://doi.org/10.1007/978-3-540-89652-4_9
18. Muth, P., Wodtke, D., Weissenfels, J., Dittrich, A.K., Weikum, G.: From centralized workflow specification to distributed workflow execution. J. Intell. Inf. Syst. **10**, 159–184 (1998)
19. Proença, J., et al.: Synchronous coordination of distributed components. Ph.D. thesis, Faculty of Science, Leiden University (2011)
20. Proença, J., Clarke, D., de Vink, E., Arbab, F.: Dreams: a framework for distributed synchronous coordination. In: Proceedings of the 27th Annual ACM Symposium on Applied Computing, pp. 1510–1515 (2012)

Testing and Fault Detection

MBT/CPN: A Tool for Model-Based Software Testing of Distributed Systems Protocols Using Coloured Petri Nets

Rui Wang(✉), Lars Michael Kristensen, and Volker Stolz

Department of Computing, Mathematics, and Physics,
Western Norway University of Applied Sciences, Bergen, Norway
{rwa,lmkr,vsto}@hvl.no

Abstract. Model-based testing is an approach to software testing based on generating test cases from models. The test cases are then executed against a system under test. Coloured Petri Nets (CPNs) have been widely used for modeling, validation, and verification of concurrent software systems, but their application for model-based testing has only been explored to a limited extent. The contribution of this paper is to present the MBT/CPN tool, implemented through CPN Tools, to support test case generation from CPN models. We illustrate the application of our approach by showing how it can be used for model-based testing of a Go implementation of the coordinator in a two-phase commit protocol. In addition, we report on experimental results for Go-based implementations of a distributed storage protocol and the Paxos distributed consensus protocol. The experiments demonstrate that the generated test cases yield a high statement coverage.

1 Introduction

Society is heavily dependent on software and software systems, and design- and implementation errors in software systems may render them unavailable and return erroneous results to their users. It is therefore important to develop techniques that can be used to ensure correct and stable operation of the software.

Model-based testing (MBT) [13] is a promising technique for using models of a system under test (SUT) and its environment to generate test cases for the system. MBT approaches and tools have been developed based on a variety of modeling formalisms, including flowcharts, decision tables, finite-state machines, Petri nets, state-charts, object-oriented models, and BPMN [6]. A test case usually consists of test input and expected output and can be executed against the SUT. The goal of MBT is validation and error-detection by finding observable differences between the behavior of an implementation and the intended behavior. Generally, MBT involves: (a) constructing a model of the SUT and its environment; (b) define test selection criteria for guiding the generation of test cases and the corresponding test oracle representing the ground-truth; (c) generation and execution of test cases; (d) comparison of the output from the test

M. F. Atig et al. (Eds.): VECoS 2018, LNCS 11181, pp. 97–113, 2018.
https://doi.org/10.1007/978-3-030-00359-3_7

case execution with the expected result from the test oracle. The component that performs (c) and (d) is known as a *test adapter* and uses the *test oracles* to determine whether a test has passed or failed.

Coloured Petri Nets (CPNs) [5] is a modeling language for distributed and concurrent systems combining Petri nets and the Standard ML programming language. Petri nets provide the primitives for modeling concurrency, synchronization and communication while Standard ML is used for modeling data. Construction and analysis of CPN models is supported by CPN Tools [2] which have been widely used for modeling and verifying models of complex systems for domains such as concurrent systems, communication protocols, and distributed algorithms [9]. Recently, work on automated code generation has also been done [8]. Comprehensive testing is an important task in the engineering of software, including the case of automated code generation, as it is seldom the case that the correctness of the model-to-text transformations and their implementation can be formally established. We have chosen CPNs as the foundation of our MBT approach due to its strong track record in modeling distributed systems, and the support for parametric models and compact modeling of data. Moreover, CPNs enables model validation prior to test case generation, and CPN Tools supports both simulation and state space exploration which is paramount for the development of our approach and for conducting practical experiments.

The main contribution of this paper is to present our approach to model-based testing using CPNs and the supporting MBT/CPN tool. MBT/CPN has been implemented on top of CPN Tools to support test case generation from CPN models. It has been developed as part of our ongoing research into MBT for quorum-based distributed systems [15]. The main idea underlying our approach is for the modeler to capture the observable input and output events (transitions) in a test case specification. A main facility of the tool is the uniform support for both state space and simulation-based test case generation. A second contribution of this paper is to experimentally evaluate the tool on a two-phase commit protocol implemented using the Go programming language, and to summarize experimental results from the application of MBT/CPN to a distributed storage protocol [15] and the Paxos distributed consensus protocol [14]. The distributed storage protocol and the Paxos protocol have both been implemented in the Go programming language [3] using a quorum-based distributed systems middleware [10]. These experiments show a high statement coverage and demonstrate in addition that the approach is able to detect programming errors via the generation and execution of unit and system tests.

The rest of this paper is organized as follows. Section 2 gives an overview of MBT/CPN and its software architecture. In Sect. 3 we introduce the two-phase commit transaction protocol that we use as a running example to present the features of MBT/CPN. Sections 4 and 5 explain how test case generation and test case execution are supported. Section 6 presents our experimental evaluation of MBT/CPN. In Sect. 7, we sum up conclusions and discuss related work. We assume that the reader is familiar with the basic concepts of Petri nets. The MBT/CPN tool is available via [11].

2 Tool Overview and Software Architecture

The MBT/CPN tool is implemented in the Standard ML programming language on top of the simulator of CPN Tools. In CPN models, Standard ML is used to define the data types of the model, to declare the colour set of places and the variables of transitions, for defining guards of transitions, and for the arc expressions appearing on the arcs connecting places and transitions. MBT/CPN provides the user with a set of Standard ML functions which can be invoked in order to perform test case generation.

Figure 1 gives an overview of the modules that constitute MBT/CPN and puts the tool into the context of model-based test case generation. The main outputs of the MBT/CPN tool are files containing Test Cases which can be read by a Reader of a test Adapter and executed by a Tester against the System Under Test (SUT). The Tester will provide the input events as stimuli to the SUT and compare the observed outputs from the SUT with the expected outputs.

The application of MBT/CPN requires the user to identify the *observable events* originating from occurrences of binding elements in the CPN model. A binding element is a pair consisting of a transition and an assignment of values to the variables of the transition. A binding element hence represents a mode in which a transition may be enabled and may occur. A test case is comprised of observable events where input events represent stimuli to the SUT and output events represent expected outputs. It is the expected outputs that are used as test oracles during test case execution to determine the overall test outcome.

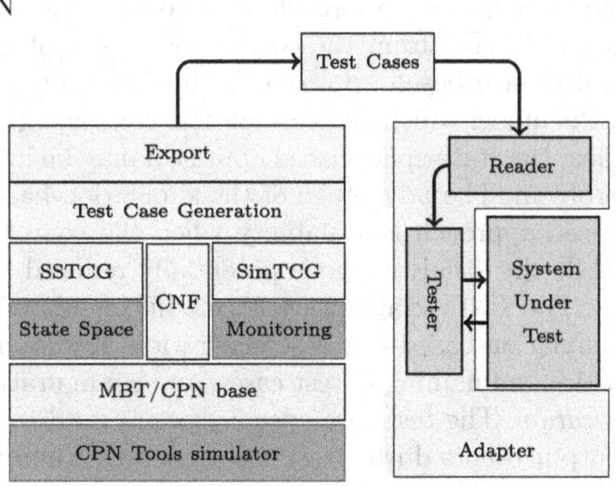

Fig. 1. Overview of MBT/CPN modules.

The MBT/CPN base module defines a generic colour set (data type) used to represent the observable events in test cases:

```
colset TCEvent = union InEvent:TCInEvent + OutEvent:TCOutEvent;
```

The definition of the colour sets `TCInEvent` and `TCOutEvent` depends on the SUT in terms of the events to be made observable. These must be defined by the user of the tool and can use the standard colour set constructors in CPN Tools. The tool supports two approaches for extracting test cases from the model:

State-space based test case generation. This approach is based on generating the state space of the CPN model and extracting test cases by considering paths in the state space. This approach is implemented in the SSTCG module on top of the state space tool of CPN Tools.

```
signature TCSPEC = sig
  val detection   : Bind.Elem -> bool;
  val observation : Bind.Elem -> TCEvent list;
  val format      : TCEvent   -> string
end;
```

Fig. 2. Standard ML interface for test case specification.

Simulation-based test case generation. This approach is based on conducting a simulation of the CPN model and extracting the test case corresponding to the execution. This approach is implemented in the SIMTCG module on top of the simulation monitoring facilities of CPN Tools.

The state-space based approach works for finite-state models and is based on computing all reachable states and state changes of the CPN model. The simulation-based approach is based on running a set of simulations and extracting test cases from the corresponding set of executions. The advantage of the state-space based approach is that it covers all the possible executions of the CPN model which gives a high test coverage. However, if the CPN model is complex, the state-space based approach may be infeasible due to the state explosion problem. The advantage of the simulation-based approach over the state-space based approach is scalability when the complexity of the CPN model is high, while the disadvantage is potentially reduced test coverage.

The CNF (configuration) module is shared between the state space- and simulation-based test case generation. It supports configuring the output directories and naming of test cases, and configuration of a *test case generation specification*. The test case specification is used to specify the observable input and output events during test case generation and is comprised of a:

Detection function constituting a predicate on binding elements that evaluates to true for binding elements representing observable events.

Observation function which maps an observable binding element into an observable input or output event belonging to the `TCEvent` colour set.

Formatting function mapping observable events into a string representation which is used in order to export the test cases into files.

The test case specification is provided by the user implementing a Standard ML structure satisfying the `TCSPEC` signature (interface) shown in Fig. 2. The type `Bind.Elem` is an existing data type in CPN Tools representing binding elements. The observation function is specified to return a list of observable events to cater for the case where one might want to split a binding element into several observable events in the test case. We will give examples of detection and observation functions for the two-phase commit protocol example in Sect. 4.

The detection and observation functions are specified independently of whether simulation-based or state space-based test case generation is employed. This allows the input from the user to be specified in a uniform way, independently of which approach will be used for the test case generation. This makes it

```
signature TCGEN = sig
  val ss  : unit -> (TCEvent list) list;
  val sim : int -> (TCEvent list) list;
  val export : (TCEvent list) list -> unit
end;
```

Fig. 3. Standard ML interface for test case generation.

easy to switch between the two approaches. The tool invokes the detection function on each arc of the state space (occurring binding element in a simulation) to determine whether the corresponding event is observable, and if so, then the observation function will be invoked to map the corresponding binding element into an observable event. The `Export` module implements the export of the test cases into files and relies on the `CNF` module for persistence and naming.

When an implementation of the test case specification has been provided by the user, the MBT/CPN tool can be used to generate test cases. The primitives available for the user to control the test case generation are provided by the Test Case Generation module which implements the `TCGEN` interface (signature) partly shown in Fig. 3. The `ss` function is used for state-space based test case generation. The `sim` function is used for simulation-based test case generation and takes an integer as a parameter specifying the number of simulation runs that should be conducted to generate test cases. Both functions return a list of test cases, where each test case is comprised of a list of test case events (`TCEvent`). The `export` function is used for exporting the test cases into files according to the settings which the user provided via the CNF configuration module (Fig. 1).

3 Example: Two-Phase Commit Transaction Protocol

We use the two-phase commit transaction (TPC) protocol from [5] to explain the use of MBT/CPN. The CPN model is comprised of four hierarchically organized modules. Figure 4 shows the CPN module for the coordinator process and Fig. 5 shows the CPN module for the worker processes. Figure 6 shows model-based test case generation and exporting. Due to space limitations, we do not show the top-level CPN module and have also omitted the submodule of the CollectVotes substitution transition in Fig. 4. Each port place (place drawn with a double border) in the coordinator module is linked via so-called port-socket assignments to the accordingly named place in the workers module. The colour sets and variable used are shown in Fig. 7.

The coordinator starts by sending a message to each worker (transition SendCanCommit), asking whether the transaction can be committed or not. Each worker votes `Yes` or `No` (transition ReceiveCanCommit). The coordinator then collects each vote as modeled by the CollectVotes submodule of the CollectVotes substitution transition. Based on the collected votes, the coordinator sends back an `abort` or `commit` decision.

The coordinator will decide on commit if and only if all workers voted yes. The workers that voted yes then receive the decision (transition ReceiveDecision) and send back an acknowledgement. The coordinator then receives all acknowledgements (transition ReceiveAcknowledgement). After having executed the protocol, the place Completed will contain a token with colour `abort` or `commit` depending on whether the transaction was to be committed or not.

When presenting MBT/CPN in the remainder of this paper, we show how it can be used to generate test cases from the TPC CPN model. These can then be executed by a test adapter against an implementation of the coordinator process in the Go programming language. The workers module is used to obtain input events (stimuli) for the coordinator implementation, and the coordinator CPN module is used to obtain expected outputs (test oracles) which in turn determine whether a test is successful or not. In that respect, the CPN module of the coordinator serves as an abstract specification of the coordinator process against which the behavior of the implementation can be compared.

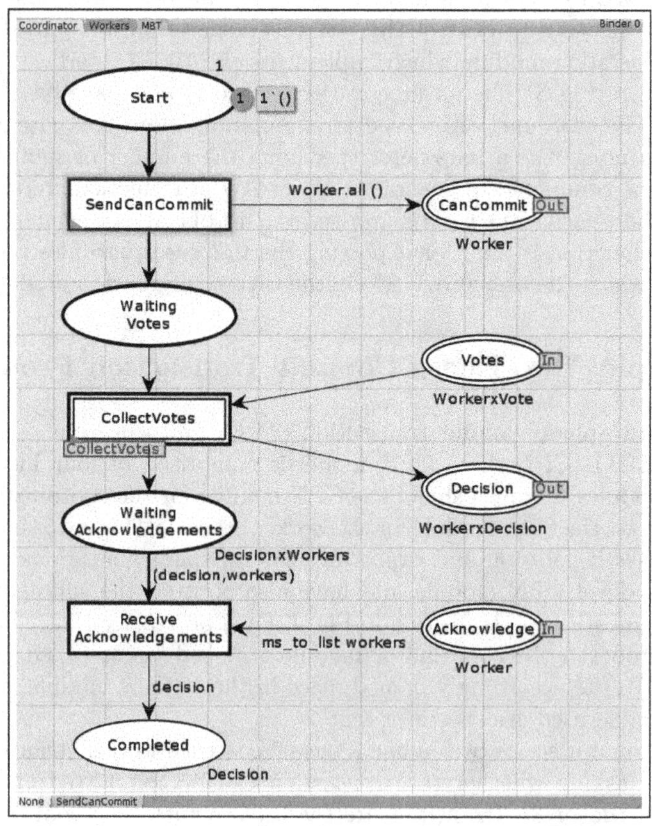

Fig. 4. MBT/CPN example in CPN Tools: Coordinator module.

4 Test Case Generation

The first step in using the MBT/CPN tool for test case generation is to extend the `TCEvent` base colour set by defining the colour sets `TCInEvent` and `TCOutEvent` according to the input and output events of the system that are to be observed. For the TPC protocol, we can define the input events to be the votes of the individual workers. The output events can be defined as the decisions sent to the individual workers and the overall decision as to whether the transaction is to be committed or aborted. Relying on the colour set definitions already in the CPN model (Fig. 7), this can be implemented as shown in Fig. 8. In the `TCOutEvent` colour set, `WDecision` is used for the decision sent to each worker while `SDecision` is used for the overall system decision.

For the TPC protocol, the input events corresponding to the votes sent by the workers can be obtained by considering occurrences of the ReceiveCanCommit transition (Fig. 5), while the output events can be obtained by considering the ReceiveDecision and ReceiveAcknowledgement transitions. This means that the

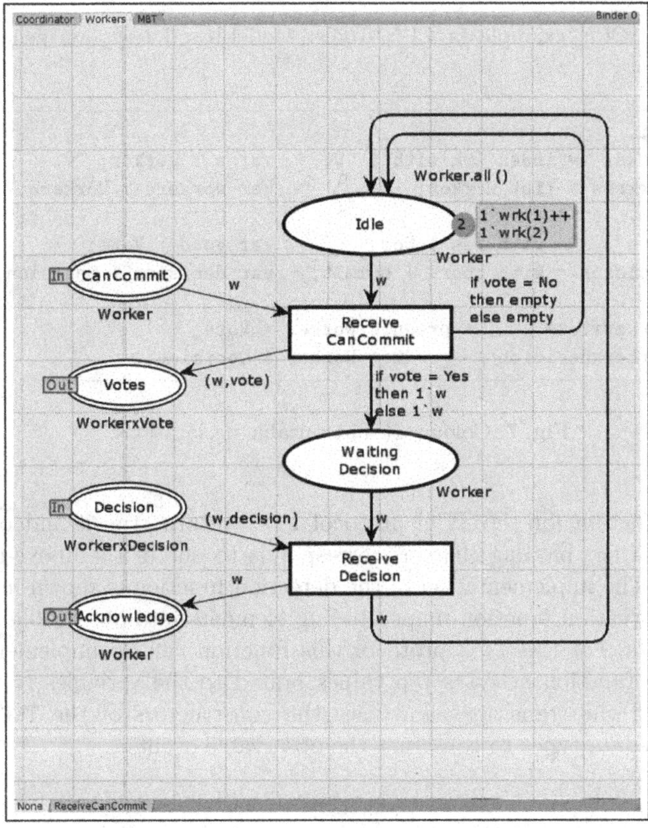

Fig. 5. MBT/CPN example in CPN Tools: Workers module.

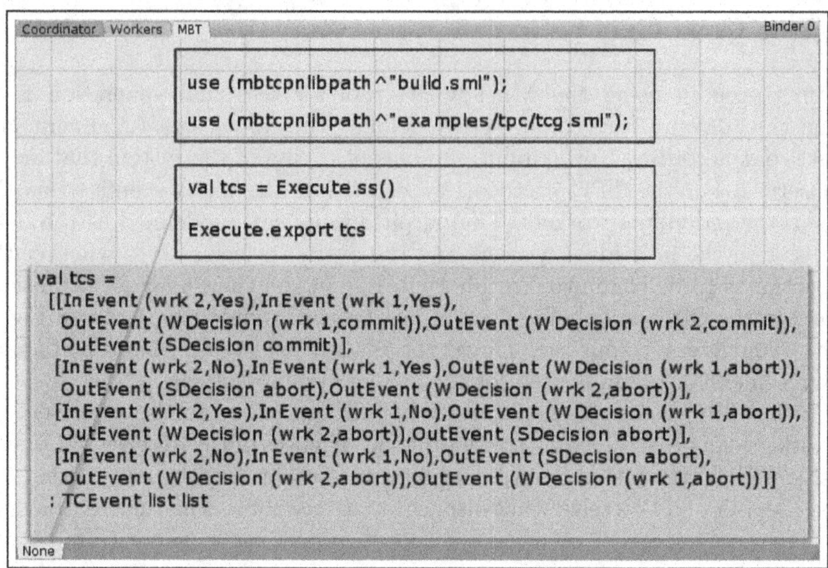

Fig. 6. MBT/CPN example in CPN Tools: Model-based test case generation and exporting.

```
val W = 2;
colset Worker  = index wrk with 1..W;     var w : Worker;
colset Workers = list Worker;             var workers : Workers;

colset Vote     = with Yes | No;          var vote : Vote;
colset Decision = with abort | commit;    var decision : Decision;

colset WorkerxVote      = product Worker * Vote;
colset WorkerxDecision  = product Worker * Decision;
```

Fig. 7. Colour set and variable declarations.

detection function for the TPC protocol must return true if and only if the occurrence of the binding element corresponds to one of the above-mentioned transitions. The implementation of the detection function is shown in Fig. 9.

The observation function maps binding elements into observable input and output events. For the TPC protocol this function can be implemented as in Fig. 10. The function accesses the values bound to the variables (`w`,`vote`, and `decision`) of the transitions and uses the constructors of the `TCEvent` and `TCOutEvent` data types to construct the observable events.

```
colset TCInEvent  = WorkerxVote;
colset TCOutEvent = union WDecision : WorkerxDecision +
                          SDecision : Decision;

colset TCEvent    = union InEvent  : TCInEvent +
                          OutEvent : TCOutEvent;
```

Fig. 8. Definitions of the colour sets TCInEvent, TCOutEvent and TCEvent.

```
fun detection (Bind.Workers'Receive_CanCommit _)  = true
  | detection (Bind.Workers'Receive_Decision _)  = true
  | detection (Bind.Coordinator'Receive_Acknowledgements _) = true
  | detection _ = false;
```

Fig. 9. The implementation of the detection function for the TPC protocol.

```
exception obsExn;
fun observation (Bind.Workers'Receive_CanCommit (_,{w,vote})) =
     [InEvent (w,vote)]
  | observation (Bind.Coordinator'Receive_Acknowledgements
     (_,{_,decision})) = [OutEvent (SDecision decision)]
  | observation (Bind.Workers'Receive_Decision (_,{w,decision})) =
     [OutEvent (WDecision (w,decision))]
  | observation _ = raise obsExn;
```

Fig. 10. The implementation of the observation function for the TPC protocol.

The MBT/CPN tool has built-in for exporting the test cases into an XML format. The use of XML makes it easy to reuse the test generator for systems under test implemented in different programming languages. The concrete XML format will depend on the observable events and hence the user needs to provide a `format` function as part of the test case generation specification that maps each observable event into a string representing an XML element. This function is typically implemented as a pattern match on the `TCEvent` data type. For the TPC protocol it would for instance map the `InEvent` corresponding to worker one (`wrk(1)`) voting `No` into the following XML element:

```
<Vote><WorkerID>1</WorkerID><VoteValue>0</VoteValue></Vote>
```

The complete formatting function for the TPC protocol is similar in complexity to the detection and the observation functions.

5 Test Case Execution

To perform model-based testing using the test cases generated by MBT/CPN, the developer (user) must implement a test Adapter as was shown in Fig. 1. The implementation of the test adapter depends on the concrete SUT, but consists of the same overall components independently of the SUT. To illustrate how MBT/CPN test cases can be used, we outline how to implement a test adapter for a Go implementation of the coordinator process. The adapter consists of a Reader and a Tester. The implementation of the Reader (around 30 lines of code) is based on the *encoding/xml* package from the Go standard library, while the implementation of the Tester (around 80 lines of code) is based on *testing* packages of the Go standard library. Go's testing infrastructure allows us to run the `go test` command to execute the test cases and it provides pass/fail information for each test case. In addition, it provides information about code coverage. The full Go implementation of the adapter and also the coordinator SUT is available together with the MBT/CPN distribution [11].

The purpose of the reader is to read the XML files containing test cases and convert them into a representation which can be used by the tester. In this case, the *encoding/xml* package of the Go standard library supports the implementation of the Reader. The purpose of the tester is to provide input and read the output from the SUT according to the test case being executed. Hence, the tester serves as an intermediate between the test cases and the SUT. In this case, our coordinator SUT is implemented in Go, and the communication between the coordinator SUT and the tester is implemented using Go channels. The tester provides input to the coordinator SUT via the channels and implements the test oracles by comparing the values received with the expected output as specified in the test case. An important property of the tester implementation is that it is transparent to the coordinator SUT that it is interacting with the tester and not a real set of worker implementations.

The messages exchanged between the tester and the coordinator SUT are defined according to the mapping between the colour sets defined for messages in the CPN model (Fig. 7) and corresponding types in Go. Figure 11 shows the declarations of messages in Go for such communication which include `CanCommit`, `Vote`, `Decision` and `Ack` (Go code organized in two columns to save space).

The Go implementation of the coordinator SUT itself follows closely the CPN module of the coordinator (Fig. 4). Figure 12 shows the coordinator interface implemented in Go, which consists of methods for sending and delivering messages through channels. The method `Start` is the entry point of the coordinator which starts the coordinator's main control flow as a goroutine (thread). Within this loop, the coordinator receives incoming `Vote` and `Ack` messages through channels, delivered by the invocations of `DeliverVote` and `DeliverACK` methods, respectively. The coordinator invokes `CollectVotes` method to collect received `Vote` messages, and invoke `SendDecision` and `SendFinalDecision` methods to send `Decision` messages and a final `Decision` message.

```
type VoteEnum int
const (
   Yes VoteEnum = iota
   No
)
const (
   Commit DecisionEnum = iota
   Abort
)
type Decision struct {
   WorkerID      WorkerID
   DecisionValue DecisionEnum
}
```

```
type DecisionEnum int
type Vote struct {
   WorkerID  WorkerID
   VoteValue VoteEnum
}
type CanCommit struct {
   WorkerID WorkerID
}

type Ack struct {
   WorkerID WorkerID
}
```

Fig. 11. Message declarations in Go.

```
type Coordinator interface {
  Start(numOfWorker int, fdChannel chan DecisionEnum)
  SendCanCommit(cc CanCommit)
  DeliverVote(v Vote)
  CollectVotes(v Vote, votes []Vote) []Vote
  SendDecision(d Decision)
  DeliverACK(a Ack)
  SendFinalDecision(fdChannel chan DecisionEnum, fd DecisionEnum)
}
```

Fig. 12. Interface of the coordinator SUT in Go.

6 Experimental Evaluation

We report on experimental results on applying the MBT/CPN tool on the two-phase commit protocol with the coordinator as the system under test. In addition, we summarize experimental results obtained using our approach on two larger case studies: a distributed storage protocol and the Paxos consensus protocol. All three systems under test have been implemented in Go and the distributed storage and consensus protocol furthermore rely on the Gorums middleware [10]. The case studies illustrate the use of both simulation- and state space based test case generation. We use statement coverage of the system under test as the quantitative evaluation criteria of the test cases generated by our approach. Other criteria exist such as branch-, condition-, and path coverage, but these are currently not supported by the Go tool chain.

6.1 Two-Phase Commit Protocol

Table 1 gives experimental results from application of our approach to the two-phase commit protocol for different number of workers W. The Gen column specifies the approach used for test case generation (state spaces (SS) or simulation

(SIM)). The Size-Steps column specifies the size of the state space (nodes/arcs) and the number of simulation runs. The Test Cases column specifies the number of test case generated and the Time gives the total time (in second) used for test case generation (including state space generation and model simulation). Finally, the Coverage gives the statement coverage obtained for the coordinator implementation. The lines of code for the coordinator is around 120 lines.

Table 1. Experimental results for the two-phase commit protocol.

W	Gen	Size - Steps	Test Cases	Time	Coverage
2	SS	59/86	4	<1	94.7%
2	SIM	5	3	<1	84.2%
2	SIM	10	4	<1	94.7%
3	SS	357/614	8	<1	94.7%
3	SIM	10	4	<1	94.7%
3	SIM	20	8	<1	94.7%
4	SS	2,811/5,957	16	5	94.7%
4	SIM	50	13	<1	94.7%
4	SIM	100	16	<1	94.7%
5	SIM	100	31	<1	94.7%
5	SIM	200	32	<1	94.7%
10	SIM	5000	1,015	13	94.7%
10	SIM	10000	1,024	25	94.7%
15	SIM	10000	8,627	91	84.2%
15	SIM	20000	14,946	265	94.7%

For simulation-based test case generation, we stopped increasing the number of simulations when reaching the same number of test cases as obtained with state space based generation which represents the maximum number of test cases that can be obtained. It can be seen that as W increases more simulations are needed in order to reach the maximum number of test cases. In general, we recommend using state-space based test case generation whenever possible as it ensures coverage of all executions of the CPN model, and resort to simulation-based test case generation if the state space is too big to be generated with the available computing power. For the two-phase commit protocol we have not pursued state space based test case generation beyond four workers as it becomes quite time consuming. It can, however, be seen that simulation-based test case generation can easily handle configurations with 5, 10, and 15 workers demonstrating the scalability of simulation-based test case generation. The coverage results show that test cases generated based on state space and simulation based approaches can both reach 94.7%. The reason why the results do not reach 100% is that the coordinator contains error handling code, which is not covered by the generated test cases, as any failures are not part of the model. The other coming two examples also have failures modeled explicitly. Further, the results also show that the statement coverage for both SIM-5 and SIM-10000 is 84.2%. This is a consequence of the simulation-based approach not covering all the possible executions of the CPN model in the absence of guided search. The longest time used for test case execution was approximately four hours (case SIM-20000) with more than 14,000 test cases.

6.2 Distributed Storage Protocol

The distributed storage protocol has been implemented by the Go language and Gorums framework. It is a single-writer, multi-reader distributed storage using read and write quorum calls and functions. The quorum calls and functions are abstractions provided by the Gorums framework/library. Clients can then invoke a write call with read calls concurrently and/or sequentially to access the distributed storage. By using our MBT/CPN tool, we have generated test cases based on the state-space based exploration to perform both system tests by invoking the read and write quorum calls concurrently and sequentially, and unit tests for quorum functions. The CPN model of the distributed storage makes it possible to generate system test cases for both successful scenarios and scenarios involving server failures and programming errors. We use a state-space based approach since the state space of the CPN testing model of the distributed storage protocol is relatively small. This is due to the fact that the CPN model describes the distributed storage system at a high level of abstraction which in turn means that we obtain all test cases without encountering state explosion.

Table 2 gives the experimental results obtained using different test drivers to invoke the read and/or write quorum calls concurrently and/or sequentially, without server failures included. The test drivers we have considered include: one read call (RD), one write call (WR), a read call followed by a write call (RD;WR), a write call followed by a read call (WR;RD), a read and a write call executed concurrently (WR||RD), a read and a write call executed concurrently and followed by a read call ((WR||RD);RD).

The results show that, for successful execution scenarios, the statement coverage for read (RD-QF) and write (WR-QF) quorum functions is 100% for both system and unit tests, as long as both read and write calls are involved. The statement coverage for read (RD-QC) and write (WR-QC) quorum calls is up to 84.4%. For the Gorums library as a whole, the statement coverage reaches 40.8%. The total number of lines of code for the system under test is approximately 2100 lines. The highest number of generated test cases for systems tests involving quorum calls is 6; the highest number of test cases for unit tests is 17. These test cases are generated within 2 s.

In addition to the successful scenarios, we has also considered to test the system under programming errors and server failures. We injected programming errors in the read and write quorum functions for the distributed storage such that the clients receive incorrectly replies from the storage system. The results show that our test adapter can capture injected errors by using generated test

Table 2. Experimental results for distributed storage protocol.

Test driver		Test case execution (coverage in percentage)				
		System			Unit	
ID	Name	Gorums library	QCs		QFs	
			RD	WR	RD	WR
S1	RD	24.6	84.4	0	100	0
S2	WR	24.6	0	84.4	0	100
S3	RD;WR	39.1	84.4	84.4	100	100
S4	WR;RD	40.8	84.4	84.4	100	100
S5	WR‖RD	40.8	84.4	84.4	100	100
S6	(WR‖RD);RD	40.8	84.4	84.4	100	100

cases from our MBT/CPN tool. For server failures scenario, we mainly test the fault tolerance of the distributed storage system. For example, a distributed storage system with three servers can tolerate one server failure. The test adapter we implemented can terminate one or more servers during the test case execution. We considered the S6 driver from Table 2 and created a scenario where S6 is executed first, then there is one or more server failures, and then S6 is repeated. The results for the scenario involving server failures show that the statement coverage for read (RD-QF) and write (WR-QF) quorum functions stay the same (100%) for both system and unit tests. The coverage for read (RD-QC) and write (WR-QC) quorum calls is increased from 84.4% to 96.7%. For the Gorums library as a whole, the statement coverage is increased from 40.8% to 52.3%.

6.3 Paxos Consensus Protocol

Paxos is a consensus protocol that can handle a group of server replicas to construct a replicated service, and ensure fault-tolerance. It is far more complex than the distributed storage system and the two-phase commit protocol. We have applied our MBT/CPN tool to validate a Go implementation of the single-decree Paxos. For such an implementation, each Paxos server replica implements a proposer, an acceptor, and a learner subsystem. In addition to these subsystems, the implementation also includes software components for failure and leader detection. Further, the communication and message handling between Paxos subsystems are implemented with quorum calls and functions (prepare, accept, and commit), which are abstractions from the Gorums framework. The total number of lines of code for the single-decree Paxos protocol is approximately 3890 lines.

The Paxos protocol is too complex for state space exploration, and we have therefore used simulation-based test case generation with up to 10 simulation runs. A summary of our experimental results is shown in Table 3. It shows the statement coverage obtained for the different Paxos subsystems, quorum calls and functions. Note that the unit tests are only for the quorum functions. The total number of generated test cases for 3 and 5 replicas configurations, respectively are given below System tests and Unit tests in the table. The time used to generate test cases for each configuration is less than 10 s, and the time used to execute each test case is less than one minute.

Table 3. Experimental results for test case generation and execution.

Subsystem	Component	System tests	Unit tests
		15/38	74/424
Gorums library		51.8%	-
Paxos core	Proposer	97.4%	-
	Acceptor	100.0%	-
	Failure Detector	75.0%	-
	Leader Detector	91.4%	-
	Replica	91.4%	-
Quorum calls	Prepare	83.9%	-
	Accept	83.9%	-
	Commit	83.9%	-
Quorum functions	Prepare	100.0%	90.0%
	Accept	100.0%	85.7%

The results show that, for unit tests, the statement coverage of Prepare and Accept quorum functions reach 90% and 85.7%, respectively. For system tests, the statement coverage of Prepare, Accept and Commit quorum calls are up to 83.9%, respectively; the statement coverage for the Failure Detector and Leader Detector modules are 75.0% and 91.4%, respectively; the statement coverage of the Paxos replica module is up to 91.4%; for the Gorums library as a whole, the highest statement coverage is 51.8%.

7 Conclusions

The MBT/CPN tool augments the CPN Tools with facilities for model-based test case generation, and is based on the user identifying observable events formalized in a test case specification. As illustrated on the TPC protocol, this entails implementing a detection, observation, and formatting function which is applied by the tool during test case generation. An important feature of our approach is the uniform support for test case generation based on state spaces and simulation. We have shown by practical experiments on the TPC protocol, the distributed storage protocol, and the Paxos consensus protocol that we can obtain a high SUT code coverage and that our approach can be used to detect implementation errors.

The application of MBT in the context of CPNs have until now been limited. Xu [16] presents the Integration and System Test Automation (ITSA) tool which supports test code generation for languages such as Java, C/C++, and C♯ based on state spaces. To obtain concrete test cases with input data, the ITSA tool relies on a separate model implementation mapping. In contrast, we obtain the input data for the system under test and call directly from the data contained in the testing model. Tretmans et al. have presented the TorX [12] tool which is used to randomly generate test cases based on a walk through the state space. The test cases can be generated either offline or on-the-fly during the test execution. There is also an adapter component in TorX to translate the inputs to be readable by the system under test, and check the actual outputs from the system under test against expected outputs. Conformiq Qtroniq [4] can be used to derive functional test cases from a system model, and can generate test cases online or offline by using a symbolic execution algorithm. Such test cases then are mapped into the TTCN-3 format. The expected outputs can also be generated from the model. The Automatic Efficient Test Generation (AETG) [1] tool is aimed at efficient generation of test cases by decreasing the number of test data required for the input test space. However, the test oracles have to be furnished manually.

There are several interesting directions to further develop the MBT/CPN tool. Related to [17], one area is to provide a higher degree of automation when implementing the test adapter such that for instance the data types required in the adapter implementation can be automatically obtained. For simulation-based test case generation investigating how a search heuristic can be specified and synthesized is an important. Such heuristics will most likely require knowledge about the SUT implementation and its CPN model specification. For the latter, we are currently investigating how to measure so-called *Modified Condition/Decision Coverage*, which is prescribed e.g. in safety critical system development [7]. Another direction for future work is to investigate if the use of partial state spaces combined with a search heuristics can provide a fruitful middle ground between simulation-based and state space-based test case generation.

References

1. Cohen, D.M., Dalal, S.R., Fredman, M.L., Patton, G.C.: The AETG system: an approach to testing based on combinatorial design. IEEE Trans. Softw. Eng. **23**(7), 437–444 (1997)
2. CPN Tools. CPN Tools homepage. http://www.cpntools.org
3. Google Inc., The Go Programming Language. https://golang.org
4. Huima, A.: Implementing conformiq qtronic. In: Petrenko, A., Veanes, M., Tretmans, J., Grieskamp, W. (eds.) FATES/TestCom -2007. LNCS, vol. 4581, pp. 1–12. Springer, Heidelberg (2007). https://doi.org/10.1007/978-3-540-73066-8_1
5. Jensen, K., Kristensen, L.: Coloured petri nets: a graphical language for modelling and validation of concurrent systems. Comm. ACM **58**(6), 61–70 (2015)
6. Jorgensen, P.: The Craft of Model-Based Testing. CRC Press, Boca Raton (2017)
7. Kelly, J.H., Dan, S.V., John, J.C., Leanna, K.R.: A Practical Tutorial on Modified Condition/Decision Coverage. Technical report (2001)

8. Kristensen, L.M., Veiset, V.: Transforming CPN models into code for TinyOS: a case study of the RPL protocol. In: Kordon, F., Moldt, D. (eds.) PETRI NETS 2016. LNCS, vol. 9698, pp. 135–154. Springer, Cham (2016). https://doi.org/10.1007/978-3-319-39086-4_10
9. Kristensen, L.M., Simonsen, K.I.F.: Applications of coloured petri nets for functional validation of protocol designs. In: Jensen, K., van der Aalst, W.M.P., Balbo, G., Koutny, M., Wolf, K. (eds.) Transactions on Petri Nets and Other Models of Concurrency VII. LNCS, vol. 7480, pp. 56–115. Springer, Heidelberg (2013). https://doi.org/10.1007/978-3-642-38143-0_3
10. Lea, T.E., Jehl, L., Meling, H.: Towards new abstractions for implementing quorum-based systems. In: Proceedings of 37th IEEE International Conference on Distributed Computing Systems (ICDCS), pp. 2380–2385 (2017)
11. MBT/CPN. Repository, January 2018. https://github.com/selabhvl/mbtcpn.git
12. Tretmans, G., Brinksma, H.: TorX: automated model-based testing. In: Hartman, A., Dussa-Ziegler, K. (eds.) 1st European Conference on Model-Driven Software Engineering, vol. 12, pp. 31–43 (2003)
13. Utting, M., Pretschner, A., Legeard, B.: A taxonomy of model-based testing approaches. Softw. Test. Verifi. Reliab. **22**, 297–312 (2012)
14. Wang, R., Kristensen, L., Meling, H., Stolz, V.: Automated test case generation for the paxos single-decree protocol using a coloured petri net model. J. Log. Algebraic Method. Programm. (JLAMP) (Submitted)
15. Wang, R., Kristensen, L., Meling, H., Stolz, V.: Application of model-based testing on a quorum-based distributed storage. In: Proceedings of PNSE 2017, CEUR Workshop Proceedings, vol. 1846, pp. 177–196 (2017)
16. Xu, D.: A tool for automated test code generation from high-level petri nets. In: Kristensen, L.M., Petrucci, L. (eds.) PETRI NETS 2011. LNCS, vol. 6709, pp. 308–317. Springer, Heidelberg (2011). https://doi.org/10.1007/978-3-642-21834-7_17
17. Xu, D., Xu, W., Wong, W.E.: Automated test code generation from class state models. Int. J. Softw. Eng. Knowl. Eng. **19**(04), 599–623 (2009)

How to Be Sure a Faulty System Does Not Always Appear Healthy?

Lina Ye[1(✉)], Philippe Dague[2], Delphine Longuet[2], Laura Brandán Briones[3], and Agnes Madalinski[4]

[1] LRI, Univ. Paris-Sud, CentraleSupélec, Univ. Paris-Saclay, Orsay, France
lina.ye@lri.fr
[2] LRI, Univ. Paris-Sud, CNRS, Univ. Paris-Saclay, Orsay, France
{philippe.dague,delphine.longuet}@lri.fr
[3] Universidad Nacional de Córdoba, Córdoba, Argentina
[4] Otto-von-Guericke-University Magdeburg, Magdeburg, Germany

Abstract. Fault diagnosis is a crucial and challenging task in the automatic control of complex systems, whose efficiency depends on the diagnosability property of a system. Diagnosability describes the system property allowing one to determine with certainty whether a given fault has effectively occurred based on the available observations. However, this is a quite strong property that generally requires a high number of sensors. Consequently, it is not rare that developing a diagnosable system is too expensive. In this paper, we analyze a new discrete event system property called manifestability, that represents the weakest requirement on observations for having a chance to identify on line fault occurrences and can be verified at design stage. Intuitively, this property makes sure that a faulty system cannot always appear healthy, i.e., has at least one future behavior after fault occurrence observably distinguishable from all normal behaviors. Then, we prove that manifestability is a weaker property than diagnosability before proposing an algorithm with PSPACE complexity to automatically verify both properties. Furthermore, we prove that the problem of manifestability verification itself is PSPACE-complete. The experimental results show the feasibility of our algorithm from a practical point of view. Finally, we compare our approach with related work.

1 Introduction

Fault diagnosis is a crucial and challenging task in the automatic control of complex systems, whose efficiency depends on a system property called diagnosability. Diagnosability is a system property describing whether one can distinguish with certainty fault behaviors from normal ones based on sequences of observable events emitted from the system. In a given system, the existence of two infinite behaviors with the same observations, where exactly one contains the considered fault, violates diagnosability. The existing work concerning discrete event systems (DESs) searches for such ambiguous behaviors, both in centralized

M. F. Atig et al. (Eds.): VECoS 2018, LNCS 11181, pp. 114–129, 2018.
https://doi.org/10.1007/978-3-030-00359-3_8

and distributed ways [10,12–14,20]. However, in reality, diagnosability turns out to be a quite strong property that generally requires a high number of sensors. Consequently, it is often too expensive to develop a diagnosable system.

To achieve a trade-off between the cost, i.e., a reasonable number of sensors, and the possibility to observe a fault manifestation, we recently introduced a new property called manifestability [21], which is borrowed from philosophy "...which I shall call the "manifestability of the mental", that if two systems are mentally different, then there must be some physical contexts in which this difference will display itself in differential physical consequences" [11]. In the domain of diagnosis, similarly, the manifestability property describes the capability of a system to manifest a fault occurrence in at least one future behavior. This should be analyzed at design stage on the system model. Under the assumption that no behavior described in the model has zero probability, the fault will then necessarily show itself with nonzero probability after enough runs of the system. In other words, given a system, if this property holds, this system cannot always appear healthy when a fault occurs in it, i.e., at least one future behavior observably distinguishes from normal behaviors. In all cases, manifestability is the weakest property to require from the system to have a chance to identify the fault occurrence. Differently, for diagnosability, all future behaviors of all fault occurrences should be distinguishable from all normal behaviors, which is a strong property and sensor demanding. Obviously one has to continue to rely on diagnosability for online safety requirements, i.e., for those faults which may have dramatic consequences if they are not surely detected when they occur, in order to trigger corrective actions. But for all other faults that do not need to be detected at their first occurrence (e.g., whose consequence is a degraded but acceptable functioning that will require maintenance actions in some near future), manifestability checking, which is cheaper in terms of sensors needed, is enough under the probabilistic assumption above.

We have several contributions in this paper. First, we define (strong) manifestability before proving that it is weaker than diagnosability. Second, we provide a sufficient and necessary condition for manifestability with a formal algorithm based on equivalence checking and prove that the manifestability problem itself is a PSPACE-complete problem. Third, the algorithm's efficiency is shown by our experimental results before comparing our approach with related work.

2 Motivating Example

In this section, we explain why it is worth analyzing the manifestability property with a motivating example.

Example 1. Figure 1 shows a modified version of a HVAC system from [13], which is a composite model that captures the interactions between the component models, i.e., a pump, a valve, and a controller. In this system, the initial state is q^0, the events $Valve\_open$, $Pump\_start$, $Pump\_stop$, $Valve\_close$ are observable and the fault event $Pump\_failed$ is not observable. Once fault event occurs, the system enters and always stays in an abnormal state.

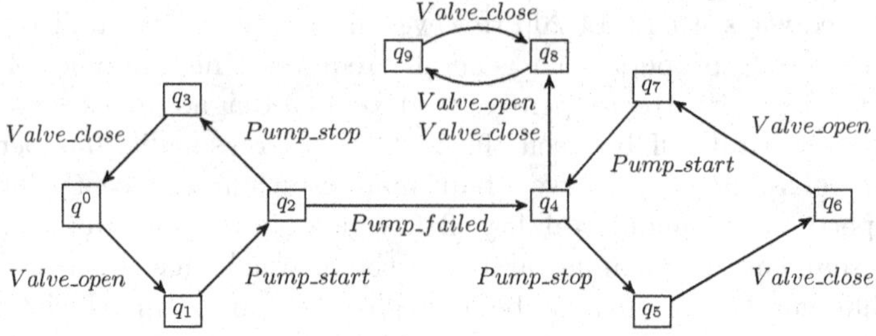

Fig. 1. A simplified HVAC system.

The correct behavior of this system is $(Valve\_open\ Pump\_start\ Pump\_stop\ Valve\_close)^\omega$, where ω denotes the infinite concatenation. After the unobservable faulty event *Pump_failed*, the system has two possibilities: either continue the execution with the same observations as the correct behavior or go to the states q_8 and q_9. Thus, this system is not diagnosable since at least one infinite future behavior of the fault occurrence is indistinguishable from the correct behavior, which is $Valve\_open\ Pump\_start\ Pump\_failed\ (Pump\_stop\ Valve\_close\ Valve\_open\ Pump\_start)^\omega$. Considering real faulty scenarios, with an assumption of nonzero probability, at one moment in the future the system will go to q_8, in which case the fault manifests itself and thus can be diagnosed. The original diagnosability property is not suitable to handle such situations. If we consider manifestability, this fault is effectively manifestable since its occurrence has at least one future that is distinguishable from the correct behavior. The manifestability property is the minimal requirement for the system to allow one to establish a diagnostic mechanism. If a fault is not manifestable, then it is totally useless to try to design a diagnoser for the system.

3 Manifestability for DESs

We now present our system model, recall diagnosability, and introduce (strong) manifestability, before giving a formal sufficient and necessary condition for this property to hold. We demonstrate that (strong) manifestability is a weaker property than diagnosability.

3.1 Models of DESs

We model a DES as a Finite State Machine (FSM), i.e., an automaton, denoted by $G = (Q, \Sigma, \delta, q^0)$, where Q is the finite set of states, Σ is the finite set of events, $\delta \subseteq Q \times \Sigma \times Q$ is the set of transitions (the same notation will be kept for its natural extension to words of Σ^*), and q^0 is the initial state. The set of events Σ is divided into three disjoint parts: $\Sigma = \Sigma_o \uplus \Sigma_u \uplus \Sigma_f$, where Σ_o is the set of observable events, Σ_u the set of unobservable normal events and Σ_f the set of unobservable fault events.

Example 2. The left part of Fig. 2 shows an example of a system model G, where $\Sigma_o = \{o1, o2, o3\}$, $\Sigma_u = \{u1, u2\}$, and $\Sigma_f = \{F\}$. Notice that for diagnosis problem, fault is predefined as an unobservable event in the model. This is different from testing, where faulty behaviors are judged against a specification.

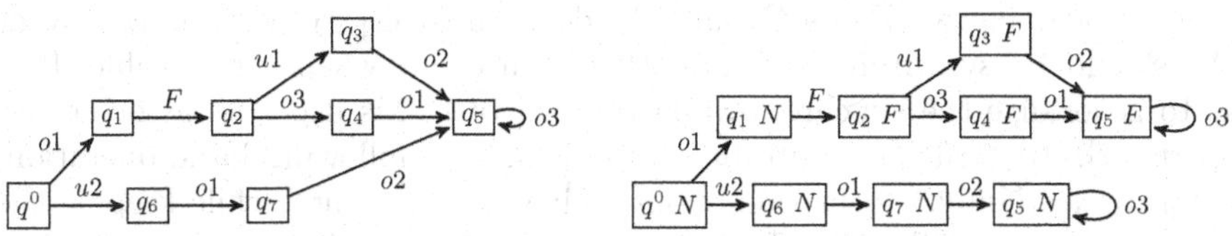

Fig. 2. A system example (left) and its diagnoser (right).

Similar to diagnosability, the manifestability algorithm that we will propose has exponential complexity in the number of fault types. To reduce it to linear complexity, as in [12,14], we consider only one fault type at a time. However, multiple occurrences of faults are allowed. The other types of faults are processed as unobservable normal events. This is justified as the system is manifestable if and only if (iff) it is manifestable for each fault type. Thus, to check the manifestability of a system with several faults, one can check its manifestability with respect to each fault type in turn. In the following, $\Sigma_f = \{F\}$, where F is the currently considered fault.

Given a system model G, its prefix-closed language $L(G)$, which describes both normal and faulty behaviors of the system, is the set of words produced by G: $L(G) = \{s \in \Sigma^* | \exists q \in Q, (q^0, s, q) \in \delta\}$. Those words containing (resp. not containing) F will be denoted by $L_F(G)$ (resp. $L_N(G)$). In the following, we call a word from $L(G)$ a trajectory in the system G and a sequence $q_0\sigma_0q_1\sigma_1\dots$ a path in G, where $q_0 = q^0$ and, for all i, $(q_i, \sigma_i, q_{i+1}) \in \delta$, whose label $\sigma_0\sigma_1\dots$ is a trajectory in G. Given $s \in L(G)$, we denote the post-language of $L(G)$ after s by $L(G)/s$, formally defined as: $L(G)/s = \{t \in \Sigma^* | s.t \in L(G)\}$. The projection of the trajectory s to observable events of G is denoted by $P(s)$, the observation of s. This projection can be extended to $L(G)$, i.e., $P(L(G)) = \{P(s) | s \in L(G)\}$, whose elements are called observed trajectories. Traditionally, we assume that each state of Q has a successor, so that $L(G)$ is live (any trajectory has a continuation, i.e., is a strict prefix of another trajectory) and that G has no unobservable cycle, i.e., each cycle contains at least one observable event. This makes it feasible to check the infiniteness of a trajectory. We will need some infinite objects. We denote by Σ^ω the set of infinite words on Σ and by $\Sigma^\infty = \Sigma^* \cup \Sigma^\omega$ the set of words on Σ, finite or infinite. We define in an obvious way infinite paths in G and thus $L^\omega(G)$ the language of infinite words recognized by G in the sense of Büchi automata [6]. As all states of G are considered as final states, those infinite trajectories are just the labels of infinite paths, and the concept of Büchi automaton coincides with that of Muller automaton, which can be determinized, according to the McNaughton theorem. We can conclude from this that $L^\omega(G)$

is the set of infinite words whose prefixes belong to $L(G)$ and that two equivalent system models, i.e., such that $L(G_1) = L(G_2)$, define the same infinite trajectories, i.e., $L^\omega(G_1) = L^\omega(G_2)$. Particularly, we use $L^\omega_F(G) = L^\omega(G) \cap \Sigma^* F \Sigma^\omega$ for the set of infinite faulty trajectories, and $L^\omega_N(G) = L^\omega(G) \cap (\Sigma \setminus \{F\})^\omega$ for the set of infinite normal trajectories, where $\setminus$ denotes set subtraction. We denote $L^\infty(G) = L(G) \cup L^\omega(G)$. In the following, we use the classical synchronization operation between two FSMs G_1 and G_2, denoted by $G_1 \|_{\Sigma_s} G_2$, i.e. any event in Σ_s should be synchronized while others can occur whenever possible. It is easy to generalize the synchronization to a set of FSMs using its associativity property [7]. To verify manifestability, we define the following basic operation, which is to keep only information about a given set of events, while keeping the same structure. It will be used to simplify some intermediate structures when checking manifestability without affecting the validity of the result obtained.

Definition 1 *(Delay Closure). Given a FSM $G = (Q, \Sigma, \delta, q^0)$, its delay closure with respect to Σ_d, with $\Sigma_d \subseteq \Sigma$, is $\mathsf{C}_{\Sigma_d}(G) = (Q_d, \Sigma_d, \delta_d, q^0)$, where: (1) $Q_d = \{q^0\} \cup \{q \in Q \mid \exists s \in \Sigma^*, \exists \sigma \in \Sigma_d, (q^0, s\sigma, q) \in \delta\}$; (2) $(q, \sigma, q') \in \delta_d$ if $\sigma \in \Sigma_d$ and $\exists s \in (\Sigma \backslash \Sigma_d)^*, (q, s\sigma, q') \in \delta$.*

3.2 Diagnosability and Manifestability

A fault F is diagnosable in a system model G if it can be detected with certainty when enough events are observed from G after its occurrence. This property is formally defined as follows [13], where s^F denotes a trajectory ending with F and $F \in p$, for p a trajectory, means that F appears as a letter of p.

Definition 2 ***(Diagnosability).*** *F is diagnosable in a system model G iff*

$$\exists k \in \mathbb{N}, \forall s^F \in L(G), \forall t \in L(G)/s^F, |t| \geq k \Rightarrow$$
$$(\forall p \in L(G), P(p) = P(s^F t) \Rightarrow F \in p).$$

The above definition states that F is diagnosable iff, for each trajectory s^F in G, for each of its extensions t with enough events, then every trajectory p in G that has the same observations as $s^F t$ should contain F. It has been proved that the existence of two indistinguishable infinite trajectories, i.e., holding the same sequence of observable events, with exactly one of them containing the given fault F, is equivalent to the violation of the diagnosability property [10].

Definition 3 ***(Critical Pair).*** *A pair of trajectories s, s' is called a critical pair with respect to F, denoted by $s \nsim s'$, iff $s \in L^\omega_F(G), s' \in L^\omega_N(G)$ and $P(s) = P(s')$.*

Theorem 1. *A fault F is diagnosable in G iff $\nexists s, s' \in L^\omega(G)$, such that $s \nsim s'$.*

The nonexistence of a critical pair w.r.t. F witnesses diagnosability of F. To design a diagnosable system, each faulty trajectory should be distinguished from normal trajectories, which is often very expensive in terms of number of sensors required. To reduce such a cost and still make it possible to show the fault after enough runs of the system, another property called manifestability has been recently introduced [21], which is much weaker than diagnosability. Intuitively, manifestability describes whether or not a fault occurrence has the possibility to manifest itself through observations. Precisely, if a fault is not manifestable, then we can never be sure about its occurrence no matter which trajectory is executed after it. Thus, the system model should be necessarily revised.

Definition 4 *(Manifestability). F is manifestable in a system model G iff*

$$\exists s^F \in L(G), \exists t \in L(G)/s^F,$$
$$\forall p \in L(G), P(p) = P(s^F t) \Rightarrow F \in p.$$

F is manifestable iff there exists at least one trajectory s^F in G, and there exists at least one extension t of s^F, such that every trajectory p that is observable equivalent to $s^F t$ should contain F. In other words, manifestability is violated iff each occurrence of the fault can never manifest itself in any future.

Theorem 2. *A fault F is manifestable in a system model G iff the following condition, denoted by $\Im$, is satisfied:*

$$\exists s \in L^{\omega}_{F}(G), \nexists s' \in L^{\omega}_{N}(G), such\, that\; s \simeq s'.$$

Proof. $\Rightarrow$ Suppose that F is manifestable in G. Thus from Definition 4, $\exists s \in L_F(G)$ such that $\nexists s' \in L_N(G)$ with $P(s) = P(s')$. By extending s with enough events, which is possible since the language is live, we obtain then $\exists s \in L^{\omega}_{F}(G)$, $\nexists s' \in L^{\omega}_{N}(G)$, such that $s \simeq s'$.
$\Leftarrow$ Suppose now that F is not manifestable in G and show that the condition $\Im$ is consequently not true. From non-manifestability of F and Definition 4, we have $\forall s^F \in L(G), \forall t \in L(G)/s^F, \exists p \in L(G), P(p) = P(s^F t)$, $p \in L_N(G)$. Thus, $\forall s^F t \in L_F(G)$, $\exists p \in L_N(G), P(p) = P(s^F t)$. This can be formulated as equality of the languages of two automata, as it will be seen in Sect. 4. It results that this equality of the languages still holds for infinite words, i.e., $\forall s^F t \in L^{\omega}_{F}(G)$, $\exists p \in L^{\omega}_{N}(G)$ such that $s^F t \simeq p$, which is $\neg\Im$, i.e., the condition $\Im$ is not true. ■

Manifestability concerns the possibility for the system to manifest at least one occurrence of the fault, i.e., there exists such an occurrence that shows itself in at least one of its futures. Now we propose a strong version of manifestability, which requires that all occurrences of the fault should show themselves in at least one of their futures.

Definition 5 *(Strong Manifestability). A fault F is strongly manifestable in a system model G iff*

$$\forall s^F \in L(G), \exists t \in L(G)/s^F,$$
$$\forall p \in L(G), P(p) = P(s^F t) \Rightarrow F \in p.$$

F is strongly manifestable iff, for each s^F in G (and not just for only one as in Definition 4) there exists at least one extension t of s^F in G, such that every trajectory p in G that is observable equivalent to $s^F t$ should contain F. Precisely, each occurrence of F should show itself in at least one of its futures. So, in a similar way as Theorem 2, we can prove the following theorem, which provides a sufficient and necessary condition for strong manifestability.

Theorem 3. *A fault F is strongly manifestable in a system model G iff the following condition, denoted by $\Im^s$, is satisfied:*

$$\forall s^F \in L(G), \exists t \in L^\omega(G)/s^F, \nexists s' \in L^\omega_N(G), \textit{such that}\, s^F t \simeq s'.$$

Theorem 4. *Given a system model G and a fault F, we have:*

1. *F is diagnosable in G implies that F is strongly manifestable in G.*
2. *F is strongly manifestable in G implies that F is manifestable in G.*

Proof. 1. Suppose that F is not strongly manifestable, then from Theorem 3, we have $\neg\Im^s$, i.e., $\exists s^F \in L(G), \forall t \in L^\omega(G)/s^F, \exists s' \in L^\omega_N(G)$ such that $s^F t \simeq s'$. This implies that there does exist at least one critical pair in the system. From Theorem 1, F is not diagnosable.
2. Suppose that F is not manifestable. From Theorem 2, we have $\forall s \in L^\omega_F(G)$, $\exists s' \in L^\omega_N(G)$, such that $s \simeq s'$. By choosing arbitrarily one $s^F \in L(G)$ and taking all s of prefix s^F, we obtain $\exists s^F \in L(G), \forall t \in L^\omega(G)/s^F, \exists s' \in L^\omega_N(G)$ such that $s^F t \simeq s'$, i.e., $\neg\Im^s$. Hence F is not strongly manifestable. ■

4 Manifestability Verification

Manifestability verification consists in checking whether the condition $\Im$ in Theorem 2 is satisfied for a given system model. In this section, we show how to construct different structures based on a system model to obtain $L^\omega_F(G)$, $L^\omega_N(G)$ as well as the set of critical pairs. The condition $\Im$ can then be checked by using equivalence techniques with these intermediate structures. Precisely, if for each infinite faulty trajectory $s \in L^\omega_F(G)$, there exists a corresponding critical pair, then the considered fault is not manifestable. Otherwise, it is manifestable. For the sake of simplicity, we concentrate on how to check manifestability, which can be extended in a straightforward way to handle strong manifestability. This extension will be explained explicitly in Sect. 4.3.

4.1 System Diagnosers

Given a system model, the first step is to construct a structure showing fault information for each state, i.e., whether the fault has effectively occurred up to this state from the initial state.

Definition 6 *(Diagnoser). Given a system model G, its diagnoser with respect to a considered fault F is the FSM $D_G = (Q_D, \Sigma_D, \delta_D, q_D^0)$, where: (1) $Q_D \subseteq Q \times \{N, F\}$ is the set of states; (2) $\Sigma_D = \Sigma$ is the set of events; (3) $\delta_D \subseteq Q_D \times \Sigma_D \times Q_D$ is the set of transitions; (4) $q_D^0 = (q^0, N)$ is the initial state. The transitions of δ_D are those $((q, \ell), e, (q', \ell'))$, with (q, ℓ) reachable from q_D^0, such that there is a transition $(q, e, q') \in \delta$, and $\ell' = F$ if $\ell = F \vee e = F$, otherwise $\ell' = N$.*

The right part of Fig. 2 shows the diagnoser for the system depicted in the left part, where each state has its own fault information. Precisely, given a system state q, if the fault has occurred on the path from q^0 to q, then the fault label for q is F. Such a state is called fault (diagnoser) state. Otherwise, the fault label is N and the state is called normal (diagnoser) state. Diagnoser construction keeps the same set of trajectories and splits into two those states reachable by both a faulty and a normal path ($q5$ in the example).

Lemma 1. *Given a system model G and its corresponding diagnoser D_G, then we have $L(G) = L(D_G)$ and $L^\omega(G) = L^\omega(D_G)$.*

In order to simplify the automata handled, the idea is to keep only the minimal subparts of D_G containing all faulty (resp., normal) trajectories.

Definition 7 *(Fault (Refined) Diagnoser). Given a diagnoser D_G, its fault diagnoser is the FSM $D_G^F = (Q_{D^F}, \Sigma_{D^F}, \delta_{D^F}, q_{D^F}^0)$, where: (1) $q_{D^F}^0 = q_D^0$; (2) $Q_{D^F} = \{q_D \in Q_D \mid \exists q'_D = (q, F) \in Q_D, \exists s' \in \Sigma_D^*, (q_D, s', q'_D) \in \delta_D^*\}$; (3) $\delta_{D^F} = \{(q_D^1, \sigma, q_D^2) \in \delta_D \mid q_D^2 \in Q_{D^F}\}$; (4) $\Sigma_{D^F} = \{\sigma \in \Sigma_D \mid \exists (q_D^1, \sigma, q_D^2) \in \delta_{D^F}\}$. The fault refined diagnoser is obtained by performing the delay closure with respect to the set of observable events Σ_o on the fault diagnoser: $D_G^{FR} = \mathbb{C}_{\Sigma_o}(D_G^F)$.*

The fault diagnoser keeps all fault states as well as all transitions and intermediate normal states on paths from q_D^0 to any fault state. Then we refine this fault diagnoser by only keeping the observable information, which is sufficient to obtain the set of critical pairs. The left (resp. right) part of Fig. 3 shows the fault diagnoser (resp. fault refined diagnoser) for Example 2.

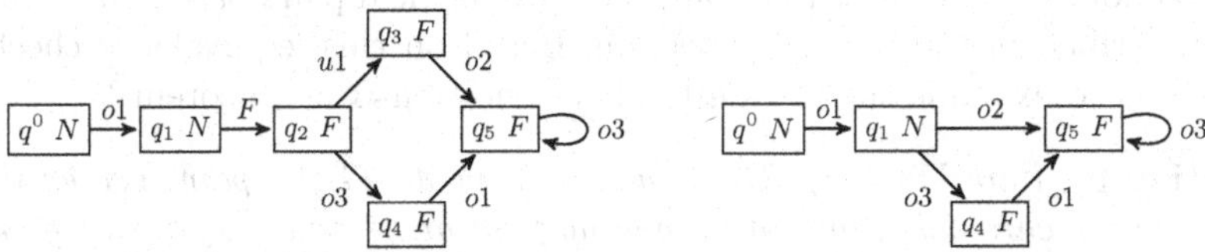

Fig. 3. Fault diagnoser (left) and its refined version (right) for Example 2.

By construction, the sets of faulty trajectories in D_G^F and in G are equal and this is still true for infinite faulty trajectories. This is also the case for infinite faulty trajectories in D_G^{FR} and infinite observed faulty trajectories in G. But take care that it may exist infinite normal trajectories in D_G^F (resp., D_G^{FR}) if it exists in G a normal cycle in a path to a fault state (e.g., adding a loop in state q_1 of the system model of Example 2).

Lemma 2. *Given a system model G and its corresponding fault diagnoser D_G^F and fault refined diagnoser D_G^{FR}, we have $L_F^\omega(G) = L_F^\omega(D_G^F)$ and $P(L_F^\omega(G)) = L_F^\omega(D_G^{FR})$.*

Similarly, we obtain the subpart of D_G containing only normal trajectories.

Definition 8 *(Normal (Refined) Diagnoser). Given a diagnoser D_G, its normal diagnoser is the FSM $D_G^N = (Q_{D^N}, \Sigma_{D^N}, \delta_{D^N}, q_{D^N}^0)$, where: (1) $q_{D^N}^0 = q_D^0$; (2) $Q_{D^N} = \{(q, N) \in Q_D\}$; (3) $\delta_{D^N} = \{(q_D^1, \sigma, q_D^2) \in \delta_D \mid q_D^2 \in Q_{D^N}\}$; (4) $\Sigma_{D^N} = \{\sigma \in \Sigma_D \mid \exists (q_D^1, \sigma, q_D^2) \in \delta_{D^N}\}$. The normal refined diagnoser is obtained by performing the delay closure with respect to Σ_o on the normal diagnoser: $D_G^{NR} = \mathfrak{C}_{\Sigma_o}(D_G^N)$.*

Lemma 3. *Given a system model G and its corresponding normal diagnoser D_G^N and normal refined diagnoser D_G^{NR}, we have $L_N^\omega(G) = L^\omega(D_G^N)$ and $P(L_N^\omega(G)) = L^\omega(D_G^{NR})$.*

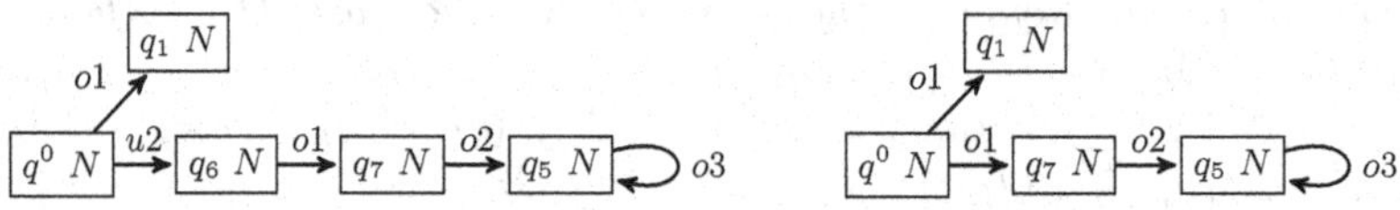

Fig. 4. Normal diagnoser (left) and its refined version (right) for Example 2.

The left (resp. right) part of Fig. 4 shows the normal diagnoser (resp. normal refined diagnoser) for Example 2.

4.2 Manifestability Checking

In this section, we show how to obtain the set of critical pairs based on the diagnosers described in the precedent section. Based on this, equivalence checking will be used to examine the manifestability condition $\Im$ in Theorem 2.

Definition 9 *(Pair Verifier). Given a system model G, its pair verifier V_G is obtained by synchronizing the corresponding fault and normal refined diagnosers D_G^{FR} and D_G^{NR} based on the set of observable events, i.e., $V_G = D_G^{FR} \parallel_{\Sigma_o} D_G^{NR}$.*

To construct a pair verifier, we impose that the synchronized events are the whole set of observable events. Then V_G is actually the product of D_G^{FR} and D_G^{NR} and the language of the pair verifier is thus the intersection of the language of the fault refined diagnoser and that of the normal refined diagnoser. In the pair verifier, each state is composed of two diagnoser states, whose label (F or N) of the first one indicates whether the fault has effectively occurred in the first of the two corresponding trajectories. If the first of these two states is a fault state, then this verifier state is called ambiguous state since, reaching this state, the first trajectory contains the fault and the second not, while both have the same observations. Infinite trajectories of V_G are thus either normal (all states labels are (N,N)) or ambiguous (all states labels from a certain state are (F,N)), the latter ones being denoted by $L^\omega_a(V_G)$.

Lemma 4. *Given a system model G with its V_G, D^{FR}_G and D^{NR}_G, we have $L^\omega_a(V_G) = L^\omega_F(D^{FR}_G) \cap L^\omega(D^{NR}_G)$.*

In the pair verifier depicted in Fig. 5, the gray node represents an ambiguous state.

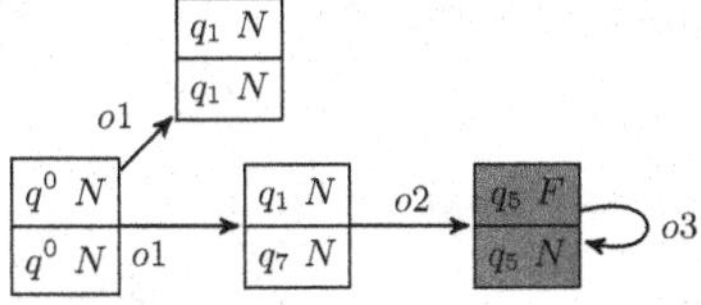

Fig. 5. The pair verifier for the system in Example 2.

Lemma 5. *Given a system model G, a fault F is diagnosable iff $L^\omega_a(V_G) = \emptyset$.*

Proof. $L^\omega_a(V_G) \neq \emptyset \Leftrightarrow L^\omega_F(D^{FR}_G) \cap L^\omega(D^{NR}_G) \neq \emptyset$ (from Lemma 4) $\Leftrightarrow P(L^\omega_F(G)) \cap P(L^\omega_N(G)) \neq \emptyset$ (from Lemmas 2 and 3) $\Leftrightarrow \exists s \in L^\omega_F(G), \exists s' \in L^\omega_N(G) P(s) = P(s') \Leftrightarrow \exists s, s' \in L^\omega(G)\ s \nsim s'$ (from Definition 3) $\Leftrightarrow F$ is not diagnosable (from Theorem 1). ■

Theorem 5. *Given a system model G, a fault F is manifestable iff $L^\omega_a(V_G) \subset L^\omega_F(D^{FR}_G)$.*

Proof. $L^\omega_a(V_G) \not\subset L^\omega_F(D^{FR}_G) \Leftrightarrow L^\omega_F(D^{FR}_G) \subseteq L^\omega(D^{NR}_G)$ (from Lemma 4) $\Leftrightarrow P(L^\omega_F(G)) \subseteq P(L^\omega_N(G))$ (from Lemmas 2 and 3) $\Leftrightarrow \forall s \in L^\omega_F(G), \exists s' \in L^\omega_N(G)$ $P(s) = P(s') \Leftrightarrow \forall s \in L^\omega_F(G), \exists s' \in L^\omega_N(G)\ s \nsim s'$ (from Definition 3) $\Leftrightarrow \neg\Im \Leftrightarrow F$ is not manifestable (from Theorem 2). ■

4.3 Algorithm

Algorithm 1 is the pseudo-code to verify manifestability, which can simultaneously verify diagnosability. Given the input (line 1) as the system model G and the fault F, we first construct the diagnoser (line 2) as described by Definition 6. We then construct fault and normal refined diagnosers (lines 3–4) as defined by Definitions 7 and 8. The next step is to synchronize D^{FR}_G and D^{NR}_G to obtain the pair verifier V_G (line 5). With D^{FR}_G and V_G, we have the following verdicts:

- if $L^\omega_a(V_G) = \emptyset$ (line 6), from Lemma 5, F is diagnosable and thus manifestable from Theorems 1 and 4 (line 7).
- if $L^\omega_a(V_G) = L^\omega_F(D^{FR}_G) \neq \emptyset$ (line 8), we can deduce from Theorem 5 that F is not manifestable. Thus, by Theorem 4 (or directly from Lemma 5), F is not diagnosable (line 9).
- if $L^\omega_a(V_G) \neq \emptyset$ and $L^\omega_a(V_G) \subset L^\omega_F(D^{FR}_G)$ (line 10), which can be deduced because of Lemma 4, the former condition means that F is not diagnosable and, by Theorem 5, the latter means that F is manifestable (line 11).

Algorithm 1. Manifestability and Diagnosability Algorithm for DESs

1: INPUT: System model G; the considered fault F
2: $D_G \leftarrow ConstructDiagnoser(G)$
3: $D^{FR}_G \leftarrow ConstructFRDiagnoser(D_G)$
4: $D^{NR}_G \leftarrow ConstructNRDiagnoser(D_G)$
5: $V_G \leftarrow D^{FR}_G \parallel_{\Sigma_o} D^{NR}_G$
6: **if** $L^\omega_a(V_G) = \emptyset$ **then**
7:     return "F is diagnosable and manifestable in G"
8: **else if** $L^\omega_a(V_G) = L^\omega_F(D^{FR}_G)$ **then**
9:     return "F is neither diagnosable nor manifestable in G"
10: **else**
11:     return "F is not diagnosable but manifestable in G"
12: **end if**

Note that $L^\omega_F(D^{FR}_G) = L^\omega(D'^{FR}_G)$ (resp., $L^\omega_a(V_G) = L^\omega(V'_G)$) where D'^{FR}_G is identical to D^{FR}_G (resp., V'_G identical to V_G), except that the final states, for Büchi acceptance conditions, are limited to fault (resp., ambiguous) states. Note also that the condition $L^\omega_a(V_G) = L^\omega_F(D^{FR}_G)$ is equivalent to $L^\omega(V_G) = L^\omega(D^{FR}_G)$ as the infinite normal trajectories are identical in V_G and in D^{FR}_G.

In Algorithm 1, the complexity of the different diagnosers constructions is linear. Building the pair verifier by synchronizing the fault and the normal refined diagnosers is polynomial with the number of system states. To finally check the manifestability, the equivalence checking (line 8) cannot be avoided, which is already demonstrated to be PSPACE, even for infinite words, in the literature [18]. Thus, the total complexity of this algorithm is PSPACE. Algorithm1 suggests that the manifestability problem is more complex than diagnosability (for which a test of language emptiness is sufficient, which implies a total NLOGSPACE complexity, a result already known), which we will formally prove later.

To verify the strong manifestability, one has to check the condition $\Im^s$ in Theorem 3. Algorithm 1 can be adapted for this with the following modifications:

- For each occurrence of the fault, we construct one fault refined diagnoser. To do this, we assume that the system has a finite number of fault occurrences (excluding thus cycles before a fault occurrence or containing a fault occurrence). To simplify, it is then enough to consider those latest occurrences of

the fault (for which no future contains another occurrence of the fault) since if such occurrence can show itself in one future, then this is the case for all earlier occurrences of the fault in the same trajectory.
- For each fault refined diagnoser, one constructs a pair verifier as described by Definition 9. Then, one has to compare the language defined by each fault refined diagnoser with the language defined by its corresponding verifier. The fault is not strongly manifestable iff there exists at least one such pair verifier and fault refined diagnoser defining the same languages for infinite words, as this violates the condition $\Im^s$ in Theorem 3.

Now we show that the problem of manifestability verification itself is a PSPACE-complete problem by the reduction to it of rational languages equivalence checking. The problem of checking non-deterministic FSM equivalence on infinite words is already proved to be PSPACE-complete [18].

Theorem 6. *Given a system model G and a fault F, the problem of checking whether F is manifestable in G is PSPACE-complete.*

Proof. The complexity of Algorithm 1 is PSPACE. Now we demonstrate that the problem of checking manifestability is PSPACE-hard. Let $G_1 = (Q_1, \Sigma, \delta_1, q_1^0)$ and $G_2 = (Q_2, \Sigma, \delta_2, q_2^0)$ be two arbitrary (non-deterministic) automata on the same vocabulary defining live languages. One can always assume that $Q_1 \cap Q_2 = \emptyset$. Based on G_1 and G_2, one can construct a new FSM, representing a system model, $G = (Q, \Sigma \cup \{F\}, \delta, q_2^0)$, where $Q = Q_1 \cup Q_2$ and $\delta = \delta_1 \cup \delta_2 \cup \{(q_2^0, F, q_1^0)\}$, with $\Sigma_o = \Sigma$, $\Sigma_u = \emptyset$ and $\Sigma_f = \{F\}$. From the construction of G, one has $L^\omega(G_1) = P(L_F^\omega(G))$ and $L^\omega(G_2) = P(L_N^\omega(G))$. From Lemmas 2, 3 and 4, one obtains $L^\omega(V_G) = P(L_F^\omega(G)) \cap P(L_N^\omega(G))$. This implies $L^\omega(G_1) \cap L^\omega(G_2) = L^\omega(V_G)$. From Theorem 5, one has $L^\omega(G_1) \cap L^\omega(G_2) \subset L^\omega(G_1) \iff F$ is manifestable in G, i.e., $L^\omega(G_1) \subseteq L^\omega(G_2) \iff F$ is not manifestable in G. So, rational languages inclusion testing on infinite words boils down to manifestability checking, which gives the result. ∎

5 Experimental Results

We have applied our algorithm on more than one hundred examples taken from literature and hand-crafted ones. The latter ones are constructed to show the scalability since the sizes of the former ones are very small. Our experimental results are obtained by running our program on a Mac OS laptop with a 1.7 GHz Intel Core i7 processor and 8 Go 1600 MHz DDR3 of memory.

Table 1 shows part of our experimental results, where verdicts (i.e., Manifes(tability), S(trong)Manifes(tability), Diagno(sability), N(on)Manifes (tability)) show the strongest property satisfied by the system. For example, if it is Manifes, then it is not SManifes nor Diagno. Diagno implies both SManifes and Manifes. We give the number of states and transitions of the system (|S|/|T|), of the pair verifier (|S|/|T|(PV)), as well as the execution time (millisecond is used as time unit). The size of the pair verifier includes all transitions

Table 1. Experimental Results

LitSys	|S|/|T|	|S|/|T|(PV)	Time	Verdict	HCSys	|S|/|T|	|S|/|T|(PV)	Time	Verdict
Ex. 2	8/10	4/4	15	SManifes	h-c1	22/24	18/18	32	SManifes
[14]	16/23	21/23	51	Manifes	h-c2	36/39	74/77	90	Manifes
[12]	16/20	7/9	25	Manifes	h-c3	46/50	105/110	120	Manifes
[9]	3/6	4/6	12	SManifes	h-c4	52/57	160/183	151	SManifes
[20]	18/21	53/57	69	SManifes	h-c5	57/69	32/37	78	SManifes
[15]	9/11	2/1	16	Diagno	h-c6	509/570	79/81	132	Manifes
[13]	12/28	45/51	68	NManifes	h-c7	320/390	1752/1791	323	NManifes

generated from the synchronization of the fault refined diagnoser and the normal refined diagnoser. The examples shown here include Example 2 in this paper with the illustrative examples of other papers that handle similar problems.

To construct the hand-crafted examples (HCSys) from those selected from the literature (LitSys), we are not interested in diagnosable examples. First, diagnosable systems are rare in the literature as well as in the industry. Second, diagnosability implies an empty language of ambiguous infinite words for the pair verifier, which can be verified without equivalence checking. The efficiency cannot be convincing by applying our algorithm on diagnosable examples. When extending the examples from the literature, we keep the same verdict. For example, for a manifestable system, an arbitrary FSM without fault is added in a place such that at least one faulty infinite trajectory can always manifest itself (and obviously critical pairs are preserved).

From our experimental results, the executed time is also dependent on the size of the pair verifier besides that of the system. To achieve a worst case, one way is to employ the example construction in the proof of Theorem 6 by setting $L^\omega(G_1) = L^\omega(G_2)$. The hand-crafted example h-c7 is constructed in such a way.

We can see that the original HVAC system in [13] is not manifestable, i.e., any faulty behavior cannot be diagnosed in all its infinite futures. It is thus necessary to go back to design stage to revise the system model. For other manifestable but not diagnosable systems, one interesting future work is to study bounded-manifestability, making sure to detect the fault in bounded time.

6 Related Work

The first approach to verify the diagnosability of DESs is to construct a deterministic FSM to check the existence of critical pairs [13], which has however exponential complexity in the number of system states. Then the authors of [10] proposed another method called twin plant with polynomial complexity. Here we adapted the twin plant plus equivalence checking to verify manifestability. Note that the existence of critical pairs, that excludes diagnosability, does not exclude manifestability. Intuitively, manifestability is a more complicated problem than diagnosability, which was demonstrated by proving that the problem itself is PSPACE instead of polynomial (actually NLOGSPACE) for diagnosability.

In [16,17], the authors proposed different variants of detectability (e.g., (strong) detectability) about state estimation. The system is detectable (resp. strongly detectable) if, based on a sequence of observations, one can be sure about the state in which is the system for some given trajectory (resp. all trajectories). They proposed a polynomial algorithm for strong detectability, for which two different trajectories with the same observations implies the violation. However, to analyze detectability, they constructed a deterministic observer that has exponential complexity with the number of system states. Our approach can be adapted to handle state estimation by considering an ambiguous state as one that contains different system states. Thus, we can improve their state estimation by using the improved equivalence checking techniques (e.g., the approach of [5] normally constructs a small part of the deterministic automaton). Furthermore, we proved that the problem of manifestability itself is PSPACE-complete.

The authors of [1,8] proposed an approach for weak diagnosability in a concurrent system by using Petri net, i.e., impose a constraint of weak fairness by disallowing the enabled transition to be perpetually ignored. The idea is to make impossible some non-diagnosable scenarios in order to upgrade the diagnosability level. They focused on how to get the more appropriate model, based on which the solution can be polynomial such as that for classical diagnosability.

Two definitions for stochastic diagnosability were introduced and analyzed in [19], which are weaker than diagnosability. A-diagnosability requires that the ambiguous behaviors have a null probability. AA-diagnosability admits errors in the provided information which should have an arbitrary small probability. Then four variants of diagnosability (FA, IA, FF, IF) were introduced and studied for different probabilistic system models [3,4]. Different ambiguity criteria were then defined according to different types of runs: for faulty runs only or for all runs; for infinite runs or for finite sub-runs. Among them IF-diagnosability (for infinite faulty runs) is the weakest one. Note that IF-diagnosability of a finite probabilistic system is equivalent to A-diagnosability.

The authors of [2,9] analyzed (safe) active diagnosability by introducing controllable actions for (probabilistic) DESs, where the complexity of these problems were also studied. The idea is to design controllers (resp. label activation strategies for probabilistic version) to enable a subset of actions in order to make it diagnosable (resp. stochastically diagnosable).

7 Conclusion and Future Work

In this paper we addressed the formal verification of manifestability for DESs. To bring an alternative to diagnosability analysis, whose satisfaction is very demanding in terms of sensors placement, we defined (strong) manifestability, a new weaker property. Then, we constructed different structures from the system model to check manifestability by using equivalence techniques. The entailment relations between different properties were proved and demonstrated on examples from the literature. Thus, engineers have a variety of criteria to design systems with optimal trade-off between safety and cost. One interesting future work is to extend our approach for distributed systems composed of a set of components, each one being modeled as a FSM with synchronization events.

References

1. Agarwal, A., Madalinski, A., Haar, S.: Effective verification of weak diagnosability. In: Proceedings of the 8th IFAC Symposium on Fault Detection, Supervision and Safety for Technical Processes (SAFEPROCESS 2012), pp. 636–641. IFAC (2012)
2. Bertrand, N., Fabre, É., Haar, S., Haddad, S., Hélouët, L.: Active diagnosis for probabilistic systems. In: Muscholl, A. (ed.) FoSSaCS 2014. LNCS, vol. 8412, pp. 29–42. Springer, Heidelberg (2014). https://doi.org/10.1007/978-3-642-54830-7_2
3. Bertrand, N., Haddad, S., Lefaucheux, E.: Foundation of diagnosis and predictability in probabilistic systems. In: 34th International Conference on Foundation of Software Technology and Theoretical Computer Science, FSTTCS 2014, 15–17 December 2014, New Delhi, India, pp. 417–429 (2014)
4. Bertrand, N., Haddad, S., Lefaucheux, E.: Diagnosis in infinite-state probabilistic systems. In: 27th International Conference on Concurrency Theory, CONCUR 2016, 23–26 August 2016, Québec City, Canada, pp. 37:1–37:15 (2016)
5. Bonchi, F., Pous, D.: Checking NFA Equivalence with Bisimulations up to Congruence. In: Proceedings of 40th ACM SIGPLAN-SIGACT Symposium on Principles of Programming Languages (POPL-2013), pp. 457–468. ACM (2013)
6. Büchi, J.R.: On a decision method in restricted second order arithmetic. Z. Math. Logik Grundlag. Math **6**, 66–92 (1960)
7. Cassandras, C.G., Lafortune, S.: Introduction To Discrete Event Systems, 2nd edn. Springer, Heidelberg (2008). https://doi.org/10.1007/978-0-387-68612-7
8. Germanos, V., Haar, S., Khomenko, V., Schwoon, S.: Diagnosability under weak fairness. ACM Trans. Embed. Comput. Syst. **14**(4), 69 (2015)
9. Haar, S., Haddad, S., Melliti, T., Schwoon, S.: Optimal constructions for active diagnosis. J. Comput. Syst. Sci. **83**(1), 101–120 (2017)
10. Jiang, S., Huang, Z., Chandra, V., Kumar, R.: A polynomial time algorithm for testing diagnosability of discrete event systems. Trans. Autom. Control **46**(8), 1318–1321 (2001)
11. Papineau, D.: Philosophical Naturalism. Blackwell Publishers, Hoboken (1993)
12. Pencolé, Y.: Diagnosability analysis of distributed discrete event systems. In: Proceedings of the 16th European Conference on Articifial Intelligent (ECAI 2004), pp. 43–47. IOS Press, Nieuwe Hemweg (2004)
13. Sampath, M., Sengupta, R., Lafortune, S., Sinnamohideen, K., Teneketzis, D.: Diagnosability of discrete event system. Trans. Autom. Control **40**(9), 1555–1575 (1995)
14. Schumann, A., Huang, J.: A scalable jointree algorithm for diagnosability. In: Proceedings of the 23rd American National Conference on Artificial Intelligence (AAAI 2008), pp. 535–540. AAAI Press, Menlo Park (2008)
15. Schumann, A., Pencolé, Y.: Scalable diagnosability checking of event-driven system. In: Proceedings of the Twentieth International Joint Conference on Artificial Intelligence (IJCAI 2007), pp. 575–580. International Joint Conferences on Artificial Intelligence Inc., Menlo Park (2007)
16. Shu, S., Lin, F.: Detectability of discrete event systems with dynamic event observation. Syst. Control Lett. **59**(1), 9–17 (2010)

17. Shu, S., Lin, F.: I-detectability of discrete-event systems. IEEE Trans. Autom. Sci. Eng. **10**(1), 187–196 (2013)
18. Sistla, A.P., Vardi, M.Y., Wolper, P.: The complementation problem for Büchi automata with applications to temporal logic. Theor. Comput. Sci. **49**(2–3), 217–237 (1987)
19. Thorsley, D., Teneketzis, D.: Diagnosability of stochastic discrete-event systems. IEEE Trans. Autom. Control **50**(4), 476–492 (2005)
20. Ye, L., Dague, P.: Diagnosability analysis of discrete event systems with autonomous components. In: Proceedings of the 19th European Conference on Artificial Intelligence (ECAI 2010), pp. 105–110. IOS Press, Nieuwe Hemweg (2010)
21. Ye, L., Dague, P., Longuet, D., Briones, L.B., Madalinski, A.: Fault manifestability verification for discrete event systems. In: Proceedings of the 22nd European Conference on Artificial Intelligence (ECAI 2016), pp. 1718–1719. IOS Press (2016)

Model Checking and State-Space Exploration

Improving Parallel State-Space Exploration Using Genetic Algorithms

Etienne Renault(✉)

LRDE, EPITA, Kremlin-Bicêtre, France
renault@lrde.epita.fr

Abstract. The verification of temporal properties against a given system may require the exploration of its full state space. In explicit model-checking this exploration uses a Depth-First-Search (DFS) and can be achieved with multiple randomized threads to increase performance.

Nonetheless the topology of the state-space and the exploration order can cap the speedup up to a certain number of threads. This paper proposes a new technique that aims to tackle this limitation by generating artificial initial states, using genetic algorithms. Threads are then launched from these states and thus explore different parts of the state space.

Our prototype implementation runs 10% faster than state-of-the-art algorithms. These results demonstrate that this novel approach worth to be considered as a way to overcome existing limitations.

1 Introduction and Related Work

Model checking aims to check whether a system satisfies a property. Given a model of the system and a property, it explores all the possible configurations of the system, i.e., the *state space*, to check the validity of the property. Typically two kind of properties are distinguished, *safety* and *liveness* properties. This paper focus on safety properties that are of special interest since they stipulate that some "bad thing" does not happen during execution. Nonetheless the adaptation of this work for liveness properties is straightforward.

The state-space exploration techniques for debugging and proving correctness of concurrent reactive systems has proven their efficiency during the last decades [3,13,18,21]. Nonetheless they suffer from the well known *state space explosion problem*, i.e., the state space can be far too large to be stored and thus explored in a reasonable time. This problem can be addressed using *symbolic* [4] or *explicit* techniques even if we only consider the latter one in this paper.

Many improvements have been proposed for explicit techniques. *On-the-fly exploration* [5] computes the successors of a state only when required by the algorithm. As a consequence, if the property does not hold, only a subset of the state space is constructed. *Partial Order Reductions (POR)* [15,19,23] avoid the systematic exploration of the state space by exploiting the interleaving semantic of concurrent systems. *State Space Caching* [9] saves memory by "forgetting" states that have already been visited causing the exploration to possibly revisit

M. F. Atig et al. (Eds.): VECoS 2018, LNCS 11181, pp. 133–149, 2018.
https://doi.org/10.1007/978-3-030-00359-3_9

a state several times. *Bit-state Hashing* [11] is a semi-decision procedure in which each state is associated to a hash value. When two states share the same hash value, one of this two states (and thus its successors) will be ignored.

The previous techniques focus on reducing the memory footprint during the state-space exploration. Combining these techniques with modern computer architectures, i.e., many-core CPUs and large RAM memories, tends to shift from a memory problem to an execution time problem which is: how this exploration can be achieved in a reasonable time?

To address this issue multi-threaded (or distributed) exploration algorithms (that can be combined with previous techniques) have been developed [2,7,12,18]. Most of these techniques rely on the *swarming* technique presented by Holzmann et al. [13]. In this approach, each thread runs an instance of a verification procedure but explores the state space with its own transition order.

Nowadays, best performance is obtained when combining swarming with *Depth-First Search* (DFS)[1] based verification procedures [3,21]. In these combinations, threads share information about states that have been *fully explored*, i.e. states where all successors have been visited by a thread. Such states are called *closed states*. These states are then avoided by other threads explorations since they can not participate in invalidating the property. These swarmed-DFS algorithms are linear but their scalability depends on two factors:

Topology problems. If the state space is linear (only one initial state, one successor per state), using more than one thread cannot achieve any speedup. This issue can be generalized to any state space that is deep but not wide.

Exploration order problems. States are tagged *closed* following the DFS postorder of a given thread. Thus, a state s can only be marked *closed* after visiting at least N states, where N is the minimal distance between the initial state and s.

	1 thread	2 threads	4 threads	8 threads	12 threads
Time in milliseconds	2 960 296	1 796 418	118 6344	981 222	978 711
Speedup	1	1.65	2.50	3.016	3.025

The table above highlights this scalability problem over the benchmark[2] used in this paper. It presents the cumulated exploration time (in a swarmed DFS fashion) for 38 models extracted from the literature. It can be observed that this algorithm achieves reasonable speedup up to 4 threads but is disappointing for 8 threads and 12 threads (the maximum we can test).

This paper proposes a novel technique that aims to keep improving the speedup as the number of threads increases and which is compatible with all memory reduction methods presented so far.

The basic idea is to use genetic algorithms to generate artificial initial states (Sects. 2 and 3). Threads are then launched with their own verification procedure

[1] It should be noted that even if DFS-based algorithms are hard to parallelize [20] they scale better in practice than parallelized Breadth-First Search (BFS) algorithms.

[2] See Sect. 6 for more details about the benchmark.

from these artificial states (Sects. 4 and 5). We expect that these threads will explore parts of the state space that are relatively deep regarding to (many) DFS order(s). Thus, some states may be marked as *closed* without processing some path between the original initial state to these states.

Our prototype implementation (Sect. 6) has encouraging performances: the proposed approach runs 10% faster (with 12 threads) than state-of-the-art algorithms (with 12 threads). These results are encouraging and show that this novel approach worth to be considered as a way to overcome existing limitations.

Related Work. To our knowledge, the combination of parallel state space exploration algorithms with the generation of artificial initial states using genetic algorithms has never been done. The closest work is probably the one of Godefroid and Khurshid [8] that suggests to use genetic programming as an heuristic to help random walks to select the *best* successor to explore. The generation of other initial states have been proposed to maximize the coverage of random walks [22]: to achieve this, a bounded BFS is performed to obtain a pool of states that can be used as seed states. This approach does not help the scalability when the average number of successors is quite low (typically when mixing with POR).

In the literature there are some work that combine model checking with genetic programming but they are not related to the work presented here: Katz and Peled [14] use it to synthesize parametric programs, while all the other approaches are based on the work of Ammann et al. [1] and focus on the automatic generation of *mutants* that can be seen as particular "tests cases".

2 Parallel State Space Exploration

Preliminaries. Concurrent reactive systems can be represented using *Transitions Systems* (TS). Such a system $T = \langle Q, \iota, \delta, V, \gamma \rangle$ is composed of a finite set of states Q, an initial state $\iota \in Q$, a transition relation $\delta \subseteq Q \times Q$, a finite set of integer variables V and $\gamma : Q \rightarrow \mathbb{N}^{|V|}$ a function that associates to each state a unique assignment of all variables in V. For a state $s \in Q$, we denote by $\texttt{post}(s) = \{d \in Q \mid (s, d) \in \delta\}$ the set of its direct successors. A *path* of length $n \geq 1$ between two states $q, q' \in Q$ is a finite sequence of transitions $\rho = (s_1, d_1) \dots (s_n, d_n)$ with $s_1 = q$, $d_i = q'$, and $\forall i \in \{1, \dots, n-1\}$, $d_i = s_{i+1}$. A state q is *reachable* if there exists a path from the initial state ι to q.

Swarming. Checking temporal properties involves the exploration of (all or some part) of the state space of the system. Nowadays, best performance is obtained by combining on-the-fly exploration with parallel DFS reachability algorithms. Algorithm 1 presents such an algorithm.

This algorithm is presented recursively for the sake of clarity. Lines 4 and 5 represent the main procedure: `ParDFS` takes two parameters, the transition system and the number n of threads to use for the exploration. Line 5 only launches n instances of the procedure `DFS`. This last procedure takes three parameters, s the state to process, *tid* the current thread number and a *color* used to tag new visited states. Procedure DFS represents the core of the exploration. This exploration relies on a shared hashmap *visited* (defined line 2) that stores all states discovered so far by all threads and associate each state with a color (line 1):

- OPEN indicates that the state (or some of its successors) is currently processed by (at least) a thread,
- CLOSED indicates that the states and all its successors (direct or not) have been visited by some thread.

Algorithm 1. Parallel DFS Exploration.

```
1  enum color = { OPEN, CLOSED }
2  visited: hashmap of (Q, color)                              // Shared variable
3  stop ← ⊥                                                    // Shared variable
4  Procedure ParDFS(⟨Q, ι, δ, V, γ⟩ : TS, n : Integer)
5    DFS(ι, 1, OPEN) || ... || DFS(ι, n, OPEN)
6  Procedure DFS(s ∈ Q, tid : Integer, status : color)
7    if s ∉ visited then visited.add(s, status)
8    else if visited[s] = CLOSED then return
9    todo ← shuffle(post(s), tid)      // Shuffle successors using tid as seed
10   while (¬stop ∧ ¬todo.isempty()) do
11     s' ← todo.pick()
12     if s' is in the current recursive DFS stack then continue
13     if (s' ∉ visited) ∨ visited[s'] ≠ CLOSED) then
14       DFS(s', tid, status)
15   visited[s] ← CLOSED
16   if (s = ι) then stop ← ⊤
```

The DFS function starts (lines 7 to 8) by checking if the parameter s has already been inserted, by this thread or another one, in the *visited* map (line 7). If not, the state is inserted with the color OPEN (line 7). Otherwise, if s has already been inserted we have to check whether this state has been tagged CLOSED. In this case, s and all its successors have been visited: there is no need to revisit them. Line 9 grabs all the successors of the state s that are then shuffled to implement the swarming. Finally lines 10 to 14 perform the recursive DFS: for each successor s' of the current state, if s' has not been tagged CLOSED a recursive call is launched. When all successors have been visited, s can be marked CLOSED.

One can note that a shared Boolean *stop* is used in order to stop all threads as soon as a thread closes the initial state. This Boolean is useless for this algorithm since, when the first threads ends, all reachable states are tagged CLOSED and every thread is forced to backtrack. Nonetheless this Boolean will be useful later (see Sect. 4). Moreover the *visited* map is thread safe (and lock-free) so that it does not degrade performances of the algorithm.

Problem Statement. The previous algorithm (or some adaptations of it [3, 21]) obtains the best performance for explicit model checking. Nonetheless this swarmed algorithm suffers from a scalability problem. Figure 1 describes a case where augmenting the number of threads will not bring any speedup[3]. This figure describes a transition system that is linear. The dotted transitions represent long paths of transitions. In this example, state x cannot be tagged CLOSED before state y and all the states between x and y have been tagged CLOSED. The problem here is that all threads start from state s. Since threads have similar throughput they will discover x and y approximately at the same time. Thus they cannot benefit from the information computed by the other threads. This example is pathological but can be generalized to any state space that is deep and narrow.

Suppose now that there are 2 threads and that the distance between s and x is the same than the distance between x and y. The only way to obtain the maximum speedup is to launch one thread with a DFS starting from s and launch the other thread from x. In this case, when the first thread reaches state x, x has just been tagged CLOSED: the first thread can backtrack and stop.

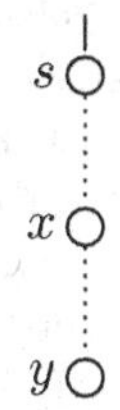

Fig. 1. Using more than one thread for the exploration is useless.

A similiar problem arise when performing on-the-fly model checking since (1) there is only one initial state and (2) all states are generated during the exploration. Thus a thread cannot be launched from a particular state. Moreover, the system's topology is only known after the exploration: we need a technique that works for any kind of topology.

The idea developed in this paper is the automatic generation of state x using genetic algorithms. The generation of *the perfect state* (the state x in the example) is a utopia. Nonetheless if we can generate a state relatively deep regarding to many DFS orders, we hope to avoid redundant work between threads, and thus maximize the information shared between threads. In practice we may generate states that do not belong to the state space, but Sect. 6 shows that more than 84% of generated states belongs to it.

3 Generation of Artificial Initial State

Genetic Algorithms. For many applications the computation of an optimal solution is impossible since the set of all possible solutions is too large to be explored. To address this problem, Holland [10] proposed a new kind of algorithms (now called genetic algorithms) that are inspired by the process of natural selection. These algorithms are often considered as optimizer and used to generate high-quality solutions to search problems. Basically, genetic algorithms start by a population of candidate solutions and improve it using bio-inspired operators:

- *Crossover*: selects multiple elements in the population (the parents) and produces a child solution from them.
- *Mutation*: selects one element in the population and alters it slightly.

[3] This particular case will certainly degrade performance due to contention over the shared hashmap.

Applying and combining these operators produces a new generation that can be evaluated using a *fitness* function. This fitness function allows to select the best elements (w.r.t the considered problem) of this new population. These best elements constitute a new population on which mutation and crossover operations can be re-applied. This process is repeated until some satisfying solution is found (or until a maximal number of generations has been reached).

Genetic algorithms rely on a representation of solutions that is chromosome-like. In the definition of a transition system we observe that every state can be seen as a tuple of integer variables using the γ function. Each variable can be considered as a gene and the set of variables can be considered as a chromosome composed of 0 and 1. For instance, if a state is composed of two variables $a = 42$ and $b = 51$ the resulting chromosome (considering 8 bits integers) would be the one described Fig. 2.

a	b
00101010	00110011

Fig. 2. Chromosome representation.

Crossover. Concurrent reactive systems are generally composed of a set of N_p processes and a set of shared variables (or channels). Given a transition system $T = \langle Q, \iota, \delta, V, \gamma \rangle$ we can define $E : V \rightarrow [0, N_p]$, such that if v is a shared variable, $E(v)$ returns 0 and otherwise $E(v)$ returns the identifier of the process where the variable v is defined.

Algorithm 2 defines the crossover operation we use. This algorithm takes a parameter S which represents the population to use for generating a new state. Line 2 instantiates a new state s that will hold the result of the crossover operation. Lines 3 to 5 set up the values of the shared variables of s: for each shared variable v, an element of S is randomly selected to be the parent. Then, at line 5, one can observe that $\gamma(s)[v]$ (the value of v in s) is set according to $\gamma(parent)[v]$ (the value of v in the *parent*). Lines 6 to 9 perform a similar operation on all the remaining variables.

These variables are treated by batch, i.e., all the variables that belong to a same process are filled using only one parent (Line 7). This choice implies that in our `Crossover` algorithm the local variable of a process cannot have two different parents: this particular processing helps to exploit the concurrency of underlying system. A possible result of this algorithm is represented Fig. 3 (with 8 bits integer variables, only one process, no shared variables, $S = \{parent1, parent2\}$ and *child* the state computed by `Crossover`(S)).

	Process 1	
	a	b
*parent*1	00000000	00000000
*parent*2	11111111	11111111
`Crossover`(S)	00000000	11111111

Fig. 3. Possible crossover.

Algorithm 2. Crossover.

```
Procedure Crossover(S ⊆ Q)
    s ← newState()
    for v ∈ V s.t. E(v) = 0 do
        parent ← pick random one of S
        γ(s)[v] ← γ(parent)[v]
    for i ∈ [0, N_p] do
        parent ← pick random one of S
        for v ∈ V s.t. E(v) = i do
            γ(s)[v] ← γ(parent)[v]
    return s
```

Algorithm 3. Mutation.

```
1 Procedure Mutation(s ∈ Q)
2     for v ∈ V do
3         r ← random(0..1)
4         if r > THRESHOLD then
5             γ(s)[v] = random_flip_one_bit_in(γ(s)[v])
6             γ(s)[v] = bound_project(γ(s)[v])
```

Mutations. The other bio-inspired operator simulates alterations that could happen while genes are combined over multiples generations. In genetic algorithms, these mutations are performed by switching the value of a bit inside of a gene. Here, all the variables of the system are considered as genes.

Algorithm 3 describes this mutation. For each variable in the state s (line 2), a random number is generated. A mutation is then performed only if this number is above a fixed threshold (line 4): this restriction limits the number of mutations that can occur in a chromosome. We can then select randomly a bit in the current variable v and flip it (line 5). Finally, line 6 exploits the information we may have about the system by restricting the mutated variable to its bounds.

Indeed, even if all variables are considered as integer variables there are many cases where the bounds are known a priori: for instance Boolean, enumeration types, characters, and so on are represented as integers but the set of value they can take is relatively small regarding the possible values of an integer. A possible result of this algorithm is represented Fig. 4 (with 8 bits integer variables and only two character variables, i.e., that have values between [0..255]).

	Process 1	
	a	b
s	00000100	00001000
Mutation(s)	00000101	00001000

Fig. 4. Possible mutation.

Fitness. As mentioned earlier, every new population must be restricted to the only elements that help to obtain a better solution. Here we want to generate states that are (1) reachable and (2) deep with respect to many DFS orders. These criteria help the swarming technique by exploring parts of the state space before another thread (starting from the real initial state) reaches them.

We face here a problem that is: for a given state it is hard to decide whether it is a *good* candidate without exploring all reachable states. For checking *deadlocks* (i.e., states without successors) Godefroid and Khurshid [8] proposed a fitness function that will only retains state with few transitions enabled[4].

Since we have different objectives a new fitness function must be defined. In order to maximize the chances to generate a reachable state, we compute the average outgoing transitions (T_{avg}) of all the states that belong to the initial population. Then the fitness function uses this value as a threshold to detect *good* states. Many fitness function can be considered:

- **equality**: the number of successors of a *good* state is exactly equal to T_{avg}. The motivation for this fitness function is that if there are $N > 1$ independent processes that are deterministic then at every time, any process can progress. Thus a good state has exactly N (equal to T_{avg}) outgoing transitions.
- **lessthan**: the number of successors of a *good* state is less than T_{avg}. The motivation for this fitness function is that if there are $N > 1$ independent deterministic processes that communicate then at any time each process can progress or two processes can be synchronized. This latter case will reduce the number of outgoing transitions
- **greaterthan**: the number of successors of a *good* state is greater than T_{avg}. The motivation for this fitness function is that if there are $N > 1$ independent and non-deterministic processes then at any time each processes can perform the same amount of actions or more.

Generation of Artificial State. Algorithm 4 presents the genetic algorithm used to generate artificial initial states using the previously defined functions.

The only parameter of this algorithm is the initial population S we want to mutate: S is obtained by performing a swarmed bounded DFS and keeping trace of all encountered states. From the initial population S, a new generation can be generated (lines 4 to 8). At any time the next generation is stored in S' (lines 7 and 3). The algorithm stops after NB_GENERATION generations (line 2). Note that this algorithm can report an empty set according to the fitness function used.

Algorithm 4. The generation of new states.

```
1 Procedure Generate(S ⊆ Q)
2   for i ← 0 to NB_GENERATION do
3     S' ← ∅
4     for j ← 0 to POP_SIZE do
5       s ← Crossover(S)
6       Mutation(s)
7       if Fitness(s) then
          S' ← S' ∪ {s}
8     S ← S'
9   return S
```

[4] Godefroid and Khurshid [8] do not generate states but finite paths and their fitness fonction analyzes the whole paths to keep only those with few enabled transitions.

4 State-Space Exploration with Genetic Algorithm

This section explains how Algorithm 1 can be adapted to exploit the generation of artificial initial states mentioned in the previous section. Algorithm 5 describes this parallel state-space exploration using genetic algorithm. The basic idea is to have a *collaborative portfollio* approach in which threads will share information about CLOSED states. In this strategy, half of the available threads runs a the `DFS` algorithm presented Sect. 2, while the other threads perform genetic exploration. This exploration is achieved by three steps:

1. Perform swarmed bounded depth-first search exploration that stores into a set $\mathcal{P}$ all encountered states (line 7). This exploration is *swarmed*, so that each thread has a different initial population $\mathcal{P}$. (Our *bounded*-DFS differs from the literature since it refers DFS that stops after visiting N states.).
2. Apply Algorithm 4 on $\mathcal{P}$ to obtain a new population $\mathcal{P}'$ of artificial initial states (line 8).
3. Apply the `DFS` algorithm for each element of $\mathcal{P}'$ (lines 9 to 11). When the population $\mathcal{P}'$ is empty, just restart the thread with the initial state ι (line 12).

One can note (line 1) that the *color* enumeration has been augmented with OPEN_GP. This new status may seem useless for now but allows to distinguish states that have been discovered by the genetic algorithm from those discovered by the traditional algorithm. In this algorithm OPEN_GP acts and means exactly the same than OPEN but: (1) this status is useful for the sketch of termination proof below and, (2) the next section shows how we can exploit similar information.

Algorithm 5. Parallel DFS Exploration using Genetic Algorithm.

1 enum *color* = { OPEN, OPEN_GP, CLOSED }
2 *visited*: hashmap of $(Q, color)$
3 $stop \leftarrow \bot$
4 **Procedure** `ParDFS_GP`$(\langle Q, \iota, \delta, V, \gamma\rangle$: TS, n : Integer)
5   `DFS`$(\iota, 1,$ OPEN$)$ $\|\ldots\|$ `DFS`$(\iota, \lfloor\frac{n}{2}\rfloor,$ OPEN$)$ $\|$ `DFS_GP`$(\iota, \lfloor\frac{n}{2}\rfloor + 1)$ $\|\ldots\|$ `DFS_GP`(ι, n)
6 **Procedure** `DFS_GP`$(\iota \in Q,\ tid$: Integer)
7     $\mathcal{P} \leftarrow$ `Bounded_DFS`$(\iota,\ tid)$ `// Swarmed exploration using` *tid* `as a seed`
8     $\mathcal{P}' \leftarrow$ `Generate`$(\mathcal{P})$ `// Described Algorithm 4`
9   **while** $\mathcal{P}'$ not empty $\wedge \neg stop$ **do**
10         $s \leftarrow$ pick one of $\mathcal{P}'$
11   `DFS`$(s, tid,$ OPEN_GP$)$
12   **if** $\neg stop$ **then** `DFS`$(\iota, tid,$ OPEN$)$

Termination. Until now we have avoided mentioning one problem: there is no reason that a generated state is a reachable state. Nonetheless even if the state is not reachable, some of its successors (direct or not) may be reachable. Since the number of unreachable states is generally much larger than the number of reachable states, we have to ensure that Algorithm 5 terminates as soon as all reachable states have been explored.

First of all let us consider only threads running the DFS algorithm. Since this algorithm has already been prove (see. [21] for more details), only the intuition is given here. When all the successors of an OPEN state have been visited, this state is tagged as CLOSED. Since all CLOSED states are ignored during the exploration, each thread will restrict parts of the reachable state space. At some point all the states will be CLOSED: even if a thread is still performing its DFS procedure, all the successors of its current state will be marked CLOSED. Thus the thread will be forced to backtrack and stop.

The problem we may have with using genetic algorithm is that all the threads performing the genetic algorithm may be running while all the other ones are idle since all the reachable states have already been visited. In this case, a running thread can see only unreachable states, i.e. OPEN_GP, or CLOSED ones. To handle this problem, a Boolean *stop* is shared among all threads (line 2). When this Boolean is set to $\top$ all threads stop regardless the exploration technique used (line 10, Algorithm 1). We observe line 9 that the use of other artificial states is also stopped, and no restart will be performed (line 12). This Boolean is set to $\top$ only when all the successors of the real initial state have been explored (line 16, Algorithm 1). Thus, one can note that even if a thread using the genetic algorithm visits first all reachable states it will stop all the other threads.

5 Checking Temporal Properties

Safety properties cover a wide range of properties: *deadlock freedom* (there is no state without successors), *mutual exclusion* (two processes execute some critical section at the same time), *partial correction* (the execution terminates in a state that does not satisfies the postcondition while the precondition of the run was satisfied), *etc.* One interesting characteristic of safety properties is that they can be checked using a reachability analysis (as described Sect. 2). Nonetheless, our genetic reachability algorithm (Algorithm 5) cannot be directly used to check safety properties. Indeed, if a thread (using genetic programming) reports an error we do not know if this error actually belongs to the state space.

Algorithm 6 describes how to adapt Algorithm 5 to check safety properties. To simplify things we focus on checking deadlock freedom, but our approach can be generalized to any safety property. This algorithm[5] relies on both Algorithms 1

[5] Main differences have been highlighted to help the reader.

and 5 The basic idea is still to launch half of the threads from the initial state ι and the remaining ones from some artificial initial state (line 7).

Algorithm 6. Parallel Deadlock Detection Using Genetic Algorithm.

```
1  enum color = { OPEN, OPEN_GP, CLOSED , DEADLOCK_GP }
2  visited: hashmap of (Q, color)
3  stop ← ⊥
4  deadlock ← ⊥
5  Procedure ParDeadlockGP(⟨Q, ι, δ, V, γ⟩ : TS, n : Integer)
6      DeadlockDFS(ι, 1, OPEN) || ... || DeadlockDFS(ι, ⌊n/2⌋, OPEN) ||
7                DeadlockDFS_GP(ι, ⌊n/2⌋ + 1) || ... || DeadlockDFS_GP(ι, n)
8  Procedure DeadlockDFS(s ∈ Q, tid : Integer, status : color)
9      if s ∉ visited then visited.add(s, status)
10     else if visited[s] = CLOSED then return
11     todo ← shuffle(post(s), tid)
12     while (¬stop ∧ ¬todo.isempty()) do
13         s' ← todo.pick()
14         if s' is in the current recursive DFS stack then continue
15         if (s' ∉ visited ∨ visited[s'] ≠ CLOSED) then
16             if s' ∈ visited ∧ visited[s'] = DEADLOCK_GP ∧ status = OPEN then
17                 deadlock ← ⊤; stop ← ⊤
18                 break
19             DeadlockDFS(s', tid, status)
20             if visited[s'] = DEADLOCK_GP ∧ status = OPEN_GP then
21                 visited[s] ← DEADLOCK_GP
22                 return
23     if post(s) = ∅ ∧ status = OPEN then deadlock ← ⊤; stop ← ⊤
24     if post(s) = ∅ ∧ status = OPEN_GP then visited[s] ← DEADLOCK_GP
25     else v[s] ← CLOSED
26     if (s = ι) then stop ← ⊤
27 Procedure DeadlockDFS_GP(ι ∈ Q, tid : Integer)
28     P ← Bounded_DFS(ι, tid) // Also check deadlock during this DFS
29     P' ← Generate(P)
30     while P' not empty ∧ ¬stop do
31         s ← pick one of P'
32         DeadlockDFS(s, tid, OPEN_GP)
33     if ¬stop then DeadlockDFS(ι, tid, OPEN)
```

- For a thread performing reachability with genetic algorithm the differences are quite few. When a deadlock state is detected (line 24) we just tag this state as DEADLOCK_GP rather than CLOSED. This new status is used to mark all states leading to a deadlock state. Indeed since we do not know if the state is a reachable one we cannot report immediately that a deadlock has been found.

Moreover we cannot mark this state CLOSED otherwise a counterexample could be lost. This new status helps to solve the problem: when such a state is detected to be reachable, a deadlock is immediately reported. The other modifications are lines 20 and 22: when backtracking, if a deadlock has been found no more states will be explored.
- For a thread performing reachability without genetic algorithm the differences are also quite few. Lines 16 to 18 only check if the next state to process has been marked DEADLOCK_GP. In this case this state is a reachable one and it leads to a deadlock state. We can then report that a deadlock has been found and stop all the other threads. A deadlock can also be reported directly (line 23), if the current state is a deadlock.

Deadlock – Sketch of Proof. Due to lack of space only the schema of a proof, that the algorithm will report a deadlock if and only if there exists a reachable state that has no successors, is given here.

Theorem 1. For all systems S, the algorithm terminates.

Theorem 2. A thread reports a deadlock iff $\exists s \in Q, post(s) = \emptyset$.

To simplify the sketch of proof, we denote by *classical thread* a thread that does not perform genetic algorithm while the other threads are called *gp threads*. The following invariants hold for all lines of Algorithm 6:

Invariant 1. If *stop* is $\top$ then no new state will be discovered.
Invariant 2. A deadlock state can only be OPEN, OPEN_GP or DEADLOCK_GP.
Invariant 3. No direct successor of a CLOSED state is a deadlock state.
Invariant 4. A state is CLOSED iff all its successors that are not on the thread's recursive stack are CLOSED.
Invariant 5. Only *gp threads* can tag a state DEADLOCK_GP.
Invariant 6. A state is DEADLOCK_GP iff it is a deadlock state or if one of its successors (direct or not) is a deadlock state.
Invariant 7. Only *classical thread* can report that a deadlock has been found.
Invariant 8. If a state is reachable then all its direct successors are reachable.

Invariants, combined to the sketch of proof of the previous section, helps to prove Theorem 1: the algorithm stops either because a deadlock is detected or because all reachable states have been explored. These invariants establish both directions of Theorem 2: invariant 7 and 8 are the most important for correctness.

Discussion. The verification of complex temporal properties involves the exploration of an automaton which is the result of the synchronous product between the state space of the system and the property automaton. Thus a state is composed of two parts: the system state and the property state. Genetic algorithms presented so far can then be applied by considering that the property state is a variable just like the other system's variables. The adaptation of Algorithm 6 for checking liveness properties is straightforward: when a *gp thread* detects an accepting cycle, all the states forming it are tagged with an ACCEPTING_CYCLE status. When a *classical thread* detects such a state, a counterexample is raised.

6 Evaluation

Benchmark Description. To evaluate the performance of our algorithms, we selected 38 models from the BEEM benchmark [16] that cover all types of models described by the classification of Pelánek [17]. All the models where selected such that Algorithm 1 with one thread would take at most 40 min on Intel(R) Xeon(R) @ 2.00 GHz with 250 GB of RAM. This six-core machine is also used for the following parallel experiments[6]. All the approaches proposed here have been implemented in Spot [6]. For a given model the corresponding system is generated on-the-fly using DiVinE 2.4 patched by the LTSmin team[7].

Reachability. To evaluate the performance of the algorithm presented Sect. 4 we conducted 9158 experiments, each taking 30 s on the average. Table 1 reports selected results to show the impact of the fitness function and the threshold over the performance of Algorithm 5 with 12 threads (the maximum we can test). For each variation, we provide *nb* the number of models computed within time and memory constraints, and *Time* the cumulated walltime for this configuration (to run the whole benchmark). For a fair-comparison, we excluded from *Time* models that cannot be processed. Table 1 also reports state-of-the-art and **random** (used to evaluate the accuracy of genetic algorithms by generating random states as seed state). This latter technique is irrelevant since it is five time slower than state-of-the-art and only process 32 models over 38.

If we now focus on genetics algorithms, we observe that the threshold highly impacts the results regardless the fitness function used: the more the threshold grows, the more models are processed within time and memory constraints.

The table also reports the best threshold[8] for all fitness function, i.e. 0.999. It appears that **greaterthan** only processed 37 models: this fitness function does not seem to be a good fitness function since (1) it tends to explore useless parts of the state-space and (2) the variations of the threshold highly impacts the performance of the algorithm. All the other fitness function provide similar results for a threshold fixed at 0.999. Nonetheless we do not recommend **equality** since a simple variation of the threshold (0.7) could lead to extremely poor results. Our preference goes to **lessthan** and **lessstrict** since they seem to be less sensitive to threshold variation while achieving the benchmark 9% faster than state-of-the-art algorithm. Thus, while the speedup for 12 threads was 3.02 for state-of-the-art algorithm, our algorithm achieves a speedup of 3.31.

Note that the results reported Table 1 include the computation of the artificial initial states. On the overall benchmark, this computation take in average slightly less than 1 s per model (30 s for the whole benchmark). This computation has a negligible impact on the speedup of our algorithm.

---

[6] For a description of our setup, including selected models, detailed results and code, see http://www.lrde.epita.fr/~renault/benchs/VECOS-2018/results.html.

[7] See http://fmt.cs.utwente.nl/tools/ltsmin/#divine for more details. Also note that we added some patches (available in the webpage) to manage out-of-bound detection.

[8] We evaluate other thresholds like 0.9999 or 0.99999 but it appears that augmenting the threshold does not increase performance, see the webpage for more details.

Table 1. Impact of the threshold and the fitness function on Algorithm 5 with 12 threads (NB_GENERATION = 3, INIT = 1000, POP_SIZE = 50). The time is expressed in millisecond and is the cumulated time taken to compute the whole benchmark (38 models); *nb* is the number of instances resolved with time and memory limits.

	THRESHOLD							
	0.7		0.8		0.9		0.999	
	nb	*Time (ms)*	*nb*	*Time (ms)*	*nb*	*Time (ms)*	*nb*	*Time (ms)*
greaterthan	35	1 041 015	35	970 248	35	1 000 184	37	900 468
equality	35	3 217 183	35	965 259	35	934 947	38	907 148
lessthan	35	972 038	35	951 767	35	928 978	38	904 776
lessstrict	35	970 668	35	983 225	35	935 319	38	894 131
	No threshold							
random	(trivial comparator to evaluate genetic algorithms)						32	5 079 869
Algorithm 1	(state-of-the-art with 12 threads)						38	978 711

We have also evaluated (not reported here, see webpage for more details) the impact of the size of the initial population and the size of each generation over the performance. It appears that augmenting (or decreasing) these two parameters deteriorate the performance. It is worth noting that the best value of all parameters are classical values regarding to state-of-the-art genetic algorithms. Finally, for each model (and **lessthan** as fitness), we compute a set of artificial initial states and run an exploration algorithm from each of these states. It appears that 84.6% of the 7 866 005 486 generated states are reachable states.

Safety Properties. Now that we have detected the best values for the parameters of the genetic algorithm we can evaluate the performance of our deadlock detection algorithm. In order to evaluate the performance of our algorithm we conduct 418 experiments. The benchmark contains 21 models with deadlocks and 17 models without. Table 2 compares the relative performance of state-of-the-art algorithm and Algorithm 6. For this latter algorithm, we only report the two fitness functions that give the best performance for reachability. Indeed, since Algorithm 6 is based on Algorithm 5 we reuse the best parameters to obtain the best performance. Results for detecting deadlocks are quite disappointing since our algorithm is 15% to 30% slower. A closer look to these results show that deadlocks are detected quickly and Algorithm 6 has degraded performance due to the computation of artificial initial states.

On the contrary we observe that our algorithm is 10% faster (regardless whether we use **lessthan** or **lesstrict**) than the classical algorithm when the system has no deadlock. One can note that this algorithm performs better than simple reachability algorithm. Indeed, even if the system has no deadlock: the algorithm can find non-reachable deadlock. In this case, the algorithm backtracks and the next generation is processed. This early backtracking force the use of a new generation that will helps the exploration of the reachable states. To achieve this speedup, we observe an overhead of 13% for the memory consumption. The use of dedicated memory reduction techniques could help to reduce this footprint.

Table 2. Comparison of algorithms for deadlock detection. Each runs with 12 threads, and we report the variation of two different fitness functions: **lessstrict** and **lessthan**. Results presents the cumulated time and states visited for the whole benchmark.

	Algorithm 1 (state-of-the-art)		Algorithm 6			
			lessthan		**lessstrict**	
	Time (ms)	States	Time (ms)	States	Time (ms)	States
Deadlocks	2 888	7.01E^6	3 713	5.87E^6	3 414	5.47E^6
No deadlocks	516 152	5.79E^8	462 881	6.73E^8	468 683	6.82E^8

Discussion. Few models in the benchmark have a linear topology, which can be considered as the perfect one for the algorithms presented in this paper. Nonetheless, we observe a global improvement of state-of-the-art algorithm. We believe that other fitness function (based on interpolation or estimation of distribution) could help to generate better states, i.e. deep with respect to many DFS orders.

7 Conclusion

We have presented some first and new parallel exploration algorithms that rely on genetic algorithms. We suggested to see variables of the model as genes and states as chromosomes. With this definition we were able to build an algorithm that generates artificial initial states. To detect if such a state is relevant we proposed and evaluate various fitness functions. It appears that these seed states improve the swarming technique. This combination between swarming and genetic algorithms has never been proposed and the benchmark show encouraging results (10% faster than state-of-the-art). Since the performance of our algorithms highly relies on the generation of good artificial states we would like to see if other strategies could help to generate better states.

This work mainly focused on checking safety properties even if we proposed an adaptation for liveness properties. A future work would be to evaluate the performance of our algorithm in this latter case. We also want to investigate the relation between artificial state generation and POR, since both rely on the analysis of processes variables. Finally, we strongly believe that this paper could serve as a basis for combining parametric model-checking with neural network.

References

1. Ammann, P.E., Black, P.E., Majurski, W.: Using model checking to generate tests from specifications. In: ICFEM 1998, pp. 46–54, December 1998

2. Barnat, J., Brim, L., Ročkai, P.: Scalable shared memory LTL model checking. STTT **12**(2), 139–153 (2010)
3. Bloemen, V., van de Pol, J.: Multi-core SCC-based LTL model checking. In: Bloem, R., Arbel, E. (eds.) HVC 2016. LNCS, vol. 10028, pp. 18–33. Springer, Cham (2016). https://doi.org/10.1007/978-3-319-49052-6_2
4. Burch, J.R., Clarke, E.M., McMillan, K.L., Dill, D.L., Hwang, L.J.: Symbolic model checking: 10^{20} states and beyond. In: Proceedings of the Fifth Annual IEEE Symposium on Logic in Computer Science, pp. 1–33. IEEE (1990)
5. Courcoubetis, C., Vardi, M., Wolper, P., Yannakakis, M.: Memory efficient algorithms for the verification of temporal properties. In: Clarke, E.M., Kurshan, R.P. (eds.) CAV 1990. LNCS, vol. 531, pp. 233–242. Springer, Heidelberg (1991). https://doi.org/10.1007/BFb0023737
6. Duret-Lutz, A., Lewkowicz, A., Fauchille, A., Michaud, T., Renault, É., Xu, L.: Spot 2.0 — a framework for LTL and ω-automata manipulation. In: Artho, C., Legay, A., Peled, D. (eds.) ATVA 2016. LNCS, vol. 9938, pp. 122–129. Springer, Cham (2016). https://doi.org/10.1007/978-3-319-46520-3_8
7. Garavel, H., Mateescu, R., Smarandache, I.: Parallel state space construction for model-checking. Technical report RR-4341, INRIA (2001)
8. Godefroid, P., Khurshid, S.: Exploring very large state spaces using genetic algorithms. In: Katoen, J.-P., Stevens, P. (eds.) TACAS 2002. LNCS, vol. 2280, pp. 266–280. Springer, Heidelberg (2002). https://doi.org/10.1007/3-540-46002-0_19
9. Godefroid, P., Holzmann, G.J., Pirottin, D.: State space caching revisited. In: von Bochmann, G., Probst, D.K. (eds.) CAV 1992. LNCS, vol. 663, pp. 178–191. Springer, Heidelberg (1993). https://doi.org/10.1007/3-540-56496-9_15
10. Holland, J.H.: Genetic Algorithms. Scientific American (1992)
11. Holzmann, G.J.: On limits and possibilities of automated protocol analysis. In: PSTV 1987, pp. 339–344. North-Holland, May 1987
12. Holzmann, G.J., Bosnacki, D.: The design of a multicore extension of the SPIN model checker. IEEE Trans. Softw. Eng. **33**(10), 659–674 (2007)
13. Holzmann, G.J., Joshi, R., Groce, A.: Swarm verification techniques. IEEE Trans. Softw. Eng. **37**(6), 845–857 (2011)
14. Katz, G., Peled, D.A.: Synthesis of parametric programs using genetic programming and model checking. In: INFINITY 2013, pp. 70–84 (2013)
15. Laarman, A., Pater, E., Pol, J., Hansen, H.: Guard-based partial-order reduction. STTT **18**, 1–22 (2014)
16. Pelánek, R.: BEEM: benchmarks for explicit model checkers. In: Bošnački, D., Edelkamp, S. (eds.) SPIN 2007. LNCS, vol. 4595, pp. 263–267. Springer, Heidelberg (2007). https://doi.org/10.1007/978-3-540-73370-6_17
17. Pelánek, R.: Properties of state spaces and their applications. Int. J. Softw. Tools Technol. Transf. (STTT) **10**, 443–454 (2008)
18. Pelánek, R., Hanžl, T., Černá, I., Brim, L.: Enhancing random walk state space exploration. In: FMICS 2005, pp. 98–105. ACM Press (2005)
19. Peled, D.: Combining partial order reductions with on-the-fly model-checking. In: Dill, D.L. (ed.) CAV 1994. LNCS, vol. 818, pp. 377–390. Springer, Heidelberg (1994). https://doi.org/10.1007/3-540-58179-0_69
20. Reif, J.H.: Depth-first search is inherently sequential. Inf. Process. Lett. **20**, 229–234 (1985)
21. Renault, E., Duret-Lutz, A., Kordon, F., Poitrenaud, D.: Variations on parallel explicit model checking for generalized Büchi automata. Int. J. Softw. Tools Technol. Transf. (STTT) **19**, 1–21 (2016)

22. Sivaraj, H., Gopalakrishnan, G.: Random walk based heuristic algorithms for distributed memory model checking. Electron. Not. Theor. Comput. Sci. **89**(1), 51–67 (2003)
23. Valmari, A.: Stubborn sets for reduced state space generation. In: Rozenberg, G. (ed.) ICATPN 1989. LNCS, vol. 483, pp. 491–515. Springer, Heidelberg (1991). https://doi.org/10.1007/3-540-53863-1_36

LTL Model-Checking for Communicating Concurrent Programs

Adrien Pommellet[1(✉)] and Tayssir Touili[2]

[1] LIPN and Université Paris-Diderot, Paris, France
pommellet@irif.fr
[2] LIPN, CNRS, and Université Paris 13, Villetaneuse, France

Abstract. Communicating Pushdown Systems (CPDSs) can be used to model multi-threaded programs with recursive procedure calls and synchronisation by rendez-vous between parallel threads. While the reachability problem for this particular class of automata is undecidable, it can be tackled using an algebraic framework for computing abstractions of context-free languages. In this paper, we combine this framework with an automata-based approach in order to approximate an answer to the model-checking problem for Linear Temporal Logic (LTL) on CPDSs: we show that, given a single-indexed LTL formula, we can accurately tell if a CPDS does not follow this formula. Finally, we show how this method can be used to find race conditions in concurrent programs.

1 Introduction

The use of parallel programs has grown in popularity in the past fifteen years, but these remain nonetheless fickle and vulnerable to specific issues such as race conditions or deadlocks. Static analysis methods for this class of programs remain therefore more relevant than ever.

The *model-checking* framework has proven to be a cornerstone of modern static analysis techniques. The program is modelled as a simpler abstract mathematical *model*. Desirable properties and forbidden behaviours are then expressed using a well-defined *logical* framework, then checked against the abstract mathematical model of the program. The *linear-time temporal logic* (also known as LTL) encodes properties about the future of execution paths, that is, the sequence of configurations the model goes through. It can be used to express safety and liveness properties.

Pushdown systems are a natural model for programs with sequential, recursive procedure calls [6]. Thus, networks of pushdown systems can be used to model multi-threaded programs, where each PDS in the network models a sequential component of the whole program.

Communicating pushdown systems (CPDSs) were introduced by Bouajjani et al. in [3] as a model for communicating multi-threaded programs. It is a natural abstraction, as each thread is modelled as a PDS, and can synchronize by rendez-vous with other threads. The reachability problem is undecidable for

M. F. Atig et al. (Eds.): VECoS 2018, LNCS 11181, pp. 150–165, 2018.
https://doi.org/10.1007/978-3-030-00359-3_10

CPDSs. Therefore, the set of execution paths cannot be computed in an exact manner. To overcome this problem, Bouajjani et al. computed an abstraction of the execution paths language, using a framework based on Kleene algebras.

Solving the model-checking problem of LTL for CPDSs would therefore be a worthy addition to the existing verification techniques. However, this problem is unfortunately undecidable. Our contributions in this paper are the following:

- we define the semantics of *single-indexed* LTL formulas for CPDS, that is, formulas of the form $\varphi = (\psi_1, \ldots, \psi_n)$, where each LTL sub-formula ψ_i must hold for the i-th process with regards to the synchronized CPDS semantics;
- we abstract the set of accepting traces of a Büchi pushdown system; to do so, we use the abstraction framework of [3] as well as the LTL model-checking methods for PDS developed by Esparza et al. in [6];
- we use this abstraction on isolated pushdown components to compute an over-approximation of the model-checking problem of single-indexed LTL for CPDSs;
- we apply this abstraction framework to detect race conditions in a toy example.

Related Work. *Multi-Stack Pushdown Systems* (MPDSs) are pushdown systems with two or more stacks that can be used to model synchronized parallel programs. In [8] Qadeer et al. solve the model-checking problem of LTL given a context-bounding constraint on runs, where context is an uninterrupted sequence of actions by a single thread. This result still holds with a weaker phase-bounding constraint, where only a single stack can be popped from during a phase, as shown by La Torre et al. in [11]. Atig introduced in [1] *Ordered Multi-Pushdown Automata*, a sub-class of MPDSs such that the stacks are ordered and only the first-non empty stack can be popped from. Given this constraint, the model-checking problem of LTL can be solved with an 2ETIME upper bound. These models depend on a bounding constraints on runs; our abstraction framework, while less accurate, does not.

Dynamic pushdown networks (DPNs) were introduced by Bouajjani et al. in [4]. A DPN models a concurrent program as a network with an unbounded number of pushdown systems that can spawn new threads, also modeled as pushdown systems. Song et al. described in [10] a model-checking framework for *single-indexed* LTL and CTL formulas. A DPN can spawn new threads according to a finite number of patterns, since it has a finite number of rules. Hence, a single-indexed formula on a DPN is of the form $\varphi = (\psi_1, \ldots, \psi_n)$, where each component ψ_i is a formula that must hold for the i-th thread pattern. While CPDSs can't model thread spawns, but DPNs do not feature synchronization between threads, an important aspect of concurrent programs.

Synchronized dynamic pushdown networks (DPNs) were later introduced by Pommellet et al. in [7]. The reachability problem for this class of automata is undecidable but can be abstracted. Abstractions for the model-checking problem, however, have yet to be defined.

Paper Outline. In Sect. 2 of this paper, we remind the reader of the definition of *communicating pushdown systems* (CPDSs). In Sect. 3, we define the *single-indexed linear-time temporal logic* for CPDSs. We describe in Sect. 4 the abstraction framework designed by Bouajjani et al. in [3] in order to over-approximate the set of execution paths of a PDS. In Sect. 5, as a main contribution of this paper, we introduce an abstract model-checking algorithm. We apply this algorithm to an example in Sect. 6. Finally, we show our conclusion in Sect. 7.

2 Communicating Pushdown Systems

2.1 Pushdown Systems

Pushdown systems are a natural model for sequential programs with recursive procedure calls.

Definition 1 (Pushdown system). *A* pushdown system *(PDS) is a tuple* $\mathcal{P} = (P, Act, \Gamma, \Delta, c_0)$ *where* P *is a finite set of control states,* Act *a finite input alphabet, also called the set of* actions, Γ *a finite stack alphabet,* $\Delta \subseteq P \times \Gamma \times Act \times P \times \Gamma^*$ *a finite set of transition rules, and* $c_0 \in P \times \Gamma^*$ *a starting configuration.*

If $d = (p, \gamma, a, p', w) \in \Delta$, we write $d = (p, \gamma) \xrightarrow{a} (p', w)$. We call a the *label* of d. We can assume without loss of generality that $\Delta \subseteq P \times \Gamma \times Act \times P \times \Gamma^{\leq 2}$.

Configurations of PDSs. A *configuration* of $\mathcal{P}$ is a pair $\langle p, w \rangle$ where $p \in P$ is a control state and $w \in \Gamma^*$ a stack content. Let $Conf_{\mathcal{P}} = P \times \Gamma^*$ be the set of configurations of $\mathcal{P}$. A set of configurations $\mathcal{C}$ of a PDS $\mathcal{P}$ is said to be *regular* if $\forall p \in P$, there exists a finite-state automaton $\mathcal{A}_p$ on the alphabet Γ such that $\mathcal{L}(\mathcal{A}_p) = \{w \mid \langle p, w \rangle \in \mathcal{C}\}$, where $\mathcal{L}(\mathcal{A})$ stands for the language recognized by an automaton $\mathcal{A}$.

In order to represent regular sets of configurations, we consider the following structure:

Definition 2 (Bouajjani et al. [2]). *Let* $\mathcal{P} = (P, Act, \Gamma, \Delta, c_0)$ *be a pushdown system. A* $\mathcal{P}$*-automaton* $\mathcal{A} = (Q, \Gamma, \delta, I, F)$ *is a finite automaton on the stack alphabet* Γ *of* $\mathcal{P}$ *where* Q *is a set of states such that* $P \subseteq Q$, $I = P$ *the set of initial states,* $F \subseteq Q$ *the set of final states, and* $\delta \subseteq Q \times \Gamma \cup \{\varepsilon\} \times Q$ *a set of transitions.*

Let $\longrightarrow_{\mathcal{A}}$ be the transition relation inferred from δ. We say that $\mathcal{A}$ *accepts* a configuration $\langle p, w \rangle$ if there is a path $p \xrightarrow{w}^*_{\mathcal{A}} f$ such that $f \in F$. Let $L(\mathcal{A}) \subseteq Conf_{\mathcal{P}}$ be the set of configurations accepted by $\mathcal{A}$. Intuitively, a $\mathcal{P}$-automaton is a finite automaton whose edges are labelled by stack symbols of $\mathcal{P}$ and whose initial states represent the states of $\mathcal{P}$. The following lemma holds:

Lemma 1 (Bouajjani et al. [2]). *A set of configurations* $\mathcal{C}$ *of a PDS* $\mathcal{P}$ *is regular if and only if there exists a* $\mathcal{P}$*-automaton* $\mathcal{A}$ *such that* $L(\mathcal{A}) = \mathcal{C}$.

The Reachability Relation. For each $a \in Act$, we define the transition relation $\xrightarrow{a}_{\mathcal{P}}$ on configurations as follows: if $(p, \gamma) \xrightarrow{a} (p', w) \in \Delta$, for each $w' \in \Gamma^*$, $\langle p, \gamma w' \rangle \xrightarrow{a}_{\mathcal{P}} \langle p', ww' \rangle$. From these relations, we can then infer the *immediate successor* relation $\rightarrow_{\mathcal{P}} = \bigcup_{a \in Act} \xrightarrow{a}_{\mathcal{P}}$. The *reachability* relation $\rightarrow^*_{\mathcal{P}}$ is the reflexive and transitive closure of the immediate successor relation $\rightarrow_{\mathcal{P}}$.

A *run* r is a sequence of configurations $r = (r_i)_{i \geq 0}$ such that $r_0 = c_0$, and $\forall i \geq 0$, $r_i \xrightarrow{a_i}_{\mathcal{P}} r_{i+1}$. The sequence $(a_i)_{i \geq 0}$ of actions is then said to be the *trace* of r. Traces and runs may be finite or infinite. Let $Runs_\omega(\mathcal{P})$ (resp. $Runs(\mathcal{P})$) be the set of all infinite (resp. finite) runs of $\mathcal{P}$. We define $Traces_\omega(\mathcal{P})$ and $Traces(\mathcal{P})$ in a similar manner.

If $\mathcal{C}$ is a set of configurations, we introduce its set of *predecessors* $pre^*(\mathcal{P}, \mathcal{C}) = \{c \in P \times \Gamma^* \mid \exists c' \in \mathcal{C}, c \Rightarrow_{\mathcal{P}} c'\}$. We may omit the variable $\mathcal{P}$ when only a single PDS is being considered.

It has been shown in [2] that the set of predecessors $pre^*(\mathcal{P}, \mathcal{C})$ is regular and can be computed by applying a saturation procedure:

Theorem 1 (Bouajjani et al. [2]**).** *Given a PDS $\mathcal{P}$ and a regular set of configurations $\mathcal{C}$, there exists a $\mathcal{P}$-automaton $\mathcal{A}_{pre^*}$ accepting $pre^*(\mathcal{C})$.*

2.2 The Model and Its Semantics

We now model each thread in a concurrent program as a PDS:

Definition 3 (Bouajjani et al. [3]**).** *A* communicating pushdown system *(CPDS) is a tuple $\mathcal{CP} = (\mathcal{P}_1, \ldots, \mathcal{P}_n)$ of pushdown systems sharing the same input alphabet Act and the same stack alphabet Γ.*

From then on, we assume that the set Act contains a special action τ that represents internal actions, and that other letters in $Lab = Act \setminus \{\tau\}$ model synchronization signals. We assume that each pair $(\mathcal{P}_i, \mathcal{P}_j)$ of pushdown systems in the network uses a dedicated set of signals $Lab_{i,j}$ disjoint from the other sets of signals.

A *global configuration* of $\mathcal{CP}$ is a tuple $g = (c_1, \ldots, c_n)$ of configurations of $\mathcal{P}_1, \ldots, \mathcal{P}_n$. Let $Conf_{\mathcal{CP}}$ be the set of global configurations of the CPDS $\mathcal{CP}$. The *global starting configuration* of $\mathcal{CP}$ is the tuple $g_0 = (c_0^1, \ldots, c_0^n)$ where c_0^i is the starting configuration of $\mathcal{P}_i$. We define a transition relation $\xrightarrow{a}_{\mathcal{CP}}$ on global configurations as follows:

- $(c_1, \ldots, c_n) \xrightarrow{\tau}_{\mathcal{CP}} (c'_1, \ldots, c'_n)$ if there is i such that $c_i \xrightarrow{\tau}_{\mathcal{P}_i} c'_i$ and $c_j = c'_j$ for all $j \neq i$; a single process applies a pushdown operation on its own stack;
- $(c_1, \ldots, c_n) \xrightarrow{a}_{\mathcal{CP}} (c'_1, \ldots, c'_n)$ if there are i and j, $i \neq j$ such that $c_i \xrightarrow{a}_{\mathcal{P}_i} c'_i$, $c_j \xrightarrow{a}_{\mathcal{P}_j} c'_j$ and $c_k = c'_k$ for all $k \neq i \neq j$; two synchronized processes perform a simultaneous action.

We define runs and traces with regards to this transition relation in a manner similar to PDSs. Given a global run g, we define g^i as its projection on its i-th component $Conf_{\mathcal{P}_i}$.

2.3 From a Program to a CPDS Model

We can assume that the program is given by a n-tuple of *control flow graphs*, whose nodes represent control points of threads or procedures and whose edges are labelled by statements. These statements can be variable assignments, procedure calls or returns, or communications between threads through unidirectional point-to point channels, where a thread sends a value x through a channel ch and another thread waits for this value then assigns it to a variable y.

Without loss of generality, we assume that threads share no global variables and instead can only synchronize through unidirectional, point-to-point channels: for all $1 \leq i, j \leq n$, $i \neq j$, there is a channel $ch_{i,j}$ that allows thread i to send values to another thread j. With a send statement $ch!(x)$, value x is sent through channel ch. With a receive statement $ch?(y)$, the value received through channel ch is bound to variable y. We also consider that both local and global variables may only take a finite number of values.

For each control flow graph, we will define a corresponding PDS $\mathcal{P} = (P, Act, \Gamma, \Delta)$. The whole program will be modelled by the tuple of these PDSs. The set of states P is the set of all possible valuations of global variables of the thread. The stack alphabet Γ is the set of all pairs (n, l) where n is a node of the flow graph and l is a valuation of the local variables of the current procedure.

The set *Act* contains an internal action τ and an action $ch(n)$ for each channel ch and value n that can be carried through it. *Lab* is a disjoint union of sets $Lab_{i,j}$ corresponding to synchronization actions of the form $ch_{i,j}(v)$ from a system $\mathcal{P}_i$ to another system $\mathcal{P}_j$.

For each statement s labelling an edge of the flow graph between nodes n_1 and n_2, we introduce the following transition rules in the corresponding PDS, where g_1 and g_2 (resp. l_1 and l_2) are the valuations of global (resp. local) variables before and after the execution of the statement:

- if s is an assignment, it is represented by rules of the form $(g_1, (n_1, l_1)) \xrightarrow{\tau} (g_2, (n_2, l_2))$; assigning new values to variables in g_1 and l_1 results in new valuations g_2 and l_2;
- if s is a procedure call, it is represented by rules of the form $(g_1, (n_1, l_1)) \xrightarrow{\tau} (g_2, (f_0, l_0)(n_2, l_2))$, where f_0 is the starting node of the called procedure and l_0 the initial valuation of its local variables;
- if s is a procedure return, it is represented by rules of the form $(g_1, (n_1, l_1)) \xrightarrow{\tau} (g_2, \varepsilon)$; we simulate returns of values by introducing an additional global variable and assigning the return value to it in the valuation g_2;
- if s is an assignment $ch?(y)$ of a value x carried through a channel c to a variable y, it is represented by rules of the form $(g_1, (n_1, l_1)) \xrightarrow{ch(v)} (g_2, (n_2, l_2))$ where g_1 and g_2 (resp. l_1 and l_2) are such that assigning the value v to the variable y in g_1 (resp. l_1) results in the new valuations g_2 (resp. l_2);
- if s is an output $ch!(x)$ through a channel c of the value x of a variable y, it is represented by rules of the form $(g_1, (n_1, l_1)) \xrightarrow{ch(v)} (g_2, (n_2, l_2))$ such that the variable y has value x in either g_1 or l_1.

Finally, we consider the starting configuration of each process $(g_{init}, (n_{init}, l_{init}))$ where g_{init} and l_{init} are respectively the initial valuations of the global and local variables of the thread, and n_{init} the starting node of its initial procedure.

3 Model-Checking LTL on CPDSs

3.1 The Linear-Time Temporal Logic LTL

Let AP be a finite set of *atomic propositions* used to express facts about a program. A *path* is an infinite word $\rho = (\rho_i)_{\geq 0}$ in the set $Paths = (2^{AP})^\omega$.

Definition 4 (LTL). *The set of* LTL *formulas is given by the following grammar:*

$$\varphi, \psi ::= \bot \mid p \in \text{AP} \mid \neg\varphi \mid \varphi \vee \psi \mid \text{X } \varphi \text{ } (Next) \mid \varphi \text{ U } \psi \text{ } (Until)$$

$\bot$ stands for the predicate 'always true'. X and U are called the *next* and *until* operators: the former means that a formula should happen at the next step, the latter, that a formula should hold at least until another formula becomes true. We consider the following semantics on paths:

Definition 5 (Semantics of LTL). *Let φ be a* LTL *formula, $\rho \in Paths$, and $i \in \mathbb{N}$. We define inductively the semantics of the relation $\rho, i \models \varphi$:*

$$\begin{aligned} \rho, i \models p \text{ where } p \in AP &\Leftrightarrow p \in \rho_i \\ \rho, i \models \text{X } \varphi &\Leftrightarrow \rho, i+1 \models \varphi \\ \rho, i \models \varphi \text{ U } \psi &\Leftrightarrow \exists j \geq i \text{ such that } \rho, j \models \psi \text{ and} \\ &\quad \forall k \in \{i, \ldots, j-1\}, \rho, k \models \varphi \end{aligned}$$

as well as the obvious interpretation of the boolean operators.

Intuitively, $\rho, i \models \varphi$ means that the path ρ verifies ϕ from it's i-th symbol onward. We consider the language $L(\varphi) = \{w \mid w \in Paths \text{ and } w, 0 \models \varphi\}$ of a LTL formula φ, that is, the set of all paths verifying φ according to the semantics outlined previously.

3.2 LTL Model-Checking for PDSs

We recall in this Section the model-checking problem for PDSs and the automata-theoretic framework introduced in [2,6].

Let $\nu : Conf_{\mathcal{P}} \to 2^{AP}$ be a valuation function on configurations of a PDS $\mathcal{P} = (P, Act, \Gamma, \Delta, c_0)$. It is said to be *simple* if for all $w, w' \in \Gamma^*$, $p \in P$, and $\gamma \in \Gamma$, we have $\nu(\langle p, \gamma w \rangle) = \nu(\langle p, \gamma w' \rangle)$. Intuitively, a simple valuation is equivalent to a function $\nu : P \times \Gamma \to 2^{AP}$ that only depends on the control state and the top stack symbol.

Let $r = (r_i)_{i \geq 0}$ be an infinite run of $\mathcal{P}$. We define the image $\nu(r) = (\nu(r_i))_{i \geq 0}$ in *Paths* of r by the valuation function ν. We write that $r \models_\nu \varphi$ if $\nu(r), 0 \models \varphi$. The *model-checking* problem is defined as follows:

Definition 6 (The model-checking problem). *Given a LTL formula φ, a PDS $\mathcal{P}$ with a starting configuration c_0, and a simple valuation ν on configurations of $\mathcal{P}$, the model-checking problem consists in determining whether $\exists r \in Runs_\omega(\mathcal{P}), r \models_\nu \varphi$.*

In order to solve this problem, we consider the following class of automata:

Definition 7 (Büchi pushdown system). *A Büchi pushdown system is a tuple $\mathcal{BP} = (P, Act, \Gamma, \Delta, c_0, G)$ such that $(P, Act, \Gamma, \Delta, c_0)$ is a PDS and $G \subseteq P$ a set of final states.*

An *accepting run* of $\mathcal{BP}$ is an infinite run of the PDS $(P, Act, \Gamma, \Delta, c_0)$ that visits infinitely often configurations whose control state is in G. To these runs, we match *accepting traces.*

A BPDS can be seen as a product automaton between a PDS and Büchi automaton. The use of this model is the following:

Theorem 2. *Given a PDS $\mathcal{P}$ and a LTL formula φ, there exists a BPDS $\mathcal{BP}$ such that t is an accepting trace of $\mathcal{BP}$ if and only if t is a trace of $\mathcal{P}$ matched to a run r such that $r \models_\nu \varphi$.*

A *repeating head* of $\mathcal{BP}$ is an element $\langle p, \gamma \rangle$ of $G \times \Gamma$ such that $\exists w \in \Gamma^*$, $\langle p, \gamma \rangle \rightarrow^+_{\mathcal{BP}} \langle p, \gamma w \rangle$. Let $Rep(\mathcal{BP})$ be the finite set of repeating heads of $\mathcal{BP}$. The following lemma characterizes accepting runs with regards to repeating heads:

Lemma 2. *r is an accepting run of a BPDS $\mathcal{BP}$ if and only if $\mathcal{BP}$ has a repeating head $\langle p, \gamma \rangle$ such that r visits configurations in $\langle p, \gamma \Gamma * \rangle$ infinitely often.*

3.3 Single-Indexed LTL for CPDSs

Let $\mathcal{CP} = (\mathcal{P}_1, \dots, \mathcal{P}_n)$ be a CPDS, ν a simple valuation function on $Conf_{\mathcal{P}_1} \cup \dots \cup Conf_{\mathcal{P}_n}$, and for $i = 1, \dots, n$, let ψ_i be a LTL formula. The formula $\varphi = (\psi_1, \dots, \psi_n)$ is said to be a *single-indexed* LTL formula. We define the following semantics for single-indexed LTL formula on CPDSs:

Definition 8 (Single-indexed LTL model-checking). *Given a CPDS $\mathcal{CP} = (\mathcal{P}_1, \dots, \mathcal{P}_n)$, a global run g of $\mathcal{CP}$, and a single-indexed LTL formula $\varphi = (\psi_1, \dots, \psi_n)$, $g \models_\nu \varphi$ if and only if for each $i = 1, \dots, n$, $g^i \models_\nu \psi_i$. Finding such a global run g is called the* model-checking *problem.*

Intuitively, each PDS $\mathcal{P}_i$ in the CPDS satisfies formula f_i, but does so while synchronizing with the others PDSs. If the model-checking problem for CPDSs were decidable, so would be the reachability problem. However, since the latter is obviously undecidable, the former is as well.

We therefore seek to get at least an approximate answer to this problem. The issue with CPDSs is the following: for each $i = 1, \dots, n$, there may be a run r of the PDS $\mathcal{P}_i$ satisfying a formula ψ_i, but a global, synchronized run on the CPDS $(\mathcal{P}_1, \dots, \mathcal{P}_n)$ satisfying $\varphi = (\psi_1, \dots, \psi_n)$ may not exist.

4 An Abstraction Framework for Traces

We seek to approximate global runs of CPDSs. To do so, we want to abstract traces of their pushdown components. We remind here the mathematical framework presented by Bouajjani et al. in [3] in order to abstract the language $\mathcal{L}_{\mathcal{P}}(\{c_0\}, C) = \{t \in Traces(\mathcal{P}) | \exists c \in C, c_0 \xrightarrow{t}{}^*_{\mathcal{P}} c\}$ of traces of a PDS $\mathcal{P}$ leading from the starting configuration c_0 to a regular set of configurations C.

4.1 Abstractions and Galois Connections

Let $\mathcal{L} = (2^{Act^*}, \subseteq, \cup, \cap, \emptyset, Act^*)$ be the complete lattice of languages on Act.

Our abstraction of $\mathcal{L}$ requires a lattice $E = (D, \leq, \sqcup, \sqcap, \bot, \top)$, from now on called the *abstract lattice*, where D is a set called the abstract domain, as well as a pair of mappings (α, β) called a *Galois connection*, where $\alpha : 2^{Act^*} \rightarrow D$ and $\beta : D \rightarrow 2^{Act^*}$ are such that $\forall x \in 2^{Act^*}$, $\forall y \in D$, $\alpha(x) \leq y \Leftrightarrow x \subseteq \beta(y)$.

$\forall L \in \mathcal{L}$, given a Galois connection (α, β), we have $L \subseteq \beta(\alpha(L))$. Hence, the Galois connection can be used to over-approximate a language such as $\mathcal{L}_{\mathcal{P}}(\{c_0\}, C)$.

Moreover, it is easy to see that $\forall L_1, \forall L_2 \in \mathcal{L}$, $\alpha(L_1) \sqcap \alpha(L_2) = \bot$ if and only if $\beta(\alpha(L)) \cap \beta(\alpha(L)) = \emptyset$. We can therefore check the emptiness of intersections of over-approximations directly in the abstract domain.

4.2 Kleene Abstractions

As defined in [3], an abstract lattice $E = (D, \leq, \sqcup, \sqcap, \bot, \top)$ is said to be compatible with a Kleene algebra $K = (A, \oplus, \odot, \overline{0}, \overline{1})$ if $D = A$, $x \leq y \Leftrightarrow x \oplus y = y$, $\bot = \overline{0}$ and $\sqcup = \oplus$.

The Kleene algebra K is an *Act*-semiring if it can be generated by $\overline{0}$, $\overline{1}$, and elements of the form $v_a \in A$, $\forall a \in Act$. A *Kleene abstraction* is an abstraction such that the abstract lattice E is compatible with the Kleene algebra and the Galois connection $\alpha : 2^{Act^*} \rightarrow D$ and $\beta : D \rightarrow 2^{Act^*}$ is defined by:

$$\alpha(L) = \bigoplus_{a_1 \ldots a_n \in L} v_{a_1} \odot \ldots \odot v_{a_n}$$

$$\beta(x) = \left\{ a_1 \ldots a_n \in 2^{Act^*} \mid v_{a_1} \odot \ldots \odot v_{a_n} \leq x \right\}$$

Intuitively, a Kleene abstraction is such that the abstract operations $\oplus$, $\odot$, and $*$ can be matched to the union, the concatenation, and the Kleene closure of the languages of the lattice $\mathcal{L}$, $\overline{0}$ and $\overline{1}$ to the empty language and $\{\varepsilon\}$, v_a to the language $\{a\}$, the upper bound $\top \in K$ to Act^*, and the operation $\sqcap$ to the intersection of languages in the lattice $\mathcal{L}$.

In order to compute $\alpha(L)$ for a given language L, each word $a_1 \ldots a_n$ in L is matched to its abstraction $v_{a_1} \odot \ldots \odot v_{a_n}$, and we consider the sum of these abstractions. Moreover, we must have $v_\tau = \overline{1}$.

A *finite-chain* abstraction is such that the lattice $(K, \oplus)$ has no infinite ascending chains. Prefix and suffix abstractions are such examples on the lattice 2^W, where $W(n) = \{w \in Act^* \mid |w| \leq n\}$ is the set of words of length smaller than n.

4.3 The Set of K-Predecessors

Let $\mathcal{P} = (P, Act, \Gamma, \Delta, c_0)$ be a PDS and $K = (A, \oplus, \odot, \overline{0}, \overline{1})$ a Kleene algebra corresponding to a Kleene abstraction of the set *Lab*. We define inductively the set Π_K of path expressions as the smallest subset of K such that:

- $\overline{1} \in \Pi_K$;
- if $\pi \in \Pi_K$, then $\forall a \in Act$, $v_a \odot \pi \in \Pi_K$.

For a given path expression π, we define its length $|\pi|$ as the number of occurrences of simple elements of the form $\dot{v}_a$ in π.

A K-configuration of $\mathcal{P}$ is a pair (c, π) in $Conf^K_{\mathcal{P}} = P \times \Gamma^* \times \Pi_K$. We can extend the transition relation $\longrightarrow_{\mathcal{P}}$ to K-configurations with the following semantics: $\forall a \in Act$, if $c \xrightarrow{a}_{\mathcal{P}} c'$, then $\forall \pi \in \Pi_K$, $(c, v_a \odot \pi) \longrightarrow_{\mathcal{P},K} (c', \pi)$; $(c, v_a \odot \pi)$ is said to be an immediate K-predecessor of (c', π). The reachability relation $\rightsquigarrow_{\mathcal{P},K}$ is the reflexive transitive closure of $\longrightarrow_{\mathcal{P},K}$.

Given a set of configurations C, we introduce the set $pre^*_K(\mathcal{P}, C)$ of K-configurations (c, π) such that $(c, \pi) \rightsquigarrow_{\mathcal{P},K} (c', \overline{1})$ for $c' \in C$:

$$pre^*_K(\mathcal{P}, C) = \{(c', \pi) \mid c' \in pre^*(\mathcal{P}, C), \pi \leq \alpha(\mathcal{L}_{\mathcal{P}}(\{c'\}, C))\}$$

As we will see later, the abstract path expression π is meant to be the abstraction of an actual trace from c' to C.

4.4 *K*-automata

$\mathcal{P}$-automata are used to represent regular sets of configurations. They can be extended to K-automata in order to handle sets of K-configurations of a PDS $\mathcal{P}$.

Definition 9 (K-automaton). *A K-automaton is a tuple $\mathcal{A} = (Q, \Gamma, \delta, I, F)$ where Q is a finite set of control states, $\delta \subseteq Q \times \Gamma \times K \times Q \times$ a finite set of transition rules, $I = P$ the set of initial states, and $F \subseteq Q$ the set of final states.*

Intuitively, a $\mathcal{P}$-automaton can be seen as K-automaton whose transitions are all labelled by $\overline{1}$.

We define $\longrightarrow_{\mathcal{A}} \subseteq Q \times \Gamma^* \times K \times Q \times$ as the smallest transition relation satisfying:

- $q \xrightarrow{(\varepsilon, \overline{1})}_{\mathcal{A}} q'$ for every $q \in Q$;
- if $(q, \gamma, e, q') \in \delta$, then $q \xrightarrow{(\gamma, e)}_{\mathcal{A}} q'$;
- if $q \xrightarrow{(w, e)}_{\mathcal{A}} q'$ and $q' \xrightarrow{(w', e')}_{\mathcal{A}} q''$, then $q \xrightarrow{(ww', e \odot e')}_{\mathcal{A}} q''$.

We say that $\mathcal{A}$ accepts a K-configuration $(< p, w >, \pi)$ if $p \xrightarrow{(w,e)}_{\mathcal{A}} q$ for $q \in F$ and some $e \in K$ such that $\pi \leq e$. Let $L_K(\mathcal{A})$ be the set of all configurations accepted by $\mathcal{A}$, and $P_K(\mathcal{A}) = \{\pi \mid \exists c \in C, (c, \pi) \in L_K(\mathcal{A})\}$ the set of abstract traces matched to these configurations.

By labelling the $\mathcal{P}$-automaton $\mathcal{A}_{pre^*}$ accepting $pre^*(\mathcal{C})$ yielded by Theorem 1, the following theorem has been proven:

Theorem 3 (Bouajjani et al. [3]). *Let P be a PDS and $\mathcal{A}$ a $\mathcal{P}$-automaton accepting a regular set of configurations C. Then we can compute a K-automaton $\mathcal{A}_{pre^*_K}$ accepting the set $pre^*_K(P, C)$.*

From there, it is possible to compute the abstract trace language using the product automaton $\mathcal{A}'$ between $\mathcal{A}_{pre^*_K}$ and a $\mathcal{P}$-automaton accepting $\langle c_0, \Gamma^* \rangle$.

5 Abstract Model-Checking of LTL for CPDSs

In this section, as a main contribution of this paper, we will introduce a semi-decision procedure for model-checking LTL on CPDSs.

5.1 Abstracting Accepting Traces of a BPDS

By Lemma 2, each accepting run of a BPDS $\mathcal{BP}$ can be matched to a repeating head it visits infinitely often, and any run visiting a repeating head infinitely often is accepting. As a consequence, if we can for each repeating head compute (resp. abstract) the set of traces visiting it infinitely often, we can compute (resp. abstract) the set of accepting traces of the BPDS.

Let $\langle p, \gamma \rangle \in Rep(\mathcal{BP})$ be a repeating head. An accepting trace visiting $\langle p, \gamma\Gamma^* \rangle$ infinitely often can be split into two parts:

(1) first, it must reach the set $\langle p, \gamma\Gamma^* \rangle$ from the initial configuration c_0;
(2) then, it must infinitely often move from $\langle p, \gamma\Gamma^* \rangle$ to $\langle p, \gamma\Gamma^* \rangle$, using a sequence of transitions of length superior or equal to one.

In order to abstract the set of accepting traces visiting $\langle p, \gamma \rangle$ infinitely often, we first compute the set $pre^*_K(\mathcal{BP}, \langle p, \gamma\Gamma^* \rangle)$ of K-predecessors of configurations with this repeating head, using Theorem 3. Then, we consider the set $pre^*_K(\mathcal{BP}, \langle p, \gamma\Gamma^* \rangle) \cap (c_0 \times \Pi_K)$ and check its emptiness.

It will be empty if the repeating head is not reachable from the starting configuration c_0. Otherwise, it will be equal to the product of c_0 with an abstraction $I_{\langle p,\gamma \rangle}$ of the set of traces from c_0 to C. Therefore, the abstraction $I_{\langle p,\gamma \rangle} = P_K(pre^*_K(\mathcal{BP}, \langle p, \gamma\Gamma^* \rangle) \cap (c^i_0 \times \Pi_K)))$ yields part **(1)** of our abstraction of the set of accepting traces of the BDPS.

Next, we want to abstract the set of paths between two occurrences of the repeating head. To do so, we use again the set $pre^*_K(\mathcal{BP}, \langle p, \gamma\Gamma^* \rangle)$ of K-predecessors of configurations with a repeating head $\langle p, \gamma \rangle$. We consider its intersection $pre^*_K(\mathcal{BP}, \langle p, \gamma\Gamma^* \rangle) \cap \langle p, \gamma\Gamma^* \rangle \times \Pi_K$ with the product of the set of configurations with a repeating head $\langle p, \gamma \rangle$ with all path expressions.

This set of K-configurations abstracts traces between two configurations with the same repeating head $\langle p, \gamma\Gamma^* \rangle$. Therefore, the abstraction $L_{\langle p,\gamma \rangle} = P_K(pre^*_K(\mathcal{BP}, \langle p, \gamma\Gamma^* \rangle) \cap \langle p, \gamma\Gamma^* \rangle \times \Pi_K))$ yields part **(2)** of our abstraction of the set of accepting traces of the BDPS.

In an accepting run of a BPDS, part **(1)** happens once, then **(2)** occurs infinitely often. Hence, $R_{\langle p,\gamma \rangle} = I_{\langle p,\gamma \rangle} \odot (L_{\langle p,\gamma \rangle})^*$ is an abstraction of the set of accepting traces using the repeating head $\langle p, \gamma \rangle$ infinitely often. This set can be computed in a finite-chain abstraction framework.

We can finally compute an abstraction $R = \bigoplus_{\langle p,\gamma \rangle \in Rep(\mathcal{BP})} R_{\langle p,\gamma \rangle}$ of the set of all accepting traces of $\mathcal{BP}$ by abstracting the set of accepting traces for each repeating head, then considering the finite sum of these sets.

5.2 Abstracting the Model-Checking Problem for CPDSs

Let $\mathcal{CP} = (\mathcal{P}_1, \ldots, \mathcal{P}_n)$ be a CPDS and $\varphi = (\psi_1, \ldots, \psi_n)$ a single-indexed LTL formula. We want to abstract the model-checking problem $\mathcal{CP} \models \varphi$. Our intuition is, for each component $\mathcal{P}_i$, to abstract the set of paths verifying ψ_i, then examine the emptiness of the intersection of these abstractions.

If $n = 2$, then for $i = 1, 2$, to each PDS $\mathcal{P}_i$ and formula ψ_i, we match a BPDS $\mathcal{BP}_i$ according to Theorem 2 and compute an abstraction of its sets of paths R^i as outlined previously. $R^1 \sqcap R^2 = \perp$ implies that we can't find a trace that is accepting for both BPDSs, hence, there is no synchronized global run verifying φ.

However, in a global run of a CPDS, the execution paths of the pushdown components are interleaved. If the CPDS has more than two threads, synchronization signals with a third thread may occur in the global run but cannot be computed by abstracting runs of each BPDS on its own. We cannot therefore study the paths of a pushdown system $\mathcal{P}_i$ in isolation from the other components. Without loss of generality, we assume that a partition of Lab such that $Lab = \bigcup_{k \neq j} L_{k,j}$ and that transitions of the component $\mathcal{P}_i$ can only be labelled by elements in $Lab_i = \bigcup_{k \neq i} L_{i,k}$. Intuitively, each pair $(\mathcal{P}_i, \mathcal{P}_j)$ of pushdown components can only synchronize by using its own set of symbols Lab_i.

For each component $\mathcal{P}_i$, we then consider a new pushdown system $\mathcal{P}'_i$ that extends $\mathcal{P}_i$ with self-loops in each control state labelled by synchronization signals between pair of other processes in $Lab_{j,k}$, $j \neq k \neq i$. The following lemma holds:

Lemma 3. *If g is a global run of $\mathcal{CP}$, then g_i is a run of $\mathcal{P}'_i$.*

We then want abstract the set of paths of $\mathcal{P}'_i$ verifying ψ_i for each i and consider the intersection of these abstractions. If it is indeed empty, the same property holds for the intersection of the actual sets of paths, and no global run satisfying φ exists in $\mathcal{CP}$.

To do so, to each PDS $\mathcal{P}'_i$ and formula ψ_i, we match a BPDS $\mathcal{BP}_i$ according to Theorem 2. We then compute an abstraction R^i of the set of traces of the BPDS $\mathcal{BP}_i$, as outlined in Sect. 5.1. The following theorem then holds:

Theorem 4. *If $R^1 \sqcap \ldots \sqcap R^n = \bot$, then there is no global run of $\mathcal{CP}$ accepting the single-indexed LTL formula φ.*

We can therefore over-approximate the model-checking problem for CPDSs.

5.3 Using Our Framework in a CEGAR Scheme

In a manner similar to the work of Chaki et al. in [5], we propose a semi-decision procedure that, in case of termination, answers exactly whether there exists a global run of a CPDS $\mathcal{CP} = (\mathcal{P}_1, \ldots, \mathcal{P}_n)$ satisfies a single-indexed LTL formula $\varphi = (\psi_1, \ldots, \psi_n)$.

We introduce the following Counter-Example Guided Abstraction Refinement (CEGAR) scheme based on the finite-domain abstraction framework detailed previously, starting from $n = 1$.

Abstraction: for each PDS $\mathcal{P}'_i$, we compute an abstraction of the set of all accepting traces R^i of $\mathcal{BP}_i$ (the product between $\mathcal{P}'_i$ and the Büchi automaton representing ψ_i), using either the prefix or suffix abstraction of rank n introduced in [3];

Verification: we then check if $R^1 \sqcap \ldots \sqcap R^n = \bot$; if it is indeed true, then we conclude that no global run of $\mathcal{CP}$ can satisfy φ;

Counter-Example Validation: if there is such a global run, we then check if our abstraction introduced a spurious counter-example; if the counter-example is not spurious, then we conclude that there exists a global run of $\mathcal{CP}$ satisfying φ;

Refinement: if the counter-example was spurious, we go back to the first step, but use this time prefix and suffix abstractions of order $n + 1$.

If this procedure ends, we can decide the model-checking problem.

6 Application to Race Conditions

A race condition is an issue peculiar to multi-threaded programs that happens when events do not occur in the order the programmer intended, such concurrent operations on a shared memory location. In this section, we show a toy example of a race condition in a CPDS that can be detected thanks to our abstraction.

6.1 The CPDS Model

We consider a network composed of three processes: one of these handles memory allocation, and the two others processes can synchronize with it in order to use memory to fulfil requests. These processes are the following:

MEMORY: handles the amount of free memory available; this amount decreases when another process uses memory; the process will send different signals depending on whether there is free memory left or not;

CONSUME: can arbitrarily use the free memory handled by the previous process;

REQUEST: has a stack of requests to fulfil, and will use memory to do so.

If MEMORY runs out of free memory and another process try to use some nonetheless, MEMORY will reach an error state.

Each process can be modelled by a PDS as follows:

The Process MEMORY. Let m and m_e be its two states. Its stack alphabet is $\{\gamma, \bot\}$. The number of γ's in the stack corresponds to the amount of memory available to other threads, a single γ being enough to handle a single request. This process will pop a γ from its stack if it receives a signal *use*. As an internal action, it can also push a γ on its stack (allocating memory) if there is no free memory left. It can send a signal *on* to other threads if there is at least one γ on the stack, and will send off otherwise. If it receive a *use* signal but there is no γ on the stack, it will instead move to the error state m_e.

MEMORY is represented by the following PDS rules:

(r_1) $(m, \gamma) \xrightarrow{on} (m, \gamma)$; the process signals that there is still free memory left;
(r_2) $(m, \bot) \xrightarrow{off} (m, \bot)$; the process signals that there is no free memory left;
(r_3) $(m, \bot) \xrightarrow{\tau} (m, \gamma\bot)$; the process allocates memory;
(r_4) $(m, \gamma) \xrightarrow{use} (m, \varepsilon)$; the amount of free memory available decreases;
(r_5) $(m, \bot) \xrightarrow{use} (m_e, \bot)$; the process reaches its error state.

The Process CONSUME. Let c, c_{check}, and c_{done} be its three states and $\bot$ its only stack symbol. This process can check if there is any free memory left by exchanging a signal *on* with MEMORY, then consume one unit by sending a signal *use*.

CONSUME is represented by the following PDS rules:

(r_6) $(c, \bot) \xrightarrow{on} (c_{check}, \bot)$; the process checks if there is any memory left;
(r_7) $(c_{check}, \bot) \xrightarrow{use} (c_{done}, \bot)$; the process uses one unit of memory;
(r_8) $(c_{done}, \bot) \xrightarrow{\tau} (c, \bot)$; the process goes back to its initial waiting state.

The Process REQUEST. Let r and r_{check} be its two states. Its stack alphabet is $\{\gamma, \bot\}$. The number of γ's in the stack corresponds to the number of requests it must handle. As an internal action, it can receive a new request and push a γ symbol on its stack. This process can check if there is any free memory left by exchanging a signal *on* with MEMORY, then handle a request and consume one unit by sending a signal *use*, popping a symbol γ from its own stack.

REQUEST is represented by the following PDS rules:

(r_{9a}) $(r, \gamma) \xrightarrow{\tau} (r, \gamma\gamma)$; the process adds a new request;
(r_{9b}) $(r, \bot) \xrightarrow{\tau} (r, \bot\gamma)$; the process adds a new request;
(r_{10}) $(r, \gamma) \xrightarrow{on} (r_{check}, \gamma)$; the process checks if there is any free memory left;
(r_{11}) $(r_{check}, \gamma) \xrightarrow{use} (r, \varepsilon)$; the process handles a request while using one unit of memory.

6.2 Using a Single-Indexed LTL Formula

Let P be the set of all states of the CPDS. We define $AP = P$ and a simple valuation ν such that for each stack symbol x and $p \in P$, $\nu(\langle p, x\rangle) = \{p\}$. We express the desirable behaviour of the CPDS as the conjunction of the three following LTL formulas:

- $\psi_{MEMORY} = G(\neg m_e)$; the process MEMORY can't reach its error state;
- $\psi_{CONSUME} = GF(c)$; the process CONSUME will always go back to its waiting state c;
- $\psi_{REQUEST} = G(r_{check}) \Rightarrow F(r)$; the process REQUEST, when it starts handling a request, must complete it and go back to its default state.

We then use a CEGAR scheme to check if there is a global run g such that the single-indexed formula $(\psi_{MEMORY}, \psi_{CONSUME}, \psi_{REQUEST})$ does not hold for g. Our algorithm finds such a counter-example in seven steps.

Intuitively, a race condition happens when both CONSUME and REQUEST try to use memory while MEMORY only has a single unit available.

6.3 An Erroneous Trace

We write $(r_i) \leftrightarrow (r_j)$ if we apply two rules that synchronize. We start from the initial configuration:

$$(\langle m, \bot\rangle, \langle c, \bot\rangle, \langle r, \bot\rangle)$$

(r_3) MEMORY allocates memory:

$$(\langle m, \gamma\bot\rangle, \langle c, \bot\rangle, \langle r, \bot\rangle)$$

$(r_6) \leftrightarrow (r_1)$ MEMORY sends *on* to CONSUME:

$$(\langle m, \gamma\bot\rangle, \langle c_{check}, \bot\rangle, \langle r, \bot\rangle)$$

(r_{9b}) REQUEST adds a new request:

$$(\langle m, \gamma\bot\rangle, \langle c_{check}, \bot\rangle, \langle r, \gamma\bot\rangle)$$

$(r_{10}) \leftrightarrow (r_1)$ MEMORY sends *on* to REQUEST:

$$(\langle m, \gamma\bot\rangle, \langle c_{check}, \bot\rangle, \langle r_{check}, \gamma\bot\rangle)$$

$(r_7) \leftrightarrow (r_4)$ CONSUME sends *use* to MEMORY and the latter process uses one unit of memory:

$$(\langle m, \bot\rangle, \langle c_{done}, \bot\rangle, \langle r_{check}, \gamma\bot\rangle)$$

(r_8) CONSUME goes back to default mode:

$$(\langle m, \bot\rangle, \langle c, \bot\rangle, \langle r_{check}, \gamma\bot\rangle)$$

$(r_{11}) \leftrightarrow (r_5)$: REQUEST sends *use* to MEMORY and the latter process reaches an error mode, violating ψ_{MEMORY}:

$$(\langle m_e, \bot\rangle, \langle c, \bot\rangle, \langle r, \bot\rangle)$$

This an erroneous execution path in 7 steps. We can find it using a prefix abstraction of order 7.

7 Conclusion and Future Works

In this paper, we study the model-checking problem of single-indexed LTL properties for CPDSs, which is unfortunately undecidable. We design an algorithm to abstract the model-checking problem that relies on the automata-theoretic approach of [2,6] and the Kleene abstraction framework of [3]. We then apply this technique to a toy example and find a race condition.

An automata-theoretic approach to the CTL model-checking problem for PDSs has been introduced in [9]. It remains to be seen if the CTL model-checking problem for CPDSs can be abstracted in a similar manner to LTL.

References

1. Atig, M.F.: Model-checking of ordered multi-pushdown automata. Log. Methods Comput. Sci. **8**(3), (2012)
2. Bouajjani, A., Esparza, J., Maler, O.: Reachability analysis of pushdown automata: application to model-checking. In: Mazurkiewicz, A., Winkowski, J. (eds.) CONCUR 1997. LNCS, vol. 1243, pp. 135–150. Springer, Heidelberg (1997). https://doi.org/10.1007/3-540-63141-0_10
3. Bouajjani, A., Esparza, J., Touili, T.: A generic approach to the static analysis of concurrent programs with procedures. In: Proceedings of the 30th ACM SIGPLAN-SIGACT Symposium on Principles of Programming Languages, POPL 2003, pp. 62–73, New York. ACM (2003)
4. Bouajjani, A., Müller-Olm, M., Touili, T.: Regular symbolic analysis of dynamic networks of pushdown systems. In: Abadi, M., de Alfaro, L. (eds.) CONCUR 2005. LNCS, vol. 3653, pp. 473–487. Springer, Heidelberg (2005). https://doi.org/10.1007/11539452_36
5. Chaki, S., Clarke, E., Kidd, N., Reps, T., Touili, T.: Verifying concurrent message-passing C programs with recursive calls. In: Hermanns, H., Palsberg, J. (eds.) TACAS 2006. LNCS, vol. 3920, pp. 334–349. Springer, Heidelberg (2006). https://doi.org/10.1007/11691372_22

6. Esparza, J., Hansel, D., Rossmanith, P., Schwoon, S.: Efficient algorithms for model checking pushdown systems. In: Emerson, E.A., Sistla, A.P. (eds.) CAV 2000. LNCS, vol. 1855, pp. 232–247. Springer, Heidelberg (2000). https://doi.org/10.1007/10722167_20
7. Pommellet, A., Touili, T.: Static analysis of multithreaded recursive programs communicating via Rendez-Vous. In: Chang, B.-Y.E. (ed.) APLAS 2017. LNCS, vol. 10695, pp. 235–254. Springer, Cham (2017). https://doi.org/10.1007/978-3-319-71237-6_12
8. Qadeer, S., Rehof, J.: Context-bounded model checking of concurrent software. In: Halbwachs, N., Zuck, L.D. (eds.) TACAS 2005. LNCS, vol. 3440, pp. 93–107. Springer, Heidelberg (2005). https://doi.org/10.1007/978-3-540-31980-1_7
9. Song, F., Touili, T.: Efficient CTL model-checking for pushdown systems. Theor. Comput. Sci. **549**, 127–145 (2014)
10. Song, F., Touili, T.: Model-checking dynamic pushdown networks. Form. Asp. Comput. **27**(2), 397–421 (2015)
11. La Torre, S., Madhusudan, P., Parlato, G.: A robust class of context-sensitive languages. In: 22nd Annual IEEE Symposium on Logic in Computer Science (LICS 2007), pp. 161–170, July 2007

Exploiting Local Persistency for Reduced State Space Generation

Kamel Barkaoui[1], Hanifa Boucheneb[2(✉)], and Zhiwu Li[3,4]

[1] Laboratoire CEDRIC, Conservatoire National des Arts et Métiers, 192 rue Saint Martin, Paris Cedex 03, France
kamel.barkaoui@cnam.fr

[2] Laboratoire VeriForm, Department of Computer Engineering and Software Engineering, École Polytechnique de Montréal, P.O. Box 6079, Station Centre-ville, Montréal, Québec H3C 3A7, Canada
hanifa.boucheneb@polymtl.ca

[3] Institute of Systems Engineering, Macau University of Science and Technology, Taipa, Macau
zhwli@xidian.edu.cn

[4] School of Electro-Mechanical Engineering, Xidian University, Xi'an 710071, China

Abstract. This paper deals with the partial order techniques of Petri nets, based on persistent sets and step graphs. To take advantage of the strengths of each method, it proposes the persistent step sets as a parametric combination of the both methods. The persistent step sets method allows to fix, for each marking, the set of transitions to be covered by the selected steps and then to control their maximal length and number. Moreover, this persistent step selective search preserves, at least, deadlocks of Petri nets.

This paper also provides two practical computation procedures of the persistent step sets based on the strong-persistent sets [5,10] and the persistent sets, respectively.

Keywords: Petri nets · Reachability analysis
State explosion problem · Persistent sets · Partial order techniques
Step graphs

1 Introduction

The state explosion problem is the main obstacle for the verification of concurrent systems, as they are generally based on an interleaving semantics, where all possible firing orders of concurrent actions are exhaustively explored. Different techniques for fighting this problem have been proposed such as structural analysis, symmetries and partial orders.

The structural analysis attempts to find a relationship between the behaviour of the net and its structure. Its results are of particular importance since initial marking is considered as a parameter. The net structure can be studied through

M. F. Atig et al. (Eds.): VECoS 2018, LNCS 11181, pp. 166–181, 2018.
https://doi.org/10.1007/978-3-030-00359-3_11

its associated incidence matrix and the corresponding net state equation leading mainly to the concept of place invariants [4] or through topological properties of the interplay between conflict and synchronisation of remarkable substructures of the net such siphons and traps leading to necessary and/or sufficient structural conditions to check general behavioural properties such as liveness [3,7] for large subclasses of place/transition nets [1,2].

The second well-accepted technique to tackle combinatorial explosion in model-checking consists into exploitation of symmetries over states and the transition relation [6] leading to the building of a quotient graph of equivalence classes of states, that may be exponentially smaller than the full state graph and preserving many behavioural properties of interest.

The partial order techniques have been proven to be the most successful in practice. We distinguish two classes of partial order techniques: partial order reduction [5,8,9,11–13] and step graph [14]. Partial order reduction techniques, such as the ample sets [8,9], the stubborn sets [11–13] and the persistent sets [5], deal with the state explosion problem by avoiding as much as possible to explore firing sequences that are equivalent w.r.t. the properties of interest (deadlock freeness, reachability, liveness, or linear properties)[1]. The step graph methods explore all the transitions of the state space but some of them are fired together in atomic steps. The common characteristics of all these methods is to reduce the state space to be explored, by selecting the actions or sets of actions (steps) to be executed from each state. The selection procedure of actions or steps relies on the notion of independent actions. Two actions are said to be independent, if whenever they are enabled, they can be fired in both orders and the firing of one of them does not inhibit the occurrence of the other. Moreover, their firing in both orders leads to the same state. Both of these conditions constitute the well known diamond property.

Each of the partial order reduction methods above provides sufficient conditions that ensure, at least, preservation of deadlocks. Thus, the set ST of the selected transitions or steps is only empty for the deadlock markings (i.e., markings with no enabled transitions). The other sufficient conditions are generally based on the structure of the model, the property to be verified and the current marking. Their aim is to ensure independency between transitions of ST and the others. Indeed, for the ample sets method [8,9], there is no transition outside ST that is firable before all transitions of ST and, at the same time, is dependent of at least a transition of ST. For the stubborn sets method [11–13], ST contains at least an enabled transition that cannot be disabled by the transitions outside ST and each of its transitions t is independent of all transitions outside ST that are firable before t. The persistent sets method [5] is considered a particular case of the stubborn sets method, where all transitions of ST are enabled. For the covering-steps graph method [14], the set of steps to be fired from each marking must cover the set of enabled transitions.

[1] Two firing sequences are equivalent w.r.t. some property, if they cannot be distinguished by the property.

To achieve more reductions, in [10], the authors have combined this technique with the persistent sets method. This combination consists to firstly compute a persistent set for the current marking and then look for firing steps within this persistent set. For these approaches, the transitions within the same step are neither in weak-conflict nor in structural conflict with the partially enabled transitions.

This paper is interested in the persistent sets and the step graphs. To take advantage of the strengths of each method, it investigates their combination and proposes persistent step sets method. Persistent-step sets method is a parametric combination of persistent sets with step graphs that allows to fix, for each marking, the set of transitions to be covered by the selected steps and then to control their maximal length and number.

The rest of the paper is organized as follows. Section 2 fixes some classical definitions and notations used throughout the paper. Section 3 presents the strong-persistent sets [5,10], the persistent sets (a weaker version of the strong-persistent sets) and the step graph methods, while pointing out their weaknesses. Section 4 provides a formal definition of persistent step sets and proves that they yield graphs preserving deadlocks of Petri nets. Section 5 establishes two computation procedures of persistent step sets that are based on strong-persistent sets and persistent sets, respectively. Conclusions are presented in Sect. 6.

2 Preliminaries

Let P be a nonempty set. A multi-set over P is a function $M : P \longrightarrow \mathbb{N}$, $\mathbb{N}$ being the set of natural numbers, defined also by the linear combination over P: $\sum_{p \in P} M(p) \times p$. We denote by P_{MS} and 0 the set of all multi-sets over P and the empty multi-set, respectively. Operations on multi-sets are defined as usual. Notice that any subset $X \subseteq P$ can be defined as a multi-set over P: $X = \sum_{p \in X} 1 \times p$.

An ordinary Petri net (PN in short) is a tuple $PN = (P, T, pre, post)$ where:

- P and T are finite and nonempty sets of places and transitions with $P \cap T = \emptyset$,
- pre and $post$ are the backward and forward incidence functions over the set of transitions T ($pre, post : T \longrightarrow 2^P$).

For $t \in T$, $pre(t)$ and $post(t)$ are the sets of input and output places of t, denoted also by ${}^\bullet t$ and $t^\bullet$, respectively. Similarly, the sets of input and output transitions of a place $p \in P$ are defined by ${}^\bullet p = \{t \in T \mid p \in t^\bullet\}$ and $p^\bullet = \{t \in T \mid p \in {}^\bullet t\}$, respectively.

Two transitions t and t' are in structural conflict, denoted by $t \perp t'$ iff $pre(t) \cap pre(t') \neq \emptyset$. We denote by $CFS(t) = \{t' \in T | t \perp t'\} = ({}^\bullet t)^\bullet$ the set of transitions in structural conflict with t. They are in weak conflict iff $t \perp^* t'$, where $\perp^*$ is the transitive closure of $\perp$. We denote by $CFS^*(t) = \{t' \in T | t \perp^* t'\}$ the set of transitions in weak conflict with t. Notice that $t \in CFS(t)$ and $CFS(t) \subseteq CFS^*(t)$.

A marking of an ordinary Petri net indicates the distribution of tokens over its places. It is defined as a multi-set over places. A marked PN is a pair $\mathcal{N} = (PN, M_0)$, where PN is an ordinary Petri net and $M_0 \in P_{MS}$ is its initial marking. Starting from its initial marking, PN evolves by firing enabled transitions. For the following, we fix a marked PN $\mathcal{N}$, a marking $M \in P_{MS}$ and a transition $t \in T$ of $\mathcal{N}$.

The transition t is enabled at M, denoted $M[t\rangle$ iff all the required tokens for firing t are present in M, i.e., $M \geq pre(t)$. The transition t is partially enabled in M iff t is not enabled in M and, at least, one of its input places is marked. In case t is enabled at M, its firing leads to the marking $M' = M - pre(t) + post(t)$. The notation $M[t\rangle M'$ means that t is enabled at M and M' is the marking reached from M by t. We denote by $En(M)$ the set of transitions enabled at M, i.e., $En(M) = \{t \in T \mid M \geq pre(t)\}$. The marking M is a deadlock iff $En(M) = \emptyset$.

For any sequence of transitions $\omega = t_1t_2...t_n \in T^+$ of $\mathcal{N}$, the usual notation $M[t_1t_2...t_n\rangle$ means that there exist markings $M_1, ..., M_n$ such that $M_1 = M$ and $M_i[t_i\rangle M_{i+1}$, for $i \in [1, n-1]$ and $M_n[t_n\rangle$. The sequence ω is said to be a firing sequence of M. The notation $M[t_1t_2...t_n\rangle M'$ gives, in addition, the marking reached by the sequence (M' is reachable from M by ω). By convention, we have $M[\epsilon\rangle M$. We denote by $\overrightarrow{M}$ the set of markings reachable from M, i.e., $\overrightarrow{M} = \{M' \in P_{MS} | \exists \omega \in T^*, M[\omega\rangle M'\}$.

A firing sequence ω of M is maximal iff it is infinite (i.e., $\omega \in T^\infty$) or it is finite and leads to a deadlock marking. The transition t is potentially firable from M if there exists a sequence $\omega \in T^*$ s.t. $M[\omega t\rangle$. Two sequences of transitions ω and ω' are equivalent, denoted by $\omega \equiv \omega'$ iff they are identical or each one can be obtained from the other by a series of permutations of transitions. If $\omega \equiv \omega'$ then $\forall M', M'' \in P_{MS}, (M[\omega\rangle M' \wedge M[\omega'\rangle M'') \Rightarrow M' = M''$. We denote by $[\omega]$ the set of transitions in ω. The firing sequences of $\mathcal{N}$ are the firing sequences of its initial marking.

The different possible evolutions of $\mathcal{N}$ are represented in a marking graph MG defined by the structure $MG = (\overrightarrow{M_0}, [\rangle, M_0)$. Let n be a natural number. The marked PN $\mathcal{N}$ is n-bounded iff for every reachable marking of M_0, the number of tokens in each place does not exceed n. It is safe iff it is 1-bounded. It is bounded iff it is k-bounded for some natural number k.

A firing step τ of $\mathcal{N}$ is a non-empty subset of transitions ($\tau \subseteq T$) fired simultaneously and atomically from a marking of $\mathcal{N}$. From an interleaving semantic point of view, it represents an abstraction of all firing orders of its transitions. For instance, $\tau = \{t_1, t_2, t_3\}$ represents the following six sequences: $t_1t_2t_3$, $t_1t_3t_2$, $t_2t_1t_3$, $t_2t_3t_1$, $t_3t_1t_2$ and $t_3t_2t_1$. The intermediate markings are abstracted to keep only the markings before and after the firing step.

Let $M \in P_{MS}$ be a marking and τ a firing step of $\mathcal{N}$. The firing step τ is enabled in M, denoted by $M[\tau\rangle$ iff $M \geq \sum_{t\in\tau} pre(t)$, which means that there are enough tokens to fire concurrently all the transitions within the step. If τ is enabled in M, its firing leads to the marking $M' = M + \sum_{t\in\tau}(post(t) - pre(t))$. The notation $M[\tau\rangle M'$ means that τ is enabled at M and M' is the marking reached from M by τ. We denote by $EnS(M)$ the set of all enabled steps in M, i.e., $EnS(M) = \{\tau \subseteq T \mid \tau \neq \emptyset \wedge M \geq \sum_{t \in \tau} pre(t)\}$. The firing step τ is maximal in M iff it is maximal for the inclusion in $EnS(M)$, i.e., $M \geq \sum_{t \in \tau} pre(t)$ and $\forall t' \in En(M) - \tau, M \not\geq pre(t') + \sum_{t \in \tau} pre(t)$.

A step graph of $\mathcal{N}$ is a structure $SG = (MM, R, M_0)$, where $MM \subseteq \overrightarrow{M_0}$ is a subset of reachable markings, M_0 is the initial marking and $R \subseteq MM \times 2^T \times MM$ is relation defined by $(M, \tau, M') \in R \Rightarrow M[\tau\rangle M'$.

For the rest of paper, we fix an ordinary Petri net $\mathcal{N} = (P, T, pre, post, M_0)$.

3 Persistent Sets and Step Graphs

3.1 Persistent Sets

Let M be a marking. Informally, a persistent set of M is a subset μ of enabled transitions such that no transition of μ can be disabled, as long as no transition of μ is fired [5,10]. A persistent graph is obtained by recursively firing from each marking a persistent set. Persistent graphs preserve deadlocks of Petri nets [10].

However, this strong definition of persistent sets can be weakened while preserving deadlocks of Petri nets. The idea comes from the stubborn sets [13]. But unlike the stubborn sets, all the transitions inside a persistent set are enabled. To distinguish between the two definitions of persistent sets, the persistent sets of [5,10] are referred to as strong-persistent sets.

Definition 1. *Let M be a marking and $\mu \subseteq En(M)$ a subset of enabled transitions.*
Formally, the subset μ is a strong-persistent set of M, if all the following conditions are satisfied:

- $En(M) \neq \emptyset \Leftrightarrow \mu \neq \emptyset$.
- $\forall t \in \mu, \forall \omega \in (T - \mu)^+, M[\omega\rangle \Rightarrow M[\omega t\rangle$.
- $\forall t \in \mu, \forall \omega \in (T - \mu)^+, M[\omega t\rangle \Rightarrow M[t\omega\rangle$.

The subset μ is a persistent set of M, if it satisfies all the following conditions:

- *D0:* $En(M) \neq \emptyset \Leftrightarrow \mu \neq \emptyset$.
- *D1:* $\exists t \in \mu, \forall \omega \in (T - \mu)^+, M[\omega\rangle \Rightarrow M[\omega t\rangle$.
- *D2:* $\forall t \in \mu, \forall \omega \in (T - \mu)^+, M[\omega t\rangle \Rightarrow M[t\omega\rangle$.

Intuitively, Condition $D0$ ensures that the persistent set of M is empty only if M is a deadlock. Conditions $D1$ means that there is at least a transition inside μ such that no transition outside μ can disable it. Condition $D2$ means that if some sequence ω with no transition from μ is firable before any transition t of μ, then it is also firable after t.

The transitions of μ that satisfy $D1$ are called the key-transitions of μ [13]. Note that in strong-persistent sets, all their transitions are key-transitions.

In the following, we investigate the combination of the persistent sets with the step graphs, in order to achieve more reduction.

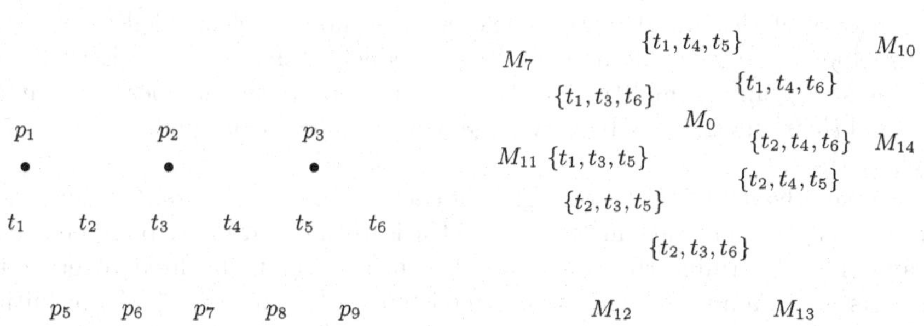

p_1 p_2 p_3
t_1 t_2 t_3 t_4 t_5 t_6
p_4 p_5 p_6 p_7 p_8 p_9

Fig. 1. Model PN1

M_8
M_9
M_7
$\{t_1, t_4, t_5\}$
M_{10}
$\{t_1, t_3, t_6\}$
$\{t_1, t_4, t_6\}$
M_0
M_{11}
$\{t_1, t_3, t_5\}$
$\{t_2, t_4, t_6\}$
M_{14}
$\{t_2, t_4, t_5\}$
$\{t_2, t_3, t_5\}$
$\{t_2, t_3, t_6\}$
M_{12}
M_{13}

Fig. 2. Step graph of PN1

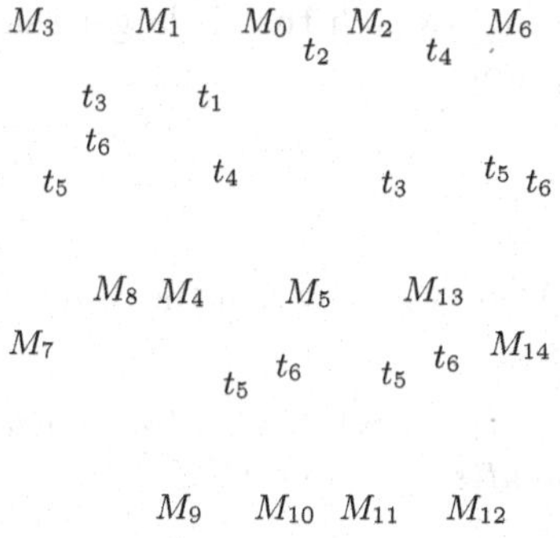

M_3 M_1 M_0 M_2 M_6
t_2 t_4
t_3 t_1
t_6
t_5 t_4 t_3 t_5 t_6
M_8 M_4 M_5 M_{13}
M_7
t_5 t_6 t_5 t_6 M_{14}
M_9 M_{10} M_{11} M_{12}

Fig. 3. A persistent set graph of PN1

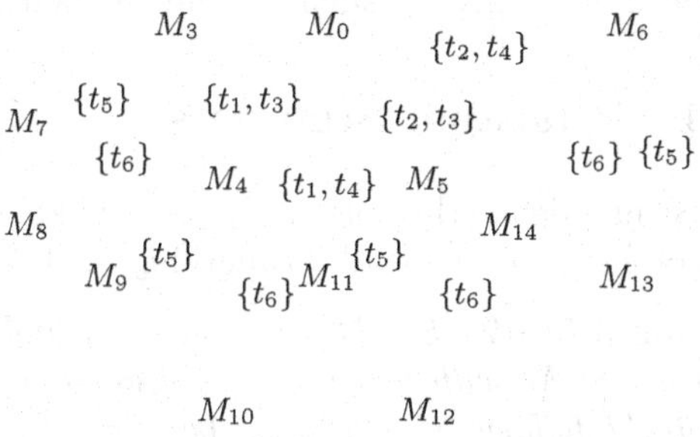

M_3 M_0 $\{t_2, t_4\}$ M_6
M_7 $\{t_5\}$ $\{t_1, t_3\}$ $\{t_2, t_3\}$
$\{t_6\}$ M_4 $\{t_1, t_4\}$ M_5 $\{t_6\}$ $\{t_5\}$
M_8 M_{14}
M_9 $\{t_5\}$ $\{t_6\}$ M_{11} $\{t_5\}$ $\{t_6\}$ M_{13}
M_{10} M_{12}

Fig. 4. A persistent step graph of PN1

3.2 Step Graphs

The aim of the step graph methods is to represent by a single path a largest possible set of equivalent maximal firing sequences of the model, by choosing appropriately, from each marking, the transitions to be fired together in steps. All transitions of the equivalent sequences are represented in the path but the concurrent ones are grouped together in steps. Step graphs allow to reduce the path depths.

However, in case there are several sets of transitions that are independent from each other, the number of steps and their lengths may be very large. For example, consider the model PN1 at Fig. 1. Its marking graph consists of 27 nodes and 54 arcs. Its initial marking M_0 has 3 persistent sets that are independent from each other: $\{t_1, t_2\}$, $\{t_3, t_4\}$ and $\{t_5, t_6\}$. A persistent graph of PN1 is shown in Fig. 3. Note that there are different persistent graphs but they have all the same size ($2^4 - 1 = 15$ nodes and $15 - 1 = 14$ arcs). Using the 3 independent persistent sets of M_0, steps can be built by picking a transition from each persistent set. Its step graph is shown in Fig. 2 and consists of $9 = 2^3 + 1$ nodes,

$8 = 2^3$ arcs and 2^3 maximal steps. It is a covering-step graph, as the set of steps selected from each marking covers all its enabled transitions. But, the number of successors of the initial marking exceeds the number of enabled transitions and is exponential with the number of independent persistent sets. Even if the covering-step graph is smaller than the persistent graph, the number of maximal steps and their lengths may be very large, which limits the usefulness of the step graph method.

To take advantage of the strengths of each method, the persistent sets and step graphs are combined in [10]. The idea is to compute a strong-persistent set and then determine the transitions within this set to be fired together in steps. As an example, for the strong-persistent set $\{t_1, t_2, t_3, t_4\}$ of the initial marking M_0, we can build 4 steps: $\{t_1, t_3\}$, $\{t_1, t_4\}$, $\{t_2, t_3\}$ and $\{t_2, t_4\}$. The resulting reduced graph is reported in Fig. 4 and consists of 13 nodes and 12 arcs. This combination allows to control the number and the length of the steps to be considered from each marking, while yielding a graph that is larger than the step graph but smaller than the persistent graph.

4 Persistent Step Sets

We first define the notion of persistent step sets. Then, we show that the resulting graphs preserve deadlock markings of Petri nets.

Definition 2. *Let M be a marking and $SS = \{\tau_1, ..., \tau_n\}$ a set of n enabled steps in M with $n > 0$. The set SS is a persistent step set in M if it satisfies all the following conditions: Let $\mu = \bigcup_{i \in [1,n]} \tau_i$.*

- *$DS0$: $En(M) \neq \emptyset \Leftrightarrow \mu \neq \emptyset$.*
- *$DS1$: $\forall (t_1, ...t_n) \in \tau_1 \times ... \times \tau_n, \forall \omega \in (T - \bigcup_{j \in [1,n]} \{t_j\})^+$,*

$$(M[\omega\rangle \Rightarrow \exists i \in [1,n], \exists t \in \tau_i, M[\omega t\rangle) \wedge (\forall i \in [1,n], M[\omega t_i\rangle \Rightarrow M[t_i \omega\rangle)$$

Condition $DS0$ is identical to $D0$. Intuitively, Condition $DS1$ means that as long as a sequence does not contain all transitions of, at least, a step (even scattered), there is always a possibility to extend this sequence with a missed transition of a step. Moreover, if a missed transition is firable after ω then it can be shifted to the front of the sequence of ω to, at the end, constitute a firing step. Note that if SS is a persistent step set of M such that all its steps are singletons, then μ is a persistent set of M. Indeed, in this case $\mu = \{t_1, ..., t_n\}$ and then $DS0 \wedge DS1$ implies $D0 \wedge D1 \wedge D2$.

Example 1. Consider the model PN1 at Fig. 1.

- The set $\mu = \{t_1, t_2, t_3\}$ is a persistent set but is not a strong-persistent set of the initial marking $M_0 = p_1 + p_2 + p_3$, as it satisfies conditions $D0$ and $D1$ (for only t_1 and t_2). There are two key-transitions in μ: t_1 and t_2.
- The step set $SS = \{\{t_1, t_3\}, \{t_2, t_3\}\}$ is not a persistent step set of M_0, as it does not satisfy Condition $DS1$. Indeed, we have $M_0[t_4 t_1\rangle$ and $\neg M_0[t_4 t_1 t_3\}\rangle$.

Theorem 1. *Let M be a marking reached in a persistent step selective search from M_0 and D a deadlock marking reachable from M in the Petri net. Then D will also be reached by the persistent step selective search from M_0.*

Proof. The marking M is reachable in the Petri net. Let ω be a firing sequence leading to the marking D from M in the Petri net. The proof is by induction on the length of ω.

(a) If $\omega = \epsilon$ then $M = D$.
(b) If $\omega = t$ and $\{t\} \in SS$ then D is reached by the persistent step selective search.
(c) If $\omega = t$ and $\{t\} \notin SS$ then, by $DS1$, D is not a deadlock marking as there is, at least, a transition from μ that is firable after t, which is in contradiction with the fact that D is a deadlock.

Suppose that Theorem 1 holds for any marking M' (reachable in a persistent step set selective search) and D reachable from M' by a sequence ω' such that $|\omega'| < |\omega|$.

- If there is no step of SS (scattered or not) in ω, then, by $DS1$, there is, at least, a missed transition of a step that is firable after ω. It means that D has, at least, a successor, which is in contradiction with the fact that D is a deadlock.
- If there is, at least a step τ of SS, scattered or not, in ω, then these transitions of this step can be shifted to the front to constitute a step firable from M. Firing this step from M leads to some marking M' that is reachable by the persistent step selective search. Moreover, D is reachable from M', in the Petri net, by a sequence ω' s.t. $|\omega'| < |\omega|$. Therefore, D is reachable by the persistent step selective search from M_0. □

5 Parametric Combination of Persistent Sets with Step Graphs

From a practical point of view, the above definition of persistent step sets is not useful. We propose, in the following, two parametric selection algorithms of persistent step sets, based on strong-persistent sets and persistent sets, respectively.

For a given marking M and a subset S of transitions enabled in M ($S \subseteq En(M)$), the idea is to compute a persistent step set that covers, at least, the transitions of S. Unlike, the approach proposed in [10], the set S is not necessarily a strong-persistent set. As we will show, according to the parameter S, the provided persistent step set is either a (strong) persistent set, a covering-step set or a set of steps that covers partially the enabled transitions in M.

We suppose that there are two available computation procedures PS and PS^+ of strong-persistent sets and persistent sets, respectively. For a given marking M and a transition t enabled in M, $PS(t, M)$ returns a persistent set of M, where at least t is a key-transition. This set can be computed from $\{t\}$ by adding recursively the enabled transitions that prevent it to satisfy $D1$ and $D2$, until reaching a fixed point. For $PS^{+}(t, M)$, the set returned is a strong-persistent set of M calculated from $PS(t, M)$ by adding recursively $PS(t', M)$, for each non key-transition t' within the set, until reaching a fixed point. Thus, the transitions of $PS^{+}(t, M)$ are all key-transitions.

5.1 Computing Strong-Persistent Step Sets

A computation procedure of strong-persistent step sets is provided in Algorithm 1. For a given marking M and a set of enabled transitions $S \subseteq En(M)$, Algorithm 1 returns a set of steps firable from M. The parameter S allows to specify the set of enabled transitions that must be, at least, covered by the set of steps. The computed set of steps is a sort of product of some disjoint strong-persistent sets ($PS^{+}(t, M)$, for t chosen from the input set S). The first term of the product is $R = PS^{+}(t, M)$, where t is chosen randomly in S' (a copy of S). Then, the transitions of R are deleted from S', to ensure that the next terms are disjoints from those computed so far. If the resulting S' is not empty, then the same process is repeated to compute the next term of the product, and so on. Theorem 2 establishes that the returned set of steps is a persistent step set.

Algorithm 1. Strong-persistent step set of a marking M covering the transitions of S

Input : A marking M and a subset S of enabled transitions such that $S \neq \emptyset$;
Output : A strong-persistent step set SS of M w.r.t. S;
$SS = \emptyset$; $S' = S$;
while $(S' \neq \emptyset)$ **do**
    Choose $t \in S'$;
    $R = PS^{+}(t, M)$;
    $S' = S' - R$;
    $SS = SS \otimes R$;
end while
return SS;
[For $X \in 2^{T}$ and a set $Y \subseteq T$, $X \otimes Y = \{x \cup \{y\} \mid x \in X \wedge y \in Y\}$. By convention, $\emptyset \otimes Y = \{\{y\} \mid y \in Y\}$]

Example 2. Consider the initial marking M_0 of the model PN1 at Fig. 1.

- For $S = \{t_1, t_2, t_3\}$, Algorithm 1 computes SS as follows. It starts by setting SS and S' to $\emptyset$ and $\{t_1, t_2, t_3\}$, respectively. If t_1 of S' is the first transition selected in the loop *while*, then $R = \{t_1, t_2\}$, $S' = \{t_3\}$ and $SS = \emptyset \otimes R = \{\{t_1\}, \{t_2\}\}$. For the second iteration, t_3 is selected, then $R = \{t_3, t_4\}$, $S' = \emptyset$ and $SS = SS \otimes \{t_3, t_4\} = \{\{t_1, t_3\}, \{t_1, t_4\}, \{t_2, t_3\}, \{t_2, t_4\}\}$. Algorithm 1 returns SS.
- For M_0 and $S = En(M_0)$, Algorithm 1 returns the set:
  $SS = (\{\{t_1\}, \{t_2\}\} \otimes \{\{t_3, t_4\}\}) \otimes \{\{t_5, t_6\}\}$.
  Indeed, initially, we have $S' = S = En(M_0)$. The loop *while* will perform

successively the following updates of R, S' and SS, for the case where the selected transitions are successively t_1, t_3 and t_5:
For t_1: $R = \{t_1, t_2\}$, $S' = \{t_3, t_4, t_5, t_6\}$ and $SS = \{\{t_1\}, \{t_2\}\}$.
For t_3: $R = \{t_3, t_4\}$, $S' = \{t_5, t_6\}$ and $SS = SS \times R$.
For t_5: $R = \{t_5, t_6\}$, $S' = \emptyset$ and then
Then, $SS = (\{\{t_1\}, \{t_2\}\} \otimes \{t_3, t_4\}) \otimes \{t_5, t_6\}$. Note that in this case, SS is a covering-step set.

- For M_0 and $S = \{t_1, t_2\}$, Algorithm 1 returns $SS = \{\{t_1\}, \{t_2\}\}$, as the transitions of S are all key-transitions. If t_1 (or t_2) is selected first then $R = S'$, $S' = \emptyset$ and $SS = \{\{t_1\}, \{t_2\}\}$.

Theorem 2. *Algorithm 1 returns a persistent step set of M.*

Proof. It suffices to show that the returned set SS by Algorithm 1 satisfies $DS0$ and $DS1$ (presented in Definition 2). It is obvious that SS satisfies $DS0$.
$DS1$? Suppose that n $(n > 0)$ iterations are needed to complete the loop *while* of the algorithm. During the ith iteration ($i \in [1, n]$, a transition t^i is selected from S'^i and $R^i = PS^+(t^i, M)$. The set R^i is a strong-persistent set where all its transitions are keys. Therefore, it holds that:

$$\forall i \in [1, n], \forall t^i \in R^i, \forall \omega \in (T - R^i)^+, M[\omega\rangle \;\Rightarrow\; M[\omega t^i\rangle \wedge M[t^i\omega\rangle.$$

Each step of SS contains one and only one transition from each R^i, for $i \in [1, n]$. Therefore, all sequences where, at least, a transition from each step is missing, is given by the union of sets $(T - R^i)^+$, for $i \in [1, n]$. Consequently, SS satisfies $DS1$. □

5.2 Computing Persistent Step Sets

The set of steps returned by Algorithm 1 is a product of some pairwise disjunct strong-persistent sets of the marking M. To achieve further reductions, Algorithm 2 computes, in SS, a product of some pairwise disjunct persistent sets, instead of strong-persistent sets. However, unlike disjunct strong-persistent sets, the product of disjunct persistent sets may contain some non enabled steps. These steps must be deleted from SS to keep only the enabled ones. According to Theorem 3, SS is a persistent step set.

Example 3. Consider the model PN2 at Fig. 5 and its initial marking M_0.
For $S = \{t_0, t_1, t_2, t_3\}$, Algorithm 2 first sets SS, S' and R' to $\emptyset$, $\{t_0, t_1, t_2, t_3\}$ and $\emptyset$, respectively. Then, if t_0 of S' is the first transition selected in the loop *while* on S', then $R = \{t_0, t_1\}$, $S' = \{t_2, t_3\}$, $SS = \emptyset \otimes R = \{\{t_0\}, \{t_1\}\}$ and $R' = \{t_0, t_1\}$. For the second iteration, t_3 is selected, as: $PS(t_2, M_0) \cap R' = \{t_1\}$ and $PS(t_3, M_0) \cap R' = \emptyset$. Therefore, $R = \{t_2, t_3\}$, $S' = \emptyset$ and

$$SS = SS \otimes \{t_2, t_3\} = \{\{t_0, t_2\}, \{t_0, t_3\}, \{t_1, t_2\}, \{t_1, t_3\}\}.$$

Finally, Algorithm 2 returns $SS \cap EnS(M_0)$, i.e., $\{\{t_0, t_2\}, \{t_0, t_3\}, \{t_1, t_3\}\}$.

Algorithm 2. Persistent-step set of a marking M covering the transitions of S

Input : A marking M and a subset S of enabled transitions such that $S \neq \emptyset$;
Output : A persistent step set SS of M w.r.t. S;
$SS = \emptyset$; $S' = S$; $R' = \emptyset$;
while $(\exists t \in S'$ s.t. $PS(t, M) \cap R' = \emptyset)$ **do**
  Choose $t \in S'$ s.t. $PS(t, M) \cap R' = \emptyset$;
  $R = PS(t, M)$;
  $S' = S' - R$;
  $R' = R' \cup R$;
  $SS = SS \otimes R$;
end while
return $SS \cap EnS(M)$;
[For $X \in 2^T$ and a set $Y \subseteq T$, $X \otimes Y = \{x \cup \{y\} \mid x \in X \wedge y \in Y\}$. By convention, $\emptyset \otimes Y = \{\{y\} \mid y \in Y\}$]

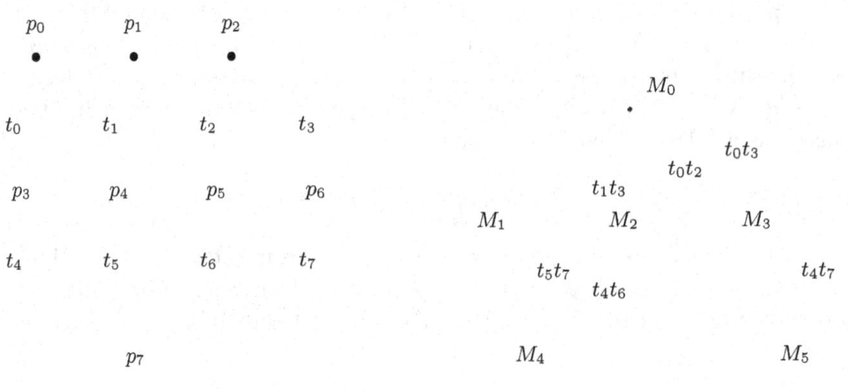

Fig. 5. Model PN2

Fig. 6. CSG of PN2

Theorem 3. *Algorithm 2 returns a persistent step set of* M.

Proof. It is obvious that the set SS returned by Algorithm 2 satisfies $DS0$. $DS1$? SS is a product of some pairwise disjunct persistent sets. Suppose that $SS = R^1 \otimes R^2 .... \otimes R^n$ with $(n > 0)$.
Then, (i) $\forall i \in [1, n], \exists t^i \in R^i, \forall \omega \in (T - R^i)^+, M[\omega\rangle \Rightarrow M[\omega t^i\rangle$ and (ii) $\forall i \in [1, n], \forall t^i \in R^i, \forall \omega \in (T - R^i)^+, M[\omega t^i\rangle \Rightarrow M[t^i \omega\rangle$.
By construction, sets R^i, for $i \in [1, n]$ are pairwise disjunct and each step of SS contains one and only one transition from each R^i, for $i \in [1, n]$. Condition (i) states that there is at least a transition t^i in R^i that is firable after each firable sequence of $(T - R^i)^+$. As the sets R^i, for $i \in [1, n]$, are pairwise disjunct, it follows that $R^j \subseteq (T - R^i)$ for $i, j \in [1, n]$ s.t. $i \neq j$.
Condition (ii) means that whenever a first transition from R^i is fired (after some sequence), it can be shifted to the front without disabling the sequence.
Let $\omega \in T^+$ be a sequence firable from M. We distinguish 3 main cases (a) ω contains no transition from $R^1 \cup ... \cup R^n$, (b) ω contains at least a transition from $R^1 \cup ... \cup R^n$ and ω contains at least a transition from each R^i for $i \in [1, n]$.

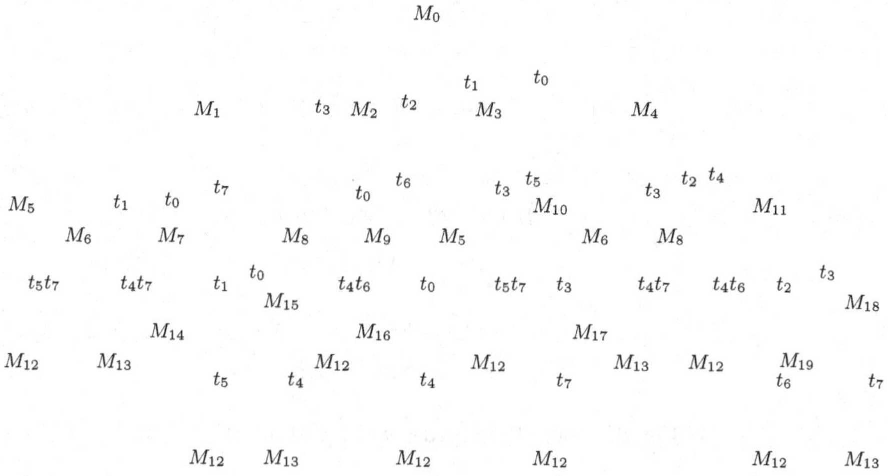

Fig. 7. MSPG of PN2 (using Algorithm 2)

For $n = 2$, the different cases are shown in Fig. 8: (a) ω has no transition from $R^1 \cup R^2$; (b1) ω has at least a transition from R^1 but no transition from R^2; (b2) ω has at least a transition from R^2 but no transition from R^1, and (c) ω has at least a transition from R^1 and from R^2.

- Case a: According to Condition (i) above, $\forall i \in [1, n], \exists t^i \in R^i, M[\omega\{t^1, ..., t^n\}\rangle$ and by Condition (ii), $M[\{t^1, ..., t^n\}\omega\rangle$. Note that $\{t^1, ..., t^n\}$ is eventually a firing step of M as each t^i is a key-transition of R^i and R^i for $i \in [1, n]$ are pairwise disjunct.
- Case b: If ω contains no transition from $R^{j_1} \cup ... \cup R^{j_k}$ but contains some transitions of $R^{l_1}, ...,$ and R^{l_m}, for some m and n such that $0 < m, 0 < k$ and $m + k = n$, then according to Condition (i), $\exists t^{j_1} \in R^{j_1}, ..., \exists t^{j_k} \in R^{j_k}, M[\omega\{t^{j_1}, ..., t^{j_k}\}\rangle$ and by Condition (ii), $M[\{t^{j_1}, ..., t^{j_k}\}\omega\rangle$.
  Let $t^{l_1}, ..., t^{l_m}$ be the first transitions of $R^{l_1}, ..., R^{l_m}$, respectively, appearing in ω. By Condition (ii), all these transitions can be shifted to the front of ω without disabling the other transitions of ω. Therefore, there is a firable sequence from M equivalent to $\omega t^{j_1} ... t^{j_k}$ that starts with a sequence of the step $\{t^{j_1}, ..., t^{j_k}, t^{l_1}, ..., t^{l_m}\}$. Note that this case is not possible, if $\{t^{j_1}, ..., t^{j_k}, t^{l_1}, ..., t^{l_m}\}$ is not a firable step of M.
- Case c: Let $t^{l_1}, ..., t^{l_n}$ be the first transitions of $R^{l_1}, ..., R^{l_n}$, respectively, appearing in ω. By Condition (ii), all these transitions can be shifted to the front of ω without disabling the other transitions of ω. Therefore, there is a firable sequence from M equivalent to ω that starts with a sequence of the step $\{t^{l_1}, ..., t^{l_n}\}$. Note that this case is not possible, if $\{t^{l_1}, ..., t^{l_n}\}$ is not a firable step of M.

Consequently, $SS \cap EnS(M)$ satisfies $DS1$. $\square$

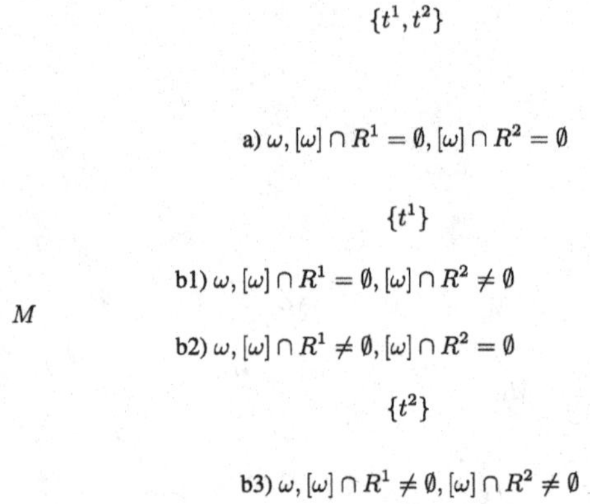

Fig. 8. Proof of $DS1$, case $n = 2$ and $M[\omega\rangle$

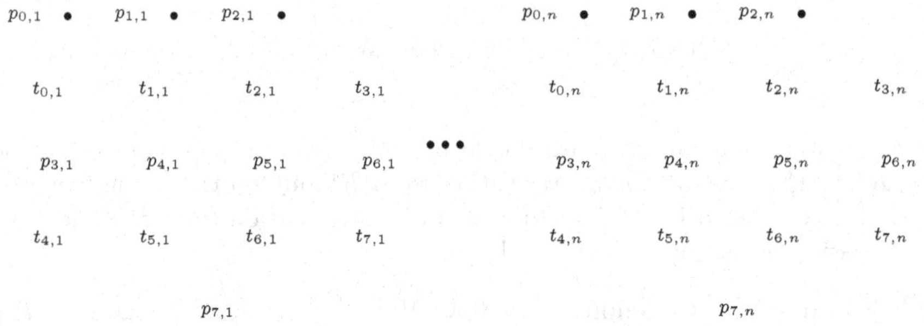

Fig. 9. Model PN3: Parallel composition of n instances of PN2 ($\|_n PN2$)

Example 4. For the model PN2 at Fig. 5, the graphs depicted at Figs. 6 and 7 are obtained using the selection Algorithms 1 and 2, respectively, for the case where all the enabled transitions are covered from each marking. Let us apply, Algorithm 1 to the initial marking M_0 for $S = En(M_0)$. It starts by $SS = \emptyset, S' = S = \{t_0, t_1, t_2, t_3\}$. If t_0 of S' is the first transition selected in the loop *while* on S', then R is set to $PS^+(t_0, M_0) = \{t_0, t_1, t_2, t_3\}$ and S' to $\emptyset$. Then, Algorithm 1 returns $SS = \emptyset \otimes R = \{\{t_0\}, \{t_1\}, \{t_2\}, \{t_3\}\}$. Note that for M_0 and $S = En(M_0)$, Algorithm 2 returns $SS = \{\{t_0, t_2\}, \{t_0, t_3\}, \{t_1, t_3\}\}$ (see Example 3).

Unlike the method in [14], which is based, as Algorithm 1, on the strong-persistent sets, the firing steps obtained by Algorithm 2 may contain some transitions that are in weak-conflict. Indeed, for the previous example, the transitions within each step of SS, returned by Algorithm 2, are not in conflict but they are in weak-conflict. The following examples shows the effectiveness of Algorithm 2 over Algorithm 1 for models where concurrency and weak-conflicts are combined.

Example 5. Consider now the model PN3 at Fig. 9 a parallel composition of PN2. We report in Table 1 for the model in Fig. 9, sizes of MG, CSG, PO, PO combined

Table 1. Parallel composition of instances of PN2

PN	MG	CSG	PO	CSG+PO	MPSG
$\Vert_2$ *PN2*					
Markings	400	194	133	125	14
Edges	1280	401	184	176	18
CPU (s)	0	0	0	0	0
$\Vert_3$ *PN2*					
Markings	8000	2072	969	929	36
Edges	38400	5393	1464	1425	54
CPU (s)	0	0	0	0	0
$\Vert_4$ *PN2*					
Markings	160000	23138	6905	6737	98
Edges	1024000	71801	11048	10880	162
CPU (s)	1.45	0	0	0	0
$\Vert_5$ *PN2*					
Markings	3200000	265640	48361	47681	276
Edges	25600000	952997	80488	79808	486
CPU (s)	50	0	0	0	0

with CSG, and MPSG. The CSG, PO, PO combined with CSG are provided by the tool TINA[2]. The MPSG is computed based on Algorithm 2 for the case where all the enabled transitions are covered from each marking. For this model, PO provides better results than CSG. Also, even if it is combined with CSG, it never gives better reduction than MPSG. One can easily check that the number of markings of the state space is of order of 3^n for MPSG while it is of order of 4^{n+1} for PO, CSG, and their combination. It stems from the fact that the selection Algorithm 2 handles in better way the weak-conflicts. For this model, the application of the selection Algorithm 2 shows an effectiveness relatively to the selection Algorithm 1, which is based, as the approach developed in [14], on the strong-persistent sets. Thus, it is not exaggerated to say that the persistent step sets method, based on persistent sets, is very promising to fight the state explosion and to address the verification of very large asynchronous concurrent systems, where the interplay between concurrency and conflict is expanded.

6 Conclusion

Although, partial order methods gained some success in coping with the state space explosion in concurrent systems with asynchronous components, the applicability of verification by state-space exploration of large systems remains as a challenge.

[2] http://projects.laas.fr/tina//home.php.

In this work, we have proposed a new parametric combination of the persistent sets with step graphs, based on a better understanding of the intricacy of the interplay between concurrency and conflict, revealing local persistency and leading to a significant reduction. The proposed approach takes into account, in a finer way, the structure of the net, while preserving deadlocks of Petri Nets. Indeed, unlike the method in [14], persistent steps may contain some transitions that are in weak-conflict. Moreover, it allows choosing the transitions to be covered while controlling the length and the number of steps to be selected from each marking.

Finally, the performed tests show the effectiveness of the proposed approach in terms of state space reduction and time execution, relatively to the covering-steps, strong-persistent sets methods or their combination implemented in the tool TINA. They also suggest that combining step graphs with any partial order technique is of very great interest for model-checking.

References

1. Barkaoui, K., Couvreur, J.-M., Klai, K.: On the equivalence between liveness and deadlock-freeness in Petri nets. In: Ciardo, G., Darondeau, P. (eds.) ICATPN 2005. LNCS, vol. 3536, pp. 90–107. Springer, Heidelberg (2005). https://doi.org/10.1007/11494744_7
2. Barkaoui, K., Pradat-Peyre, J.-F.: On liveness and controlled siphons in Petri nets. In: Billington, J., Reisig, W. (eds.) ICATPN 1996. LNCS, vol. 1091, pp. 57–72. Springer, Heidelberg (1996). https://doi.org/10.1007/3-540-61363-3_4
3. Chen, Y.F., Li, Z.W., Barkaoui, K.: New Petri net structure and its application to optimal supervisory control: Interval inhibitor arcs. IEEE Trans. Syst. Man Cybern. **44**(10), 1384–1400 (2014)
4. Desel, J., Juhás, G.: "What is a Petri net?" Informal answers for the informed reader. In: Ehrig, H., Padberg, J., Juhás, G., Rozenberg, G. (eds.) Unifying Petri Nets. LNCS, vol. 2128, pp. 1–25. Springer, Heidelberg (2001). https://doi.org/10.1007/3-540-45541-8_1
5. Godefroid, P. (ed.): Partial-Order Methods for the Verification of Concurrent Systems. LNCS, vol. 1032. Springer, Heidelberg (1996). https://doi.org/10.1007/3-540-60761-7
6. Junttila, T.: On the symmetry reduction method for Petri nets and similar formalisms. Ph.D. dissertation, Helsinki University of Technology, Espoo, Finland (2005)
7. Li, Z.W., Zhao, M.: On controllability of dependent siphons for deadlock prevention in generalized Petri nets. IEEE Trans. Syst. Man Cybern. **38**(2), 369–384 (2008)
8. Peled, D.: All from one, one for all: on model checking using representatives. In: Courcoubetis, C. (ed.) CAV 1993. LNCS, vol. 697, pp. 409–423. Springer, Heidelberg (1993). https://doi.org/10.1007/3-540-56922-7_34
9. Peled, D., Wilke, T.: Stutter-invariant temporal properties are expressible without the next-time operator. Inf. Process. Lett. **63**(5), 243–246 (1997)
10. Ribet, P.-O., çois, F., Berthomieu, B.: On combining the persistent sets method with the covering steps graph method. In: Peled, D.A., Vardi, M.Y. (eds.) FORTE 2002. LNCS, vol. 2529, pp. 344–359. Springer, Heidelberg (2002). https://doi.org/10.1007/3-540-36135-9_22

11. Valmari, A.: A stubborn attack on state explosion. Form. Methods Syst. Des. **1**(4), 297–322 (1992)
12. Valmari, A.: The state explosion problem. In: Reisig, W., Rozenberg, G. (eds.) ACPN 1996. LNCS, vol. 1491, pp. 429–528. Springer, Heidelberg (1998). https://doi.org/10.1007/3-540-65306-6_21
13. Valmari, A., Hansen, H.: Can stubborn sets be optimal? Fundam. Inform. **113**(3–4), 377–397 (2011)
14. Vernadat, F., Azéma, P., Michel, F.: Covering step graph. In: Billington, J., Reisig, W. (eds.) ICATPN 1996. LNCS, vol. 1091, pp. 516–535. Springer, Heidelberg (1996). https://doi.org/10.1007/3-540-61363-3_28

Stochastic and Probabilistic Systems

Analysis of a Road/Tramway Intersection by the ORIS Tool

Laura Carnevali, Alessandro Fantechi(✉), Gloria Gori, and Enrico Vicario

Department of Information Engineering, University of Florence, Florence, Italy
{laura.carnevali,alessandro.fantechi,gloria.gori,enrico.vicario}@unifi.it

Abstract. Intelligent Transportation Systems for urban mobility aim at the grand objective of reducing environmental impact and minimize urban congestion, also integrating different mobility modes and solutions. However, the different transportation modalities may end in a conflict due to physical constraints concerned with the urban structure itself: an example is the case of intersection between a public road and a tramway right-of-way, where traffic lights priority given to trams may trigger road congestion, while an intense car traffic can impact on trams' performance. These situations can be anticipated and avoided by accurately modeling and analyzing the possible congestion events. Typically, modeling tools provide simulation facilities, by which various scenarios can be played to understand the response of the intersection to different traffic loads. While supporting early verification of design choices, simulation encounters difficulties in the evaluation of rare events. Only modeling techniques and tools that support the analysis of the complete space of possible scenarios are able to find out such rare events. In this work, we present an analytical approach to model and evaluate a critical intersection for the Florence tramway, where frequent traffic blocks used to happen. Specifically, we exploit the ORIS tool to evaluate the probability of a traffic block, leveraging regenerative transient analysis based on the method of stochastic state classes to analyze a model of the intersection specified through Stochastic Time Petri Nets (STPNs). The reported experience shows that the frequency of tram rides impacts on the road congestion, and hence compensating measures (such as sychronizing the passage of trams in opposite directions on the road crossing) should be considered.

Keywords: Intelligent Transportation Systems
Transportation modeling · Integrated traffic model
Stochastic state classes · Markov Regenerative Processes

1 Introduction

By the year 2030, urban mobility will have changed due to sociodemographic evolution, urbanization, increase of the energy costs, implementation of environmental regulations, and further diffusion of Information and Communication Technology (ICT) applications. The demand for public and collective modes of

M. F. Atig et al. (Eds.): VECoS 2018, LNCS 11181, pp. 185–199, 2018.
https://doi.org/10.1007/978-3-030-00359-3_12

transport will increase considerably. Part of the answer will come from the public transport that will evolve as an integrated combination of buses, cars, metros, tramways and trains [1,13]. In general, right-of-way (ROW) is the defining characteristic of public transportation modes and we can list three ROW types:

1. *Exclusive:* Transit vehicles operate on fully separated and physically protected ROW. Tunnels, elevated structures, or at-grade tracks are such examples. This ROW type offers very high capacity, speed, reliability and safety. All heavy rail transit systems, like the Metrorail of the Washington Metropolitan Area Transit Authority, belong to this category.
2. *Semi-Exclusive:* Transit ways are longitudinally separated from other traffic, such as private vehicles and pedestrians. Light rail transit (LRT) systems, like the Florence tramway in Italy, are mostly built according to this ROW type.
3. *Fully-Shared:* Transit vehicles share ROW with other traffic, for examples buses, taxi and cars. This ROW type requires the least infrastructure investment, but operations are relatively unreliable due to roadway congestion.

Exclusive ROW needs major investment, thus often semi-exclusive or fully-shared modes are chosen. The drawback of this choice is that the different transportation modalities may end in a conflict due to physical constraints concerned with the urban structure itself. For example, this is the case of an intersection between a public road and a tramway right-of-way, where traffic lights priority given to trams may trigger road congestion, while an intense car traffic can impact on trams' performance. These situations can be anticipated and avoided by accurately modeling and analyzing the possible congestion events. Typically, modeling tools provide simulation facilities, by which various scenarios can be played to understand the response of the intersection to different traffic loads. Simulation techniques are used to support early verification of design choices, but can analyze a limited, yet high, number of different scenarios, and encounter difficulties in the evaluation of rare events. Only modeling techniques and tools that support the analysis of the complete space of possible scenarios are able to find out such rare events [4,7].

In this work, we present an analytical approach to model and evaluate a critical intersection for the Florence tramway, where frequent traffic blocks used to happen. This work was funded by Fondazione Cassa di Risparmio di Firenze, with the kind help of GEST[1], the company running the Florence tramway, in providing important data on which to base the study.

Figure 1 shows the route of line 1, which has been put in service in 2010 and links Santa Maria Novella central station to Scandicci (Florence suburbs). This line has overall good performance, with trams running regularly from the end of the line in Scandicci to almost the other end in the city center, but there is a consistent source of delay just a few meters short of the last scheduled stop, near Santa Maria Novella train station [10]. The root cause for these issues is the Diacceto-Alamanni intersection, where both via Iacopo da Diacceto, a

[1] https://www.ratpdev.com/en/references/italy-florence-tramway.

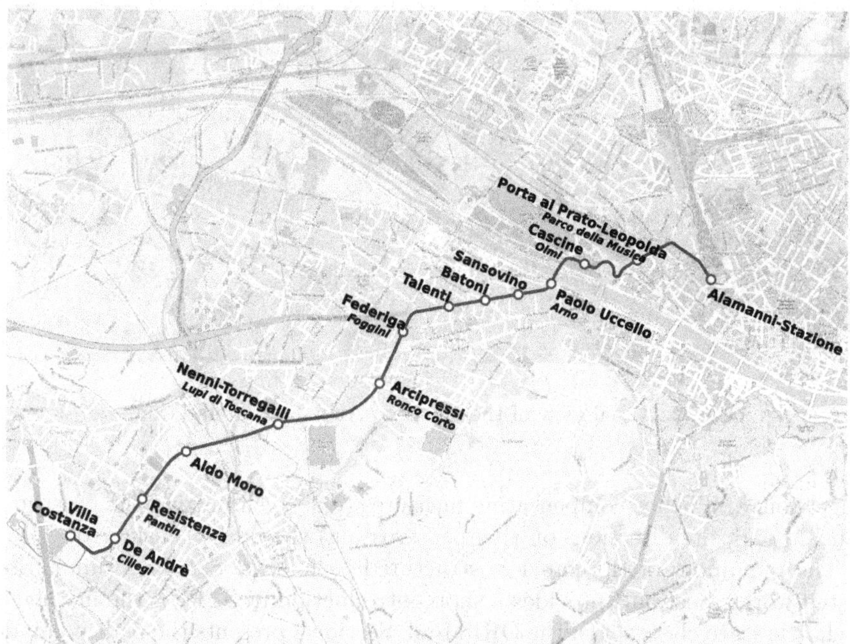

Fig. 1. Map of tram route from Villa Costanza (Scandicci) to Alamanni-Stazione (Santa Maria Novella station). The route is 7720 m long with 14 tram stops.

street with dedicated tracks for tramways, and via Luigi Alamanni, a street for private transport, head to Santa Maria Novella train station.[2]. An aerial view of this intersection is shown in Fig. 2. The darker stripe that crosses the tracks represents the (unidirectional) private traffic flow from Alamanni street that is the source of the analyzed conflict.

Taking this intersection as a case study, we exploit the ORIS tool to evaluate the probability of a traffic block, leveraging regenerative transient analysis based on the method of stochastic state classes to analyze a model of the intersection specified by Stochastic Time Petri Nets (STPNs). Note that ORIS supports the analysis of models with multiple concurrent temporal parameters associated with a general (i.e., non-exponential) distribution. In particular, the model of the Diacceto Alamanni intersection includes timers associated with a deterministic value (e.g., tram interleaving period), a uniform distribution (e.g., tram delay time), and an exponential distribution (e.g., private vehicles arrival rate). The reported experience shows that the frequency of tram rides impacts on the road

[2] The construction works of the new tramway lines (due to be opened soon) have consistently changed the geometry of the considered intersection, partially removing the car traffic. Anyway, the analysis presented in this work refers to a relevant scenario, typical of intersections between a public road and a tramway right-of-way, which will occur more frequently in Florence as new tramway lines will be built.

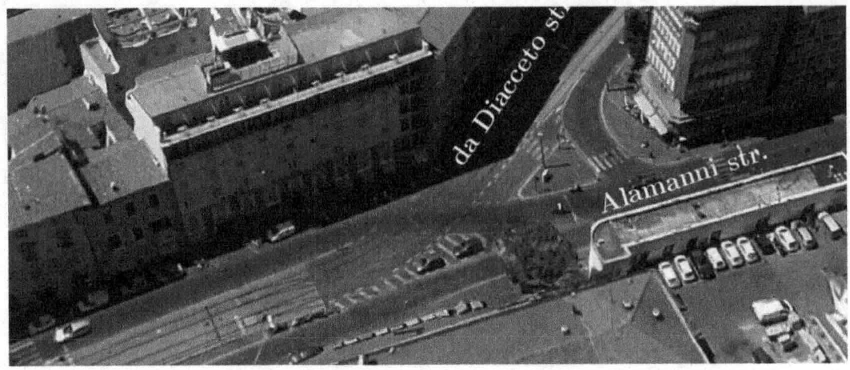

Fig. 2. Aerial view of the Diacceto-Alamanni intersection.

congestion, and hence compensating measures (e.g., sychronizing the passage of trams in opposite directions on the road crossing) should be considered.

The remainder of the paper is structured as follows. Section 2 summarises related works. Section 3 provides a short introduction to STPNs, the method of stochastic state classes, and the ORIS tool. Section 4 presents the realized model and Sect. 5 the obtained results. Finally, Sect. 6 concludes the paper.

2 Related Works

Earliest research on integrated control for traffic management at network level can be traced back to the 1970 s. The first railway timetables were planned based on the experience and knowledge of dispatchers in resolving train conflicts [17]. This manual scheduling practice proved its low efficiency with the increase of traffic congestion and exacerbated train delays.

An integrated policy for priority signals at intersections is required, given that trams operate in a *semi-exclusive* ROW environment. In the literature, we can find two different streams of studies: the first aiming at optimizing tram schedules without considering their effects on other traffic flows; the second aiming at manipulating the tram schedule so that trams always clear the intersection during green phases, thus reducing influences on other traffic flows. In [27], the tradeoffs between tram travel times and roadway traffic delays are explored. Literature counts several works applying different simulation techniques. Microscopic models, i.e., models in which each vehicle is modeled by itself as a particle, can be divided according to the representation of road structure in greater detail. In the continuous road model group, a base structure of road space is modeled as a continuous one dimensional (1D) link. The behavior of car agents is often implemented by applying car-following theories [26,28,35]. In the cell-type road model group, road space is discretized by homogeneous cells in which the behavior of car agents is expressed using transition rules such as cellular automata

[19,29]. In a queuing model group, road networks are modeled as queuing networks [2,15]. Most commercial microscopic traffic simulators employ the continuous road model. In addition, several researchers have proposed simulation frameworks for mixed traffic of two or more models. For example, Yang et al. [32] proposed a framework for pedestrian road crossing behavior in Chinese cities in which they determined the criterion used by pedestrians to decide whether to start crossing a road after considering vehicle flows. Meanwhile, Zeng et al. [34] modeled pedestrian-vehicles interactions at crosswalks in order to minimize pedestrian-vehicle collisions.

Dobler and Lämmel [12] integrated multi-modal simulation modules to the existing framework of MATSim, a large scale traffic simulation framework based on the queuing model [8]. Their integration approach was based on locally replacing simple queue structures with continuous 2D space at sections with higher traffic flows. The behavior rules of agents in the 2D space are based on the social force model (SFM). Krajzewicz et al. [20] introduced pedestrian and bicycle agent models into SUMO, which is a widely used traffic simulator belonging to the continuous road model group [21]. Finally Fujii et al. [14] introduced an agent-based framework for mixed-traffic of cars, pedestrians and trams by using the simulator MATES [33]. To our knowledge, there is no work that leverages analytic, non simulative, techniques for the analysis of traffic models.

3 Background

In this section, we provide some background on STPNs (Sect. 3.1), the method of stochastic state classes (Sect. 3.2), and the ORIS tool (Sect. 3.3).

3.1 Stochastic Time Petri Nets

An STPN is a tuple $\langle P, T, A^-, A^+, A^{\cdot}, m_0, F, W, E, U\rangle$ where: P is the set of places; T is the set of transitions; $A^- \subseteq P\times T$, $A^+ \subseteq T\times P$ and $A^{\cdot} \subseteq P\times T$ are the sets of precondition, postcondition, and inhibitor arcs, respectively: $m_0 : P \to \mathbb{N}$ is the initial marking; $F : T \to [0,1]^{[EFT_t, LFT_t]}$ associates each transition t with a Cumulative Distribution Function (CDF) $F(t) : [EFT_t, LFT_t] \to [0,1]$, where $EFT_t \in \mathbb{Q}_{\geq 0}$ and $LFT_t \in \mathbb{Q}_{\geq 0} \cup \{\infty\}$ are the *earliest* and *latest firing time*, respectively; $W : T \to \mathbb{R}_{>0}$ associates each transition with a weight; E and U associate each transition t with an enabling function $E(t) : \mathbb{N}^P \to \{true, false\}$ and an update function $U(t) : \mathbb{N}^P \to \mathbb{N}^P$, which associate each marking with a boolean value and a new marking, respectively.

A place p is an *input*, *output*, or *inhibitor* place for a transition t if $\langle p,t\rangle \in A^-$, $\langle t,p\rangle \in A^+$, and $\langle p,t\rangle \in A^{\cdot}$, respectively. A transition t is *immediate* (IMM) if $EFT_t = LFT_t = 0$ and *timed* otherwise; a timed transition t is *exponential* (EXP) if $F_t(x) = 1 - e^{-\lambda x}$ over $[0,\infty]$ with $\lambda \in \mathbb{R}_{>0}$, and *general* (GEN) otherwise; a general transition t is *deterministic* (DET) if $EFT_t = LFT_t > 0$ and *distributed* otherwise; for each distributed transition t, we assume that F_t is the integral function of a Probability Density Function (PDF) f_t, i.e., $F_t(x) =$

$\int_0^x f_t(y)dy$. IMM, EXP, GEN, and DET transitions are represented by thick white, thick gray, thick black, or thin black bars, respectively.

The state of an STPN is a pair $\langle m, \tau \rangle$, where m is a marking and $\tau : T \rightarrow \mathbb{R}_{\geq 0}$ associates each transition with a time-to-fire. A transition is *enabled* by a marking if each of its input places contains at least one token, none of its inhibitor places contains any token, and its enabling function evaluates to true; an enabled transition t is *firable* in a state if its time-to-fire is equal to zero. The next transition t to fire in a state $s = \langle m, \tau \rangle$ is selected among the set of firable transitions $T_{f,s}$ with probability $W(t)/\sum_{t_i \in T_{f,s}} W(t_i)$. When t fires, s is replaced with $s' = \langle m', \tau' \rangle$, where:

- m' is derived from m by: removing a token from each input place of t, which yields an intermediate marking m_{tmp}; adding a token to each output place of t, which yields a second intermediate marking m'_{tmp}; and, applying the update function $U(t)$ to m'_{tmp};
- τ' is derived from τ by: (*i*) reducing the time-to-fire of each *persistent* transition (i.e., enabled by m, m_{tmp} and m') by the time elapsed in s; (*ii*) sampling the time-to-fire of each *newly-enabled* transition t_n (i.e., enabled by m' but not by m_{tmp}) according to F_{t_n}; and, (*iii*) removing the time-to-fire of each *disabled* transition (i.e., enabled by m but not by m').

3.2 The Method of Stochastic State Classes

The method of stochastic state classes [6,18,31] permits the analysis of STPNs with multiple concurrent GEN transitions. Given a sequence of firings, a *stochastic state class* encodes the marking and the joint PDF of the times-to-fire of the enabled transitions and the absolute elapsed time τ_{age}. Starting from an initial stochastic state class, the *transient tree* of stochastic state classes that can be reached within a time $t_{\max}$ is enumerated, enabling derivation of continuous-time transient probabilities of markings (*forward transient analysis*), i.e., $p_m(t) := P\{M(t) = m\} \; \forall \; 0 \leq t \leq t_{\max}, \; \forall \; m \in \mathcal{M}$, where $M(t)$ is the *marking process* describing the marking $M(t)$ of an STPN for each time $t \geq 0$ and $\mathcal{M}$ is the set of reachable markings.

If the STPN always reaches within a bounded number of firings a *regeneration*, i.e., a state satisfying the Markov condition, its marking process is a Markov Regenerative Process (MRP) [9], and its analysis can be performed enumerating stochastic state classes between any two regenerations. This results in a set of trees that permits to compute a local and a global kernel characterizing the MRP behavior, enabling evaluation of transient marking probabilities through the numerical solution of Markov renewal equations (*regenerative transient analysis*). Trees also permit to compute conditional probabilities of the Discrete Time Markov Chain (DTMC) embedded at regenerations and the expected time spent in any marking after each occurrence of any regeneration [22], supporting derivation of steady-state marking probabilities according to the Markov renewal theory (*regenerative steady-state analysis*).

While stochastic state classes support quantitative evaluation of an STPN model, the set Ω of behaviors of the STPN can be identified with simpler and more consolidated means through non-deterministic analysis of the underlying TPN model. In this case, the state space is covered through the method of *state classes* [11,30], each made of a marking and a joint support for τ_{age} and the times-to-fire of the enabled transitions. In this approach, enumeration of state classes starting from an initial marking provides a representation for the continuous set of executions of an STPN, enabling verification of qualitative properties of the model, e.g., guarantee, with certainty, that a marking cannot be reached within a given time bound (*non-deterministic transient analysis*).

3.3 ORIS Overview

ORIS [5][3] is a software tool for qualitative verification and quantitative evaluation of reactive timed systems. ORIS supports modeling and evaluation of stochastic systems governed by timers (e.g., interleaving or service times, arrival rate, timeouts) with general probability density functions (PDFs). The tool adopts Stochastic Time Petri Nets (STPNs) as a graphical formalism to specify stochastic systems, and it efficiently implements the method of stochastic state classes, including regenerative transient, regenerative steady-state and non-deterministic analysis.

The software architecture of ORIS decouples the graphical editor from the underlying analysis engines. Given the many variants of Petri net features, ORIS was developed with extensibility in mind: new features can be defined by implementing specific interfaces, so that they can be introduced in the graphical editor and made available to the analysis engines. In turn, analysis engines implement a specific interface that allows them to cooperate with the graphical interface, i.e., to collect analysis options from the user, to start/stop analysis runs, to record and display analysis logs, and to show time series and tabular results. The following analysis engines are available.

Non-deterministic Analysis is based on the theory of Difference Bound Matrix (DBM) and supports the identification of the boundaries of the space of feasible timed behaviors, producing a compact representation of the dense set of timed states that can be reached by the model [30]. The state space is displayed as a directed graph, where edges represent transition firings while nodes are *state classes* comprising a marking and a DBM zone of timer values. This analysis is useful to debug STPNs models and ensure that their state space M is finite.

Transient and Regenerative Analysis computes transient probabilities in Generalized Semi-Markov Processes (GSMPs) and Markov Regenerative Processes (MRPs), respectively. These methods evaluate trees where edges are

[3] ORIS is available for download at the webpage https://www.oris-tool.org/.

labeled with transitions and their firing probabilities, while nodes are *stochastic state classes* [18] comprising a marking, the PDF of timers, and their support (a DBM zone). For a given *time limit* T, the enumeration proceeds until the tree covers the transition firings of the STPN by time T with probability greater than $1 - \epsilon$, where $\epsilon > 0$ is an *error* term. While standard transient analysis enumerates a single, very large tree of events, regenerative analysis avoids the enumeration of repeated subtrees rooted in the same *regeneration point* (where all general timers are reset or have been enabled for a deterministic time). A *time step* Δt is used to select equispaced time points where transient probabilities are evaluated (directly or by solving Markov renewal equations).

Regenerative Steady-State Analysis computes steady-state probabilities in MRPs (and thus Semi-Markov Processes (SMPs) and Continuous Time Markov Chains (CTMCs)) with irreducible state space. This method uses trees of stochastic state classes between regeneration points to compute steady-state probabilities of markings: expected sojourn times in each tree are combined with the steady-state probability of regenerations at their roots [22]. As for transient analysis, this method can be applied to STPNs allowing multiple general timers enabled in each state.

Transient Analysis Under Enabling Restriction computes transient probabilities in MRPs with at most one general transition enabled in each state [16].

ORIS engines support instantaneous (transient or steady-state) and cumulative (transient) rewards. A *reward* is a real-valued function of markings $r : M \rightarrow \mathbb{R}$ that is evaluated by substituting place names with the number of contained tokens in order to compute the instantaneous expected reward $I_r(t) = \sum_{i \in M} r(i) p_i(t)$ at each time t, its steady-state value $\overline{I}_r = \lim_{t \to \infty} I_r(t) = \sum_{i \in M} r(i) \overline{p}_i$ or its cumulative value over time $C_r(t) = \int_0^t I_r(t) dt$. In addition, the user can specify a *stop condition*, i.e., a Boolean predicate on markings such as $(\mathtt{p_0} == \mathtt{1}) \&\& (\mathtt{p_1} == \mathtt{1})$, that is used to halt the STPN. This feature can be used to compute first-passage probabilities [18] or reach-avoid objectives equivalent to bounded until operators [25].

4 Diacceto-Alamanni: An STPN Model

In this section, we describe the STPN model of the Diacceto-Alamanni intersection. Figure 3 shows the model which is composed of two submodels: the tramway submodel (blue box) and the private traffic submodel (red box).

4.1 Tramway Submodel

The portion of the tramway submodel in the dotted blue box represents the direction from Santa Maria Novella train station (Alamanni-Stazione), while the one in the dashed blue box represents the opposite direction. GEST provided the

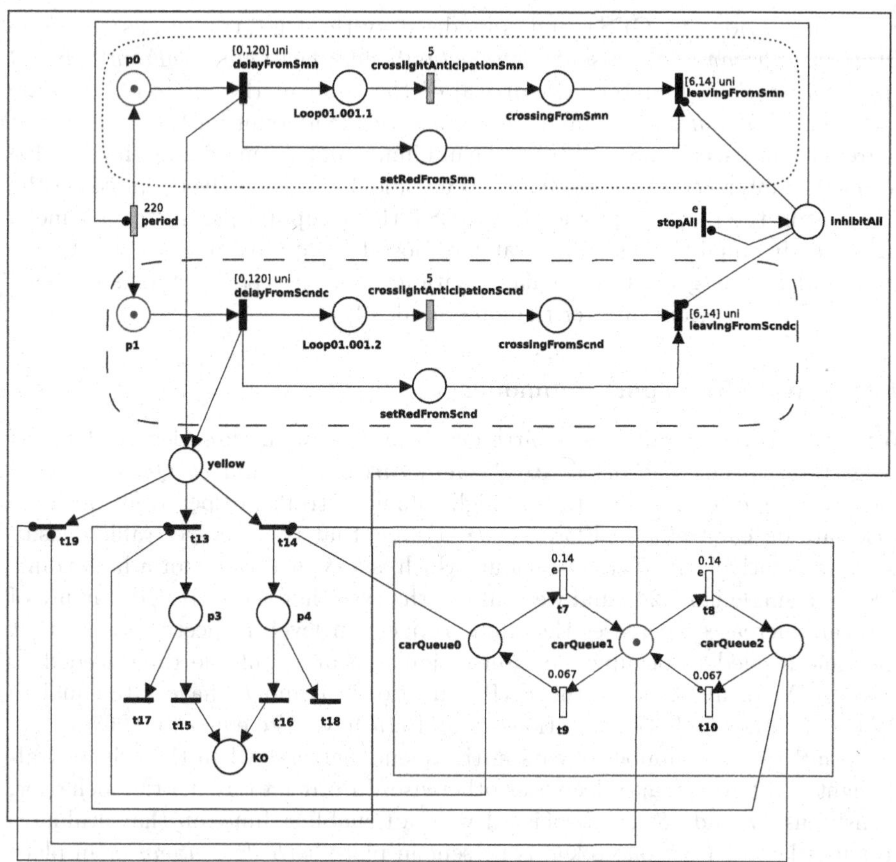

Fig. 3. Intersection model. The tramway submodel is highlighted by the blue box, the private traffic queue submodel is highlighted by the red one. Transitions associated with an enabling function are marked by a label "e". (Color figure online)

interleaving period of trams, which is equal to 220 s; the transition *period*, which models tram departures, fires a new token periodically and is enabled with continuity until place *KO* receives a token. Places *p0* and *p1* represent a tramway departing from Alamanni-Stazione and Villa Costanza, respectively. Transitions *delayFromSmn* and *delayFromScndc* represent the delays cumulated by the two trams, respectively; note that 120 s is an upper bound on the maximum delay observed in the available data set and, given that data are few and their distribution is unknown, this parameter is modeled using a uniform distribution [3].

When the tramway is approaching the intersection, dedicated wayside systems (i.e., two loops placed under the railway tracks) are activated (places *Loop01.001.1* and *Loop01.001.2*) and the corresponding traffic lights are set to red (places *setRedFromSmn* and *setRedFromScnd*). The traffic lights are in fact set to red 5 s before the arrival of the tram at the intersection; this parameter has been provided by GEST and is modeled by the DET transitions *crosslightAnticipationSmn* and *crosslightAnticipationScnd.* Places *crossingFromSmn* and *crossingFromScnd* represent the arrival of the tram at the intersection, while transitions *leavingFromSmn* and *leavingFromScndc* account for the time needed to free the intersection. Specifically, the minimum and the maximum time needed to free the intersection are set equal to 6 s and 14 s, respectively, based on the fact that in the data set provided by GEST this temporal parameter has mean value nearly equal to 10 s and a standard deviation approximately equal to 4 s. Also in this case, given that available data are few, this parameters is modeled by a uniform distribution over the interval [6, 14] [3].

4.2 Private Transport Submodel

We model private traffic as a birth-death process with three levels of traffic congestion: specifically, places *carQueue0*, *carQueue1*, and *carQueue2* model the condition of low, moderate, and high volume of traffic, respectively. Since we lack data on car traffic in Florence, we assume that the average traffic density is approximatively 1000 cars per hour, which is a typical value for a high traffic flow on a single lane [24], and we consider the case that the arrival/departure of two cars increases/decreases the traffic congestion level, respectively, and that the time needed to occupy the intersection is nearly half the time needed to leave it. According to this, the EXP transitions *t7* and *t8* have rate equal to 0.14 s^{-1}, while the EXP transitions *t9* and *t10* have rate equal to 0.067 s^{-1}.

Intuitively, the number of cars in the queue increases when the private traffic light is set to red and decreases otherwise. In order to model this behavior, transitions *t7* and *t8* are associated with an enabling function that evaluates to true when at least one token is present in place *setRedFromSmn* or in place *setRedFromScnd* (i.e. *setRedFromSmn+setRedFromScnd>0*). Conversely, transitions *t9* and *t10* are associated with an enabling function that evaluates to true when no token is present in places *setRedFromSmn* and *setRedFromScnd* (i.e., *setRedFromSmn+setRedFromScnd==0*).

4.3 Interaction Between the Tramway Submodel and the Private Transport Submodel

Road congestion may cause cars to stand for a while on the tracks after the private traffic light has turned to red, thus blocking trams. Place *yellow* models the private traffic light set to yellow, while place *KO* actually models the case that a tram ride is blocked by private vehicles on the lane. When place *KO* receives a token, transition *stopAll* becomes enabled (given that it is associated with an enabling function *KO>0*) and fires, depositing a token in place *inhibitAll.* This finally disables transitions *period*, *leavingFromSmn*, and *leavingFromScndc*, due to the inhibitor arcs from *inhibitAll* to each of these transitions.

Transitions *t13* through *t19* model the possibility that a tram ride is blocked by private vehicles stopping on the tracks. If the traffic congestion level is low (i.e., *carQueue0* > 0), the tram runs regularly and transition *t19* is enabled, so that no token is deposited in place *KO*. If traffic congestion increases to a moderate level (*carQueue1* > 0) or to a high level (*carQueue2* > 0), transition *t13* or transition *t14* becomes enabled and fires, respectively. In the former case (*p3* > 0), transitions *t15* and *t17* fire with probability 0.3 and 0.7, respectively, given that they have weight equal to 30 and 70, respectively; in the latter case, transitions *t16* and *t18* fire with probability 0.4 and 0.6, respectively, given that they have weight equal to 40 and 60, respectively. In doing so, the probability of a traffic block is 0.3 and 0.4 in the case of moderate and high traffic congestion, respectively. These parameters have been estimated from tram delays observed in the data set provided by GEST.

5 Analysis and Results

In this section, we report the results obtained from the analysis of the model of Sect. 4. In all the experiments, we performed regenerative transient analysis of the model through the ORIS tool using the following parameters:

- *Time limit* $T = 7200$ s (corresponding to 2 h);
- *Time step* $\Delta t = 20$ s.
- *Error* $\epsilon = 0.01$;

The first experiment has been performed with average traffic density equal to 1000 cars per hour (i.e., the EXP transitions *t7* and *t8* have rate equal to 0.14 s^{-1}, and the EXP transitions *t9* and *t10* have rate equal to 0.067 s^{-1}, as shown in Fig. 3) and crosslight anticipation equal to 5 s (i.e., the value of the DET transitions *crosslightAnticipationSmn* and *crosslightAnticipationScnd* is 5 s, as also shown in Fig. 3). Figure 4 shows the probability of the private traffic queue status in a time interval of 2 h, obtained computing the instantaneous rewards "*carQueue0* > 0", "*carQueue1* > 0", and "*carQueue2* > 0". Due to the high value of average traffic density, the car queue tends to be filled quite rapidly. As we can see, the reward "*carQueue2* > 0" (high traffic volume) tends to 1 s, while the rewards "*carQueue0* > 0" (low traffic volume) and "*carQueue1* > 0" (moderate traffic volume) tend to 0 s (note that the sum of tokens in places *carQueue0*, *carQueue1*, and *carQueue2* is 1).

Figure 5 shows the KO probability for different values of the crosslight anticipation parameter, obtained computing the instantaneous reward "*KO* > 0". We observe that the probability of reaching the KO state increases every 220 s for all the displayed curves, due to periodic tram departures. We also note that the probability of reaching the KO state increases when the crosslight anticipation is higher: intuitively, when the anticipation time increases, the time during which private traffic should flow away from the intersection decreases, thus degrading the queue status and consequently increasing the KO probability.

Finally, Fig. 6 shows the KO probability (obtained computing the instantaneous reward "*KO* > 0") for different values of the private traffic density. The probability of reaching the KO state increases when the traffic density is higher and reaches 0.7 in less than half an hour with extremely congested private traffic

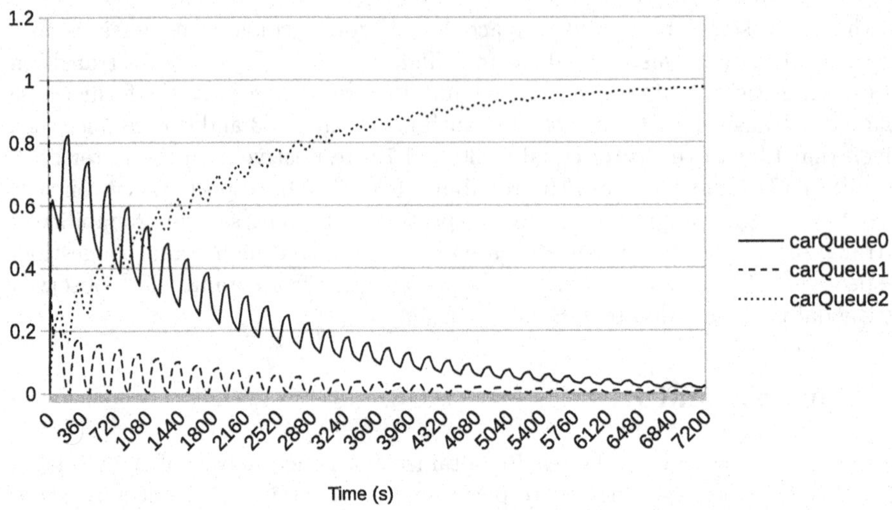

Fig. 4. Transient probability of the traffic queue status.

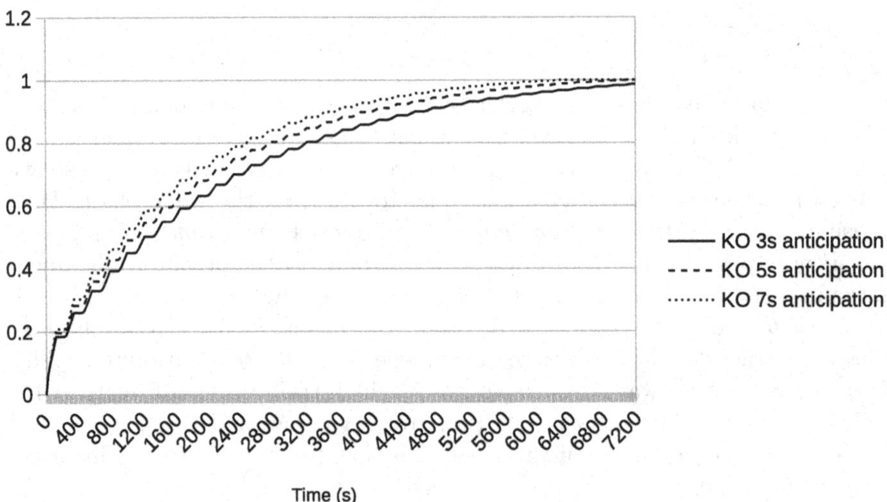

Fig. 5. Transient probability of the KO state for different values of the crosslight anticipation parameter.

(i.e., 1500 cars per hour), while the same value is reached in more than a hour with moderately congested private traffic (i.e., 500 cars per hour).

We also argue that, for the planning of both tram timetables and traffic light timings, it is important to consider the correlation between the time of red signal, the time of green signal, and the tram headway, pointing out the need of an integrated management of the different transport systems in order to have a more robust and higher quality service. Furthermore, a more detailed analysis is needed to accurately model the behavior of private traffic during the day.

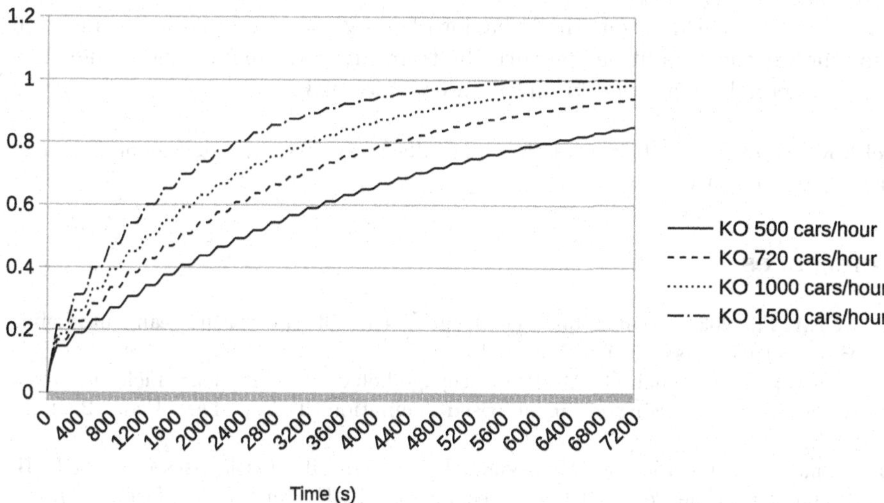

Fig. 6. Transient probability of the KO state for different values of traffic density.

6 Conclusion

Modeling and analysis of complex intersections for the integration of private and public transport supports the evaluation of the perceived availability of public transport and the identification of robust traffic light plans and tram timetables. In this work, we presented an analytical approach to model and evaluate a critical intersection for the Florence tramway. Specifically, we used the ORIS tool to evaluate the probability of a traffic block, leveraging regenerative transient analysis based on the method of stochastic state classes to analyze a model of the intersection specified through Stochastic Time Petri Nets (STPNs). The analysis results showed a correlation between the frequency of tram rides, the traffic light plan, and the status of the queue of private vehicles, pointing out that the frequency of tram rides impacts on the road congestion. Therefore, compensating measures should be considered, such as synchronizing the passage of trams in opposite directions on the road crossing.

Within the context of modeling techniques to optimize the integration of public and private traffic, our work will go towards the following directions:

- analyze other road/tramway intersections, also considering the new tramway lines that will be opened in Florence, so as to compare differences and similarities and generalize the modeling methodology;
- improve the scalability of the approach by combining numerical solution of the tramway submodel through the ORIS tool with analytical evaluation of the traffic congestion level, which could permit to model private traffic more accurately (e.g., considering a larger number of congestion levels) without incurring in the state space explosion problem;

- evaluate to which extent the behavior of passengers and pedestrians as well as the weather conditions perturb the tramway performance, including them in the model of the road/tramway intersection [23].

Acknowledgements. This work was partially supported by Fondazione Cassa di Risparmio di Firenze.

References

1. ACEA: The 2030 urban mobility challenge. Technical report, European Automobile Manufacturers Association, May 2016
2. Agarwal, A., Lämmel, G.: Modeling seepage behavior of smaller vehicles in mixed traffic conditions using an agent based simulation. Transp. Dev. Econ. **2**(2), 12 (2016)
3. Bernardi, S., Campos, J., Merseguer, J.: Timing-failure risk assessment of UML design using time Petri net bound techniques. IEEE Trans. Ind. Inform. **7**(1), 90–104 (2011)
4. Biagi, M., Carnevali, L., Paolieri, M., Vicario, E.: Performability evaluation of the ERTMS/ETCS - Level 3. Transp. Res. C-Emerg. **82**, 314–336 (2017)
5. Bucci, G., Carnevali, L., Ridi, L., Vicario, E.: Oris: a tool for modeling, verification and evaluation of real-time systems. Int. J. Softw. Tools Technol. Transf. **12**(5), 391–403 (2010)
6. Carnevali, L., Grassi, L., Vicario, E.: State-density functions over DBM domains in the analysis of non-Markovian models. IEEE Trans. Softw. Eng. **35**(2), 178–194 (2009)
7. Carnevali, L., Flammini, F., Paolieri, M., Vicario, E.: Non-Markovian performability evaluation of ERTMS/ETCS level 3. In: Beltrán, M., Knottenbelt, W., Bradley, J. (eds.) EPEW 2015. LNCS, vol. 9272, pp. 47–62. Springer, Cham (2015). https://doi.org/10.1007/978-3-319-23267-6_4
8. Charypar, D., Axhausen, K., Nagel, K.: Event-driven queue-based traffic flow microsimulation. Transp. Res. Rec. **2003**, 35–40 (2007)
9. Choi, H., Kulkarni, V.G., Trivedi, K.S.: Markov regenerative stochastic Petri nets. Perform. Eval. **20**(1–3), 333–357 (1994)
10. Ciuti, I.: Jean-Luc Laugaa: Ingorgo-trappola alla stazione, un rischio anche per la linea 2. Repubblica.it (2014). http://goo.gl/QxrXR4
11. Dill, D.L.: Timing assumptions and verification of finite-state concurrent systems. In: Sifakis, J. (ed.) CAV 1989. LNCS, vol. 407, pp. 197–212. Springer, Heidelberg (1990). https://doi.org/10.1007/3-540-52148-8_17
12. Dobler, C., Lämmel, G.: Integration of a multi-modal simulation module into a framework for large-scale transport systems simulation. In: Weidmann, U., Kirsch, U., Schreckenberg, M. (eds.) Pedestrian and Evacuation Dynamics 2012, pp. 739–754. Springer, Cham (2014). https://doi.org/10.1007/978-3-319-02447-9_62
13. ERTRAC: ERTRAC road transport scenario 2030+ "road to implementation". Technical report, European Road Transport Research Advisory Council, October 2009
14. Fujii, H., Uchida, H., Yoshimura, S.: Agent-based simulation framework for mixed traffic of cars, pedestrians and trams. Transp. Res. C-Emerg. **85**, 234–248 (2017)
15. Gawron, C.: An iterative algorithm to determine the dynamic user equilibrium in a traffic simulation model. Int. J. Mod. Phys. C **9**(3), 393–407 (1998)

16. German, R.: Performance Analysis of Communication Systems with Non-Markovian Stochastic Petri Nets. Wiley, Hoboken (2000)
17. Higgins, A., Kozan, E., Ferreira, L.: Optimal scheduling of trains on a single line track. Transp. Res. B-Methodol. **30**(2), 147–161 (1996)
18. Horváth, A., Paolieri, M., Ridi, L., Vicario, E.: Transient analysis of non-Markovian models using stochastic state classes. Perform. Eval. **69**(7–8), 315–335 (2012)
19. Kerner, B.S., Klenov, S.L., Wolf, D.E.: Cellular automata approach to three-phase traffic theory. J. Phys. A: Math. Gen. **35**(47), 9971–10013 (2002)
20. Krajzewicz, D., Erdmann, J., Härri, J., Spyropoulos, T.: Including pedestrian and bicycle traffic into the traffic simulation SUMO. In: ITS 2014, 10th ITS European Congress, 16–19 June 2014, Helsinki, Finland (2014)
21. Krajzewicz, D., Hertkorn, G., Rössel, C., Wagner, P.: SUMO (simulation of urban mobility) - an open-source traffic simulation. In: 4th Middle East Symposium on Simulation and Modelling, pp. 183–187 (2002)
22. Martina, S., Paolieri, M., Papini, T., Vicario, E.: Performance evaluation of Fischer's protocol through steady-state analysis of Markov regenerative processes. In: 2016 IEEE 24th International Symposium on MASCOTS, pp. 355–360 (2016)
23. Nagy, E., Csiszár, C.: Analysis of delay causes in railway passenger transportation. Period. Polytech. Transp. Eng. **43**(2), 73–80 (2015)
24. Ondráček, J., et al.: Contribution of the road traffic to air pollution in the Prague city (busy speedway and suburban crossroads). Atmos. Environ. **45**(29), 5090–5100 (2011)
25. Paolieri, M., Horváth, A., Vicario, E.: Probabilistic model checking of regenerative concurrent systems. IEEE Trans. Softw. Eng. **42**(2), 153–169 (2016)
26. Peng, G., Cai, X., Liu, C., Cao, B., Tuo, M.: Optimal velocity difference model for a car-following theory. Phys. Lett. A **375**(45), 3973–3977 (2011)
27. Shi, J., Sun, Y., Schonfeld, P., Qi, J.: Joint optimization of tram timetables and signal timing adjustments at intersections. Transp. Res. C-Emerg. **83**, 104–119 (2017)
28. Tang, T., Wang, Y., Yang, X., Wu, Y.: A new car-following model accounting for varying road condition. Nonlinear Dyn. **70**(2), 1397–1405 (2012)
29. Tonguz, O.K., Viriyasitavat, W., Bai, F.: Modeling urban traffic: a cellular automata approach. IEEE Commun. Mag. **47**(5), 142–150 (2009)
30. Vicario, E.: Static analysis and dynamic steering of time dependent systems using time Petri nets. IEEE Trans. Softw. Eng. **27**(1), 728–748 (2001)
31. Vicario, E., Sassoli, L., Carnevali, L.: Using stochastic state classes in quantitative evaluation of dense-time reactive systems. IEEE Trans. Softw. Eng. **35**, 703–719 (2009)
32. Yang, J., Deng, W., Wang, J., Li, Q., Wang, Z.: Modeling pedestrians' road crossing behavior in traffic system micro-simulation in China. Transp. Res. A-Policy **40**(3), 280–290 (2006)
33. Yoshimura, S.: MATES : multi-agent based traffic and environmental simulator-theory, implementation and practical application. Comput. Model. Eng. Sci. **11**(1), 17–25 (2006)
34. Zeng, W., Chen, P., Nakamura, H., Iryo-Asano, M.: Application of social force model to pedestrian behavior analysis at signalized crosswalk. Transp. Res. C-Emerg. **40**, 143–159 (2014)
35. Zheng, L.J., Tian, C., Sun, D.H., Liu, W.N.: A new car-following model with consideration of anticipation driving behavior. Nonlinear Dyn. **70**(2), 1205–1211 (2012)

Toward Implicit Learning for the Compositional Verification of Markov Decision Processes

Redouane Bouchekir(✉) and Mohand Cherif Boukala

MOVEP, Computer Science Department, University of Science and Technology Houari Boumediene, BP 32 El-Alia, Algiers, Algeria
{rbouchekir,mboukala}@usthb.dz

Abstract. In this paper, we propose an automated compositional verification using implicit learning to verify Markov Decision Process (MDP) against probabilistic safety properties. Our approach, denoted *ACVuIL* (Automatic Compositional Verification using Implicit Learning), starts by encoding implicitly the MDP components by using compact data structures. Then, we use a sound and complete symbolic assume-guarantee reasoning rule to establish the compositional verification process. This rule uses the CDNF learning algorithm to generate automatically the symbolic probabilistic assumptions. Experimental results suggest promising outlooks for our approach.

Keywords: Probabilistic model checking
Compositional verification · Symbolic model checking
Assume-guarantee paradigm · Machine learning · CDNF Learning

1 Introduction

An important feature of modern systems is their complexity. This characteristic makes the design, implementation and verification of complex systems extremely difficult. This difficulty is enhanced by the often critical role of these systems (avionics control process, nuclear power plants, etc.). *Probabilistic verification* is a set of techniques for formal modelling and analysis of such systems. *Probabilistic model checking* [1–3] involves the construction of a finite-state model augmented with probabilistic information, such as Markov chains or probabilistic automaton [17,26]. This is then checked against properties specified in probabilistic extensions of temporal logic, such as Probabilistic Computation Tree Logic (PCTL) [18].

Formal methods, including the Probabilistic Model Checking [1–3] suffer from the problem of state space explosion. This problem constitutes, even after several years of research, the main obstacle of probabilistic model checking. *Compositional verification* [14,15,19,24] and *Symbolic model checking* [7,27] are two promising approaches to cope with this problem. Compositional verification suggests a divide and conquer strategy to reduce the verification task into simpler

M. F. Atig et al. (Eds.): VECoS 2018, LNCS 11181, pp. 200–217, 2018.
https://doi.org/10.1007/978-3-030-00359-3_13

subtasks. A popular approach is the *assume-guarantee* paradigm [9,11,29], in which individual system components are verified under *assumptions* about their environment. Once it has been verified that the other system components do indeed satisfy these assumptions, proof rules can be used to combine individual verification results, establishing correctness properties of the overall system. The success of assume-guarantee reasoning approach depends on discovering appropriate assumptions. The process of generating automatically assumptions can be solved by using machine learning [9,14], such as $CDNF$ learning algorithm [6]. Symbolic model checking is also a useful technique to cope with the state explosion problem. In symbolic model checking, system states are implicitly represented by Boolean functions, as well as the initial states and transition relation of the system. To verify probabilistic systems encoded using Boolean function, the Boolean function should be converted to another data structures such as Binary Decision Diagrams(BDD) or Multi Terminal BDD(MTBDD) [16], this is due to the absence of SAT-based model checking for probabilistic systems.

In this paper, we present a novel approach for the compositional verification for probabilistic systems through implicit learning. Our aim is to reduce the size of the state space. For that, we propose to encode the system components using Boolean functions and Multi Terminal BDD. This encoding allows to store and explore a large number of states efficiently [9]. We use the Boolean functions as input of the CDNF learning algorithm. This algorithm generates an assumption which simulates a set of MDP component. The idea is to use this assumption for the verification instead of the real system components. Thus, if the size of this assumption is much smaller than the size of the corresponding MDP component, then we can expect significant gain of the verification performance. In our work, Interval Markov Decision Processes (IMDP) are used to represent assumptions. To establish the verification process and guarantee that the generated assumption simulates all the possible behaviour of the set of components, we proposed a sound and complete symbolic assume-guarantee reasoning rule. This rule defines and establish the compositional verification process. We have illustrated our approach using a simple example, and we have applied our approach in a several case studies derived from PRISM benchmarks. Experimental results suggest promising outlooks for the implicit learning of the compositional verification.

The remainder of this paper is organized as follows: In Sect. 2 we provide the most relevant works to our work. Section 3 provides some background knowledge about MDP, Interval MDP and the parallel composition MDP || IMDP. In Sect. 4, we present our approach, where we detail the process of encoding MDP using Boolean function, our symbolic assume-guarantee reasoning proof rule and the application of the CNDF learning algorithm to generate assumptions. Section 6 concludes the paper and talks about future works.

2 Related Works

In this section, we review some research works related to the symbolic probabilistic model checking, compositional verification and assume-guarantee reasoning.

Verification of probabilistic systems have been addressed by Vardi and Wolper [32–34], and then by Pnueli and Zuck [30], and by Baier and Kwiatkowska [3]. The symbolic probabilistic model checking algorithms have been proposed by [10,28]. These algorithms have been implemented in a symbolic probabilistic model checker PRISM [22]. The main techniques used to generate counterexamples was detailed in [21]. A recent work [12] proposed to use causality in order to generate small counterexamples, the authors of this work propose to used the tool DiPro to generate counterexamples, then they applied an aided-diagnostic method to generate the most indicative counterexample. For the compositional verification of non-probabilistic systems, several frameworks have been developed using the assume-guarantee reasoning approach [9,11,29]. The compositional verification of probabilistic systems has been a significant progress in these last years [14,15,19,23]. Our approach is inspired by the work of [14,15]. In this work, they consider the verification of Discrete Time Markov Chains, and they proposed to use CDNF learning algorithm to infer assumptions. Another work relevant to ours is [19]. This work proposed the first sound and complete learning-based composition verification technique for probabilistic safety properties, where they used an adapted L^* learning algorithm to learn weighted automata as assumptions, then they transformed them into MTBDD.

3 Preliminaries

In this section, we give some background knowledge about MDP and IMDP. MDP are often used to describe and study systems exhibit non deterministic and stochastic behaviour.

Definition 1. *Markov Decision Process (MDP) is a tuple $M = (States_M, s_0^M, \Sigma_M, \delta_M)$ where $States_M$ is a finite set of states, $s_0^M \in States_M$ is an initial state, Σ_M is a finite set of actions, $\delta_M \subseteq States_M \times (\Sigma_M \cup \{\tau\}) \times Dist(States_M)$ is a probabilistic transition relation, where where τ denotes a "silent" (or "internal") action.*

In a state s of MDP M, one or more transitions, denoted $(s, a) \rightarrow \mu$, are available, where $a \in \Sigma_M$ is an action label, μ is a probability distribution over states, where $\mu \neq 0$, and $(s, a, \mu) \in \delta_M$. A path through MDP is a (finite or infinite) sequence $(s_0, a_0, \mu_0) \rightarrow (s_1, a_1, \mu_1) \rightarrow ....$ An example of two MDP M_0 and M_1 is shown in Fig. 1.

Interval Markov Chains (IMDP) generalize ordinary MDP by having interval-valued transition probabilities rather than just probability value. In this paper, we use IMDP to represent the assumptions used in our compositional verification.

Definition 2. *Interval Markov Chain (IMDP) is a tuple $I = (States_I, i_0^I, \Sigma_I, P^l, P^u)$ where $States_I, i_0^I$ and Σ_I are respectively the set of states, initial state and the set of actions. $P^l, P^u : States_I \times \Sigma_I \times States_I \mapsto [0, 1]$ are matrices representing the lower/upper bounds of transition probabilities such that: $P^l(i, a)(i') \leq P^u(i, a)(i')$ for all states $i, i' \in States_I$ and $a \in \Sigma_I$.*

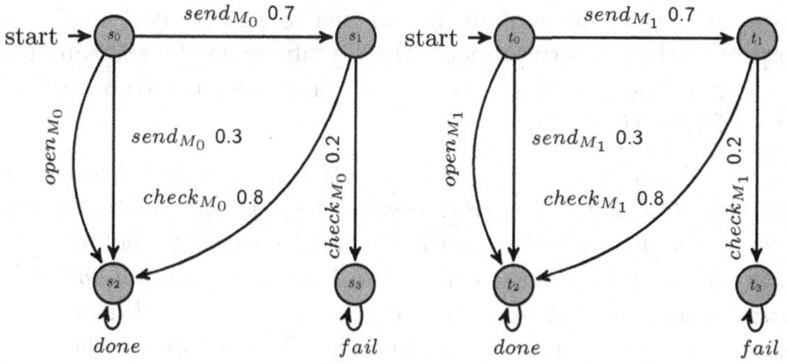

Fig. 1. Example of two MDP, M_0 (left) and M_1 (right).

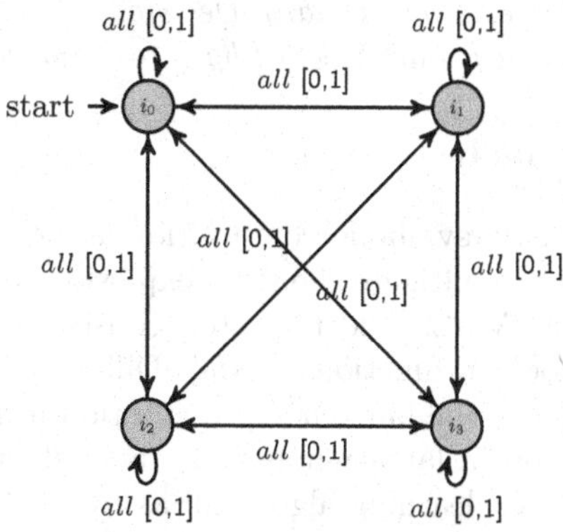

Fig. 2. Example of IMDP I.

An example of IMDP I is shown in Fig. 2, where *all* represents the set of actions : $\{open_{M_0}, send_{M_0}, check_{M_0}, done, fail\}$ with the probability interval value equal to $[0, 1]$.

In Definition 3, we describe how MDP and IMDP are composed together. This is done by using the asynchronous parallel operator ($\|$) defined by [31], where MDP and IMDP synchronise over shared actions and interleave otherwise.

Definition 3. *Parallel composition $MDP \parallel IMDP$*
Let M and I be MDP and Interval MDP, respectively. Their parallel composition, denoted by $M \parallel I$, is an Interval MDP MI. $MI = \{States_M \times States_I, (s_0^M, s_0^I), \Sigma_M \cup \Sigma_I, P^l, P^u\}$, where P^l, P^u are defined such that: $(s_i, s_j) \xrightarrow{a} [P^l(s_i,a)(s_j) \times \mu_i, P^u(s_i,a)(s_j) \times \mu_i]$ if and only if one of the following conditions holds: Let $s_i,\ s_i' \in States_M$ and $s_j,\ s_j' \in States_I$: (i) $s_i \xrightarrow{a,\mu_i} s_i', s_j \xrightarrow{P^l(s_j,a)(s_j'),P^u(s_j,a)(s_j')} s_j'$, where $a \in \Sigma_M \cap \Sigma_I$, (ii) $s_i \xrightarrow{a,\mu_i} s_i'$, where $a \in \Sigma_M \setminus \Sigma_I$, and (iii) $s_j \xrightarrow{P^l(s_j,a)(s_j'),P^u(s_j,a)(s_j')} s_j'$, where $a \in \Sigma_M \setminus \Sigma_I$.

In this work we use the symbolic model checking to verify if a system $M_0 \parallel I$ satisfies a probabilistic safety property. The symbolic Model checking uses BDD and MTBDD to encode the state space. It is straightforward to convert a Boolean function to a BDD/MTBDD.

Definition 4. *A Binary Decision Diagram (BDD) is a rooted, directed acyclic graph with its vertex set partitioned into non-terminal and terminal vertices (also called nodes). A non-terminal node d is labelled by a variable $var(d) \in X$, where X is a finite ordered set of Boolean variables. Each non-terminal node has exactly two children nodes, denoted $then(d)$ and $else(d)$. A terminal node d is labelled by a Boolean value $val(d)$ and has no children. The Boolean variable ordering $<$ is imposed onto the graph by requiring that a child d' of a non-terminal node d is either terminal, or is non-terminal and satisfies $var(d) < var(d')$.*

Definition 5. *A Multi-Terminal Binary Decision Diagram (MTBDD) is a BDD where the terminal nodes are labelled by a real number.*

4 ACVuIL Approach

Our approach, probabilistic symbolic compositional verification using implicit learning (ACVuIL), aims to mitigate the state explosion problem. Figure 3 illustrates an overview of ACVuIL. The first step consists to encode the system component M_0 using Boolean functions $\beta(M_0)$. Different from the explicit representing of the state space, the implicit representation using Boolean functions allows to store and explore a large number of states efficiently. $\beta(M_0)$ will be used as input of the CDNF learning algorithm as target language. The second step aims to generate an appropriate assumption S_{I_i}, which needs to abstract the behaviour of the original competent M_0. In our approach, we use the $CDNF$ learning algorithm to generate automatically the assumptions. The second step starts by calling the $CDNF$ learning algorithm, with $\beta(M_0)$ as input. At each iteration, the CDNF learns a new assumption $\beta(I_i)$ represented as Boolean functions. For the first iteration ($i = 0$), the CDNF generates $true$ as assumption, for that, we generate a special initial assumption S_{I_0}. For ($i \geq 1$) iterations, we convert the generated assumption $\beta(I_i)$ to MTBDD S_{I_i}, then we refine the initial assumption S_{I_0} using S_{I_i}. We use the symbolic probabilistic model checking algorithm ($SPMC$) to verify if $S_{I_0} \parallel S_{M_1}$ satisfies the probabilistic safety property $P_{\leq P}[\psi]$. If $SPMC(S_{I_0}, S_{M_1})$ returns true, then we can conclude that $M_0 \parallel M_1 \models P_{\leq P}[\psi]$ is true i.e. $P_{\leq P}[\psi]$ satisfies $M_0 \parallel M_1$, otherwise, we generate a counterexample Ctx illustrated why $P_{\leq P}[\psi]$ is violated. Ctx can be a real counterexample of the system $M_0 \parallel M_1$ or a spurious counterexample due to the generated assumption. Thus, at each iteration, we analyse if Ctx is real or not. If Ctx is real, then we can conclude that $M_0 \parallel M_1 \not\models P_{\leq P}[\psi]$ i.e. $P_{\leq P}[\psi]$ does not satisfy the system $M_0 \parallel M_1$, otherwise, we return Ctx to CDNF to generate a new assumption. Our compositional verification process is sound and complete. The soundness and completeness is guaranteed by the use of an assume-guarantee reasoning rule. All steps of our approach are described in details in the next sections.

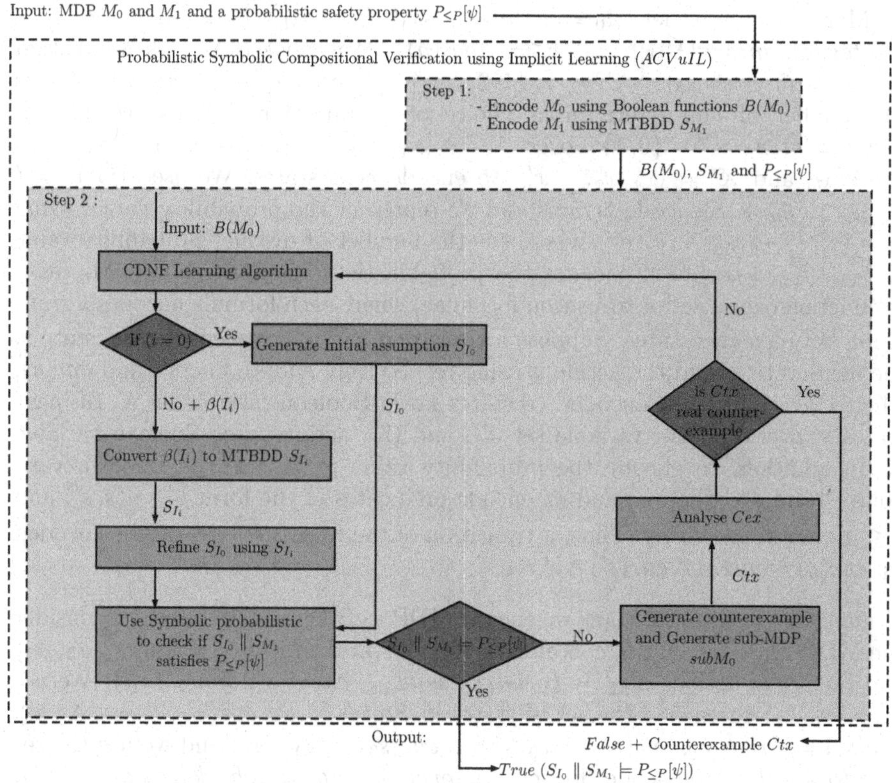

Fig. 3. An overview of our approach (ACVuIL).

4.1 Encoding MDP Using Boolean Functions

MDP can be encoded implicitly as Boolean functions, we denote by $\beta(M_0)$ the Boolean functions encoded MDP M_0. The encoding process of MDP using Boolean functions aims to reduce the size of the state space. Indeed, many works such as [7,16,27,28] show that the implicit representation is often more efficient than the explicit representation. In addition, this Boolean functions will be used as input of the CDNF learning algorithm. In this section we describe the process of encoding MDP using Boolean functions.

Definition 6. *$\beta(M_0) = (Init_{M_0}, f_{M_0}\ (yxx'e^le^u))$ is a pair of Boolean functions encoded the MDP M_0, where $Init_{M_0}$ is predicate encoding the initial state $s_0^{M_0}$ over the set X and $f_M(yxx'e^le^u)$ is a transition predicate over $Y \cup X \cup X' \cup E$ where y, x, x', e^l, e^u are predicates of receptively Y, X, X' and E. Y, X, X' and E are finite ordered set of Boolean variables with $Y \cap X \cap X' \cap E = \emptyset$. The set X encodes the states of M_0, X' next states, Y encodes actions and E encodes the probability values.*

More concretely, let $M_0 = (States_{M_0}, s_0^M, \Sigma_{M_0}, \delta_{M_0})$ be a MDP. Let $n = |States_{M_0}|$, $m = |\Sigma_{M_0}|$ and $k = \lceil log_2(n) \rceil$. We can see δ_{M_0} as a function of the form $States_{M_0} \times \Sigma_{M_0} \times \{1, 2, ..., r\} \times States_{M_0} \rightarrow [0, 1]$, where r is the number of non-deterministic choice of a transition. We use a function $enc : States_{M_0} \rightarrow \{0, 1\}^k$ over $X = \langle x_1, x_2, ..., x_k \rangle$ to encode states in $States_{M_0}$ and $X' = \langle x'_1, x'_2, ..., x'_k \rangle$ to encode next states. We use also $Y = \langle y_1, y_2, ..., y_m \rangle$ to encode actions and we represent the probability values using $E = \langle e^l_1, e^u_1, e^l_2, e^u_2, ..., e^l_t, e^t \rangle$, where t is the number of distinct probability value in δ_{M_0}. $f_{M_0}\ (yxx'e^le^u)$ encodes the probabilistic transition relation δ_{M_0} as a disjunction over a set of transition formulae, where each formula encodes a transition between two states. Suppose a transition $s \xrightarrow{a,p} s'$, we encode the state s, the next state s' and the action a using respectively $enc(s)$, $enc(s')$ and $enc(a)$, where enc is a function encodes: (i) states s over Boolean variable set X, (ii) next states s' over Boolean variable set X', and (iii) actions over Boolean variable Y. In addition, to encode the probability value p, we use the Boolean variables e^l and e^u, where e^l and e^u encode predicates of the form $p \geq \mu(s, s')$ and $p \leq \mu(s, s')$ respectively. Thus, a transition of the from $s \xrightarrow{a,p} s'$ can be encoded as: $enc(y) \wedge enc(s) \wedge enc(s') \wedge e^l \wedge e^u$.

Example 1. To illustrate how we encode MDP as Boolean functions, we consider the MDP M_0 (Fig. 1). M_0 contains the set of states $States_{M_0} = \{s_0, s_1, s_2, s_3\}$ and the set of actions $\Sigma_{M_0} = \{open_{M_0}, send_{M_0}, check_{M_0}, done, fail\}$. We use $X = \langle x_0, x_1 \rangle$ to encode the set of states in $States_{M_0}$ as: $enc(s_0) = \neg x_0 \wedge \neg x_1$, $enc(s_1) = \neg x_0 \wedge x_1$, $enc(s_2) = x_0 \wedge \neg x_1$, $enc(s_3) = x_0 \wedge x_1$; and we use the set $Y = \langle o, s, c, d, f \rangle$ to encode the actions $\{open_{M_0}, send_{M_0}, check_{M_0}, done, fail\}$, respectively. Table 1 summarizes the process of encoding the transition function δ_{M_0}. $\beta(M_0) = (Init_{M_0}, f_{M_0}\ (yxx'e^le^u))$ encoded M_0 is $Init_{M_0} = \neg x_0 \wedge \neg x_1$ and

$$
f_{M_0}(yxx'e^le^u) = \begin{array}{l}
((s \wedge \neg x_0 \wedge \neg x_1 \wedge \neg x'_0 \wedge x'_1 \wedge e^l_3 \wedge e^u_3) \\
\vee(s \wedge \neg x_0 \wedge \neg x_1 \wedge x'_0 \wedge \neg x'_1 \wedge e^l_2 \wedge e^u_2) \\
\vee(o \wedge \neg x_0 \wedge \neg x_1 \wedge x'_0 \wedge \neg x'_1 \wedge e^l_5 \wedge e^u_5) \\
\vee(c \wedge \neg x_0 \wedge x_1 \wedge x'_0 \wedge \neg x'_1 \wedge e^l_4 \wedge e^u_4) \\
\vee(c \wedge \neg x_0 \wedge x_1 \wedge x'_0 \wedge x'_1 \wedge e^l_1 \wedge e^u_1) \\
\vee(d \wedge x_0 \wedge \neg x_1 \wedge x'_0 \wedge \neg x'_1 \wedge e^l_5 \wedge e^u_5) \\
\vee(f \wedge x_0 \wedge x_1 \wedge x'_0 \wedge x'_1 \wedge e^l_5 \wedge e^u_5))
\end{array}
$$

4.2 Encoding MDP Using MTBDD

In this paper, we also consider the implicit representation using MTBDD. MTBDD are used to encode components M_1 and to perform the probabilistic model checking. In Definition 7, we introduce Symbolic MDP (SMDP) and we provide the different data structures used to encode MDP. We denoted by S_{M_1} the SMDP encoded the MDP M_1.

Definition 7. *Symbolic MDP (SMDP) is a tuple* $S_M = (X, Init_M, Y, f_{S_M}(yxx'))$ *where* X, X' *and* Y *are finite ordered set of Boolean variables with*

Table 1. Encoding the set of states and the probability values of MDP M_0 (Fig. 1).

$e_i \in E$	Predicate	$e_i \in E$	Predicate	$s_i \in \Sigma_{M_0}$	$enc(s_i)$
e_0^l	≥ 0	e_2^l	≥ 0.3	s_0	$\neg x_0 \wedge \neg x_1$
e_0^u	≤ 0	e_2^u	≤ 0.3	s_1	$\neg x_0 \wedge x_1$
e_1^l	≥ 0.2	e_3^l	≥ 0.7	s_2	$x_0 \wedge \neg x_1$
e_1^u	≤ 0.2	e_3^u	≤ 0.7	s_3	$x_0 \wedge x_1$
e_4^l	≥ 0.8	e_5^l	≥ 1		
e_4^u	≤ 0.8	e_5^u	≤ 1		

$X \cap X' \cap Y = \emptyset$. $Init(X)$ is a BDD encoded the initial state and $f_{S_M}(yxx')$ is an MTBDD encoded the transition relation. The sets X, X' and Y are used to encode respectively the set of states, next states and the set of actions of M, and y, x, x' are valuations of receptively, Y, X, X'.

The encoding of MDP as SMDP follows the same process as the encoding using Boolean functions.

Example 2. We consider the MDP M_1 (Fig. 1) to illustrate the encoding of MDP using SMDP. M_1 contains the set of states $States_{M_1} = \{t_0, t_1, t_2, t_3\}$ and the set of actions $\Sigma_{M_1} = \{open_{M_1}, send_{M_1}, check_{M_1}, done, fail\}$. We use the set $X = \langle x_0, x_1 \rangle$ to encode the set of states $States_{M_0}$ as: $enc(t_0) = (00)$, $enc(t_1) = (01)$, $enc(t_2) = (10)$, $enc(t_3) = (11)$; and we use the set $Y = \langle s, o, c, d, f \rangle$ to encode the actions $\{open_{M_1}, send_{M_1}, check_{M_1}, done, fail\}$, respectively.

Following the same process to encode MDP implicitly as SMDP, we can encode Interval MDP as SIMDP.

Definition 8. *Symbolic Interval MDP (SIMDP) is a tuple $S_I = (X, Init_I, Y, f^l_{S_I}(yxx'), f^u_{S_I}(yxx'))$ where X, X' and Y are finite ordered set of Boolean variables with $X \cap X' \cap Y = \emptyset$. $Init_I$ is a BDD encodes the initial state and $f^l_{S_I}(yxx')$ and $f^u_{S_I}(yxx')$ are MTBDD encode the transition relation over $Y \cup X \cup X'$. The MTBDD $f^l_{S_I}(yxx')$ encodes the lower probability bound and $f^u_{S_I}(yxx')$ encodes the lower. The sets X, X' and Y encode respectively, the set of states, next states and the set of actions, and y, x, x' are valuations of receptively, Y, X, X'.*

4.3 Symbolic Assume-Guarantee Reasoning Rule

To establish the compositional verification process we propose an assume-guarantee reasoning proof rule, where assumptions are represented using IMDP. As described before, the compositional verification aims to generate a symbolic assumption I_i represented using IMDP, where M_0 is embedded in I_i ($M_0 \preceq I_i$).

Definition 9. *Let* $M_0 = (States_{M_0}, s_0^{M_0}, \Sigma_{M_0}, \delta_{M_0})$ *and* $I_i = (States_{I_i}, s_0^{I_i}, \Sigma_{I_i}, P^l, P^u)$ *be MDP and IMDP, respectively. We say* M_0 *is embedded in* I_i*, written* $M_0 \preceq I_i$*, if and only if: (1)* $States_{M_0} = States_{I_i}$*, (2)* $s_0^{M_0} = s_0^{I_i}$*, (3)* $\Sigma_{M_i} = \Sigma_{I_i}$*, and (4)* $P^l(s,a)(s') \leq \mu(s,a)(s') \leq P^u(s,a)(s')$ *for every* $s, s' \in States_M$ *and* $a \in \Sigma_M$.

Example 3. Consider the MDP M_0 shown in Fig. 1 and IMDP I shown in Fig. 2. They have the same number of states, identical initial state (s_0, i_0) and the same set of actions $\Sigma_{M_1} = \{open_{M_1}, send_{M_1}, check_{M_1}, done, fail\}$. In addition, the transition probability between any two states in M_0 lies within the corresponding transition probability interval in I by taking the same action in Σ_{M_1}. For example, the transition probability between s_0 and s_1 is $s_0 \xrightarrow{send_{M_0}, 0.7} s_1$, which falls into the interval $[0, 1]$ labelled the transition $i_0 \xrightarrow{send_{M_0}, [0,1]} i_1$ in I. Thus, we have $M_0 \preceq I$; (M_0 is embedded in I).

Theorem 1. ***Symbolic assume-guarantee reasoning rule***
Let M_0, M_1 *be MDP and* $P_{\leq P}[\psi]$ *a probabilistic safety property, then the following proof rule is sound and complete:* ***if*** $M_0 \preceq I$ ***and*** $I \parallel M_1 \models P_{\leq P}[\psi]$ ***then*** $M_0 \parallel M_1 \models P_{\leq P}[\psi]$*. This proof rule means, if we have a system composed of two components* M_0 *and* M_1*, then we can check the correctness of a probabilistic safety property* $P_{\leq P}[\psi]$ *over* $M_0 \parallel M_1$ *without constructing and verifying the full state space. Instead, we first generate an appropriate assumption* I*, where* I *is an IMDP, then we check if this assumption could be used to verify* $M_0 \parallel M_1$ *by checking the two promises: (i) Check if* M_0 *is embedded in* I*,* $M_0 \preceq I$*, and (ii) Check if* $I \parallel M_1$ *satisfies the probabilistic safety property* $P_{\leq P}[\psi]$*,* $I \parallel M_1 \models P_{\leq P}[\psi]$*. If the two promises are satisfied then we can conclude that* $M_0 \parallel M_1$ *satisfies* $P_{\leq P}[\psi]$.

Proof (Soundness). *Consider* M_0 *and* M_1 *be MDP, where* $M_0 = (States_{M_0}, s_0^{M_0}, \Sigma_{M_0}, \delta_{M_0})$*,* $M_1 = (States_{M_1}, s_0^{M_1}, \Sigma_{M_1}, \delta_{M_1})$*, and IMDP* I*,* $I = (States_I, s_0^I, \Sigma_I, P^l, P^u)$. If $M_0 \preceq I$ *and based on Definition* 9 *we have* $States_M = States_I$*,* $s_0^M = s_0^I$*,* $\Sigma_M = \Sigma_I$*, and* $P^l(s,a)(s') \leq \mu(s,a)(s') \leq P^u(s,a)(s')$ *for every* $s, s' \in States_{M_0}$ *and* $a \in \Sigma_{M_0}$*. Based on Definitions* 3 *and* 9*,* $M_0 \parallel M_1$ *and* $I \parallel M_1$ *have the same state space, initial state and actions. Since* $P^l(s,a)(s') \leq \mu(s,a)(s') \leq P^u(s,a)(s')$*, and we suppose the transition probability of* $M_0 \parallel M_1$ *as:* $\mu_{M_0 \parallel M_1}((s_i, s_j), a)(s_i', s_j') = \mu_{M_0}((s_i), a)(s_i') \times \mu_{M_1}((s_j), a)(s_j')$ *for any state* $s_i, s_i' \in States_{M_0}$ *and* $s_j, s_j' \in States_{M_1}$*. Thus,* $P^l((s_i, s_j), a)(s_i', s_j') \leq \mu_{M_0 \parallel M_1}((s_i, s_j), a)\ (s_i', s_j') \leq P^u((s_i, s_j), a)(s_i', s_j')$ *for the probability between two states* (s_i, s_i') *and* (s_j, s_j'). In $I \parallel M_1$ *the probability interval between any two states* (s_i, s_j) *and* (s_i', s_j') *is restricted by the interval* $[P^l((s_i, a)(s_i') \times \mu_{M_1}(s_j), a)(s_j'),\ P^u((s_i, a)(s_i') \times \mu_{M_1}(s_j)\ , a)(s_j')]$*, this implies, if* $M_0 \preceq I$ *and* $I \parallel M_1 \models P_{\leq P}[\psi]$ *then* $M_0 \parallel M_1 \models P_{\leq P}[\psi]$ *is guaranteed.*

Proof (Completeness). *The completeness of our approach is guarantee since we always generate a new assumption to refine the initial one. In the worst case, the CDNF will learn a final assumption equivalent to the original component.*

4.4 CDNF Learning Algorithm

The CDNF learning algorithm [6] is an exact learning algorithm for Boolean functions. It learns a Boolean formula in conjunctive disjunctive normal form (CDNF) for a target Boolean function over a fixed set of Boolean variables x. In this paper, we use this algorithm to learn the symbolic assumptions I for MDP represented by Boolean functions. During the learning process, the CDNF learning algorithm interacts with a Teacher to make two types of queries: (i) *membership queries* and (ii) *equivalence queries*. A membership queries are used to check whether a valuation v over Boolean variables x satisfies the target function. Equivalence queries are used to check whether a conjectured Boolean function is equivalent to the target function.

4.5 ACVuIL: Automatic Compositional Verification Using Implicit Learning Algorithm

Algorithm ACVuIL highlighted the main steps of our approach. ACVuIL accepts the system components MDP M_0, M_1 and the probabilistic safety property $\varphi = P_{\leq P}[\psi]$ as input. ACVuIL starts by encoding M_0 using Boolean functions and M_1 using SMDP. Then, it calls the CDNF learning algorithm to learn the initial assumption I_0. For the first iteration, CDNF learns *true* as initial assumption. For that, ACVuIL calls the function *GenerateInitialAssumption* to generate S_{I_0}. The process of generating the SIMDP S_{I_0} is described in the next section.

4.6 Generate Initial Assumption

The ACVuIL calls the function *GenerateInitialAssumption* to generate the initial assumption S_{I_0}. This function accepts MDP M_0 and the Boolean functions I_0 as inputs, and returns SIMDP S_{I_0}. The process of generating S_{I_0} is described in Algorithm 2.

GenerateInitialAssumption creates a new IMDP $Initial\_I_0$ equivalent to M_0, with transitions equal to $[0, 1]$ between all states, and the set of actions are hold in each transition. Then it encodes the IMDP of $Initial\_I_0$ as SIMDP. The aim behind the generation of S_{I_0} with transition equal to $[0, 1]$ between all states is to reduce the size of the implicit representation of the state space. Indeed, for large probabilistic system, when we use uniform probabilities (0 and 1 in our case) this will reduce the number of terminal nodes as well as non-terminal nodes. Adding transition between all states, will keep our assume-guarantee verified for the initial assumption, since M_0 is embedded in $Initial\_I_0$, in addition, this process will help to reduce the size of the implicit representation of $Initial\_I_0$ and this by combining any isomorphic sub-tree into a single tree, and eliminating any nodes whose left and right children are isomorphic.

Example 4. To illustrate our approach, we consider the verification of $M_0 \parallel M_1$ (Fig. 1) against the probabilistic safety property $P_{\leq 0.0195}[\Diamond \text{“}err\text{”}]$, where “*err*” stands for the state (s_3, t_3). This property means that the maximum probability that the system $M_0 \parallel M_1$ should never fails, over all possible adversaries,

Algorithm 1. ACVuIL

1: **Input:** M_0, M_1 and $\varphi = P_{\leq P}[\psi]$
2: **output:** $SIMDP\ I_i$, set of counterexamples and a Boolean value
3: **Begin**
4: $\beta(M_0) \leftarrow$ Encode M_0 as a Boolean functions;
5: $S_{M_1} \leftarrow$ Encode M_1 as SMDP;
6: $I_0 \leftarrow$ CDNF $(\beta(M_0))$;
7: $S_{I_0} \leftarrow$ GenerateInitialAssumption(M_0, I_0);
8: $result \leftarrow$ SPMC$(S_{I_0}, S_{M_1}, \varphi)$;
9: **while** $(result == false)$ **do**
10: $\quad i \leftarrow i + 1$;
11: $\quad Ctx \leftarrow$ GenerateCounterexample $(S_{I_{i-1}}, S_{M_1}, \varphi)$;
12: $\quad subM_0 \leftarrow$ GenerateSub-MDP (M_0, Ctx);
13: $\quad$ real $\leftarrow$ AnalyseCounterexample $(subM_0, S_{M_1}, \varphi)$;
14: $\quad$ **if** $(real == true)$ **then**
15: $\qquad$ return $(S_{I_{i-1}}, Ctx, false)$;
16: $\quad$ **else**
17: $\qquad \beta(I_i) \leftarrow$ return $false$ to CDNF to generate new assumption;
18: $\qquad S_{I_i} \leftarrow Refine\_S_{I_i}(S_{I_0}, \beta(I_i), \beta(M_0))$.
19: $\qquad result \leftarrow$ SPMC$(S_{I_i}, S_{M_1}, \varphi)$;
20: $\quad$ **end if**
21: **end while**;
22: return $(S_{I_i}, NULL, true)$;
23: **End**

is less than 0.0195. ACVuIL starts by encoding M_0 using Boolean functions $\beta(M_0)$. $\beta(M_0)$ encoded M_0 is illustrated in Sect. 4.1. In addition, The encoding process of M_1 as SMDP is illustrated in Sect. 4.2. After encoding the system components using implicit representation, ACVuIL calls the function *GenerateInitialAssumption* to generate the initial assumption. The explicit representation of the initial assumption $Initial\_I_0$ is illustrated in Fig. 2.

Symbolic Probabilistic Model Checking (SPCV). In line 8 and 19, ACVuIL calls the function Symbolic probabilistic model checking (SPCV). To model checking $S_{I_i} \parallel S_{M_1} \models P_{\leq P}[\psi]$, SPCV computes the parallel composition $S_{I_i} \parallel S_{M_1}$, where the result is SIMDP, because S_{I_i} is SIMDP. Indeed, model checking algorithm for IMDP was considered in [4,8], where it was demonstrated that the verification of IMDP is often more consume, in time as well as in space, than the verification of MDP. In this work, our ultimate goal is reducing the size of the state space. Therefore, the verification of IMDP needs to be avoided. Thus, we propose rather than verifying SIMDP $S_{I_i} \parallel S_{M_1}$, we verify only a restricted SMDP *RI*, which is an MTBDD contains the upper probability value of the probability interval associate in each transition of S_{I_i}. This can be done by taking the MTBDD $f^u_{S_{I_i}}$ of S_{I_i}. Then, the verification of $RI \parallel S_{M_1}$ can be done using the standard probabilistic model checking proposed in [19]. The symbolic probabilistic model checking used in this work was proposed in [28].

Algorithm 2. *GenerateInitialAssumption*

Input: *MDP* M_0, Boolean functions I_0
output: *SIMDP* S_{I_0}
BEGIN
Create a new IMDP *Initial_I*$_0$ equivalent to M_0, with transitions equal to $[0, 1]$ between all states. The set of actions in M_0 are hold in each transition of I_0.
$S_{I_0} \leftarrow$ Encode *Initial_I*$_0$ as SIMDP;
return S_{I_0};
End

Example 5. To analyse if S_{I_0} could be used to establish the compositional verification, ACVuIL calls the symbolic model cheeking (SPCV) to check if $S_{I_0} \parallel S_{M_1} \models P_{\leq 0.0195}[\Diamond\text{"}err\text{"}]$. This latter returns $false$. In practice, to verify $S_{I_0} \parallel S_{M_1} \models P_{\leq 0.0195}[\Diamond fail]$ we used the model PRISM with the engine *"MTBDD"* [22].

Generate Probabilistic Counterexamples. The probabilistic counterexamples are generated when a probabilistic property φ is not satisfied. They provide a valuable feed back about the reason why φ is violated.

Definition 10. *The probabilistic property* $\varphi = P_{\leq \rho}[\psi]$ *is refuted when the probability mass of the path satisfying* φ *exceeds the bound* ρ*. Therefore, the counterexample can be formed as a set of paths satisfying* φ*, whose combined measure is greater than or equal to* ρ*.*

As denoted in Definition 10, the probabilistic counterexample is a set of finite paths, for example, the verification of the property "*a fail state is reached with probability at most* 0.01" is refused by a set of paths whose total probability exceeds 0.01. The main techniques used for the generation of counterexamples are described in [21]. The probabilistic counterexamples are a crucial ingredient in our approach, since they are used to analyse and refine the conjecture symbolic assumptions. Thus, our need consist to find the most indicative counterexample. A most indicative counterexample is the minimal counterexample (which has the least number of paths). A recent work [12] proposed to use causality in order to generate small counterexamples.

Example 6. Since $PSCV(S_{I_0} \parallel S_{M_1} \models P_{\leq 0.0195}[\Diamond\text{"}err\text{"}])$ returns false, the ACVuIL calls the function *GenerateCounterexample* to generate Ctx, which shows the reason why $P_{\leq 0.0195}[\Diamond\text{"}err\text{"}])$ is violated. In addition Ctx will be used to check if it is a *real counterexample or not.* In practice, we used the tool DiPro to generate counterexamples. This returns $Ctx = \{(s_0, t_0) \xrightarrow{open_{M_1}, 1} (s_3, t_0) \xrightarrow{send_{M_2}, 0.7} (s_3, t_1) \xrightarrow{check_{M_2}, 0.2} (s_3, t_3)\}$.

Generate Sub-MDP and Analyse the Probabilistic Counterexamples. To analyse if the counterexample Ctx is *real* or not, ACVuIL generates a sub-MDP, where this latter represents a fragment of the MDP M_0 based on the probabilistic counterexample Ctx, where the MDP fragment $SubM_0$ contains only transitions present in Ctx. Thus, the fragment $SubM_0$ is obtained by removing from M_0 all states and transitions not appearing in any path of the set Ctx. Since we use symbolic data structures to encode the state space, we encode the MDP fragment $SubM_0$ using SMDP (following the same process to encode MDP). The function $GenerateSubMDP$ is described in Algorithm 3.

Algorithm 3. $GenerateSub - MDP$

```
Input: MDP M_0 and a set of counterexample Ctx
output: SMDP subM_0
Begin
Sub-MDP M_0^{Ctx} = remove from M_0 all states and transitions not appearing in any
    path of the set Ctx;
SMDP SubM_0 = Encode M_0^{Ctx} as SMDP;
return SubM_0;
End
```

Then ACVuIL calls the function $AnalyseCounterexample$. This function aims to check whether the probabilistic counterexample Ctx is *real* or not. Ctx is a *real* counterexample of the system $M_0 \parallel M_1 \models P_{\leq P}[\psi]$ if and only if $SubM_0 \parallel S_{M_1} \models P_{\leq \rho}[\psi]$ does not hold i.e. $AnalyseCounterexample$ returns $true$ if and only if the symbolic probabilistic model cheeking of $SubM_0 \parallel S_{M_1} \models P_{\leq \rho}[\psi]$ returns $false$, or $false$ otherwise.

Example 7. To analyse the counterexamples, ACVuIL generates a $sub - MDP$ containing only states and transitions exist in Ctx. For our example, the set Ctx contains transition $s_0 \xrightarrow{open_{M_1},1} s_3$, where this transition is not present in M_0. Thus, $AnalyseCounterexample$ returns false, since no sub-MDP was generated for this counterexample. After a few iterations, ACVuIL returns the final assumption S_{I_f} equivalent to the original component M_0. In this example, ACVuIL was not able to generate a final assumption more compact than the original component. Indeed, in the worst case, ACVuIL returns the original component as a final assumption.

If the probabilistic counterexample Ctx is not real, then ACVuIL returns $false$ to the CDNF learning algorithm. When ACVuIL returns $false$ to CDNF, this means that the generated assumption is not equivalent to the target Boolean functions. Thus, CDNF generates a new assumption $\beta(I_i)$ $(i \geq 1)$. In line 18, the ACVuIL calls the functions $Refine\_S_{I_i}$ to refine the initial assumption. The function $Refine\_S_{I_i}$ is described in the next section (Sect. 4.6).

Refinement Process of the Conjecture Symbolic Assumption S_{I_i}. At each iteration of the ACVuIL, the generated assumption S_{I_i} converges to the target Boolean functions ($\beta(M_0)$). The function $Refine\_S_{I_i}$ aims to refine the initial assumption S_{I_0} using the new generated assumption. This is done by removing from the initial assumption all transitions between two states, if these states are present in the new generated assumption, and add transitions from the original component between these states.

Algorithm 4. $Refine\_S_{I_i}$

Input: S_{I_0}, $\beta(I_i)$, $\beta(M_0)$
output: S_{I_i}
Begin
SIMDP $S_{I_{tmp}} \leftarrow$ convert $\beta(I_i)$ to SIMDP.
We consider $f^u_{S_{I_{tmp}}}(yxx')$ the MTBDD encoding the lower probability values of $S_{I_{tmp}}$ and $f^u_{S_{I_0}}$ the MTBDD encoding the lower probability values of S_{I_0};
Let $v_{I_{tmp}} = (y_{I_{tmp}}, x_{I_{tmp}}, x'_{I_{tmp}})$, $v_{I_0} = (y_{I_0}, x_{I_0}, x'_{I_0})$;
Let $v_{M_0} = (y_{M_0}, x_{M_0}, x'_{M_0}, e^u_{M_0})$;
for each valuation $v_{I_{tmp}} \in f^u_{S_{I_{tmp}}}$ **do**
  remove from S_{I_0} all valuations v_{I_0} if ($x_{I_{tmp}} = x_{I_0}$ & $x'_{I_{tmp}} = x'_{I_0}$);
  add all valuations $v_{M_0} \in \beta(M_0)$ to $f^u_{S_{I_i}}$ if ($x_{I_{tmp}} = x_{M_0}$ & $x'_{I_{tmp}} = x'_{M_0}$);
end for
optimise $f^u_{S_{I_0}}$;
return S_{I_0};
End

5 Implementation and Experimental Results

We have implemented a prototype tool to evaluate our approach. Our tool accepts MDP specified using PRISM code and a probabilistic safety property as input, and returns either *true* if the MDP satisfies the probabilistic safety property, or *false* and a counterexample otherwise. To implement our tool, we have used the library BULL[1], which impelements the CDNF learning algorithm and the tool Dipro[2] to generate counterexamples. In this section, we give the results obtained for the application of our approach in a several case studies derived from the PRISM benchmark[3]. For each case study, we check the model against a probabilistic safety property using: (i) symbolic monolithic probabilistic model checking and (ii) compositional verification (our approach). The tests

[1] https://sourceforge.net/projects/bull/.
[2] https://se.uni-konstanz.de/research1/tools/dipro/.
[3] http://www.prismmodelchecker.org/casestudies/index.php.

were carried on a personal computer with Linux as operating system, 2.30 GHz I5 CPU and 4 GB RAM.

For each case study, we compare the size of the original component M_0 and the final assumption I_f and this by considering the number of clauses (*#Clauses*) and the number of nodes (MTBDD nodes). In addition, we compare the symbolic non-compositional verification (SMV) with our approach ACVuIL. For SMV, we report the size (number of MTBDD nodes) and the time for model construction (T4MC) for the model $S_{M_0} \parallel S_{M_1}$. For ACVuIL, we report the number of iterations for ACVuIL algorithm to learn the final assumption S_{I_f} (*#ite.*), total time to generate S_{I_f} (T. Gen. S_{I_f}), as well as the size and T4MC to model checking $S_{I_f} \parallel S_{M_1}$.

The results are reported in Table 2. The case studies considered in our experimental results are:

(i) Randomized dining philosophers [13,25], for this case study we check the property $\varphi_1 =$ *the probability that philosophers do not obtain their shared resource simultaneously is at most* 0.1, formally: $P_{\leq 0.1}[\lozenge``err"]$, where label *"err"* sands for every states satisfy: $[(s_N \geq 8)\&(s_N \leq 9)]$, and N is the component number, (ii) The second case study is Israeli and Jalfon [20] solution for the randomized Self stabilising algorithm, we check the system against property: $\varphi_2 =$ *the probability to reach a stable configuration for all algorithms is at most 0.999*, (iii) The third case study is a variant of the client-server model from [29]. It models a server and N clients. The server can grant or deny a client's request for using a common resource, once a client receives permission to access the resource, it can either use it or cancel the reservation. Failures might occur with certain probability in one or multiple clients, causing the violation of the mutual exclusion property (i.e. conflict in using resources between clients). In this case study, we consider the property: $\varphi_3 =$*the probability a failure state is reached is at most 0.98*.

The overall results show that ACVuIL successfully generates assumptions for all case studies. As shown in Table 2, CDNF learns assumption $\beta(I_f)$ smaller than the original component $\beta(M_0)$. For the case studies R.D. Philos and Client-Server, the implicit representation of the final assumption using MTBDD is more compact than the implicit representation of the original components. However, for R.S. Stab. is the same size, this is due to the fact that ACVuIL had refined all transitions of the initial assumption, therefore, the final assumption is equal to the original component. For the verification time, the symbolic monolithic verification (non-compositional) verifies the system faster than our approach ACVuIL. Indeed, our approach takes more time to generate and refine the assumptions, as well as, the time necessary to generate counterexamples at each iteration.

Table 2. Experimental results for the case studies randomized dining philosophers, randomized Self stabilising algorithm and Client-server

Case study	N.	P.	# Clauses		MTBDD nodes		SMV		ACVuIL			
							S_{M_0}	S_{M_1}	#Ite.	T. gen S_{I_f}	S_{I_f}	S_{M_1}
			$\beta(M_0)$	$\beta(I_f)$	S_{M_0}	S_{I_f}	T4MC	Size			T4MC	Size
R.D. Philos	6	φ_1	3696	467	910	340	0.883	5008	237	30.57	0.110	1816
	8		48656	3486	1958	670	2.573	9215	308	67.28	0.128	3711
	10		599600	24677	3335	1062	7.353	14570	381	103.62	0.259	6164
R.S. Stab.	6	φ_2	21	12	7	7	0.001	63	12	2.14	0.001	63
	10		140	80	31	31	0.007	1023	29	7.05	0.007	1023
	14		784	448	127	127	0.016	16383	59	17.25	0.016	16383
	18		4032	2304	511	511	0.034	262143	102	39.52	0.034	262143
Client Server	5	φ_3	3348	3122	917	911	0.114	5962	12	17.02	0.091	5855
	6		12069	11052	1282	1274	0.146	7439	19	25.08	0.139	7129
	7		42282	38947	1707	1697	0.130	10684	28	41.06	0.181	8433

6 Conclusion and Future Works

In this paper, we proposed a fully-automated probabilistic symbolic compositional verification to verify probabilistic systems, where each component is an MDP. Our approach ACVuIL is based on complete and sound symbolic assume-guarantee reasoning rule. The first step aims to encode the system components using compact data structures such as Boolean functions and MTBDD, then we use the compositional verification to model checking the system against the probabilistic safety property. In addition, we proposed to use the CDNF to learn automatically assumptions used in the verification process. We evaluated our approach using three case studies derived from PRISM benchmark, that are R.D. Philos, R.S. Stab. and Client-Server. The overall results show that our approach successfully generates assumptions. For two of the listed case studies, the CDNF learns assumption with implicit representation smaller than the original competent. For the future works, we plan to proposed other assume-guarantee reasoning rule such as asymmetric rule or circular rule to handle more large and complex systems. In addition, the research present in this paper can be extended to verify other probabilistic properties such as liveness. Furthermore, we plan to evaluate our approach using real-life complex systems such as the verification of the composition of inter-organisational Workflows [5].

References

1. Abate, A., Prandini, M., Lygeros, J., Sastry, S.: Probabilistic reachability and safety for controlled discrete time stochastic hybrid systems. Automatica **44**(11), 2724–2734 (2008)
2. Baier, C., Katoen, J.-P.: Principles of Model Checking. MIT press, Cambridge (2008)

3. Baier, C., Kwiatkowska, M.: Model checking for a probabilistic branching time logic with fairness. Distrib. Comput. **11**(3), 125–155 (1998)
4. Benedikt, M., Lenhardt, R., Worrell, J.: LTL model checking of interval markov chains. In: Piterman, N., Smolka, S.A. (eds.) TACAS 2013. LNCS, vol. 7795, pp. 32–46. Springer, Heidelberg (2013). https://doi.org/10.1007/978-3-642-36742-7_3
5. Bouchekir, R., Boukhedouma, S., Boukala, M.C.: Automatic compositional verification of probabilistic safety properties for inter-organisational workflow processes. In: 2016 6th International Conference on Simulation and Modeling Methodologies, Technologies and Applications (SIMULTECH), pp. 1–10. IEEE (2016)
6. Bshouty, N.H.: Exact learning boolean functions via the monotone theory. Inf. Comput. **123**(1), 146–153 (1995)
7. Burch, J.R., Clarke, E.M., McMillan, K.L., Dill, D.L., Hwang, L.-J.: Symbolic model checking: 1020 states and beyond. Inf. Comput. **98**(2), 142–170 (1992)
8. Chatterjee, K., Sen, K., Henzinger, T.A.: Model-checking ω-regular properties of interval markov chains. In: Amadio, R. (ed.) FoSSaCS 2008. LNCS, vol. 4962, pp. 302–317. Springer, Heidelberg (2008). https://doi.org/10.1007/978-3-540-78499-9_22
9. Chen, Y.-F., Clarke, E.M., Farzan, A., Tsai, M.-H., Tsay, Y.-K., Wang, B.-Y.: Automated assume-guarantee reasoning through implicit learning. In: Touili, T., Cook, B., Jackson, P. (eds.) CAV 2010. LNCS, vol. 6174, pp. 511–526. Springer, Heidelberg (2010). https://doi.org/10.1007/978-3-642-14295-6_44
10. Ciesinski, F., Baier, C., Größer, M., Parker, D.: Generating compact MTBDD-representations from Probmela specifications. In: Havelund, K., Majumdar, R., Palsberg, J. (eds.) SPIN 2008. LNCS, vol. 5156, pp. 60–76. Springer, Heidelberg (2008). https://doi.org/10.1007/978-3-540-85114-1_7
11. Cobleigh, J.M., Giannakopoulou, D., PĂsĂreanu, C.S.: Learning assumptions for compositional verification. In: Garavel, H., Hatcliff, J. (eds.) TACAS 2003. LNCS, vol. 2619, pp. 331–346. Springer, Heidelberg (2003). https://doi.org/10.1007/3-540-36577-X_24
12. Debbi, H., Debbi, A., Bourahla, M.: Debugging of probabilistic systems using structural equation modelling. Int. J. Crit. Comput.-Based Syst. **6**(4), 250–274 (2016)
13. Duflot, M., Fribourg, L., Picaronny, C.: Randomized dining philosophers without fairness assumption. Distrib. Comput. **17**(1), 65–76 (2004)
14. Feng, L.: On learning assumptions for compositional verification of probabilistic systems. Ph.D. thesis, University of Oxford (2013)
15. Feng, L., Kwiatkowska, M., Parker, D.: Compositional verification of probabilistic systems using learning. In: 7th International Conference on Quantitative Evaluation of Systems (QEST 2010), p. 133 (2010)
16. Fujita, M., McGeer, P.C., Yang, J.C.-Y.: Multi-terminal binary decision diagrams: an efficient data structure for matrix representation. Form. Methods Syst. Des. **10**(2–3), 149–169 (1997)
17. Hart, S., et al.: Probabilistic temporal logics for finite and bounded models. In: Proceedings of the sixteenth annual ACM symposium on Theory of computing, pp. 1–13. ACM (1984)
18. Hasson, H., Jonsson, B.: A logic for reasoning about time and probability. Form. Asp. Comput. **6**, 512–535 (1994)
19. He, F., Gao, X., Wang, M., Wang, B.-Y., Zhang, L.: Learning weighted assumptions for compositional verification of markov decision processes. ACM Trans. Softw. Eng. Methodol. (TOSEM) **25**(3), 21 (2016)

20. Israeli, A., Jalfon, M.: Token management schemes and random walks yield self-stabilizing mutual exclusion. In: Proceedings of the Ninth Annual ACM Symposium on Principles of Distributed Computing, pp. 119–131. ACM (1990)
21. Jansen, N., et al.: Symbolic counterexample generation for large discrete-time markov chains. Sci. Comput. Program. **91**, 90–114 (2014)
22. Kwiatkowska, M., Norman, G., Parker, D.: PRISM 4.0: verification of probabilistic real-time systems. In: Gopalakrishnan, G., Qadeer, S. (eds.) CAV 2011. LNCS, vol. 6806, pp. 585–591. Springer, Heidelberg (2011). https://doi.org/10.1007/978-3-642-22110-1_47
23. Kwiatkowska, M., Norman, G., Parker, D., Qu, H.: Assume-guarantee verification for probabilistic systems. In: Esparza, J., Majumdar, R. (eds.) TACAS 2010. LNCS, vol. 6015, pp. 23–37. Springer, Heidelberg (2010). https://doi.org/10.1007/978-3-642-12002-2_3
24. Larsen, K.G., Pettersson, P., Yi, W.: Compositional and symbolic model-checking of real-time systems. In: Proceedings of 16th IEEE Real-Time Systems Symposium 1995, pp. 76–87. IEEE (1995)
25. Lehmann, D., Rabin, M.O.: On the advantages of free choice: a symmetric and fully distributed solution to the dining philosophers problem. In: Proceedings of the 8th ACM SIGPLAN-SIGACT Symposium on Principles of programming languages, pp. 133–138. ACM (1981)
26. Lehmann, D., Shelah, S.: Reasoning with time and chance. Inf. Control **53**(3), 165–198 (1982)
27. McMillan, K.L.: Symbolic model checking. In: McMillan, K.L. (ed.) Symbolic Model Checking, pp. 25–60. Springer, Boston (1993). https://doi.org/10.1007/978-1-4615-3190-6_3
28. Parker, D.A.: Implementation of symbolic model checking for probabilistic systems. Ph.D. thesis, University of Birmingham (2003)
29. Pasareanu, C.S., Giannakopoulou, D., Bobaru, M.G., Cobleigh, J.M., Barringer, H.: Learning to divide and conquer: applying the l^* algorithm to automate assume-guarantee reasoning. Form. Methods Syst. Des. **32**, 175–205 (2008)
30. Pnueli, A., Zuck, L.: Verification of multiprocess probabilistic protocols. Distrib. Comput. **1**(1), 53–72 (1986)
31. Segala, R.: Modeling and verification of randomized distributed real-time systems (1996)
32. Vardi, M.Y.: Automatic verification of probabilistic concurrent finite state programs. In: 26th Annual Symposium on Foundations of Computer Science (SFCS 1985) (FOCS), pp. 327–338, October 1985
33. Vardi, M.Y.: Probabilistic linear-time model checking: an overview of the automata-theoretic approach. In: Katoen, J.-P. (ed.) ARTS 1999. LNCS, vol. 1601, pp. 265–276. Springer, Heidelberg (1999). https://doi.org/10.1007/3-540-48778-6_16
34. Vardi, M.Y., Wolper, P.: Reasoning about infinite computations. Inf. Comput. **115**(1), 1–37 (1994)

Author Index

Printed in the United States
By Bookmasters